THE
BOTANY
OF
THE VOYAGE OF H.M.S SULPHUR,

UNDER THE COMMAND OF

CAPTAIN SIR EDWARD BELCHER, R.N., C.B., F.R.G.S., ETC.

DURING THE YEARS 1836-42.

PUBLISHED UNDER THE AUTHORITY OF
THE LORDS COMMISSIONERS OF THE ADMIRALTY.

Edited and Superintended by

RICHARD BRINSLEY HINDS, ESQ., SURGEON, R.N.,

ATTACHED TO THE EXPEDITION.

THE BOTANICAL DESCRIPTIONS

BY

GEORGE BENTHAM, ESQ.

LONDON:
PUBLISHED BY SMITH, ELDER AND CO., 65, CORNHILL.
MDCCCXLIV.

BOTANY

OF THE

VOYAGE OF THE SULPHUR.

I. NORTH-WEST AMERICA.

THE portion of country visited, and which may be accepted under this popular denomination, extends from 60° 21′ to 46° 19′ N. lat. Port Etches, in King William's Sound, and the Columbia River are situated at the extremes, and Port Mulgrave, Sitka, and Nootka Sound, are intermediate. These places were severally visited during the autumn of 1837, with the exception of the Oregon or Columbia River, the examination of which was deferred till the months of August and September in 1839. The whole territory, though extensive, is remarkably uniform in its physical character and natural productions. The climate is far more moderate than on the eastern coast, not being liable to those great vicissitudes, nor ever known to display any great range of temperature. The number of rainy days in the year is very great, and at Sitka only thirty-seven really fine clear days were recorded throughout this period. At this Russian settlement some extended observations gave the mean temperature of the year as 45° 5′, and the range from 2° 3′ to 81° 9′. The whole country is bold and mountainous, intersected by deep and moist valleys, and is every where covered by a gloomy forest of spruce. These vast forests offer a scene which powerfully arrests attention. The trees are often of enormous dimensions; stretching upwards, with scarcely a branch, to where the eye almost fails to follow them, with enormous trunks, very deceptive till brought within the scope of our experience by means of the tape-line; beneath, a most luxuriant undergrowth everywhere abounds, and has an exuberance and charm about it which is rarely supposed to be possible beyond the tropics. But over these the influence of the moist climate is unceasing. It most probably hurries through a rapid existence the more lowly shrubs, and its effect on the trees is very marked. None are seen to attain any great age, that is, none have that appearance; but when the vigour of life is past, they rapidly yield to the constant influence of the moist atmosphere, soil, and investment of mosses and lichens, and soon fall to the ground, which in some places they occupy in great numbers. But as is everywhere observable where the climate is uniform, the variety in species is not great; and some will occur with multitudes of individuals covering a very large space. It is curious to observe how tenaciously some genera extend throughout this territory, though continually represented by a different species. This is particularly conspicuous with *Vaccinium*, *Rubus*, *Ribes*, *Rosa*, and *Lupinus*. The former has several deciduous species towards the northern portion, but towards the south they become neat evergreen shrubs, with a myrtle-like foliage. To a European, the general features of the vegetation are entirely such as he is familiar with, only modified by the character of the climate and country; with the exception, that there are two common plants, *Panax horridum* and *Dracontium camtschaticum*, which differ so entirely from the surrounding vegetation, as to exert a very considerable influence on the physiognomy.—Ed.

The number of species collected at these several places was altogether about 200; many of them are as yet very scarce in herbaria, but none entirely new, the whole line of coast having been already pretty well explored by English, American, and Russian botanists. They have also been well described in several works, amongst which we may particularly refer to Hooker's Flora Boreali-Americana, Bongard's Végétation de l'Isle de Sitcha, and to two general works now in the course of publication, Ledebour's Flora Rossica for the Russian possessions, and Torrey and Gray's Flora of North America, which includes the whole of the territory visited. An enumeration of the species collected by the Expedition would therefore be superfluous.

II. CALIFORNIA.

It usually happens, that the season most favourable for the nautical examination of a country, is that which is least so from acquaintance with its vegetation; and this proved particularly the case with California. Indeed, the residents would almost check our pursuits, by representing that the season was past when Botany should be pursued, whilst they dwelt with much animation on the rich vesture the country assumed after the period of the rains. It was late in the autumn of 1837, when an Expedition up the Rio Sacramento penetrated from San

Francisco some distance into the interior. The country exhibited a vast plain, rich in a deep soil, and subject to periodical submersion. Occasional clumps of fine oaks and planes imparted an appearance of park-land. They were already shedding their leaves; a small grape was very abundant on the banks; and we sometimes obtained a dessert from the fruit of a juglans. We had scarcely returned, when a storm covered the maritime range of hills with snow; and this set the final seal on the year's vegetation. On quitting the coast for the interior, we exchanged the evergreen oaks for deciduous species. The latter grow to fine trees, with wood of great specific gravity. But the natives have a very pernicious practice of lighting their fires at the bases; and as they naturally select the largest, it was really a sorrowful sight to behold numbers of the finest trees thus prematurely and wantonly destroyed. And it is not a country where wood is superabundant; for no sooner is the Oregon crossed than the spruce forests disappear, and the prevailing trees are oaks, which towards the South become gradually less abundant.

But Upper California had already been tolerably examined; and it was our good fortune to touch rapidly at several places on the coast of Lower, or New California, during October and November, 1839, and here we trod in no footsteps, as none had preceded us. I shall confine myself to a few brief abstracts of notes written at the time, as they may convey fresher and more correct impressions; merely premising, that the two Californias are countries differing in many essential particulars, and that San Diego is their political place of separation.

New California, Oct. 15th.—We have touched already at several places on the coast. Everywhere it has much the same character, being almost destitute of wood or even of shrubs; where there happens to be any of the former, consisting of evergreen oak. At this season the soil is dried and cracked, and the vegetation extremely arid. Yet even here after a day's wanderings we return with a dozen or more different species in flower, and I very much doubt this being a common event in the Tropics during the dry season. The prevalence of *Compositæ* is truly great, and one is surprised at the variety of aspect their flowers are capable of assuming. They are not all blue Asters, or yellow Coreopsis, as is seen in an English garden, but have very varied colours and tints. At different places on the coast the species vary, and their total is perhaps considerable. My attention has been directed to the distribution of *Cacteæ*, by meeting with two species for the first time at San Pedro, as we are descending the coast. Their limit here then may be stated at 34° N.; but in the Rocky Mountains, a species has been recorded at 49°. On the plains of the Missouri four species attain to 48°. In Europe we have a representative in 44°. And in Chiloe they probably cease at about 42° S.

San Diego, 32° 29' N. lat. The vegetation generally is highly aromatic, not certainly always fragrant or agreeable, but abounding in strongly scented properties. It continues to consist of a low shrubby character, amongst which multitudes of quail, rabbits, and hares love to nestle. *Compositæ* greatly prevail, and are numerous even as species. *Cacteæ* are now common, and three species have been noticed; there are a few lactescent plants, and many of the shrubs have tough leathery leaves—intelligible indices of the prevailing climate. *Ricinus communis* is seen for the first time, and a few trees of *Phœnix dactylifera*. The latter bears no fruit fit for eating, it being very sour. One of the trees was tall and fine grown, and stood a solitary vegetable monument amid a lowly growth. None of the stunted evergreen oak have been seen below Santa Barbara, and their Northern limit is the waters of San Francisco; thus ranging on the coast between 38° and 34° N. lat.

San Quentin, 30° 21' N. lat. We had heard that Lower California was "Muy Arenoso," but this place did not quite coincide with our conceptions; it was, however, extremely arid. In one place sand abounds, in another plenty of vesicular lava and volcanic ashes: there is still some vegetation. Our species of *Cacteæ* are increased to seven; there is an herbaceous *Compositæ* with aromatic and excessively clammy leaves. *Abronia umbellata* is a relief to the eye, and protects the sand, whose surface is ever on the move; and thus each plant is seated over a little dome, which it has shielded from the winds. Its flowers get deeper coloured as we gain the south. The long taper roots are an article of food on the Oregon; and having had some cooked, I must confess I have tasted a worse vegetable.

San Bartolomè, 27° 40' N. lat., Oct. 29th. Nothing can exceed the rugged and dreary condition of its shores, yet here and there is a straggling shrub, and at nearly every spot we land is some peculiar plant. I remarked here, what will generally apply to California, that many plants have the habit of bearing their leaves and flowers at different periods; we saw a few in flower of which it was impossible to obtain leaves, and these flowers unequalled for the brilliancy of their colours.

Bay of Mugdalena, 24° 38' N. lat., Nov. 2nd. I was yesterday greatly surprised to find that the vegetation here is so truly varied, beautiful, and engaging. A distant view of the hills yields nothing but a dreary prospect, apparently solely broken by a few cactus; and on approaching nearer appearances do not improve. But on landing, and climbing over the rocks and stones and threading the ravines, we behold the surface diversified by clusters of the most interesting and brilliant flowers, and we are surprised that they should thus flourish amongst so much aridity. It is even more singular that they nearly all should be strangers to us, since we have touched so much on the coast. *Compositæ* now cease to be so abundant, but a few herbaceous species were collected. *Euphorbiaceæ* are very numerous and equally curious, and they rank next to *Compositæ* in the physionomy of the vegetation. *Cacteæ* are next in prominence, with new additions to their species. *Leguminosæ, Scrophularineæ* and *Labiatæ*, are all feebly represented. Tropical features are becoming decidedly developed. A solitary cruciferous plant flourishes on the arid sides of the hills.—Nov. 10th. Two days since our surveyors returned from the examination of an *estero* or creek. They had been also searching for water, a stream of which we have scarcely seen in lower California, and were unsuccessful; they, however, brought me some news of the vegetation. The mangrove abounds on the margins, and this is the most northern station of our observation. The *Cactus* was growing to an enormous size, and more species were seen and collected. The trunk of one tree measured upwards of six feet in circumference, and each of the three branches into which it was divided between four and five feet.—Nov. 19th. Since the above I have gathered the mangrove, *Rhizophora Mangle*, myself. Like the rest of the vegetation it is stunted, not usually exceeding four feet, never six. I have also seen some attempts at trees; imagine what the bones and muscles of a giant would be distorted into three feet, such looked these trees. They twisted and twirled, but could not assume the erect position. Their diameters were far from inconsiderable.

But my brief notes are already too copious. As we left the Bay of Magdalena thin fleecy clouds began to spread over its clear sky, and indicated the near approach of the rainy season; and then would be called into active life and vigour a host of beautiful flowers, which we were not to gather. Indeed our visit was in the most inopportune month of the whole year, so far as vegetation was concerned.

We afterwards landed at Cape San Lucas, and not without profit. The *Cacteæ* here, as elsewhere, were studiously sought after, and behind the raised beach is a fine array of trees, with all their singularity and interest. The afterpart of the vessel by this time presented a small forest of them, but though tended with much care, and with a due regard to their constitutions, they one by one pined and died during the subsequent voyage.—ED.

The flora of this country is particularly interesting, as forming the connecting link between the north-west and the tropical vegetation. The species collected in Upper California are for the most part already published in the Botany of Captain Beechey's Voyage, or in Torrey and Gray's Flora. As species they are generally peculiar to the districts where they are found, but belong chiefly to the same genera or groups as the north-western plants. But the Lower Californian plants, especially the interesting collection, made at the Bay of Magdalena and the Cape San Lucas, are almost all either tropical or Mexican forms, but chiefly new as to species. The specimens, owing to the season at which the country was visited, were often only found in fruit, or with very young flowers, and there is no doubt but that, were this hitherto unexplored district examined at a period of full vegetation, a very rich harvest might be made. I am not aware of any South Californian plants having been yet published.

In the following enumeration, the species already described are merely mentioned, with a reference to some work where their character may be found. The new species will be described as fully as the state of the specimens admits of.

Cruciferæ.

1. Arabis? sp. n., *A. petræa* affinis, sed glaberrima foliis omnibus petiolatis pinnatifidis.—The specimens are barely in flower, and therefore the genus is uncertain in this difficult order.—Stony hills 400 to 500 feet high on the Bay of Magdalena.

Capparideæ.

2. Isomeris *arborea* Nutt. in Torr. et Gr. Fl. N. Amer. 1. p. 124.—The genus appears to me to be scarcely sufficiently distinct from Cleome, unless the several sections of that genus are separated from it.—San Pedro and San Diego.

Polygalaceæ.

3. Krameria *parvifolia* sp. n. (Plate I.) frutescens, adpresse pubescens, foliis linearibus obtusis vel vix acutis, pedicellis medio bracteatis paucis folio longioribus, capsula cordato-globosa subdidyma breviter acuminata, aculeis tenuibus apice hamulosis.—Bay of Magdalena.

Rami divaricati, rigidi, ramosissimi. Ramuli et folia pube adpressa more Heliotropiorum canescentia. Folia inferiora semipollicaria, summa multo minora, sæpius falcata et apice obtusa vel mucrone subrecurvo acutata. Flores parvi, in speciminibus suppetentibus fere omnes a vermibus exesi, sed, tanquam e fragmentis judicare potes, filamenta petaloidea basi interne connata videntur, a staminibus fertilibus libera. Capsula sua sponte indehiscens, in valvulas duas separabilis, utrinque ad suturam obscure costata, apice breviter acuminata, nec ut in plerisque speciebus depressa.

This species is probably allied to *K. pauciflora* DC., very imperfectly described from a drawing of a Mexican plant; but in his short character the leaves are said to be oblong-linear, which is scarcely applicable to the *K. parvifolia*.

VIOLACEÆ.

4. IONIDIUM *fruticulosum*, sp. n. (Plate II.) humile, erectum, ramosissimum, pubescens, foliis alternis linearibus integerrimis, stipulis parvis, floribus breviter pedunculatis, sepalis ovatis obtusiusculis, labello subsessili calyce dimidio longiore, staminum filamentis brevibus, 2 anticis supra basin glandula gibbis, squamulis ovatis, capsulis trigonis glabris calyce duplo longioribus.—Cape San Lucas.

Fruticulus habitu Thesii, ramulis 3-4-pollicaribus, viridibus, pilis adpressis puberulis. Folia basi in petiolum angustata, 6-10 lin. longa. Flores parvi. Sepala margine membranacea. Petala parum inæqualia, quatuor superiora calycem æquantia, labellum vix dimidio longius. Semina plerumque sex, obovoideo-compressa, pallida.

Plate II. fig. 1, flower; fig. 2, petals; fig. 3, stamens; fig. 4, style, all magnified.

FRANKENIACEÆ.

5. FRANKENIA *grandifolia*, Cham. et Schlecht. Linnæa, 1. p. 35.—San Pedro.

MALVACEÆ.

6. HIBISCUS (Bombicella) *denudatus*, sp. n. (Plate III.) suffruticosus? dense stellato-tomentosus, foliis lato-ovatis orbiculatisve crenatis, pedunculis axillaribus petiolo vix longioribus, involucello nullo vel ad bracteolas tuberculiformes reducto.—Bay of Magdalena.

Rami divaricati, uti folia pedunculi et calyces tomento denso flavicantes. Folia 1-$1\frac{1}{2}$-pollicaria, distantia, mollia, sub-5-nervia, basi cuneata vel rotundata, petiolo 2-4 lin. longo. Pedunculi semi-pollicares. Involucellum nunc omnino nullum, nunc ejus loco tuberculi adsunt in lana fere absconditi. Calyx profunde 5-fidus, laciniis lanceolatis fere 4 lin. longis. Petala pollicaria, tenuiter ciliata. Columna staminea pistillo dimidio brevior, a basi tecta antheris stipitatis, stipitibus sæpe 2-3-furcatis. Stylus apice breviter 5-fidus. Capsula calyce paullo brevior, depresso-globosa, 5-angularis, 5-valvis, valvulis medio septiferis, a columna centrali tenui persistente (ut in plerisque Bombicellis) solutis. Semina in quoque loculo pauca, angulo centrali affixa, lana involuta.

Plate III. fig. 1, bud; fig. 2, staminal column and style; fig. 3, capsule; fig. 4, the same, cut open; fig. 5, seed, all magnified.

The technical character derived from the calyx and capsule would almost place this plant in *Lagunea*, of which it has neither the stamens and stigmata, nor yet the habit or station. It has the habit and, with the exception of the want of an involucellum, the character of *Bombicella*, which ought perhaps rather to be considered as a distinct genus than as a section of *Hibiscus*. In some other species, however, of *Bombicella*, as in some *Fugosiæ*, the involucellum is reduced to small setiform appendages, slight traces of which may be observed on the young bud of the present species.

7. Gossypium, sp. foliis omnibus integris late cordato-ovatis subtus uni-glandulosis.—Bay of Magdalena.

These specimens do not agree with any of the published forms of Cotton with which I am acquainted, but the seeds are wanting; and, according to those who have classified these varieties or species in the least unsatisfactory manner, it is only from the seed that any positive character can be drawn, and I therefore abstain from giving a new name to the present one.

8. Abutilon *californicum*, sp. n., undique stellato-tomentosum, foliis late cordato-ovatis crenatis subangulatisque concoloribus, pedunculis petiolo longioribus, capsulæ calycem æquantis vel vix superantis stellato-tomentosæ loculis 10 trispermis lanceolato-rostratis.—Bay of Magdalena.

This species is very like the *A. commune*, but the peduncles are longer, the calyxes larger, the capsules smaller, and covered with a short cottony down instead of long hairs.

9. Sida *malvæflora*, DC.—Torr. et Gr. Fl. N. Amer. 1. p. 234.—San Francisco and the Rio Sacramento.

10. Melochia *tomentosa*, Linn.—DC. Prod. 1. p. 290.—Bay of Magdalena.

A common West Indian and Central American plant, of which this is probably the northern limit.

MALPIGHIACEÆ.

11. Janusia *californica*, sp. n., (Plate IV.) foliis ovatis lanceolatisve acutis basi subcordatis utrinque ramulisque sericeo-pilosis, petiolis eglandulosis, pedunculis axillaribus dichotome vel umbellatim 2-8-floris.—Bay of Magdalena.

Ramuli volubiles, tenuiores quam in *J. guaranitica*, pilis albidioribus. Folia pleraque semipollicaria, vix unquam pollicem æquantia, nunc anguste ovato-lanceolata acutissima, nunc ovata acumine brevi acuto, margine glandulis minutis dentiformibus raris plus minusve notata. Petioli 1-2 lin. longi. Loco stipularum glandulæ adsunt in caule minutæ. Pedunculi subsesquipollicares, apice bifoliolati, pedicellos ferunt 2 ad 6 pedunculo ipso longiores, semel iterumque bibracteolatos, simplices unifloros vel bifurcatos bifloros, rarius iterum umbelliferos. Flores quam in *J. guaranitica* minores. Calycis laciniæ lanceolatæ, obtusiusculæ, basi pilosæ, apice glabræ, quorum 4 basi glandulas 2 parvas obovoideas ferunt. Petala calyce duplo longiora, lamina lata, carinata, margine vix dentata. Stamina vidi 1-3 antherifera, et interdum 1-2 parva, sterilia. Ovaria 3, basi coalita, hirsutissima. Styli vulgo 2-3, valde inæquales, uno semper validiore, stigmate capitato. Samaræ sæpius 2-3, dorso superne compressæ in alam margine superiore crassiorem, inferne crista brevissima callosa marginatæ.

Plate IV. fig. 1, flower; fig. 2, stamens and style; fig. 3, fruit; fig. 4, single carpel, all magnified.

This species agrees perfectly both in habit and in character with Ad. de Jussieu's genus *Janusia*, of which, however, all the species hitherto known are from South Brazil and adjoining countries.

12. GALPHIMIA *angustifolia*, sp. n., (Plate V.) suffruticosa, humilis, ramis erectis sericeo-pilosis, foliis petiolatis oblongis linearibusve prope basin 1-2-glandulosis glabris (subtus glaucis?), racemis paucifloris, petalis calyce subdimidio longioribus.—Cape San Lucas.

Caules numerosi, ramosi, vix semipedales, pilis longis mollibus albidis vel in ramulis novellis ferrugineis obtecti. Stipulæ parvæ, ferrugineo-pilosæ. Folia semipollicaria, utrinque angustata, obtusa vel acutiusculа, margine siccitate revoluta, prope basin laminæ uno latere vel rarius utrinque glandulifera, petiolo 1-2 lin. longo. Racemi terminales, laxi, 3-6-flori. Bracteæ sub pedicellis parvæ, ferrugineæ, acutissimæ. Pedicelli vix 2 lin. longi, sericei. Sepala 1¼ lin. longa, lanceolata, glabriuscula, eglandulosa. Petala obovato-oblonga, carinata. Filamenta glabra, basi leviter dilatata at inter se libera, omnia antherifera, antheris inappendiculatis. Styli tres, filiformes, acuti, stigmatibus vix incrassatis punctiformibus. Capsulæ calyce parum breviores, glabræ.

Plate V. fig. 1, flower; fig. 2, stamens and style; fig. 3, fruit, all magnified.

SAPINDACEÆ.

13. CARDIOSPERMUM *tortuosum*, sp. n., (Plate VI.) fruticosum, tortuoso-ramosissimum, ramulis flexuosis vix volubilibus incanis, foliis bi-tri-ternatis subbipinnatisve, foliolis trifidis, segmentis integerrimis incisisve parvis glabris vel pilis paucis hirtellis, paniculis paucifloris, glandulis ovatis, fructibus parvis inflatis turbinato-trigonis glabris vel minute tomentellis.—Bay of Magdalena.

Frutex ramulis rigide flexuosis tenuibus a cæteris speciebus facile distinctus. Rami lignosi, albidi. Tomentum in ramulis pedunculisque brevissimum, canescens. Folia longiuscule petiolata, cum petiolo 2-3-pollicaria; pinnæ 3-5, semel vel bis ternatim sectæ; rhachides sæpius anguste alatæ; segmenta ultima ovata vel oblonga, obtusissima vel acutiuscula et mucronulata, integra vel 3-5-fida, basi cuneata et sæpe in petiolum decurrentia, 2-8 lin. longa, 1-4 lin. lata, crassiuscula, utrinque viridia et glabra nonnisi ad venas pilis paucis brevibus rigidulis hirtella. Pedunculi 1-1½-pollicares, rigidi, sub panicula bicirrhosi. Panicula more *C. halicacabi* subcymosa, floribus raro plus quam sex. Flores magnitudine eorum *C. halicacabi*, abortu polygama, pedicellis brevissimis. Petalorum squamæ vix petalis ipsis breviores. Glandulæ breves, ovato-conicæ. Capsula magnitudine *C. microcarpi*, apice depresso-truncata, angulis acutissimis, basi in stipitem superne triangulato-subalatam attenuata.

Plate VI. fig. 1, male flower; fig. 2, fertile flower, with the petals removed; fig. 3, ovary cut open, all magnified.

ÆSCULACEÆ.

14. ÆSCULUS *californica*, Nutt. in Torr. et Gr. Fl. N. Amer. 1. p. 251.—Rio Sacramento.

VITICEÆ.

15. VITEX *californica*, sp. n., foliis subrotundis acutiusculis grosse dentatis integris, 3-5-lobisve basi profunde cordatis, supra glabris subtus ramulisque floccoso-tomentosis.—*V. Caribæa*, Hook et Arn. in Bot. Beech. Suppl. p. 327 non DC.—Rio Sacramento.

Folia latiora quam in *V. caribæa*, nunquam acuminata, sinu baseos profundiore angustiore. Baccæ parvæ, nigræ.

ZYGOPHYLLACEÆ.

16. FAGONIA *californica*, sp. n., ramis diffusis repetito-dichotomis, foliis trifoliolatis, foliolis ovato vel oblongo-lanceolatis articulatis margine nudis petiolo brevioribus.—Bay of Magdalena.

α. *Hindsiana*, glabra, stipulis brevissimis.

β. *Barclayana*, puberula, stipulis setaceo-spinescentibus petiolo paullo brevioribus.

The long slender excessively-branched stem, the elongated petioles and small flowers, distinguish this as well from *F. cretica* as from *F. chilensis*, with both of which it has considerable affinity, but is more distinct from either than they are from one another. Perhaps, however, they may all be mere forms of one species.

RHAMNACEÆ.

17. RHAMNUS *oleæfolius*, Hook. Fl. Bor. Am. 1. p. 123. t. 44.—Rio Sacramento.

18. CEANOTHUS *thyrsiflorus*, Eschsch.—Torr. et Gr. Fl. N. Amer. 1. p. 266.—Rio Sacramento.

19. CEANOTHUS *verrucosus*, Nutt. in Torr. et Gr. Fl. N. Amer. 1. p. 267.—San Diego.

BURSERACEÆ.

20. ELAPHRIUM *rhoifolium*, sp. n., (Plate VII.) ramis tortuosis, foliis trifoliolatis, foliolis ovatis obtusis crenatis utrinque pubescentibus, terminali basi in petiolum alatum contracto, lateralibus basi rotundatis, pedunculis fructiferis brevibus, 1-2-carpicis.—Bay of Magdalena.

Frutex ramis crassis teretibus rigide tortuosis glabris, ramulis brevibus, junioribus puberulis. Folia fere *Rhois aromatici*. Petiolus communis 1-1½-pollicaris. Foliolum terminale subrhombeum, 9-18 lin. longum, lateralia ovalia, minora, sessilia. Flores non vidi. Pedunculi fructiferi vix semipollicares, medio articulati, monocarpici vel ad articulationem in pedicellos duo monocarpicos divisi. Drupæ ovoideo-globosæ, axi 4 lin. longo, cortice crasso carnoso bivalvi, putamine subangulato lævi basi albido apice nigro biloculari, loculo altero vel utroque perfecto monospermo, altero sæpe effæto. Semen facie plana affixum, testa membranacea, cotyledonibus crassis trilobis plicatis, radicula brevi.

Plate VII. fig. 1, fruit cut across; fig. 2, seed; fig. 3, embryo, all magnified.

21. ELAPHRIUM *Hindsianum*, sp. n., (Plate VIII.) ramis tortuosis, foliis simplicibus ovatis obtusis crenatis basi late subcordatis utrinque pubescentibus, pedunculis brevibus 1-2-carpiis.—Bay of Magdalena.

Habitus, pubescentia et fructus *E. rhoifolii*, sed folia constanter simplicia. Petiolus fere pollicaris, lamina 1-1½-pollicaris, inciso-crenata vel obscure lobata. Flores non vidi, sed sub fructu vestigia observavi staminum octo.

Plate VIII. fig. 1, fruit cut across, with two perfect cells; fig. 2, the same, where one cell is abortive, both magnified.

ANACARDIACEÆ.

22. SCHINUS? *discolor*, sp. n., (Plate IX.) foliolis 1-7 parvis ovatis obtusissimis supra puberulis subtus incano-tomentosis, terminali inciso crenato subtrilobo, inferioribus multo minoribus integris crenatisve, paniculis abbreviatis, pedicellis fasciculatis.—Bay of Magdalena.

Rami tortuosi, rigidi, cortice cinereo; ramuli breves tomentoso-canescentes. Folia alterna vel in ramulis brevissimis fasciculata, vix cum petiolo sesquipollicaria. Foliolum terminale sæpius semipollicare, lateralibus bijugis 3-4 lin. longis; nonnunquam præsertim in foliis superioribus terminale usque ad 8-10 lin. longum, lateralibus multo minoribus vel omnino nullis. Panicula terminalis foliata, ramulis axillaribus 6-12 lin. longis; fasciculi in quoque ramulo 2-4, sessiles, 8-15-flori. Pedicelli puberuli, 2 lin. longi. Sepala 5, puberula, colorata, siccitate rubra. Petala 5, calyce longiora (vix lineam excedentia) ovata, in alabastro carinato-concava, æstivatione valde imbricata. Stamina 10, petalis breviora, in disco 10-crenato inserta. Ovarii rudimentum stylis 3 brevibus terminatum. Flores hermaphroditos vel fæmineos non vidi.

Plate IX. fig 1, flower; fig. 2, the same, with the petals removed, both magnified.

This plant has a very different aspect from most others of this genus; but in the male flowers, the only ones which I have seen, I can find no character to distinguish it.

23. RHUS *laurina*, Nutt. in Torr. et Gr. Fl. N. Amer. 1. p. 219.—San Diego.

24. STYPHONIA *integrifolia*, Nutt. in Torr. et Gr. Fl. N. Amer. 1. p. 220.—Sea-side at San Quentin and other places.

LEGUMINOSÆ.

25. LUPINUS *sericeus*, Pursh.—Torr. et Gr. Fl. N. Amer. 1. p. 379.—Rio Sacramento.

26. PSORALEA *orbicularis*, Lindl.—Torr. et Gr. Fl. N. Amer. 1. p. 304.—Santa Clara.

27. PSORALEA *macrostachya*, DC.—Torr. et Gr. Fl. N. Amer. 1. p. 304.—Rio Sacramento.

28. DALEA *ramosissima*, sp. n., (Plate X.) fruticulosa, ramosissima, diffusa, glabra, foliolis 11-13 parvis cuneatis glaucis subtus ramulisque insigniter nigro-punctatis, spicis terminalibus pedunculatis ovatis villosis, bracteis ovatis acuminatis calyce subbrevioribus, calycis villosi dentibus subulatis tubo æquilongis.—Bay of Magdalena.

Rami cinerascentes; ramuli floriferi semipedales ad pedales, tenues, rigidi, rubicundi, punctis elevatis conspersi. Folia inferiora sesquipollicaria, foliolis distantibus fere 3 lin. longis, ramorum floralium vix pollicaria, foliolis 1-1½ lin. longis obtusis basi angustatis, petiolulis brevissimis. Stipulæ setaceæ, stipellæ inconspicuæ. Pedunculus floriger supra folium ultimum pollicare. Spica nunc 8-9 lin. longa, densa, nunc duplo longior, basi interrupta. Bracteæ membranaceæ, glandulosæ, fuscæ, longiuscule acuminatæ. Calyx sessilis, tubo 1 lin. longo, extus undique piloso, intus glabro, 10-nervio, glanduloso-punctato, laciniis plumosis. Corolla ex sicco violacea; carina calyce plus duplo longior, petalis dorso leviter cohærentibus, lateraliter prope basin concavo-appendiculatis; alæ breviores plicatæ; vexillum alas superans, orbiculatum. Stamina monodelpha. Antheræ consimiles, apice glanduliferæ. Ovarium biovulatum. Legumen calyce brevius, compressum, ovato-triangulare, pilosum, monospermum.

Plate X. fig. 1, bractea; fig. 2, flower; fig. 3, vexillum; fig. 4, one of the alæ; fig. 5, carina laid open; fig. 6, stamens and style; fig. 7, anther: fig. 8, ovary cut open; fig. 9, pod, all magnified.

29. DALEA *divaricata*, sp. n., herbacea, diffusa, tenuis, glabra, foliolis 15-21 parvis obovato-oblongis obcordatisve, glandulis paucis marginalibus, racemis oppositifoliis dissite paucifloris, calycibus glabris 10-costatis pauciglandulosis, dentibus 4 brevibus obtusis, imfimo longiore acuto.—Bay of Magdalena.

Habitu et foliis *D. hypoglottideæ* affinis, inflorescentia et floribus distincta. Caulis annuus videtur, a basi ramosus, ramis tenuibus rigidis divaricato-ramosis nigro-punctatis. Folia 1-1½-pollicaria, fere a basi foliolosa, foliolis brevissime petiolulatis 1-2 lin. longis obtusis retusis vel emarginatis basi rotundatis crassiusculis enerviis vel obscure uninerviis, margine integerrimis vel raro glandulis subimmersis obsolete crenulatis. Stipulæ minutæ setaceo-acuminatæ. Stipellæ nullæ. Racemi vix pollicares, pedunculo rigidulo divaricato 9-12 lin. longo. Flores in spica 12-18, subsessiles, parvi. Bracteæ lanceolatæ, acuminatæ, calyce breviores. Calyx 1 lin. longus, rubescens, costis elevatis transverse scabriusculis, inter costas pauci-glandulosus; dentes 4 superiores æquales, late rotundati, glabri vel rarius ciliati, infimus angustior, duplo longior. Corollæ vexillum calyce dimidio, alæ duplo, carina triplo longiora. Legumen glabrum.

30. DALEA *canescens*, sp. n., herbacea, diffusa, pusilla, tota canescenti-hirtella, foliolis 11-15 cuneato-vel obovato-oblongis obtusis vel retusis, spicis densis ovatis pedunculatis oppositifoliis, calycis hirsuti dentibus lanceolatis acutis, infimo paullo longiore.—Bay of Magdalena.

Habitus *D. divaricatæ* sed gracilior, ramulis filiformibus. Caules, folia, pedunculi, calyces et ovaria pilis albidis brevibus rigidis copiose tecta. Folia 6-9 lin., foliola 1 lin. longa, basi angustata, sub villis raro glandulifera. Stipulæ lineari-subulatæ, vix lineam longæ. Stipellæ adsunt sæpe minutissimæ. Pedunculi graciles, circa 9 lin. longi. Spica imbricata, semipollicaris. Bracteæ ovatæ, acutæ, acuminatæ. Calyx lineam longus, costis obscuris glandulisque parvis sub pube reconditis. Dentes tubo dimidio breviores. Vexillum calyce vix longius, alæ ei plus dimidio, carina plus triplo longiores. Ovarium villosum.

31. DALEÆ? sp. n., suffruticosa, divaricato-ramosa. Ramuli dense niveo-tomentosi et punctis elevatis glandulosis conspersi. Stipulæ parvæ, subulatæ, acutæ. Foliola 5-11, orbiculata, 1½-3 lin. longa et lata, terminali sæpius cæteris majore, utrinque cum petiolo niveo-tomentosa, supra venosa impunctata, subtus nigro-punctata, marginibus recurvis. Pedunculi oppositifolii, 2-4-pollicares, niveo-tomentosi et punctati.—Bay of Magdalena.

Of this plant I have seen but a single specimen in Mr. Barclay's collection, from which all the flowers are fallen off. I have very little doubt that it belongs to *Dalea*, in which genus it would form a very distinct species, unlike any one I am acquainted with, excepting an unpublished Chilian one. As, however, without the flower, the genus cannot be ascertained, I have refrained from giving it a specific name.

32. PHACA *candidissima*, sp. n., decumbens, tota pube adpressa subsericea candidissima, stipulis minutis latis acutis, foliolis 18-17 obovatis obtusissimis basi cuneatis, pedunculis folia superantibus, spicis oblongis laxiusculis, bracteis brevissimis, calycis ovati dentibus lato-subulatis brevibus rectis subæqualibus, legumine sessili ovato-inflato membranaceo incano.—Bay of Magdalena.

Rami flexuosi, obtuse subangulati, uti foliorum pagina utraque pedunculi et calyces argenteo-candidissimi. Stipulæ vix semilineam longæ. Folia bipollicaria, foliolis 3-4 lin. longis. Spica 1-1½-pollicaris in pedunculo subtripollicari. Flores sessiles, primum imbricati, inferioribus tandem subdissitis. Bracteæ persistentes, vix semilineam longæ, acutæ. Calyx 2 lin. longus. Corolla glabra, (violacea?); vexillum calyce triplo longius; alæ paullo breviores, prope basin intus concavo-gibbæ, carinæ æquilongæ lævissime adhærentes, non plicatæ. Stamen vexillare a basi liberum, cætera alte connata. Antheræ inter se consimiles, oblongæ, versatiles, eglandulosæ. Legumen valde inflatum, 9 lin. longum, sutura seminali breviter intromissa. Semina plurima, orbiculari-reniformia.

33. PHACA *vestita*, sp. n., decumbens? pube brevi densa candidissima, stipulis brevibus membranaceo-tomentosis inferioribus in unicam oppositifoliam connatis, foliolis 25-39 ovatis orbiculatisve, pedunculis folio longioribus, spica oblonga laxa, bracteis parvis, calycis ovati dentibus late subulatis brevibus, ovario sessili villoso.—Bay of Magdalena, and San Quentin.

Habitu præcedenti affinis, et pariter candidissima, sed pubes minus appressa. Stipulæ inferiores 3-4 lin. longæ, acutæ, ad medium concretæ, superiores multo minores. Folia demum 4-pollicaria. Foliola inferiora 3-4 lin. longa, acutiuscula, superiora gradatim minora et latiora; ultima fere orbicularia, obtusa, 1-1½ lin. longa, omnia mollissima, basi rotundata. Flores fere *P. candidissimæ* sed in spica minus densi, et corolla ex sicco flava videtur. Legumen non vidi.

34. PHASEOLUS (Drepanospron) *filiformis*, sp. n., volubilis, glabra, ramis gracillimis, foliolis hastato-trilobis lobo medio productiore oblongo, vel rarius ovato-deltoideis subrhombeisve, pedunculis folio longioribus supra medium interrupte paucifloris, bracteis bracteolisque minimis lanceolatis, pedicellis calyce minimo vix duplo longioribus, calycis labio superiore truncato vix emarginato, dentibus lateralibus latis brevibus, infimo acuto tubo dimidio breviore, legumine pendulo falcato glabro.—Bay of Magdalena.

Affinis *P. leptostachyo*. Annuus videtur, ramulis filiformibus. Stipulæ minutæ, oblongæ, striatæ. Petioli 1-1½-pollicares, tenues. Foliola sæpius profunde triloba, lobis oblongis, intermedia 6-12 lin. longa, lateralibus dimidio brevioribus, interdum late subrhombeo-ovata, integra vel sinnato-triloba, 6-9 lin. longa, ramulorum sæpe multo minora. Stipellæ minutæ, oblongæ, acutiusculæ, striatæ. Pedunculi filiformes, 2-2½-pollicares. Florum nodi pauci, distantes, 2-3 flori. Pedicelli floriferi lineam longi, fructiferi paullo longiores, recurvi. Bracteæ minutissimæ, lanceolatæ. Calyx linea brevior, bracteolis dimidio brevioribus appressis. Corolla fere *P. paniculati*, sed multo minor. Vexillum late orbiculatum, basi intus biappendiculatum, medio leviter callosum. Alæ vexillo paullo longiores, oblique oblongæ. Carina apice anfractibus completis spiraliter torta, acuta. Stamen vexillare basi geniculatum, inappendiculatum. Ovarium puberulum. Stylus apice valde incrassatus, stigmate laterale. Legumen forma fere *P. lunati* sed quadruplo minus, vix enim semipollicem longum, lunatum, utrinque acutum, glaberrimum, læve, intus nudum, 6-8-spermum. Semina reniformia, subquadrata, lævia.

35. DESMANTHUS *virgatus*, Willd.—DC. Prod. ii. p. 444.—Bay of Magdalena.

This is probably the Northern limit on the Pacific side of this common South American plant, which extends also into the Southern States of the North American Union, and is found not uncommonly in tropical Asia, but perhaps not originally indigenous to the Old World.

36. CALLIANDRA *californica*, sp. n., (Plate XI.) ramulis petiolisque appresse pilosis demum glabratis, stipulis lanceolato-subulatis rigidis, foliis eglandulosis, pinnis 2-4-jugis, foliolis 8-15-jugis oblongis obtusiusculis utrinque appresse pilosis demum coriaceis nitidis, pedunculis tenuibus petiolo paullo longioribus, calycibus corolla pubescente multoties brevioribus.—Bay of Magdalena.

Species *C. eriophyllæ* et *C. Cumingii* affinis, sed ab utraque distincta. Frutex videtur, rigide ramosissimus, ramulis teretibus. Pubes appressa, brevis, in partibus junioribus canescens, demum rara. Stipulæ persistentes, lineam longæ, interdum subpungentes. Petioli communes tenues, 6-12 lin. longi, partiales paullo longiores. Foliola in ramulis junioribus 2 lin. longa, in ramis fere 3 lin. longa, demum rigida. Flores fere *C. Cumingii*.

Plate XI. fig. 1. flower; fig. 2. stamens; fig. 3. anther; fig. 4. pollen mass; fig. 5. style, all magnified.

The beautiful genus *Calliandra*, consisting of a few of Willdenow's *Acaciæ* and *Ingæ*, with a considerable number of species lately discovered, is almost exclusively South American, a very few species only being found in the West Indies or Mexico, and none in the United States. The Californian one now described is thus the most northern species yet discovered.

ROSACEÆ.

37. ADENOSTOMA *fasciculata*, Hook et Arn. Bot. Beech. p. 139. t. 30.—San Diego.
38. FRAGARIA *chilensis*, Eschsch.—Torr. et Gr. Fl. N. Amer. 1. p. 448.—San Francisco.
39. RUBUS *ursinus*, Cham. et Schlecht.—Torr. et Gr. Fl. N. Amer. 1. p. 456.—San Francisco.
40. ROSA *californica*, Cham. et Schlecht. Linnæa 2. p. 35.—San Francisco.
41. PHOTINIA *arbutifolia*, Lindl.—Torr. et Gr. Fl. N. Amer. 1. p. 473.—San Francisco.

COMBRETACEÆ.

42. LAGUNCULARIA *racemosa*, Gærtn.—DC. Prod. 3. p. 17.—Bay of Magdalena. A tropical maritime shrub, the limits of which appear to be nearly the same as those of the Mangrove.

RHIZOPHOREÆ.

43. RHIZOPHORA *Mangle*, Linn.—Torr. et Gr. Fl. N. Amer. 1. p. 484.—Cape San Lucas, and thence to lat. 24° 38′, which is its northern limit on this coast.

ONAGRACEÆ.

44. ŒNOTHERA (Godetia) *Lindleyana*, Dougl.—Torr. et Gr. Fl. N. Amer. 1. p. 502.—Bodegas, Upper California.

45. ŒNOTHERA (Godetia) *purpurea*, Curt.—Torr. et Gr. Fl. N. Amer. 1. p. 504.—Bodegas.

46. ŒNOTHERA (Sphærostigma) *cheiranthifolia*, Hornem.—Torr. et Gr. Fl. N. Amer. 1. p. 509.—Bodegas.

47. GAURA ? *fruticulosa*, sp. n., fruticosa, humilis, ramosissima, foliis oblongo-linearibus integerrimis basi longe angustatis crassis glabris, spicis foliatis abbreviatis, calycis tubo longissimo tenui, laciniis anguste lanceolatis acutis reflexis, stigmate capitato, (ovario fructuque cauli immersis).—Bay of Magdalena.

Frutex humilis, tortuoso-ramosus, cortice ramorum albido lævi, ramulorum cicatricibus foliorum delapsorum verrucoso. Folia pollicaria, 1-2 lin. lata, subcarnosa, enervia, basi in petiolum angustata, floralia omnia caulinis conformia, 6-8 lin. longa. Ramuli floriferi 3-4-pollicares, dense foliati, superne (difformes?) incrassati. Flores in axillis superioribus solitarii. Ovarium ramo incrassato immersum, parvum, biloculare, ovulis in quoque loculo solitariis pendulis. Tubus calycis filiformis, 9-10 lin. longus; laciniæ limbi 4 lin. longæ, membranaceo-virides. Petala (ex sicco rosea) obovata, 2 majora semipollicaria basi breviter angustata, 2 paullo minora. Stamina 8, parum declinata, 4 petalis alterna paullo longiora. Antheræ oblongæ, prope basin affixæ, circinnato-revolutæ. Stylus staminibus et petalis subæquilongus, stigmate late capitato obsolete 4-lobo. In ramis vetustis fructus nonnullos vidi difformes, in ramo semiarticulato immersos, induratos, biloculares, seminibus in loculis solitariis linearibus incurvis imperfectis. Specimina alia glaberrima, alia superne molliter pubescentia.

In all the specimens there is the same semiarticulation and thickening of the flowering part of the branches so as to enclose the ovaria, which Chamisso and Schlchtendal observed in an allied Mexican species, and which appeared to them to justify the constituting a distinct genus under the name of *Gongylocarpus*. It is, however, much more probably the effect of some disease or parasite. I could not indeed, any more than the above quoted authors, discover any traces of fungus or insect, but the distortion of the ovaries, as well as of the more enlarged capsules and seeds which may be found still remaining in their hardened state in the old woody branches, show that this is not the healthy natural form of the plant. The flowers appear in all other respects perfect, and are evidently showy.

48. ZAUSCHNERIA *californica*, Presl.—Torr. et Gr. Fl. N. Amer. 1. p. 486.—San Pedro and Estrecho de Carquines.

One or two *Cucurbitaceæ*, from Magdalena Bay, are not in a state to enable their being determined.

LOASACEÆ.

49. MENTZELIA *adhærens*, sp. n., caule erecto a basi ramoso albo, foliis petiolatis ovatis grosse dentatis vel sinuato-lobatis basi cuneatis, floralibus oppositis, filamentis 30-40 omnibus filiformibus, capsula oblongo-turbinata, seminibus 10-12.—Magdalena Bay.

Pili crebri, biformes, iis cæterum specierum similes. Caules 1-2-pedales, basi opposite superne dichotome ramosi, ut in *M. albicauli* cortice tenui albido demum detergibili tecti. Folia subbipollicaria, basi in petiolum 3-6 lin. longum angustata, sæpius irregulariter 3-5-loba, interdum simpliciter et inæqualiter dentata, floralia conformia sed gradatim minora. Flores in dichotomiis breviter pedicellati, minores quam in *M. hispida*. Calycis tubus 4 lin. longus, turbinatus, valde hispidus. Laciniæ lanceolato-lineares, reflexæ, tubo parum breviores, interdum subdentatæ. Petala oblonga, basi angustata, semipollicaria. Stamina parum inæqualia, petalis breviora. Capsula (nondum matura) 6 lin. longa, calycis limbo coronata, 5-valvis, placentis duabus.

This species, from the whiteness of its stem, resembles the *M. albicaulis* Dougl. and *M. albescens* Gill., but is very different in foliage and flowers from either. It is remarkable from the adhesiveness of its barbed hairs, which most of the *Loasaceæ* have, it is true, but few of them to such a degree as the present species.

FOUQUIERIACEÆ.

50. BRONNIA *spinosa*, Humb. et Kunth, Nov. Gen., et Sp. vi. p. 84. t. 528.—Cape San Lucas.

This remarkable plant, forming the second genus in an anomalous natural order, consisting as yet but of two genera and three species, was only seen by Humboldt and Bonpland in fruit. The specimens in the present collection have a few flowers, resembling those of *Fouquiera* in general aspect, though of a smaller size, and offering the following characters:

Sepala 5, rigide scariosa, colorata, glabra, ovata, obtusa cum mucrone, valde imbricata interioribus latioribus, 2 lin. longa. Corolla 8 lin. longa, tubo cylindrico superne paullo ampliore rectiusculo, limbi laciniis late ovatis acutis convoluto-imbricatis. Stamina 10, disco subperigyno cum corolla inserta, corolla longiora; filamenta glabra, antheræ oblongo-lineares, dorso affixæ, biloculares, loculis parallelis, basi liberis, rima longitudinali dehiscentibus, connectivo apice apiculato. Ovarium ovato-conicum, triloculare, columna placentifera crassiuscula centrali facile a dissepimentis secedente. Ovula in quoque loculo pauca, e basi anguli centralis adscendentia. Stylus filiformis, exsertus, apice trifidus, laciniis truncatis apice stigmatosis.

PARONYCHIACEÆ.

51. DRYMARIA *holosteoides*, sp. n., humilis, cæspitosa, subglauca, florum et foliorum fasciculis paucis remotis, foliis longiuscule petiolatis ovatis basi cuneatis integerrimis crassiusculis, pedicellis unifloris petiolum vix æquantibus, capsulis calycem æquantibus.—Cape San Lucas.

Herba humilis a cæteris *Drymariis* habitu distincta. Caules e collo plures, 4-6-pollicares, simplices, fasciculos foliorum et florum 1-3 inter se distantes ferentes, inter fasciculos nudi. Stipulæ scariosæ, parvæ, fugaces. Petioli 2-3 lin. longi; lamina foliorum vix longior, obscure sub-5-nervia. Pedicelli numerosi, petiolum vix æquantes. Calyx profunde 5-fidus, laciniis $1\frac{1}{4}$ lin. longis ovatis margine membranaceis, æstivatione imbricata. Petala 5, perigyna, calycem vix æquantia, lineari-cuneata, semibifida, laciniis incisis. Stamina 5, perigyna, laciniis calycinis opposita. Ovarium uniloculare, ovulis paucis, placentæ centrali brevi affixis. Stylus simplex, apice brevissime trifidus, laciniis intus stigmatosis. Capsula oblonga, triquetra, ad angulos in valvulas 3 cartilagineo-subhyalinas dehiscens. Semina pauca vel abortu solitaria, orbiculato-cochleata. Testa coriacea, Embryo circa albumen farinaceum linearis, hemicyclicus.

52. DRYMARIA *crassifolia*, sp. n., humilis, cæspitosa, ramosissima, glauca, florum et foliorum fasciculis numerosis, foliis petiolatis ovatis basi cuneatis integerrimis crassis, pedicellis unifloris folia æquantibus, capsulis calyce subdimidio longioribus.—Cape San Lucas.

This species is near *D. holosteoides*, but forms dense tufts covered with leaves and flowers; the leaves are thicker and more glaucous, and the flowers larger, and on longer stalks. Both species differ considerably in habit from the more common *D. cordifolia*, but they have all the essential characters of the genus.

53. SPERGULARIA *rupestris*, Camb. in St. Hil. Fl. Bras. Mer. ii. p. 176. t. 110.—Cape San Lucas. The same species extends over a great part of tropical America, as far as South Brazil, from whence it was first described.

PHYTOLACCACEÆ.

54. STEGNOSPERMA *halimifolia*, gen. nov., (Plate XII.)—Cape San Lucas.

CHAR. GEN. Sepala 5, ovata, margine membranacea, æstivatione imbricata. Petala 5, perigyna, calyce minora, orbiculata, integra, brevissime unguiculata. Stamina 10, in annulum perigynum basi connata, filamentis e basi latiore filiformibus, antheris bilocularibus. Ovarium sessile, subglobosum, uniloculare, columna centrali percursum. Ovula 5, anatropa, e basi columnæ centralis erecta. Styli 5, breves, recurvi, intus fere a basi stigmatosi. Capsula pentagona, unilocularis, ad angulos in valvulas 5 dehiscens. Semina 5 vel abortu pauciora, singula arilla alba e funiculo orta intus aperta involuta, erecta, testa crassiuscula fusca, embryone annulari?

Species unica, *S. halimifolia*. Frutex ramosissimus, glaberrimus, glaucus, ramis adscendentibus, cortice pallido. Stipulæ nullæ. Folia alterna, petiolata, 1-1½-pollicaria, ovata vel oblonga, obtusissima, integerrima, basi angustata vel rotundata, carnosula, uninervia. Racemi terminales, simplices, floribundi, subtripollicares. Pedicelli 3 lin. longi, singuli ex axilla bracteæ minutæ scariosæ orti et ima basi bibracteolati, bracteolis bracteis consimilibus. Flores iis *Limei capensis* subsimiles, sed paullo majores.

The nearest affinity of this very distinct genus is with *Limeum*. The calyx and petals are the same, but the number of stamens appears to be constantly complete, the carpels are five instead of two, and are completely united into an unilocular ovary and fruit without any dissepiments, and the seeds are enclosed in a very remarkable thick white arillus. I regret much that there are none of them quite ripe enough in the specimens gathered, to ascertain the form of the embryo.

Plate XII. fig. 1, flower; fig. 2, petal; fig. 3, stamens; fig. 4, ovary; fig. 5, ovary cut open; fig. 6, capsule; fig. 7, capsule open; fig. 8, a seed in the arillus; fig. 9, a seed taken out of the arillus.

GROSSULACEÆ.

55. RIBES (Grossularia) *Menziesii*, Pursh.—Torr. et Gr. Fl. N. Amer. 1. p. 545.—San Francisco.

56. RIBES (Ribesia) *malvaceum*, Sm.—Torr. et Gr. Fl. N. Amer. 1. p. 552.—San Francisco.

57. RIBES (Ribesia) *tortuosum*, sp. n., ramis brevibus tortuoso-ramosissimis per anthesin aphyllis glabris, foliis basi cordatis 5-lobis junioribus puberulis, bracteis pedicellos æquantibus, calycis limbo tubuloso apice 5-fido, laciniis ovatis reflexo-patentibus.—San Quentin.

Fruticulus ante foliorum explicationem florens. Ramuli crassi, cortice cinereo glabro, vegetiores 2-3-pollicares, plerique multo breviores. Internodia (ex cicatricibus foliorum delapsorum) pauca. Ad apices ramulorum, e gemma squamis fuscis persistentibus suffulta, racemi oriuntur 6-12 lin. longi, 8-12-flori, minute puberuli, et hinc inde folia pauca parva explicari incipiunt. Pedicelli divaricati, lineam longi. Calycis tubus fere 2 lin. longus, cylindricus, crassiusculus, glaber; laciniæ semilineam longæ. Petala ovata, calycis laciniis dimidio breviora, ad faucem inserta. Stamina 5, petalis æquilonga. Ovarium in fundo calycis brevessimum, placentis 2 parietalibus, ovulis numerosis. Stylus apice brevissime bilobus, lobis intus stigmatosis, placentis contrariis. Fructus jam paullo grandefactus siccus videtur.

A scrubby leafless shrub, with small but very pretty and highly fragrant flowers.

UMBELLIFERÆ.

58. ERYNGIUM *petiolatum*, Hook.—Torr. et Gr. Fl. N. Amer. 1. p. 604.—Rio Sacramento.

CORNACEÆ.

59. CORNUS *glabrata*, sp. n., ramulis erectis cymisque glabris vel vix minute puberulis, foliis ovatis acuminatis basi angustatis supra sparse minuteque puberulis subtus glaberrimis, cymis parvis depressis, drupis globosis.—San Francisco.

Resembles the *C. stricta* in habit and in the form of the leaves, but has a somewhat glaucous foliage and inflorescence; the cymes are much more compact and the flowers fewer; they appear also to be smaller, from the vestiges remaining on the specimens which are in ripe fruit.

LORANTHACEÆ.

60. VISCUM *flavescens*, Pursh.—Torr. et Gr. Fl. N. Amer. 1. p. 654.—San Francisco, on the oak, ash, walnut, willow, and birch, but never on the plane, although that tree be very common.

61. ARCEUTHOBIUM *oxycedri*, Bieb.—Torr. et Gr. Fl. N. Amer. 1. p. 654.—On pine trees in Upper California.

Besides the stations already known for this parasite on the coniferæ of N. W. America, Southern Europe, and Southern Russia, it has been found by Linden on pine trees on the Peak of Orizaba in Mexico; and on the closest examination of the dried specimen, I am unable to detect any difference between the European and Mexican specimens. Botanists do not, however, agree about the colour of the fruits. In California they were found to be nearly black, with a yellow top.

CAPRIFOLIACEÆ.

62. LONICERA *involucrata*, Banks.—Torr. et Gr. Fl. N. Amer. ii. p. 9.—San Francisco.

RUBIACEÆ.

63. Hedyotis (Ericotis) asperuloides, sp. n., (Plate XIII.) erecta, pusilla, divaricato-ramosa, glabra, stipulis minutis ciliatis, foliis lineari-subulatis, pedicellis elongatis filiformibus, calycis tubo ovato-turbinato, capsula apice brevissime libera.—Cape San Lucas.

Herba annua, tripollicaris vel vix semipedalis, ramis dichotomis filiformibus obscure tetragonis scabriusculis. Folia vix semipollicaria, infima et superiora breviora, angustissima vel rarius supra medium subdilatata. Stipulæ vix conspicuæ, utrinque breviter ciliato-2-3-fidæ. Pedunculi in axillis vel dichotomiis superioribus vel ad apices ramulorum 4-8 lin. longi, gracillimi. Flores quam in *H. cærulea* graciliores. Calycis tubus 1 lin. longus, dentes anguste lanceolati, tubo paullo breviores, per anthesin approximati, in fructu inter se distantes. Ovarium fere ad apicem adnatum. Corollæ tubus tenuis, 2 lin. longus, superne paullo ampliatus, limbi laciniæ patentes, obovato-oblongæ. Antheræ oblongo-lineares. Capsula ovata, apice obtusa, vix emarginata, valvulis 4 brevissimis cruciatim dehiscens. Semina in quoque loculo pauca.

In placing this little plant in *Hedyotis*, I have adopted the extended view of that genus taken by St. Hilaire and others, as well as by Torrey and Gray. There is much doubt, it is true, whether such natural groups as *Kadua*, *Kohautia*, &c., might not be sufficiently well characterised to be maintained as separate genera; but it is clear that the greater or lesser degree of adherence of the ovary and capsule will not give any positive line of demarcation between *Houstonia* and *Anotis*, and that the characters by which these have been distinguished from *Hedyotis* and *Oldenlandia* are of little importance, and not always consonant with habit. The species now described, as well as the following, would belong to the section *Houstonia* of Torrey and Gray, except that the stipules, though very minute, are not always perfectly entire, but it might be better to restrict that section to those species which have the ovary free, at least from the middle upwards, and to adopt De Candolle's section *Ericotis*, for those which like this one as well as *H. minima*, Torr. and Gr., have the calyx adherent almost to the summit of the ovary, as their narrow heathlike leaves give them all at the same time a peculiar habit.

Plate XIII. fig. 1, pair of leaves showing the stipules; fig. 2, flower; fig. 3, corolla cut open; fig. 4, longitudinal section of the ovary; fig. 5, capsule; fig. 6, seed, all magnified.

64. HEDYOTIS (Ericotis) *mucronata*, sp. n., fruticulosa, erecta, ramosa, glaberrima, stipulis minutis, foliis linearibus subfasciculatis mucronato-acutis margine subrevolutis crassiusculis, floribus subsessilibus in cymis terminalibus paucis.—Bay of Magdalena.

Fruticulus semipedalis ad pedalis, subdichotome ramosus. Ramuli tetragoni. Folia subsemipollicaria, internodiis sæpius breviora, carnosula, vix semilineam lata, pleraque abrupte in mucronem brevem acutata. Stipulæ minimæ, integræ aut 2-3-fidæ, sæpe vix conspicuæ. Cymæ dichotomæ, foliosæ, laxæ vel congestæ. Pedicelli sæpius brevissimi, rarius 1-2 lin. longi. Calycis tubus usque ad apicem ovarii adnatus, limbi laciniæ lanceolatæ, foliaceæ, acutissimæ. Corolla infundibuliformis, calyce duplo longior, intus glabra. Filamenta brevia. Antheræ oblongo-lineares. Styli lobi oblongi. Ovarii loculi oligospermi.

This plant has something of the habit of the Cape *Thesia*, and it is evidently allied to some of the Peruvian species of *Ericotis*. The flowers in the specimens before me are most of them too much deformed, apparently by the effect of some insect, to admit of any very accurate description.

65. MITRACARPIUM *lineare*, sp. n., annuum, erectum, glabriusculum, foliis linearibus, calycis laciniis 2 majoribus corollæ tubo subdimidio brevioribus, 2 multo minoribus.—Cape San Lucas.

Herba pusilla, parum ramosa, 4-6-pollicaris. Caulis tetragonus, pube minuta scabriusculus vel demum glaber. Folia flavescenti-viridia, crassiuscula, margine recurva, obscure uninervia, majora pollicaria. Stipulæ glabræ, vagina albida 1 lin. longa, setis utrinque 3-5 inæqualibus, intermediis vaginæ æquilongis, lateralibus brevioribus. Capitula sæpius ad apices ramulorum solitaria, majuscula, foliis floralibus quatuor caulinis similibus. Calyx glaber vel minute ciliato-puberulus, laciniis 2 lanceolato-linearibus acutis viridibus, 2 parvis hyalinis. Corollæ tubus $1\frac{1}{2}$ lin. longus, glaber, laciniæ limbi ovatæ, acutæ, tubo dimidio breviores. Calyx fructifer auctus. Semina ventre sulco cruciato notata.

COMPOSITÆ.

66. PECTIS *multiseta*, sp. n., caule diffuso ramosissimo puberulo, foliis lanceolato-linearibus acuminato-piliferis per totam longitudinem dentibus aristatis ciliatis, crebre gianduloso-punctatis, pedunculis folia superantibus ebracteatis monocephalis, involucri squamis 5 late lineari-oblongis carinatis, pappo radii 2-3-setoso, disci coroniformi unisetoso vel mutico.—Cape San Lucas.

Herba annua, pedalis. Rami flexuoso-diffusi, oppositi, graciles, pube minutissima albida conspersi. Folia pleraque pollicaria, basi angustata, margine subrecurva, utroque latere denticulis piliferis 6-8 subæquidistantibus notata, supra viridia, subtus pallida. Glandulæ plurimæ majusculæ, sparsæ, in pagina inferiore prominulæ, aliæ numerosæ minores immersæ, omnes pellucidæ. Pedunculi solitarii, terminales, floridi ramulos superant; demum ramulis elongatis in dichotomiis persistunt, basi foliorum paribus 2-3 approximatis suffulti. Involucrum 2 lin. longum, insigniter 5-costatum, minute puberulum. Squamæ inter se leviter cohærentes, apice breviter liberæ, acutiusculæ. Corollæ radii 5, squamis involucri oppositæ et arcte appressæ, ligulis luteis patentibus integris acutis 2 lin. longis. Corollæ disci fere 20, tubulosæ, ligulis breviores, ex sicco luteæ, dentibus lanceolatis obscure bilabiatis. Achænia linearia, teretia, minute appresso-puberula, pappo coroniformi brevissimo. Aristæ rigidæ, pilis brevibus paucis obverse ciliatæ, achænio breviores, in radio sæpissime tres parum inæquales divergentes, in disci achæniis exterioribus solitariæ, in interioribus nullæ.

67. HELOGYNE *fasciculata*, gen. nov. (Plate XIV.)—Bay of Magdalena.

CHAR. GEN. Capitulum multiflorum, homogamum. Involucrum imbricatum squamis linearibus acutissimis numerosis. Receptaculum planum, nudum. Flores hermaphroditi tenuissime tubulosi, 5-dentati. Pappi paleæ 2-3 breves hyalinæ sublaceræ et aristæ 2-3 scabridæ corollam superantes.—Genus e tribu *Eupatoriacearum Ageratearum*.

H. fasciculata, suffrutex? humilis, subcæspitoso-ramosus, ramulis brevibus glaberrimis glaucescentibus. Folia alterna, superiora sub pedunculo approximata subfasciculata, in ramis vetustis marcide persistentia, omnia longe petiolata, profunde trisecta vel pinnatisecta, laciniis paucis cruciato-divaricatis inter se distantibus, ovatis lanceolatisve, inciso-dentatis vel pinnatifidis acutis basi subconfluentibus carnosis enerviis glauco-viridibus 3-8-lin. longis, petiolo 1-2-pollicari. Pedunculi terminales, solitarii, semipedales, nudi, monocephali. Involucrum ovatum, fere 4 lin. longum. Squamæ numerosissimæ, acutissime acuminatæ, dorso virides, exteriores sublanceolato-lineares breves, interiores lineari-subulatæ elongatæ, intimæ paullo breviores, scariosæ. Receptaculum brevissime alveolatum. Flores tenuissimi. Corollæ superne paullo ampliatæ, dentibus 5 brevibus conniventibus. Styli rami longe exserti, apice clavati, extus papillosi. Antheræ angustæ, ecaudatæ.

There is no doubt that this plant belongs to the *Agerateæ* of De Candolle, but it does not agree with any of the described genera in those minute characters upon which they are distinguished among *Compositæ*, and still less in habit. The involucre is nearly that of *Ageratum* or *Anisochæta*, but with much sharper squamæ, and it differs essentially from the former in the pappus, and from the latter in the corolla. The pappus is that of some *Steviæ*, but the involucres, and number of flowers, remove it at once from them. It is probable that *Phania urenifolia*, Hook. et Arn. Bot. Beech. p. 297, which I have not seen, is a second species of *Helogyne*. The *Phania? dissecta*, of the same work, has some slight resemblance in habit; but the involucre, flowers, and pappus do not appear to me to differ from those of *Eupatorium*.

Plate XIV. fig. 1, flower; fig. 2, anthers; fig. 3, pappus; fig. 4, pappus with aristæ.

68. CARPHEPHORUS *junceus*, sp. n., caule erecto ramoso glabro, foliis remotis plerisque oppositis anguste linearibus patentibus, pedunculis longis monocephalis subcorymbosis, achæniis subpentagonis puberulis, pappo plumoso.—Bay of Magdalena.

Herba perennis, vel forte basi fruticosa, bipedalis. Rami oppositi, elongati, virgati, subteretes. Internodia pluripollicaria. Folia 1-2-pollicaria, crassiuscula, integerrima, glabra. Pedunculi 3-6-pollicares, sæpius alterni, nudi vel superne bracteolis 1-3 parvis stipati. Capitulum hemisphæricum. Involucri squamæ imbricatæ, pauciseriatæ, exteriores ovatæ, margine vix membranaceæ, extus tomento farinoso canescentes; interiores longiores, angustiores, latius membranaceæ, gradatim abeunt in paleas receptaculi lineari-lanceolatas scariosas sublaceras apice ciliatas floribus breviores. Receptaculum subplanum. Flores ultra 30, vix pappo longiores, tubulosæ, dentibus 5 brevibus recurvo-patentibus. Antheræ breviter exsertæ. Styli rami exserti, longi, acutiusculi, brevissime hispiduli. Achænium 1½ lin. longum, molliter villosulum. Pappus 3 lin. longus, setis circa 15, longe et molliter plumosis.

69. BRICKELLIA (Bulbostyles) *hastata*, sp. n., fruticosa? ramis canescenti-tomentosis, foliis oppositis petiolatis hastato-trilobis, supra scabriusculis, subtus reticulato-rugosis tomentellis dense glandulosis, capitulis conferte corymbosis ovatis sub-12-floris, styli rami longe exsertis. — Bay of Magdalena.

Ramuli floriferi pedales, subteretes, tomento brevissimo denso sordide canescente vel flavicante obtecti. Folia caulina omnia opposita, 3-5-nervia, hastato-triloba, lobo intermedio 2-3-pollicari, lateralibus divaricatis 6-12 lin. longis, omnibus obtusis subintegerrimis penninerviis, vel intermedio trinervio et rarius in sinu lobulo altero brevi utrinque aucto. Venæ in pagina superiore vix conspicuæ, in inferiore prominentes, minute tomentosæ. Glandulæ paginæ inferioris parvæ, creberrimæ. Corymbus terminalis, polycephalus; rami 2 infimi oppositi, axillares, cœteri alterni, bracteis minimis vel inferioribus majoribus foliaceis subtensi. Pedicelli ultimi abbreviati. Capitula 4 lin. longa. Squamæ involucri pauciseriales, lato-lineares, vix acutæ, striatæ, margine scariosæ; exteriores abbreviatæ, dorso puberulæ; interiores pappos et corollas subæquantes, glabræ, intimæ scariosæ. Corollæ tenuiter tubulosæ, dentibus 5 extus parce glandulosis. Stylus basi villoso-bulbosus; rami longe exserti, superne incrassati, obtusi. Achænia villosula, striis circa 10. Pappus caducissimus, albus, setis circa 30 uniserialibus barbato-serrulatis.

The genus *Brickellia* was first established by Elliott, for a plant which appeared to him to approach the (N. American) *Vernoniæ* in habit, but distinguished from *Eupatorium* by very slight characters only, amongst which he did not advert to the bulbous base of the style. De Candolle, to whom Elliott's plant was unknown, established under the name of *Bulbostyles*, a genus distinguished from *Eupatorium* chiefly by the last named character, but with some general resemblance amongst the several species, in habit and involucre. Torrey and Gray have since ascertained that both *Brickellia* and *Bulbostyles* have the bulbous style, and are in other respects closely allied to each other. Accordingly they are placed in their Flora next to each other, with detailed generic characters, but with the observation that they are perhaps not sufficiently distinct,—a circumstance so far confirmed by the examination of the present and of some other species, that I have been induced to consider both as one genus under Elliott's older name of *Brickellia*, taking that of *Bulbostyles* as a sectional name for those species which have from ten to twenty, or rarely twenty-five flowers in each head. The species now described has usually about twelve flowers; in other respects it is shrubby, as the true *Bulbostyles* are said to be, but has the exserted style of Torrey and Gray's *Brickellia*, and also, in common with many Brazilian species, has the corymbose inflorescence attributed to the latter genus. The whole group is certainly, as observed by Torrey and Gray, very near *Eupatorium*, yet if the bulbous style proves as constant as it appears to be, it may be found to be a sufficient distinction where the species are so very numerous that recourse is necessarily had to very slight characters for the formation of genera.

70. CORETHROGYNE *obovata*, sp. n., caule procumbente albo-lanato, foliis caulinis obovatis in petiolum longum angustatis apice subdentatis laxe albo-lanatis, ramulorum superioribus parvis, pedunculis involucrisque minutissime glanduloso-puberulis lana orbatis.—Bodegas.

Suffrutex videtur ramis elongatis flagelliformibus, ramulis floriferis ad apices ramorum plurimis brevibus adscendentibus monocephalis. Folia caulina pollicaria, bullato-rugosa, lana laxa utrinque alba, ætate rarius denudata, petiolo longo alato; ramorum floralium parva, sessilia, viridia, bracteæformia. Capitula quam in *C. californica* minora, minus glandulosa, squamis acutioribus angustioribus. Receptaculum nudum. Flores cærulei, pulchelli. Ligulæ circa 20, lineari, stylo nullo, achænii rudimento parvo apice pappum ferente paucisetum. Flores disci numerosi, tubulosi, dentibus vix extus glandulosis. Styli rami ut in *C. californica* penicillati. Achænia villosa. Pappus rufescens, multisetus.

71. Corethrogyne *virgata*, sp. n., caule erecto rigido superne paniculato-ramoso tenuiter arachnoideo-lanato, foliis oblongo-lanceolatis amplexicaulibus arachnoideo-lanatis, ramealibus parvis bracteæformibus squamisque involucri viridibus glanduloso-viscosis, receptaculo nudo. — San Pedro.

Rami adsunt sesquipedales, apice paniculato-polycephali. Folia subadpressa, caulina vix pollicaria, integerrima vel obscure dentata, rarius infra medium contracta, basi caulem amplectentia vel interdum brevissime decurrentia, superiora et suprema in ramulis paniculæ 1-3 lin. longa, integerrima. Capitula quam in præcedente multo minora. Involucri squamæ numerosæ, in seriebus circa sex imbricatæ, margine scariosæ, apice virides, acutiusculæ, glandulis stipitatis sessilibusque viscosæ, interiores apice subsquarrosæ, exteriores gradatim breviores in bracteas abeunt. Ligulæ circa 20, lineares, ovarii rudimento setis paucis brevissimis coronato. Corollæ disci pappum rufum æquantes. Styli rami apice penicillati. Achænia oblongo-linearia, compressa, villosa.

72. Aster *chilensis*, Nees.—Torr. et Gr. Fl. N. Amer. 2. p. 112.—San Francisco.

73. Erigeron *glaucum*, Ker.—Torr. et Gr. Fl. N. Amer. 2. p. 172.—Bodegas.

74. Perityle *californica*, gen. nov. (Plate XV.)—Bay of Magdalena.

Char. Gen. Capitulum hemisphæricum, radiatum. Involucrum subbiseriale, squamis æquilongis oblongo-linearibus, exterioribus hirtis, interioribus subscariosis. Receptaculum planum, epaleaceum. Corollæ extus glandulosæ, radii uniseriales, tubo tenui, ligula oblonga apice 2-3-dentata, disci tubulosæ, 4-dentatæ. Styli rami apice dilatati, breviter appendiculati, obtusiusculi, hirti. Achænia radii et disci conformia, compressa, hirtella, margine calloso cincta. Pappus e squamellis brevibus hyalinis fimbriatis constans, adjecta sæpe arista exteriore longa hirtella et nonnunquam setis 2-3 brevissimis.

Species unica: *P. californica*. Herba annua, erecta, pubescens, divaricato-ramosa, semipedalis vel vix altior. Folia opposita, superiora alterna, longe petiolata, lato-ovata vel suborbiculata, grosse dentata vel inciso-lobata, basi truncata trinervia, tenuiter membranacea, utrinque sparse puberula, inferiora sesquipollicaria, superiora multo minora. Pedunculi elongati, terminales, pauci, laxe subcorymbosi, monocephali. Capitula 3-4 lin. diametro. Involucri squamæ exteriores nervosæ, ciliato-hispidæ, interiores margine subscariosæ, disco breviores. Ligulæ circa 12, breves, ex sicco flavæ videntur. Corollæ disci luteæ, numerosæ et semper quadrifidæ.

The place of this genus is uncertain, neither the form of the style nor the habit being very decidedly that of any of the great tribes of *Compositæ*. The technical characters bring it nearest to *Boltonia*, but the habit is totally different, resembling that of some *Agerateæ*. It has also some affinity with some of the *Senecionidæ*, and may possibly be near to the imperfectly known genus *Rosilla* of Lessing.

Plate XV. fig. 1. involucre and receptacle; fig. 2. floret of the ray; fig. 3. floret of the disk; fig. 4, anthers; fig. 5, summit of the style; fig. 6, achænium; fig. 7, pappus.

75. Ericameria *microphylla*, Nutt. in Torr. et Gr. Fl. N. Amer. 2. p. 236. Variat foliis puberulis siccis vel glabris glutinosis, squamis omnibus obtusis vel exterioribus acutis, achænio glabro vel juniore adpresse puberulo.—San Francisco.

76. Ericameria *diffusa*, sp. n., glabra, laxe ramosissima, subglutinosa, foliis lineari-subulatis canaliculatis, floribus disci 4-5, ligula solitaria, achæniis villosis.—Bay of Magdalena.

Fruticulus humilis, diffuse ramosissimus. Folia majora semipollicaria, obtusiuscula, multo laxiora quam in *E. microphylla*, raro fasciculata. Capitula ad apices ramulorum 3-4, parva, oblonga, in paniculam corymbosam foliosam polycephalam disposita. Involucrum *E. microphyllæ* sed minus. Corolla radii disco brevior, ligula basi sæpe laciniis duabus linearibus brevibus aucta, subbilabilata; flores disci profunde 5-dentati. Receptaculi alveolæ sæpe in paleas subsetiformes hyalinas achænia superantes productæ. Achænia sublinearia, leviter compressa, villis albis obtecta. Pappus *E. microphyllæ*.

77. APLOPAPPUS (Blepharodon) *baccharoides*, sp. n., glaber, erectus, virgato-ramosus, foliis linearibus acutis integerrimis margine scabriusculis, capitulis dense corymbosis numerosis parvis, ligulis circa 15 involucrum vix superantibus, floribus disci 8-10, achænio villoso.—Santa Clara.

Caules 1-1½-pedales, ramis teretibus lævibus. Folia majora pollicaria, ramealia multo minora, omnia acuta et basi angustata, crassiuscula, sub lente trinervia, margine dentibus minutissimis scabriuscula, vel omnino integerrima, leviter glutinosa. Capitula ad apices ramorum numerosa, vix 2 lineis longiora, ovata. Involucri campanulati squamæ subtriseriatim imbricatæ, lineari-lanceolatæ, margine scariosæ, acutæ, dorso virides, leviter glutinosæ. Receptaculum parvum, convexum, alveolatum, alveolis fimbriatis. Ligulæ disco non longiores, biseriales, tubo gracili, lamina lanceolata acuta subpatente; styli ramis subulatis glabris. Corollæ disci tubulosi, tubo tenui glabro, fauce paullo ampliata tubo vix longiore in lacinias 5 lineari-lanceolatas ultra medium divisa. Antheræ ecaudatæ, appendice lanceolata. Styli rami exserti, subulato-compressi, appendicibus parte stigmatifera multo brevioribus. Achænia oblongo-turbinata, villosa. Pappus e setis plurimis inæqualibus uniserialibus constans.

The habit of this plant, resembling in some respects that of *Isopappus*, and still more that of several *Baccharides*, is very different from that of most *Aplopappi*, of which it has all the essential characters.

78. APLOPAPPUS (Blepharodon) *arenarius*, sp. n., suffruticosus, divaricato-ramosus, breviter pubescens, viscosissimus, foliis oblongis lanceolatisve obtusis sinuato-dentatis undulatis, dentibus obtusis rarius aristulatis, involucri hemisphærici squamis linearibus apice foliaceis squarrosis. — Cape San Lucas.

Caules rigide ramosissimi, ramis semipedalibus divaricatis in arena prostratis. Folia crassiuscula, semipollicaria vel paullo longiora, superiora minora, uninervia, dentibus paucis sæpe valde undulatis, basi sessilia vel amplexicaulia, utrinque viridia, pube brevi viscosissima obtecta. Capitula ad apices ramulorum solitaria, magnitudine *Grindeliæ squarrosæ*. Squamæ involucri numerosæ, pluriseriatim imbricatæ, lineares, basi scariosæ, apice virides, acutiusculæ, squarroso-patentes, extus glanduloso-puberulæ. Receptaculum brevissime alveolato-fimbrilliferum. Ligulæ ultra 30. Achænia turbinato-compressa, sericeo-villosa. Pappi setæ numerosæ, inæquales, rufescentes.

A low plant, with something of the habit of some of the European *Pulicariæ* or *Francœuriæ*, and not much resembling the generality of *Aplopappi*, of which however it has all the technical characters.

79. GRINDELIA *cuneifolia*, Nutt. in Torr. et Gr. Fl. N. Amer. 2. p. 247 ?—The specimens resemble much those of *G. squarrosa*, gathered by Douglas on the Red River; but the leaves are but slightly and remotely toothed. The flowers are too much eaten up by worms to show the structure of the pappus.—San Francisco.

80. HETEROTHECA *floribunda*, sp. n., erecta, elata, hispida et viscoso pubescens, dense foliosa, foliis ovatis grosse dentatis inferioribus petiolatis, supremis sessilibus oblongis, panicula oblonga

apice corymbosa conferta polycephala, involucri squamis linearibus acutis, disci pappo exteriore brevi setoso.—San Pedro and San Quentin.

Habitus fere *Inulæ viscosæ*. Caules bipedales, crassi, rigidi, simplices, erecti, pilis longis albidis et pube brevi viscosa vestiti, foliis numerosis obtecti. Ramuli florales in parte superiore caulis numerosi, 2-3-pollicares, oligocephali, inferiores secus caulem racemosi, superiores confertim corymbosi. Folia caulina 1-2-pollicaria, crassiuscula, reticulato-rugosa, utrinque pube glandulosa viscosa vestita, pilis albis longis intermixtis. Petioli foliorum inferiorum pollicares, basi auriculato-dilatati. Folia ramulorum floralium parva, oblonga, subintegerrima. Capitula quam in *H. scabra* majora, multo tamen minora quam in *H. inuloide*. Involucra dense glanduloso-puberula, pilis paucis albis intermixtis. Squamæ pluriseriales. Ligulæ plus quam 20, angustæ. Corollæ disci numerosæ, tenues, glabræ. Styli ramorum appendiculæ breves, hirtæ. Achænia radii parva, compressa, glabra nisi ad margines ciliolata; disci obovata, compressa, sericeo-pubescentia; pappi interioris setæ numerosæ rufæ, exterioris breves numerosæ.

81. CHRYSOPSIS *echioides*, sp. n., undique pilis longis albis hispidissima, subramosa, foliosa, foliis oblongis lanceolatisve basi rotundatis, capitulis confertis subcorymbosis, involucri campanulati squamis lineari-subulatis pilosis, achæniis obovato-oblongis adpresse villosis, pappo exteriore setoso squamellato.—Bodegas.

Affinis *C. villosæ*, Nutt., sed imprimis distinguitur pilis longis rigidis albis subadhærentibus, in caule ramis foliorumque pagina utraque creberrimis, iis *Echii italici* subsimilibus. Caules duri, pedales, superne confertim ramosi. Folia inferiora desunt, superiora 1-1½-pollicaria, sessilia vel semi-amplexicaulia; pili paginæ inferioris sæpe quam cæteræ molliores, at semper longi et densissimi; folia suprema multo minora. Ramuli floriferi breves, ultimi bracteolati, vix semipollicares, monocephali. Capitula quam in *C. villosa* minora, squamis involucri acutioribus. Ligulæ 12-15. Styli ramorum appendices longæ hirsutæ. Achænia subsericeo-villosa, compressiuscula, basi longe, apice brevissime attenuata. Pappus setosus, barbellatus, sordidus, exterior brevis e setis squamellisve linearibus paucis constans.

82. BACCHARIS *pilularis*, DC.—Torr. et Gr. Fl. N. Amer. 2. p. 259.—San Francisco.

83. BACCHARIS *consanguinea*, DC.—Torr. et Gr. Fl. N. Amer. 2. p. 259.—Santa Clara.

Good specimens of both sexes of the two last species appear to be constantly distinct. The leaves of *B. consanguinea* are usually narrower than in *B. pilularis*, the heads of flowers more ovoid and fewer flowered, and the foliaceous bracts or floral leaves on the outside not so large, nor so closely appressed.

84. BACCHARIS *Douglassii*, DC.—Torr. et Gr. Fl. N. Amer. 2. p. 259.—Santa Clara.

The leaves of the flowering branches are as in Douglas's specimens, and as described by Torrey and Gray. Some of the stem-leaves are, however, four to five inches long, nearly an inch broad, and often slightly serrulate. The species appears to me perfectly distinct from *B. glutinosa*.

85. AMBROSIA *artemisiæfolia*, Linn.—Torr. et Gr. Fl. N. Amer. 2. p. 291.—San Francisco.

86. FRANSERIA, *hispida*, sp. n., foliis bipinnatisectis, segmentis dentato-pinnatifidis utrinque hirsutis viridibus, capitulis confertis spicatis, involucris masculis 6-fidis, fœmineis ovoideis brevissime aculeatis 2-4-floris.—Bay of Magdalena.

Specimen unicum vidi semipedale, durum. Caulis teres, erectus, undique pilis longis albis hispidissimus.

Folia alterna, petiolata, 2 poll. longa et lata, fere ad costam mediam bis dissecta, lobulis lineari-lanceolatis acutis, dentibus obtusiusculis brevibus crispis, rhachi alata et lobulis dentibusve crispis inter segmenta additis, pagina utraque virescente pube utprimum densa viscosa vestita, in foliis adultis pilis albidis erectis numerosis intermixtis. Racemi breves, conferti, alii masculi videntur alii fœminei, sed in specimine incompleti sunt; capitula tamen utriusque sexus numerosa sunt, sessilia, et valde approximata. Involucra mascula patentia, 2 lin. lata, valde obliqua, fere ad medium in lacinias 6 ovatas acutas divisa, viscoso-puberula. Paleæ receptaculi lineares, apice paullo latiores, flores superantes, viscoso-hirtæ. Corollæ subinfundibuliformes, tubi parte attenuata brevissima, fauce longa campanulata brevissime 5-dentata. Stamina inclusa; filamenta brevissima; antheræ oblongæ, appendice ovata acuta vix setifera antheræ loculis æquilonga. Styli rudimentum breve, apice penicillatum. Involucra fœminea ovata, arcte clausa, extus viscoso-pubescentia, 2-4-flora. Ovaria inclusa, ovoidea, glabra. Styli rami exserti, elongati, obtusi, glabri, stigmatis seriebus prominulis fere ad apicem extensis. Capitula matura vix 2 lin. longa, aculeis paucis brevissimis sæpius tuberculiformibus, intus 3-4-locularia.

Allied probably to *F. pumila*, Nutt. which is very imperfectly described, but is said to be silky-canescent, which the present species certainly is not. The *F. pumila* is, moreover, placed by Torrey and Gray in a section with uniflorous female heads, but it does not appear whether that character had been in this instance verified.

87. FRANSERIA *chenopodiifolia*, sp. n., suffruticosa? humilis, foliis petiolatis ovatis dentatis subincisis utrinque albo-tomentosis, spica interrupta, capitulis superioribus masculis involucro 8-10-dentato, inferioribus fœmineis paucis subglobosis tri-floris tomentosis, aculeis elongatis numerosis.—Bay of Magdalena.

Specimen semipedale, ramosum. Caulis basi lignosus videtur, glaber, purpureus; apices ramorum cano-tomentosæ. Folia alterna 1-1½-pollicaria, acuta vel vix obtusiuscula, dentibus inæqualibus sæpe duplicatis subcrispis, basi latiora truncata vel in petiolum breviter angustata, crassiuscula, penninervia et basi subtrinervia, utrinque præsertim in pagina inferiore tomento brevi laxiusculo albida; petioli graciles fere pollicares. Spica tripollicaris. Capitula mascula in parte superiore circa 10, sessilia, late hemisphærica, involucro tomentello membranaceo venoso breviter et inæqualiter 8-10-dentato. Flores fere 30. Receptaculi paleæ lineari-spathulatæ, floribus paullo breviores, apice ciliato-hirtæ. Corollæ anguste turbinato-tubulosæ, involucrum superantes, apice breviter 5-dentatæ, extus vix puberulæ. Antheræ corollam æquantes, singulæ filamento suo paullo longiores, appendice ovata acuta apice breviter pilifera inflexa. Styli rudimentum corollam æquans, apice penicillatum. Capitula fœminea ad basin spicæ pauca. Stylus exsertus, ramis longissimis, fere *F. hispidi*. Fructus depresso-globosus, 2 lin. diametro, intus (in speciminibus duo scalpello subjectis) trilocularis, loculis in uno specimine omnibus fertilibus, in altero duobus abortivis. Aculei lineam longi, basi subdilatati, apice sæpe hamati, glabriusculi. Tomentum seu lana inter aculeis breve, laxum, album.

88. ENCELIA *conspersa*, sp. n., diffusa, ramis adscendentibus junioribus albo-tomentosis, foliis alternis ovatis oblongisve adultis viridibus pube rara conspersis, pedunculis longis 2-3-cephalis, involucri squamis lineari-lanceolatis ciliolatis, achæniis planis faciebus fere glabris marginibus longe villosis.—Bay of Magdalena.

Caules basi lignosi, ramosissimi. Rami floriferi adscendentes vel erecti, ½-1-pedales, striati, pube farinosa albidi, demum glabrati. Folia omnia alterna, petiolata, pollicaria vel paullo longiora, nunc lato-ovata margine sinuata, nunc oblonga integerrima, omnia obtusa, basi cuneata, crassiuscula, trinervia, pilis brevissimis albis sparsis utrinque punctato-scabriuscula, cæterum viridia vel primo juventute alba. Pedunculi semipedales, in ramos 2-3 monocephalos divisi, ramis bractea oblonga parva subtensis. Capitula hemisphærica, magnitudine

E. canescentis. Involucri squamæ 2-3-seriales, inæquales, virides, membranaceæ, minute puberulæ, margine præsertim basi ciliatæ, interiores discum subæquantes. Ligulæ circa 12, oblongæ, extus pubescentes, neutræ. Receptaculum planum. Paleæ membranaceæ, naviculares, floribus disci paullo breviores. Corollæ disci glabræ, tubi parte tenui brevissima, fauce tubulosa elongata, dentibus brevibus incrassatis. Styli rami appendice subulato-conica superati. Achænia margine villis longis mollibus dense ciliata, faciebus villis similibus raris onustis.

Allied to *E. californica*, but neither the form of the leaves, nor the clothing of the involucres agree with the character given to that species.

89. ENCELIA *nivea*, sp. n., procumbens, tomento subsericeo niveo, foliis plerisque oppositis petiolatis ovatis obovatisve, pedunculis elongatis 1-2-cephalis, involucri squamis ovato-lanceolatis extus sericeo-tomentosis, achæniis compressiusculis breviter villosis marginibus vix ciliatis.—San Quentin.

Rami laxiores et longiores quam in *E. conspersa*, tomento molli albo obtecti, vix demum subnudi. Folia vix pollicaria, obtusissima, integerrima, margine subundulata, basi in petiolum 3-6 lin. longum angustata, crassiuscula, molliter niveo-tomentosa, nervis 3 subtus prominulis; fere omnia opposita, pauca hinc inde præsertim sub pedunculis alterna. Pedunculi semipedales, rigiduli, sæpius 1-2-bracteati at simplices, rarius ramo monocephalo ad axillam bracteæ aucti. Capitula hemisphærica, quam in *E. conspersa* paullo majora. Squamæ involucri biseriales, exteriores paullo breviores, subfoliaceæ, apice subpatentes, cano-tomentosæ. Ligulæ circa 10; lamina 4 lin. longa, ovato-oblonga, integra, multinervis, glabra. Paleæ lineari-lanceolatæ, carinatæ, disco paullo breviores. Corollæ disci et genitalia? *E. conspersæ.* Achænia vix perfecta vidi, sed multo minus compressa sunt quam in specie præcedente, villis minus inæqualibus.

This species differs slightly from other *Enceliæ*, in having its leaves mostly opposite, and the achænia, so far as can be ascertained from very young ones, and from a few others very old and somewhat injured, are much less compressed, with the hairs more equally diffused. These characters bring it near to *Gymnopsis*, but the habit is in other respects that of *Encelia*, and I can see no trace of any coroniform pappus. Perhaps the two genera are not sufficiently distinct.

90. VIGUIERA *subincisa*, sp. n., suffruticosa, foliis oppositis inferioribus approximatis ovato-lanceolatis grosse dentatis subincisisve, superioribus sub panicula oligocephala remotis parvis linearibus, involucri squamis biseriatis obtusiusculis cano-pubescentibus, receptaculo conico.—Bay of Magdalena.

Caules basi lignosi, ramosissimi, breves, foliosi, glaberrimi. Folia ad basin ramorum floralium conferta, longiuscule petiolata, late vel anguste ovato-lanceolata, subbipollicaria, acuminata, valde inæqualiter paucidentata vel sublobata, basi angustata, glabra vel rarius pube minuta scabriuscula. Rami floriferi erecti, subpedales, superne alternatim paniculati, oligocephali. Folia remota, inferiora opposita, suprema alterna bracteæformia. Pedunculi apice uti involucra pilis brevibus rigidulis appressis plus minus canescentes. Capitula quam in *V. helianthoide* minora. Involucri squamæ lanceolatæ, inæquales, interiores floribus et paleis breviores. Receptaculum parvum, solidum, conicum. Paleæ anguste oblongæ, membranaceæ, margine involutæ, achænium includentes. Ligulæ circa 10, neutræ; lamina late oblonga, integra, multinervis, extus puberula. Corollæ disci numerosæ, laxiuscule tubulosæ, basi brevissimæ contractæ. Styli rami appendice subulato-conica terminati. Achænia pilis longis sericeo-villosa, squamellis pappi oblongis apice laceris achænio subdimidio brevioribus, aristis 2 inæqualibus squamellas paullo superantibus.

91. HELIANTHUS *californicus*, DC.—Torr. et Gr. Fl. N. Amer. 2. p. 325 ?—The specimen is too much injured to determine accurately.—San Francisco.

92. HELIANTHUS *scaberrimus*, sp. n., caule elato scabro-hispido, foliis inferioribus oppositis supremis alternis petiolatis ovato-lanceolatis acuminatis integerrimis basi cuneatis supra scaberrimis obscure triplinerviis, involucri squamis ovatis scabris ciliatis longe acuminatis, achæniis puberulis demum glabratis, pappo bipaleaceo.—Bodegas.

Rami adsunt superiores, pilis brevibus rigidis asperati. Ramuli floriferi elongati uti folia superiora alterna. Folia caulina opposita 2-3-pollicaria, longiuscule petiolata, nervis subtus tantum prominulis. Capitula magnitudine *H. californici*. Squamæ involucri foliaceæ, exteriores 1-2 interdum elongatæ, foliiformes, omnes longe subulato-acuminatæ et pilis rigidis ciliatæ. Paleæ receptaculi apice sæpius tridentatæ, dente medio elongato acute acuminato. Achænia juniora pube adpressa plus minus vestita, matura glabrescunt. Pappi paleæ lato-lanceolatæ, concavæ, acutæ vel apice fimbriatæ, caducissimæ.

This certainly much resembles my specimens of *H. californicus* from Douglas, but the leaves are shorter and broader, and the scales of the involucre are very different. It is, however, very difficult, from dried specimens, to distinguish accurately the species of a genus like this, where the size of our herbaria will only admit of mere fragments of the larger species.

93. COREOCARPUS *parthenioides*, gen. nov. Verbesinearum, (Plate XVI.)—Bay of Magdalena.

CHAR. GEN. Capitulum hemisphæricum, multiflorum, radiatum. Involucri squamæ circa 5, ovatæ, subæquales, leviter imbricatæ. Paleæ receptaculi lineares. Ligulæ circa 5, fœmineæ. Flores disci numerosi, tubulosi, 5-dentati. Styli rami appendice longa acuta superati. Achænia obcompressa, radii margine crasso rugoso cincta et aristis 2 brevibus retrorsum hispidis coronata, disci anguste marginata, calva.

Species unica: *C. parthenioides*. Herba perennis? ramosa, suberecta, semipedalis, glabra vel partibus junioribus vix canescentibus. Folia opposita, petiolata, pinnatisecta, segmentis obovatis oblongisve grosse inciso-dentatis pinnatifidisve crassiusculis. Pedunculi pauci monocephali. Capitula magnitudine et forma fere *Unxiæ*. Involucri campanulati squamæ lineam longæ, ovatæ vel obovatæ, brevissime acuminatæ, juniores opacæ marginatæ, demum membranaceæ, venosæ. Receptaculi paleæ exteriores ovali-oblongæ, interiores oblongo-lanceolatæ vel lineares, floribus disci breviores. Ligulæ sæpissime 5, interdum 6, tubo glabro involucrum æquante; lamina ovali-oblonga, 4-nervis, vix apice dentata, 2 lin. longa. Corollæ disci involucro paullo longiores, tubi parte tenui brevissima, fauce tubulosa ampliore basi extus annulo squamellarum aucta. Antheræ inclusæ, ecaudatæ. Styli ramorum appendicula sublinearis hirsuta. Ovaria omnia compressa, marginata, apice nuda, aristis achæniorum radii vix ante grossificationem conspicuis. Achænia disci læviuscula, radii dorso lævia, facie interiore tuberculosa.

This little plant is evidently allied to *Parthenium* and *Mendezia*, approaching the former in habit, the latter in character, and with it should be transferred, as suggested by De Candolle, to the *Verbesineæ*. The central flowers, though often sterile, are always hermaphrodite, and frequently fertile.

Plate XVI. fig. 1, floret of the ray; fig. 2, floret of the disk; fig. 3, anthers; fig. 4, summit of the style; fig. 5, achænium of the ray seen from the inner face; fig. 6, the same seen from the back; fig. 7, achænium of the disk.

94. ACOMA *dissecta*, gen. nov. Verbesinearum (Plate XVII.)—Cape San Lucas.

CHAR. GEN. Capitula ovoidea, pluriflora, radiata. Involucrum imbricatum, squamis paucis latis obtusis. Receptaculum parvum, planum; paleæ lanceolatæ, acutæ. Flores radii 1-2, fœminei, fertiles; disci plures, hermaphroditi, tubulosi, 5-dentati. Styli rami appendice sublanceolata acuta vix puberula terminati. Achænia obcompressa, bialata, apice emarginata, calva; interiora sæpe abortiva.

Species unica: *A. dissecta.* Suffrutex 1-1½ pedalis, glaberrimus, a basi ramosus. Folia opposita, petiolata, bipinnatisecta; segmentis linearibus acutis integerrimis crassiusculis, superioribus subconfluentibus. Corymbi longiusculi pedunculati, oligocephali. Capitula 3 lin. longa. Involucrum fere *Latreilleæ* vel *Clibadii*, squamæ circa 5, valde imbricatæ, læves, extimæ paullo breviores. Ligula sæpius solitaris, tubo gracili, lamina oblonga 5-nervi apice vix emarginato-dentata. Paleæ floribus disci paullo breviores.

The deeply cut, narrow, somewhat fleshy leaves give this plant the habit of some *Senecios* and *Chrysanthema*. The heads of flowers have some resemblance to those of *Clibadium* and *Latreillea*, but the flowers of the disk are hermaphrodite though often sterile. The genus would, therefore, belong to the *Verbesineæ*, amongst which none are published with the same combination of characters as in our plant.

Plate XVII. fig. 1, floret of the ray; fig. 2, floret of the disk and palea; fig. 3, anthers; fig. 4, style; fig. 5, achænium, all magnified.

95. DYSODIA *anthemidifolia*, sp. n., erecta, glabra, foliis pinnatisectis, segmentis remotis linearibus integerrimis, involucri ebracteati hemisphærici squamis 8 apice obovato-scariosis.—Bay of Magdalena.

Herba annua, pedalis, habitu fere *Anthemidis cotulæ*. Folia alterna vel infima opposita, 1-2-pollicaria, anguste linearia, crassiuscula, glabra, laciniis utrinque 2-4 inter se distantibus 3-6 lin. longis. Glandulæ orbiculatæ, hinc inde ad apices foliorum vel laciniarum solitariæ; folii apex glandulifera sæpius paullo dilatata et mucronulata. Pedunculi terminales, superne parum incrassati, monocephali, bracteis paucis parvis linearibus sparsis a capitulo remotis. Capitula hemisphærica, radio neglecto 6-7 lin. diametro. Involucri squamæ glaberrimæ læves, basi incrassato-cartilagineæ, superne membranaceæ, apice latæ, obtusissimæ, scariosæ, dorso glandulis 3-4 majusculis onustæ. Ligulæ 8, lamina ovata obtusissima. Flores disci numerosi, involucrum paullo superantes; corolla tubulosa basi breviter attenuata, fauce elongato-tubulosa, dentibus 5 lanceolatis acuminatis. Genitalia inclusa. Styli rami apice truncati penicillati. Achænia lineari-turbinata, basi pedicello brevissimo hispido stipitata, striata, sparse puberula, apice truncata. Pappus achænio sublongior, constans e squamellis numerosis (circa 20) basi in annulum brevissimum subcoalitis, ultra medium in setas plurimas barbellatas fissis.

This very distinct species cannot be referred to any of De Candolle's sections. The want of bracteæ under the involucre would place it in *Gymnolæna*, but the habit, the foliage, and the form of the involucre are totally different from those of *D. serratifolia*. Our plant has, however, all the essential characters of the genus *Dysodia*.

96. POROPHYLLUM *gracile*, sp. n., suffruticosum, glabrum, foliis oppositis alternisque anguste linearibus integerrimis, glandulis paucis vel nullis, involucri cylindracei squamis muticis margine anguste scariosis, achænio rostrato scabriusculo.—Bay of Magdalena.

Affine quidem *P. lineari DC*, sed multo gracilior et involucrum diversum. Rami floriferi semipedales ad pedales, tenues, striati, riguli, apice in ramulos 2-3 breves monocephalos divisi. Folia 1-1½-pollicaria, pleraque angustissime linearia, acuta, viridia, eglandulosa; nonnulla paullo latiora, utrinque acutata, et hinc inde glandula una alterave majuscula notata. Pedunculi fructiferi vix apice dilatati. Involucrum 4 lin. longum; squamæ a basi ad apicem subæquilatæ, obtusæ, margine anguste scariosæ, non mucronatæ, dorso gerentes glandulas circa 6 parvas lineares sæpe per paria dispositas. Flores in capitulo 12-15, involucro subdimidio longiores, tubo longo infundibuliformes, extus scabriusculi, dentibus 5 æqualibus lanceolatis patentibus. Antheræ breviter exsertæ. Styli rami longi, subulati, hispidi. Achænia tenuia, angulata, longiuscule rostrata, pilis minutis appressis scabrella. Pappus sordidus, multisetus.

The form of the involucres, corolla, and seed are those of De Candolle's first group, but the scales of the involucre are blunt and slightly scariose at the top, as in his second group.

97. POROPHYLLUM *tridentatum*, sp. n., fruticosum, humile, ramosissimum, glabrum, foliis lanceolatis cuneatisve, inferioribus pinnatilobatis, superioribus tridendatis trilobisve, lobis dentibusve plerisque glandula setigera terminatis, capitulis ovato-oblongis, squamis apice scariosis, achænio erostri vix scabriusculo.—Bay of Magdalena.

Frutex semipedalis vel paullo altior, basi rigide ramosus; rami floriferi 3-4 poll. longi, foliosi, apice in ramulos 2-4 breves monocephalos divisi. Folia pleraque 3-5 lin. longa, basi angustata; supra medium paullo latiora, apice in dentes vel lobulos 3 lanceolatos divisa; pauca vegetiora 6-8 lin. longa et præter dentes terminales utrinque secus marginem lobulis dentibusve 1-2 remotis aucta; dentes omnes lanceolati, glandula globosa breviter setigera terminati, vel rarius acuti mutici eglandulosi; folia cæterum crassiuscula, eglandulosa. Involucra 4 lin. longa. Squamæ latiusculæ, margine scariosæ, apice scarioso-appendiculatæ, obtusæ, dorso gerentes glandulam unam alteramve majusculam prominentem ad basin partis scariosæ. Flores numerosi (circa 40), involucrum vix superantes; corollæ tubulosæ, dentibus subpatentibus obscure bilabiatis. Achænia brevia, striatula, pilis minimis vix scabrella. Pappi setæ numerosæ, serrulato-barbellatæ. Styli rami subulati, hispidi.

98. BAHIA *latifolia*, sp. n., procumbens, araneoso-lanata, foliis oppositis trilobis, lobis obovatis cuneatisve subincisis, pedunculis elongatis monocephalis tomentosis.—Bodegas.

Habitus fere *B. lanatæ*. Caules elongati, procumbentes, ramulis apice adscendentibus, lana araneosa densa nivea obtecti. Folia 6-15 lin. longa, petiolo alato basi amplexicauli dilatato, ultra medium trifida, laciniis latis dentatis vel iterum trifidis, rugosa, supra tenuiter subtus dense araneoso-lanata, rarius demum denudata, novella lana gossypina involuta. Inflorescentia *B. lanatæ*. Pedunculi crassiores. Capitula paullo majora, late campanulata. Involucri squamæ oblongo-lanceolatæ, arcte appressæ, biseriales, subæquilongæ, extus albo-tomentosæ. Ligulæ circa 12, tubo viscoso-hirto, lamina oblonga apice vix 2-3-dentata. Flores disci numerosi; corollæ tubus infra medium tenuis viscoso-hirtus, superne in faucem tubulosam subglabram ampliatus, dentes 5, breves. Genitalia subinclusa. Styli rami truncati, exappendiculati. Achænia tetragona, glabra. Pappi squamellæ 4, brevissimæ, ovatæ, hyalinæ.

99. HELENIUM *puberulum*, DC.—Torr. et Gr. Fl. N. Amer. 2. p. 385.—San Francisco.

100. HEMIZONIA *ramosissima*, sp. n., glabra vel pilis raris subhispida, glanduloso-viscosa, caule diffuso intricato-ramosissimo ramulis fasciculato-polycephalis, foliis lanceolatis linearibusve integerrimis vel paucidentatis, ligulis 5, paleis receptaculi ad medium connatis, pappi disci squamellis laceris.—San Diego.

H. fasciculatæ affinis, sed imprimis capitulis floribusque duplo minoribus distincta. Caules 1-2-pedales, ramis insigniter paniculato-ramosissimis dense foliosis et floriferis. Folia inferiora lanceolata, pollicaria, obtusiuscula, basi late rotundata et arcte sessilia, margine revoluto integra vel dentibus lobulisve paucis remotis aucta, uti caules hinc inde pilis paucis rigidis hirta; superiora parva, linearia, integerrima, glandulis crebris sessilibus stipitatisve viscosa. Capitula ad apices ramulorum dense et irregulariter corymbosa. Involucra 2 lin. longa; squamæ 5, lanceolatæ, acutæ, extus glandulosæ, basi concavæ, achænia radii semi-includentes, extus squamis bracteisve 2-3 foliaceis linearibus squamis ipsis æquilongis suffultæ. Paleæ receptaculi 5, squamas æquantes, lanceolatæ, acutæ, carinatæ, ad medium connatæ in cupulam 5-fidum, 5-costatum, flores disci includentem. Ligulæ 5, squamis involucri oppositæ et basi subinclusæ, paleis alternæ, tubo hirtello, lamina obovata 1 lin. longa apice trifida, lacinia media lineari, lateralibus ovatis. Flores disci sæpius 6, quorum 5 paleis oppositi, sextus paullo longior in medio capitulo, omnes infundibuliformes, hermaphroditi, steriles, extus minute glandulosi, tubo brevi, fauce subcampanulata 5-dentata. Antheræ corollam æquantes, appendicibus acutis. Styli rami subulati, hispidi. Achænia radii obovata, leviter incurva, matura nigra, extus rugosa, calva, glabra, areola obliqua; disci abortiva, glabra, pappo coronata e squamellis circa 10 apice laceris constante.

This species, as well as the *H. fasciculata*, are unlike the other *Hemizoniæ* in habit, and are intermediate in their characters between *Hemizonia* aud *Calycadenia*.

101. HEMIZONIA *pungens*, Torr. et Gr. Fl. N. Amer. 2 p. 399.—San Francisco.

102. HEMIZONIA *rudis*, sp. n., erecta, paniculato-ramosissima, undique glanduloso-pubescens, foliis linearibus sublanceolatisve integerrimis, capitulis numerosis ad apices ramulorum solitariis, ligulis 5, floribus disci circa 15, receptaculo undique paleaceo, achæniis omnibus epapposis.—Santa Clara.

Caules e basi perenni plures, erecti, 1-2 pedales, ramis virgatis paniculato-ramosissimis. Pubes brevis glanduloso-viscosa, graveolens, in caule ramis foliis involucrisque copiosa, pilis nonnullis brevibus rigidulis siccis præsertim in parte inferiore plantæ intermixtis. Folia radicalia in speciminibus detrita, conferta, elongata et subpetiolata; caulina inferiora pollicaria, basi dilatata, semiamplexicaulia; ramealia multo minora, ultima sub capitulis 2-3 lin. longa, sparsa vel vix sub capitulis conferta. Capitula in ramulis ultimis brevibus foliatis solitaria paniculam formant amplam irregulariter corymbosam; singula ovoideo-subglobosa, magnitudine *H. fasciculatæ*. Involucri squamæ 5, uniseriales, liberæ, ovali-oblongæ, acutiusculæ, discum subæquantes, virides, dorso glanduloso-pubescentes, marginibus involutis scariosis achænia radii semi-includentes. Paleæ receptaculi cuneato-oblongæ, membranaceæ, apice ciliato-hirtæ, exteriores inter ligulos et flores disci ultra medium in cupulam connatæ. Ligulæ 5, tubo brevissimo lato villoso, lamina lata profunde trifida, lacinia media angustiore. Flores disci sæpissime 15, subinfundibuliformes, glabri, tubo tenui, limbo 5-dentato. Antheræ oblongæ, fuscæ, appendice ovata. Styli rami breves, cono hispido superati. Achænia obovato-compressa, nigra, lævia, areola laterali.

103. MADARIA *corymbosa*, DC.—Torr. et Gr. Fl. N. Amer. 2. p. 404.—Santa Clara.

104. AMAURIA *rotundifolia*, gen. nov. Madiearum.—San Quentin.

CHAR. GEN. Capitulum multiflorum, radiatum, ligulis fœmineis, floribus disci hermaphroditis, fertilibus. Involucri squamæ subbiseriales, lineares, exteriores glutinosæ, interiores scariosæ. Receptaculum planum, epaleaceum. Antheræ ecaudatæ. Styli rami subulati, acuti, fere a basi hispidi, stigmatis seriebus fere ad apicem extensis. Achænia oblongo-linearia, tetragona, compressiuscula, calva.

Species unica: *A. rotundifolia*. Suffrutex? humilis, undique pube fusca glanduloso-viscosissima obtectus. Caules erecti, semipedales vel paullo altiores, apice laxe corymboso-ramosi. Folia inferiora opposita, superiora alterna, petiolata, orbiculata, inciso-dentata vel lobata, lobis dentatis, basi late cordata, trinervia, utrinque viscosissima; floralia in ramis corymbi pauca, parva, subsessilia, ovata, dentata. Corymbus oligocephalus, ramis apice monocephalis, inferioribus elongatis. Capitula hemisphærica, vix semipollicem diametro, iis *Hemizoniarum* multiflorarum subsimilia. Squamæ involucri exteriores flores disci subæquantes, margine subscariosæ, dorso viscoso-pubescentes, interiores fere omnino scariosæ, omnes acutiusculæ. Corollæ radii circa 20, tubo dense glanduloso-hispido, ligula 4 lin. longa apice tridentata, styli ramis glabris. Corollæ disci numerosæ, fere ad apicem dense glanduloso-hispidæ, dentibus 5 brevibus. Styli rami exserti, longi. Achænia radii et disci conformia, nigra, acutangula, ad angulos minute subglanduloso-serrulata, cæterum glabra.

Although the number of genera of *Compositæ* with radiate heads, without chaff on the receptacle or pappus to the achænia, be but very few, this plant does not agree with any of them, and the structure of the style being as it were intermediate between that of the *Vernoniaceæ* and of the *Senecionideæ*, it is difficult to place it. The general appearance is that of some *Astereæ*, but the lower leaves are opposite, and the involucre, flowers, and style are very nearly those of the *Hemizoniæ*. The receptacle being entirely free from chaff, does not agree with the technical character of the *Madieæ*, yet, on the whole, it appears to be amongst them, and next to *Hemizonia*, that the genus should be placed.

105. ACHILLEA *millefolium*, Linn.—Torr. et Gr. Fl. N. Amer. 2. p. 409.—San Francisco.

106. ARTEMISIA *pachystachya*, DC.—Torr. et Gr. Fl. N. Amer. 2. p. 422.—Bodegas.

Certainly the same as the plant gathered by Douglas, upon which De Candolle established his *A. pachystachya*. I find, however, in these specimens, as well as in Douglas's, more or less of long white hairs on the hermaphrodite florets. All the specimens are too young to ascertain whether these florets are fertile or not, but they certainly appear to me to be infertile; and it is matter of great doubt whether the species be not referable to the *A. pycnocephala* (DC. Torr. et Gr. l. c. p. 416), gathered by Chamisso in the same locality as Douglas's specimens.

107. ARTEMISIA *vulgaris*, Linn.—Torr. et Gr. Fl. N. Amer. 2. p. 421.—Santa Clara.

108. GNAPHALIUM *Sprengelii*, Hook. et Arn.—Torr. et Gr. Fl. N. Amer. 2. p. 427.—San Francisco.

109. GNAPHALIUM *palustre*, Nutt.—Torr. et Gr. Fl. N. Amer. 2. p. 427.—San Francisco.

110. TRIXIS *frutescens*, P. Br.—DC. Prod. 7. p. 68.—Bay of Magdalena.—A tropical genus, of which this appears to be the northern limit.

111. STEPHANOMERIA *virgata*, sp. n., caule erecto elato virgato paniculato, capitulis secus ramos fasciculatis 8-10-floris, achæniis tuberculoso-rugosis.

Caules 2-3-pedales vel altiores, teretes, striati, crassiusculi, glabri, intus cavi, ramulis floriferis numerosis virgatis paniculati. Folia inferiora desunt, superiora linearia vel lineari-lanceolata, apice subulata, acuta, integerrima vel prope basin argute inciso-dentata, glabra. Capitula in ramulis brevissimis 2-3-cephalis secus ramos paniculæ fasciculata, subsessilia, floribus sæpius 10. Involucra 3 lin. longa; squamæ interiores sæpius 5, oblongo-lineares, acutiusculæ, virides, extus squamellis bracteolisve pluribus brevibus suffulta. Ligulæ roseæ, involucro paullo longiores. Achænia anguste oblonga, leviter incurva, apice truncata, tetragona, tuberculis numerosis rugosa, glabra. Pappi setæ achænio subduplo longiores, numerosæ, niveæ, elegantissime plumosæ.

A very pretty species when recent, with numerous small pinkish flowers.

Ericaceæ.

112. Arbutus *Menziesii*, Pursh.—DC. Prod. 7. p. 582.—San Francisco.

There were two varieties found, one quite smooth, with the leaves nearly entire, the other with a few hairs on the branches and petioles, and the leaves more serrate; neither were in flower, but both apparently belong to this species.

Oleaceæ.

113. Fraxinus *latifolia*, sp. n., petiolis villosulis, foliolis 5, lateralibus sessilibus late ovato-ellipticis, terminali obovato, omnibus integerrimis supra glabris subtus pilosulis, samaris elongatis angustis emarginatis.—San Francisco.

Pubes e pilis patentibus mollibus sparsis constans, in petiolis ramulisque junioribus copiosa, in pagina inferiore foliorum rarior, præcipue in venis et marginibus sita. Petioli usque ad foliolum terminale 4-6 poll. longi, angulati. Foliola lateralia in folio adulto $2\frac{1}{2}$-3 poll. longa, 2 poll. lata, obtusa cum acumine brevissimo, basi rotundato-cuneata, membranacea, penninervia; terminale 3-$3\frac{1}{2}$ poll. longum, $2\frac{1}{2}$ poll. latum, basi in petiolo angustatum. Flores non vidi. Paniculæ fructiferæ infra folia fasciculatæ, foliis breviores, parce ramosæ, pedicellis ultimis 3 lin. longis. Calyx sub fructu persistens, dentatus, et fructus grossificatione fissus. Samaræ pars seminifera 7-8 lin. longa, subcylindrica; ala 9-10 lin. longa, vix 3 lin. lata, apice profunde emarginata. Species *F. pubescenti* affinis videtur, sed foliorum forma et pube diversa.

Apocynaceæ.

114. Vallesia *dichotoma*, Ruiz et Pav. Fl. Per. ii. p. 26. t. 151.—Precisely similar to the South American specimens.

Asclepiadiaceæ.

115. Metastelma *californicum*, sp. n., (Plate XVIII.) glabrum, caule filiformi volubili, foliis ovato-oblongis breviter acuminato-mucronatis, basi rotundato-subcordatis, pedunculis subnullis, pedicellis glabris, corollæ laciniis ovatis intus incano-papillosis, coronæ stamineæ foliolis lanceolatis acutiusculis gynostegium sessile paullo superantibus, stigmate planiusculo.—Bay of Magdalena.

M. parvifloro simile. Folia brevius mucronata et basi sæpius late subcordata. Flores paullo minores.

My friend M. Decaisne, who has described the Asclepiadiaceæ in the eighth volume of De Candolle's Prodromus, has kindly examined this and the following species, both of which he has pronounced to be new. He has also furnished me with accurate drawings of the minute parts of the flower, which have been copied into the accompanying plate.

Plate XVIII. fig. 1, bud; fig. 2, expanded flower; fig. 3, anther seen from outside, *a*, leaflet of the corona; fig. 4, anther seen from inside, *b*, terminal membrane of the anther, *c*, cells; fig. 5, pollen mass; all magnified.

116. SARCOSTEMMA *arenarium*, sp. n., volubile, ramis puberulis, foliis lineari-spathulatis acutulis carnosulis utrinque aveniis pube brevissima inspersis, pedunculis folium vix æquantibus multifloris, corollæ laciniis patulis ciliatis extrorsum calycibusque pubescentibus, introrsum atro-violaceis papillosis, corona staminea exteriore integra, interioris foliolis gynostegium vix æquantibus. (Decaisne MSS).—Bay of Magdalena.

Caules elongati, crassitie *Convolvuli arvensis*, teretes vel compressi, virides, striatuli, juniores præsertim sub nodis adpresse puberuli, cæterum glabri. Folia 1-1½ poll. longa, 1-2 lin. lata, apice breviter acutata, basi longiuscule angustata subpetiolata; floralia minora. Pedunculi floridi 6-9 lin. longi, axillares, apice umbellatim 12-15 flori, pedicellis tenuibus 4-5 lin. longis. Flores illis *Gomphocarpi fruticosi* paullo majores. Calyx 5-partitus, laciniis brevibus lanceolatis dense hispidis. Corolla patula, laciniis latis obtusis, crassiusculis, extus hirsutis, intus glabriusculis. Corona staminea gynostegio paullo brevior.

POLEMONIACEÆ.

117. GILIA *capitata*, Dougl. in Bot. Mag. t. 2698.; forma humilis, hinc inde puberula.—Bodegas.

118. GILIA *pharnaceoides*, Benth. in Bot. Reg., sub tab. 1622.—Santa Clara.

CONVOLVULACEÆ.

119. JACQUEMONTIA *abutiloides*, sp. n., humilis, undique molliter et dense tomentosa, foliis late ovato-cordiformibus acutis, pedunculis folio longioribus capitato-3-5-floris, sepalis ovato-lanceolatis acuminatis exterioribus paullo majoribus.—Bay of Magdalena.

Planta semipedalem ad pedalem, in speciminibus suppetentibus non volubilis; ramuli tamen apice leviter flexuosi et forte in solo pinguiore volubiles evaderent. Ramuli, petioli, foliorum utraque pagina, pedunculi et sepala tomento obtecta denso molli ferrugineo-flavescente vel subcanescente, e pilis substellatis intertextis constante. Petioli inferiores laminam æquant, superiores multo breviores. Folia majora vix pollicaria, crassiuscula, venis primariis subtus prominulis, acuta vel vix mucronulata. Pedunculi omnes folia superant, post anthesin bipollicares, apice flores ferunt tres vel rarissime quinque, subsessiles ad axillas bractearum lineari-subulatarum. Sepala omnia basi angustata vel rotundata nec cordata, multo minus quam in *J. violacea* inæquales. Corolla fere *J. violaceæ*. Styli lobi oblongo-elliptici, divaricati, supra undique stigmatosi.

Although Choisy unites to the *J. violacea* the *Convolvulus canescens* of Humboldt and Kunth, as a tomentose variety, yet I cannot but consider that the plant now described must remain distinct, although the chief differences are the same as those which Kunth relied upon for his *C. canescens*, but in a much greater degree. The appearance of the plant is very dissimilar to that of any form of *J. violacea* I have seen. The form of the leaves, and especially of the sepals, are also different from those of the common *J. violacea*.

120. Cuscuta *patens*, sp. n., cymis paucifloris laxiusculis, calyce pentagono laxe campanulato, laciniis latis obtusissimis, corollæ urceolato-globosæ laciniis brevibus obtusis, filamentis anthera brevioribus, squamis ovatis fimbriatis conniventibus.—Bay of Magdalena.

Caules filiformes, tenuissimi, implexo-ramosissimi, squamis perpaucis parvis. Cymæ 3-5-floræ, irregulares, pedicellis flore brevioribus. Flores quam in *C. epilino* paullo majores, 5-meri vel rarius 4-meri. Calyx laxe et late campanulatus, patens, ut in *C. pentagono*, Engelm. angustatus, tenuiter membranaceus, non verrucosus, lobis latissimis tubo multo brevioribus. Corolla tenuiter membranacea, tubo subgloboso calyce paullo longiore, ore contracta; laciniæ tubo duplo breviores, erecto-patentes, ovatæ, obtusæ. Antheræ in sinubus fere sessiles; filamenta tamen in tubo corollæ evidenter decurrunt usque ad squamam. Ovarium globosum. Styli breves, inclusi, apice capitato-stigmatosi. Capsula corolla persistente inclusa, abortu sæpius monosperma, in speciminibus tamen maturam non vidi.

The calyx of this dodder is like that of *C. pentagona*, described by Engelmann in the London Journal of Botany, but the flowers are much larger, the lobes of the corolla shorter and more obtuse, and the filaments and styles shorter. The specimens are large, much matted, and full of flower, but there are no traces of the plant on which they grew, unless it be an *Ipomæa* (unknown to me), of which there are some fragments in the mass, but not enough to characterise it.

Hydroleaceæ.

121. Eriodictyon *crassifolium*, gen. nov., dense tomentoso-villosum, foliis crassis oblongis dentatis basi angustatis supra canescentibus subtus ramisque rufescentibus, floribus villosis, corolla calycem vix superante.—San Diego.

Char. Gen. Calyx 5-partitus, persistens. Corolla tubulosa, limbo parvo subpatente. Stamina inclusa. Ovarium uniloculare, placentis 2 parietalibus in medio ovario bifidis inter se liberis vel vix cohærentibus pluriovulatis. Styli 2, a basi distincti, apice capitato-stigmatosi. Capsula dehiscentia 4-partita, (incomplete dicocca, coccis bipartitis,) partitionibus oligospermis.—Frutices Californici, undique vel in pagina inferiore foliorum tomentosi. Folia alterna, integra, inferiora vel omnia dentata, basi in petiolum angustata, penninervia, venulis crebre reticulatis subtus prominulis. Cymæ terminales, 2-3-chotome ramosæ, ramis subscorpioideis, floribus numerosis sessilibus.

E. crassifolium. Frutex dense foliatus, ramulis subteretibus, pube densa rufescente vestitis. Folia 2-2½ poll. longa, 6-10 lin. lata, acutiuscula, grosse et subæqualiter dentata, basi longiuscule angustata et integerrima, crassa, rigida, utrinque dense tomentoso-villosa, supra canescentia, subtus reticulato-venosa et plus minus præsertim juniora rufescentia. Cymæ breviter pedunculatæ, ramis 2-3-chotomis divaricatis, ultimis breviter scorpioideis. Flores sessiles. Calycis laciniæ lineares, hispidæ, 2 lin. longæ. Corolla extus et intus sub insertione staminum hispida, calyce sublongior, tubo ampliato et ut videtur ad faucem contracto, omnes tamen corollæ quæ in specimine unico supersunt plus minus monstruosæ sunt, et varie inflato-deformatæ. Limbi laciniæ parvæ, obtusæ, erecto-patentes, intus glabræ. Stamina 5, inæqualia, inclusa; filamenta brevia, hirsuta; antheræ glabræ, ovatæ, loculis parallelis. Ovarium villosum. Styli glabriusculi, corollam subæquantes. Fructus calyce inclusus, conicus, villosus, secedit in valvulas seu semicoccos (vel si mavis nuces incomplete clausas) 4, consistentia dura fere ossea, quibus margo altera inflexa semina fert 2-3 ovoidea, testa castanea striato-rugosa, albumine subcarnoso, embryone recto.

A Californian genus consisting now of three species, one of which has been figured by Hooker and Arnott under the name of *Wigandia? californica* (Bot. Beech. p. 364, t. 88). It is there observed how very unlike that plant is to the South American *Wigandiæ*, but it was supposed that in the absence of the fruit no essential distinctive characters could be found to remove it from that genus. Choisy, however, in his monograph of *Hydroleaceæ*, observes that *Wigandia*, however distinct in habit, only differs from *Hydrolea* in the shape of the corolla and the exserted stamens, and in both these respects *Wigandia* differs also from these Californian plants. Thus, even if the difference in the conformation of the fruit should not prove so striking in Douglas's plant as it is in our *Eriodictyon crassifolium*, still the characters derived from the flower are sufficient to maintain the genus now established. I regret much that in the only specimen I have seen of this *E. crassifolium* (in Mr. Barclay's collection), the corollas are all more or less deformed, apparently by the effect of some insect, so that it is impossible to ascertain its precise form. Even the fruits are not in so satisfactory a state as could have been wished. The two other species, which I refer to *Eriodictyon*, are both from Douglas's collection, and are in excellent flower, but not yet in fruit. They may be characterised as follows:—

E. tomentosum, undique niveo-vel subflavescenti-tomentosum, foliis ovali-oblongis dentatis basi angustatis, supremis oblongis vix dentatis, cymis pedunculatis densis, floribus villosis, corolla calycem vix excedente.— Folia paullo latiora quam in *E. crassifolio*. Flores numerosissimi, multo minores.

E. glutinosum, ramis glabriusculis, foliis lanceolatis vix dentatis basi angustatis supra glabris glutinosis subtus albo-tomentosis, floribus parce hirtis, corolla calyce 2-3-plo longiore.—*Wigandia californica*, Hook. et Arn. l. c.

HYDROPHYLLACEÆ.

122. PHACELIA *circinnata*, Jacq.—Hook. et Arn. Bot. Beech. p. 374.—San Pedro.

123. PHACELIA *distans*, sp. n., scabro-pubescens vel hispida, foliis pinnatisectis, segmentis

oblongis lanceolatisve obtusis pinnatifidis, calycis laciniis obovatis oblongisque obtusis inæqualibus viridibus hispidis, staminibus corollam vix superantibus.—Bodegas.

Hinc *P. ciliatæ*, hinc *P. ramosissimæ* affinis, ab utraque tamen distincta. Planta humilis, divaricato-ramosa. Foliorum segmenta plurima, infima a caule et inter se distantia, superiora approximata, suprema interdum confluentia; inferiora 6-7 lin. longa, ad medium pinnatifida lobis obtusis subdentatis, utrinque hispida, juniora subtus subcanescentia. Spicæ densifloræ, circinnatæ, demum pluripollicares. Pedicelli brevissimi. Calyces floriferi 2 lin. longi, sepalo exteriore late obovato obtusissimo, interioribus angustioribus, omnibus tamen obtusis dense hispidis. Corolla *P. ramosissimæ*; genitalia breviora.

Boragineæ.

124. Cordia (Varronia) *angustifolia*, Rœm. et Schult. Syst. v. 4. p. 460.—Bay of Magdalena. —An imperfect specimen, but apparently identical with the West Indian plant.

125. Heliotropium *curassavicum*, Linn.—Rœm. et Schult. Syst. v. 4. p. 32.—Common on the sea coast throughout California.

126. Myosotis *californica*, Fisch. et Mey. Ind. 2. Sem. Hort. Petrop. p. 42.—San Pedro.

The leaves are rather broader, and the flowers perhaps a little larger than in the specimens raised from seeds received from Dr. Fischer, but in every other respect precisely the same. Probably the *M. Scouleri* adverted to by Hooker and Arnott (Bot. Beech. p. 370), belongs also to the same species.

Pedaliaceæ.

127. Martynia *altheæfolia*, sp. n., foliis alternis cordato-ovatis sinuato-3-7-lobis, calyce obliquo 5-lobo antice fisso corollæ tubo plus duplo breviore, staminibus fertilibus quatuor.—Bay of Magdalena.

Herba rudis, diffusa, more generis hispida et viscosa, bis terve dichotome ramosa, et in axillis foliorum ramulis brevibus prædita. Folia omnia alterna vidi; caulina in petiolo 2-4-pollicari 1-1½-pollicaria, obtusissima, irregulariter sinuato-crenata vel in lobos breves latos divisa, basi profunde cordata, crassa et utrinque viscosissimo-puberula pilisque paucis præsertim novella hispida, basi 3-7-nervia, nervis tamen venisve ob consistentia foliorum vix aut non prominentibus; folia ramulorum multo minora, ovata vel suborbiculata. Racemi ad apices ramorum breves. Pedunculi pauci, inter se distantes, 2-3 poll. longi, hispidi, singuli ad axillam bracteæ minutæ squamæformis solitarii, uniflori. Calyx, forma *M. proboscideæ* sed multo minor, vix enim 6 lin. longus, hirsutus, basi bracteolis duo ovatis vix 2 lin longis appressis instructus. Corollæ tubus 12-13 lin. longus, puberulus, basi decurvus, superne ampliatus, minus tamen quam in *M. proboscidea*; limbi laciniæ breves, latæ, patentissimæ. Stamina inclusa, didynama; antheræ per paria leviter cohærentes, lineares, divaricato-biloculares. Stylus staminibus longior, lobis divaricatis obovatis obtusissimis supra undique stigmatosis post anthesin conniventibus. Drupa oblonga, rostro neglecto 2 poll. longa; rostrum 4 poll. longum, incurvum, apice subhamatum, acutum. Cortex spongiosus, ferrugineus, villosus, demum basi circumscissus, secedens in valvulas 2, diutius a cornubus putaminis dependentes. Putamen coriaceo-sublignosum, drupæ conforme sed postice et antice serie duplici dentium longitudinaliter armatum, rostro mox in cornua 2 divaricata fisso, et maturitate usque ad basin in valvulas 2 dehiscens; dentes per dehiscentiam ad margines valvulorum alternatim persistunt, postici 3-4 lin. longi, duri, sublignosi, apice dilatati et sæpe breviter lobati, supremum utriusque valvulæ in rostrum productum brevius tamen quam cornu terminalis valvulæ; dentes antici minores, omnes erostres. Fructus intus unilocularis; placentæ 2, medio valvularum longitudinaliter adnatæ, basi simplices steriles angustæ, supra basin bifido-dilatatæ usque ad parietes fructus utrinque attingentes et ibidem utrinque seminiferæ, dissepimenta formant spuria fructum dividentia in loculos 5 omnes seminiferos, quorum 4 inter placentas et parietes fructus, quintum in medio fructu inter placentas sita. Semina cujusve placentæ circa 15, infima pendula, cætera plus minus transversa, omnia obovoidea, testa spongiosa rugosa, albumine nullo. Embryo membrana tenui inclusa, cotyledonibus carnosis plano-convexis obovatis, radicula brevissima ad hilum spectante.

The fruit of *Martynia* is described by Endlicher (Gen. Pl. p. 724) and others as 4-locular, with a perforate axis, which can scarcely be considered as organically correct, or yet in conformity with the apparent structure. It is, strictly speaking, unilocular, and most clearly so in the lower part of the fruit; but in the upper part it is distinctly divided into *five* cells, all of them containing seeds, for the parietal placentæ of the ovarium bear ovules both on their inner and outer edge, some of which are matured in the space intervening between the two placentæ, designated by Endlicher as a perforate axis. Gærtner, who has very accurately figured the fruit of *M. proboscidea* (Carp. v. 2, t. 10), correctly denominates this space a fifth spurious cell, although he terms it empty (inanis), whereas he certainly represents it (fig. c.) as bearing seeds, as I have also found to be the case. The perforate axis of some *Verbenaceæ*, sometimes designated as a third cell, is very different, being really an empty space intervening between two perfectly closed carpella.

The species now described is probably near *M. triloba*, Cham. and Schlecht. a Mexican plant unknown to me, but of which the description does not agree with our plant either in the form, texture, or position of the leaves. The *M. proboscidea* differs again in the form and proportion of the calyx and corolla, the form of the leaves, and the absence of any crest or teeth on one side of the putamen of the fruit, as well as the want of the horn to the upper tooth on the other side.

ACANTHACEÆ.

128. BELOPERONE *californica*, sp. n., ramulis pubescentibus, foliis petiolatis ovatis vel ovato-lanceolatis basi truncatis vel late cordatis utrinque breviter puberulis, racemis brevibus terminalibus, bracteis minutis, bracteolis lineari-subulatis calyce brevioribus, corollæ profunde bilabiatæ labio superiore emarginato inferiore apice breviter trifido.—Cape San Lucas.

Frutex ramosus, paucifoliatus, ramulis albidis teretibus, junioribus subflavescenti-pubescentibus. Folia pleraque pollicaria, sæpius triangularia vel cordato-ovata, obtusa vel plus minus acuminata, crassiuscula, mollia, paucivenia, petiolo 3-6 lin. longo. Racemi 1-2-pollicares, simplices vel subramosi, in paniculam pyramidatam dispositi. Flores oppositi, subsessiles. Calyces puberuli, 2½ lin. longi, sepalis lineari-lanceolatis acutis, postico paullo minore. Corolla 13-14 lin. longa, glabra; tubus superne paullo ampliatus; labia tubo æquilonga, angusta; superius concavum, apice emarginatum, erectum; inferius erecto-patens, superne paullo dilatatum et breviter et obtuse trilobum. Stamina 2, corolla paullo breviora. Antheræ loculi connectivo latiusculo disjuncti, paralleli, altero minore altius affixo mutico, altero majore basi mucronato. Ovarium basi sterile, paullo contractum, stipitiforme, superne biloculare, loculis biovulatis. Capsulam non vidi.

Solanaceæ.

129. Solanum (Leprophora) *Hindsianum*, sp. n., undique tomento denso stellato subleproso flavicans, aculeis rectis, foliis ovato-vel oblongo-lanceolatis obtusis integerrimis, pedunculis lateralibus brevibus 1-3-floris, corollæ extus floccoso-tomentosæ lobis latissime ovatis.—Bay of Magdalena.

Frutex divaricatus, ramulis teretibus. Aculei sparsi, recti, acerosi, in ramulis sæpe 2-3 lin. longi, in petiolis calycibusque parvi, rari. Tomentum oculo nudo subleprosum, sub lente stellatum, multo densius quam in *S. elæagnifolio et S. leproso*, in ramulis rufescenti-flavicans, in foliorum pagina inferiore albido-flavescens, interdum micans, in pagina superiore laxius, viridi-flavescens, in floribus subfloccosum. Folia longiuscule petiolata, pleraque 1½-2-poll. longa, prope basin 6-9 lin. lata, margine plana, integra, basi rotundata truncata vel rarius subcordata sæpe inæqualia, juniora in axillis breviora obtusiora. Peduculi laterales, brevissimi, vulgo triflori. Pedicelli floriferi 2-3 lin. longi. Calyx turbinato-campanulatus, 5-angulatus, dentibus acuminatis mollibus tubo suo per anthesin brevioribus, post anthesin acutis. Corolla circa pollicem diametro; laciniæ vix ad medium limbi separatæ, 6 lin. latæ, obtusæ cum mucronula parva. Pedicelli fructiferi paullo elongati. Calycis fructiferi laciniæ lanceolatæ, 5-6 lin. longæ. Bacca globosa, 4-5 lin. diametro. Semina orbiculata, plana, nitida, immarginata.

Allied on the one hand to the Peruvian and Chilian *S. leprosum* and *elæagnifolium*, but with a coarse and thicker tomentum, and differently formed leaves and corolla, and on the other to a Texas plant (n. 266 of Drummond's 2nd Collection), which is probably as yet unpublished, but this appears to be scarcely shrubby, it is almost unarmed, has the leaves sharper and usually undulate or sinuate, the peduncles longer, &c., than in our plant. The *S. obtusifolium* of Humb. and Kunth, a Mexican species unknown to me, is also probably nearly allied, but the description does not quite agree with ours in several respects, especially as to the form of the corolla.

130. Solanum *nigrum*, Linn.—San Francisco.

131. Physalis *glabra*, sp. n., perennis, glaberrima, caulibus elongatis prostratis, foliis crassiusculis ovato-lanceolatis obtusis sinuatis vel obtuse subtrilobis hastatisve, floribus parvis immaculatis, calyce fructus subgloboso pentagono glabro, dentibus parvis conniventibus.—Cape San Lucas.

Caules e radice crassa perenni numerosi, 2-3-pedales, dichotome ramosi, tenues, subangulati, virides, nitiduli. Folia sæpius gemina, altero majore et longius petiolato; majora 6-9 lin. longa vel rarius sub-pollicaria, superiora multo minora, pleraque lanceolata, obtusa, basi ovato-dilatata. Flores solitarii, pedicellis gracilibus 6-8 lin. longis. Calyx per anthesin 1½ lin. longus, inflato-campanulatus, basi intrusus, glaber, membranaceus, viridis, dentibus brevissimis. Corolla latiuscule campanulata, 3 lin. longa, basi attenuata, glabra, margine obsolete denticulata. Stamina corollam subæquantia. Calyx fructifer 6-7 lin. longus, valde inflatus, glaber, membranaceus, baccam globosam omnino includens. Semina numerosa, orbiculata, plana.

132. PHYSALIS *crassifolia*, sp. n., perennis, junior minute canescenti-puberula demum glabrata, caulibus prostratis, foliis crassis ovatis undulatis sinuatisve, floribus immaculatis, calycis puberuli dentibus per anthesin vix tubo brevioribus.—Bay of Magdalena.

Specimen unicum vidi nondum fructiferum, *P. glabro* affine quidem, at distinctum foliis latioribus et præsertim floribus majoribus puberulis, calycis dentibus longioribus patentibus. Flores fere *P. hygrophilæ* Mart. sed folia et habitus diversa.

The small thick leaves give the above two species a different aspect from that of any other *Physalis* I am acquainted with.

133. LYCIUM *brevipes*, sp. n., spinosissimum, glabrum, foliis cuneato-oblongis subobovatisve obtusis, floribus subaxillaribus brevissime pedicellatis solitariis, calyce campanulato 5-dentato, corollæ infundibuliformis limbo 5-fido subpatente, genitalibus inclusis.—Bay of Magdalena.

Rami breves, divaricati, ramosissimi, ramulis spinescentibus numerosis brevibus basi sæpius foliatis. Folia 4-6 lin. longa, solitaria vel rarius fasciculata, basi in petiolum angustata, in speciminibus Hindsianis 1-1½ lin. lata oblonga, in Barclayanis 2 lin. lata fere obovata, crassiuscula, obsolete uninervia. Pedicelli solitarii, calyce breviores. Calyx vix linea longior, anguste campanulatus, crassiusculus, viridis, glaber, dentibus 5 subæqualibus lanceolatis acutis. Corolla 5 lin. longa, tubo basi tenui superne in limbum campanulatum 5-fidum dilatato, laciniis ovatis subpatentibus. Bacca parva, polysperma.

A scrubby looking shrub, apparently allied to *L. horridum*, Humb. et Kunth, and to *L. chilense*, Bert.; but, besides the shortness of the pedicels and the smaller flowers, the corolla is less tubular than in *L. horridum*, and much more so than in *L. chilense*. The specimens are not, however, perfect enough for a complete description of the flower and fruit.

SCROPHULARIACEÆ.

134. SCROPHULARIA *nodosa*, Linn. var. *Californica*.—*S. californica*, Cham. Linnæa. 2. p. 585.—San Francisco.

135. ANTIRRHINUM (Orontium) *cyathiferum*, sp. n., (Plate XIX.) humile, erectum, viscoso-pubescens, foliis petiolatis ovatis vel supremis oblongis vel lato-lanceolatis puberulis, floribus axillaribus, calycis laciniis tubo corollæ multo brevioribus.—Bay of Magdalena.

Herba annua, semipedalis, a basi ramosa, tota pube viscidula vestita. Folia alterna vel ima opposita, longiuscule petiolata, majora pollicaria, superiora gradatim minora, omnia integerrima. Flores brevissime pedicellati, fere in omnibus axillis nascentes. Calyx florifer 1½ lin. longus, segmentis linearibus parum inæqualibus viscoso-pubescentibus. Corolla 4 lin. longa, fere *A. Orontii*. Capsula fere *A. Asarinæ*, depresso-globosa, subdidyma, parum obliqua, loculis subæqualibus poro irregulari dehiscentibus. Semina iis *A. Orontii* subsimilia sed majora, cyatho faciei interioris majore profundiore.

A very remarkable species, as being closely allied to our *A. Orontium* in inflorescence, flowers, and seed, and with that species alone (including its variety *A. calycinum*) forming a distinct section in the genus, but abundantly characterised as a species by the foliage and capsule.

Plate XIX. fig. 1, flower; fig. 2, corolla cut open; fig. 3, anther; fig. 4, style; fig. 5, capsule; fig. 6, side view of the seed; fig. 7, front view of the seed; fig. 8, embryo and albumen; all magnified.

136. MAURANDIA *juncea*, sp. n., erecta, glabra, ramis junceis ramosissimis rigidis, foliis paucis parvis oblongo-linearibus, pedicellis brevibus oppositis, corollæ tubulosæ palato prominulo piloso.—From San Diego to the Bay of Magdalena.

Habitus *Russeliæ equisetiformis*. Caules erecti, elati, crassiusculi, ramulis numerosis oppositis vel ternatim verticillatis erectis strictis, supremis paniculatis. Folia opposita vel ternatim verticillata, vix unquam semipollicaria, crassa, integerrima, superiora minuta squamæformia. Flores versus apices ramulorum pauci, per paria inter se distantia dispositi, vel interdum ternatim verticillati. Pedicelli flexuosi, vix semipollicares. Calycis laciniæ vix 1½ lin. longæ, lato-lanceolatæ, acutæ, glabræ, crassæ. Corollæ tubus 8 lin. longus, rectus et subæqualis, basi leviter gibbus, extus viscidulus; labia brevia, superius erectum, bifidum, inferius patens trifidum, palato prominulo at faucem non claudente. Stamina corollam subæquantia. Antherarum loculi divergentes. Stylus superne paululum incrassatus, integer. Capsula ovoidea, 3-4 lin. longa, loculis æqualibus apice dentibus circa sex dehiscentibus. Semina numerosa, profunde rugosa et tuberculoso-subechinata, iis *M. Barclayanæ* similia.

This plant is, at first sight, so very unlike the *Maurandiæ* in cultivation, that it seems unnatural to associate them in the same genus, but the characters derived from the flowers and fruit are the same, and the *Maurandia stricta*, Hook. et Arn., is an intermediate species in habit. The genus altogether is perhaps too closely allied to *Antirrhinum*, in which also very great dissimilarities in habit may be observed, as for instance between *A. Orontium* and *A. Asarina*.

VERBENACEÆ.

137. VERBENA *lasiostachys*, Link.—Hook. et Arn. Bot. Beech. p. 156 et 383.—Santa Clara.

These specimens are certainly identical as to species with Douglas's, referred to by Hooker and Arnott, and also with others from the Berlin Garden, where the species was originally described.

138. VERBENA *paniculata*, Lam.—Hook. Fl. Bor. Amer. 2. p. 117.—San Francisco.

There is little doubt that this plant, as suggested by Hooker, as well as the

V. polystachya, Humb. et Kunth, from Mexico, should be united with *V. hastata*, Linn.

LABIATÆ.

139. HYPTIS (Umbellaria) *laniflora*, sp. n., (Plate XX.) fruticosa, junior minute cano-tomentosa, mox glabrata, foliis petiolatis late ovatis acutis grosse dentatis basi cuneatis truncatisve crassiusculis glabris, cymis umbellæformibus longe pedunculatis paniculatis, bracteis minutis setaceis, calycibus breviter pedicellatis tubuloso-campanulatis longe et dense albo-lanatis, dentibus æqualibus subulatis. —Cape San Lucas.

Frutex divaricato-ramosus, ramis teretibus glabris, cortice albido lœvi. Ramuli juniores tetragoni, tomento tenui mox evanido canescentes. Folia 6-12 lin. longa, longiuscule petiolata, vix longiora quam lata, rigidula, venis parum conspicuis, juniora tomento tenuissimo canescentia, adulta glaberrima vix punctata, superiora sub panicula multo minora, floralia suprema in panicula minima. Pedunculi axillares vel supra-axillares, filiformes, rigidi, pollicem circiter longi, glaberrimi, nitidi. Cymæ ad apices pedunculorum in umbellulam vel fere in capitulum contractæ, 8-12-floræ, rarius brevissime dichotomæ. Bracteæ vix conspicuæ. Pedicelli inæquales, 1-3 lin. longi, albolanati. Calyces 4 lin. longi, lana nivea molli densissima et longa immersi, dentibus vix tubo brevioribus. Corollæ tubus calycem vix æquans, glaber, laciniæ limbi 4 superiores ovatæ, obtusæ, æquales, extus breviter lanatæ, infima ut in omni genere stipitata, stipite incrassato abrupte deflexo, lamina saccata extus breviter lanata. Antheræ ovato-reniformes, loculis confluentibus. Gynophorum crassum, hinc glandula auctum ovarii lobulis dimidio breviore. Stylus apice breviter bifidus, lobo postico obtuso apice stigmatoso, inferiore subdilatato intus et margine stigmatoso. Carpidia oblonga, obtusa, glabra, nuda, plurima sæpius abortiva. Semina exalbuminosa. Cotyledones crassiusculæ basi emarginatæ. Radicula brevis recta.

The genus *Hyptis*, consisting of above two hundred species from the warmer regions of America, and more especially from the Brazilian territories, is remarkable as well from the great diversity of habit, foliage, inflorescence, and calyx observable in different species, as by the constancy of the essential characters derived from the corolla and stamens. But amongst all the various forms hitherto observed, the present species is at once distinguished by the long thick snow-white wool which envelopes the flowers, whilst the rest of the plant is perfectly smooth. Its nearest affinity is perhaps with *H. tomentosa*, Poit., but it differs so much in aspect, even from that one, that, without examining the corolla, one would hardly place it in the same genus.

Plate XX. fig. 1, flower; fig. 2, corolla; fig. 3, the same cut open; fig. 4, anther; fig. 5, calyx cut open, shewing the style; fig. 6, ovary; fig. 7, upper portion of the style; fig. 8, carpidium; fig. 9, seed; fig. 10, embryo; all magnified.

140. MONARDELLA *villosa*, sp. n., (Plate XXI.) caule basi procumbente, foliis ovatis obsolete crenatis ramisque villosis, verticillastris dense globosis magnis solitariis, bracteis exterioribus ovatis foliaceis villosis, calycibus tubulosis elongatis subæqualiter dentatis.—Bodegas.

Caules basi lignosi. Rami breves, adscendentes, ramosi, pilis patentibus villosi. Folia fere *Calaminthæ Nepetæ*, breviter petiolata, semipollicaria vel paullo longiora, obtusa, cuneata, margine recurva, venoso-rugosa, utrinque hirsuta. Pedunculi terminales, verticillastro vel capitulo coronati ultra pollicem diametro, flores continente fere 100 sessiles. Bracteæ sessiles, exteriores foliis similes, interiores minores. Calyces 4 lin. longi, medio paullo ampliati, basi attenuati, membranaceo-foliacei, extus hirsuti, 13-nervii, dentibus 5 brevibus erectis vel demum patentibus, ore intus nuda. Corollæ tubus calycem vix superans; limbi tubo æquilongi labium superius bifidum, inferius tripartitum, laciniis omnibus elongato-linearibus. Stamina exserta, divergentia. Antherarum loculi demum divaricati. Carpidia ovoidea, obtusa, glabra, nuda.

This species has the habit of the three North Californian ones already described, but is very distinct in the form of the leaves, and in the hairiness.

Plate XXI. fig. 1, flower; fig. 2, calyx laid open, showing the style; fig. 3, corolla laid open; fig. 4, anther; fig. 5, ovary; fig. 6, upper part of the style.

141. MICROMERIA *Douglasii*, Benth. Lab. Gen. et Sp. p. 372.—San Francisco.

142. STACHYS *ajugoides*, Benth. Lab. Gen. et. Sp. p. 545.—Santa Clara.

143. STACHYS *Macræi*, Benth. Lab. Gen. et Sp. p. 545.—San Francisco.

PLUMBAGINEÆ.

144. ARMERIA *vulgaris*, Willd. var.—*A. humilis*, Link.—Ebel. Prod. Armer. p. 28.—Bodegas.

145. STATICE *Limonium*, Linn.—Santa Clara.

Found frequently on the eastern and western coasts of North America, as well as on the Chilian and South Brazilian coasts, and always apparently the same as our common European *S. Limonium*.

NYCTAGINEÆ.

146. BOERHAAVIA *polymorpha*, A. Rich.—Hook. et Arn. Bot. Beech, p. 308.—Bay of Magdalena.

This is a perfectly smooth form, common on the western coast of tropical America, in the South Sea Islands, &c., and probably the same as *B. mutabilis*, Br., as well as the several Linnæan and other species included by A. Richard under the above name; but the limits of the species in this difficult and most uninteresting genus are far from being as yet ascertained.

147. ABRONIA *arenaria*, Menzies in Hook. Exot. Fl. t. 193.—Bodegas to the Bay of Magdalena.

148. ABRONIA *umbellata*, Lam.—Hook. l. c. t. 194.—Common in the sands near the sea, from the Oregon to the Bay of Magdalena.

149. ABRONIA *gracilis*, sp. n., pubescenti-vicosa, foliis ovatis oblongisve obtusissimis sinuato-lobatis.—Bay of Magdalena.

A. umbellatæ affinis quidem, sed distincta videtur caule petiolis pedunculisque multo gracilioribus, et præsertim foliis tenuibus omnibus obtusissimis, et margine utroque in lobos 2-4 latos breves obtusissimos inciso.

150. OXYBAPHUS *lævis*, sp. n., glaberrimus, foliis petiolatis cordato-ovatis, involucro unifloro, perigonio florido paullo breviore, staminibus 5 exsertis.—Bay of Magdalena.

Folia et habitus fere *O. glabrifolii*, sed undique, etiam in inflorescentia, glaberrimus. Caulis basi albidus. Folia longiuscule petiolata, inferiora sesquipollicaria, late cordata, obtusiuscula, integerrima vel vix sinuata, crassa, enervia, cujusve paris sæpius æqualia; superiora minora, angustiora, acutiora, sessiliora. Flores ad apices ramulorum pauca. Involucrum calyciforme, breviter pedicellatum, 3-4 lin. longum, profunde 5-fidum, laciniis lanceolatis acutis valde inæqualibus. Flos sessilis, tubo subgloboso, fauce constricta; limbus late campanulatus, 4 lin. longus, brevissime 5-lobus. Stamina 5, ad faucem inserta, distincta, corolla longiora. Ovarium in fundo tubi inclusum. Stylus exsertus, apice crasse capitato-stigmatosus. Fructus non vidi.

In the generic character of *Oxybaphus*, it is usual to give the number of stamens as three, but they vary from two to five in this as well as in some other Nyctagineous genera.

151. ALLIONIA (Wedelia) *malacoides*, sp. n., hirsuta, foliis ovatis sinuatis, involucro triphyllo trifloro.—Bay of Magdalena.

Caules e radice perenni plures, tenues, ramosi, pedales vel longiores, pilis albis subviscosis hirsuti. Folia opposita, cujusve paris valde inæqualia, fere *Erodii malacoidis*, majora semipollicem ad pollicem longa, obtuse et obscure sinuato-lobata vel rarius subintegerrima, apice acuta vel obtusa, basi rotundata sæpius inæquilatera, utrinque viridia et hirsuta, peliolo 2-6 lin. longo. Folium alterum ejusdem paris triplo quadruplove minus. Pedunculi axillares, 3-6 lin. longi, monocephali, in racemos axillares foliatos breves dispositi. Involucri foliola ovata, hirsuta, 2 lin. longa. Flores involucro breviores, sessiles. Perigonii tubus brevis glaber; limbus obovoideo-inflatus, hirtus, ore obliquo, dentibus 4 brevibus conniventibus. Caryopsides involucro paullo breviores, ovoideæ, glabræ, dorso convexæ læves, facie interna cyathiformes, marginibus inflexis dentatis. Semen perfectum non vidi.

POLYGONEÆ.

152. PTEROSTEGIA *macroptera*, sp. n., ramulis junioribus cano-tomentosis, foliis obovatis spathulatisve apice obtusis integerrimis, involucro fructifero maximo hyalino reticulato dorso late bialato apice obsolete trilobo.—Bay of Magdalena.

Caules tenues, rigiduli, dichotome ramosi, ramulis junioribus pube brevi incanis, demum glabratis rubescentibus, ad nodos tumidulis. Folia opposita, membrana angustissima subconnata, exstipulata, 4-6 lin. longa, obtusa, integerrima, basi in petiolum brevissimum contracta, crassiuscula, subcarnosa, enervia vel vix basi uninervia. Involucra axillaria, sessilia, diphylla, uniflora, florida rubida vix lineam longa, foliolis late reniformibus apice obtusissime sinuatis vel obscure rotundato-trilobis, basi trinerviis, nervis mox in rete venarum ramosissimum anastomosantibus. Flos brevissime stipitatus. Perigonium profunde sexfidum, laciniis oblongo-linearibus obtusis, interioribus ut primum paullo minoribus, post anthesin omnibus subæqualibus. Stamina sex?

antheræ tamen in omnibus quos examinavi floribus etiam inapertis delapsæ vel destructæ, et nil inveni nisi filamentorum reliquias breves ad basin laciniarum perigonii insertas. Ovarium brevissime stipitatum, trigonum. Styli tres breves, divergentes, apice capitato-stigmatosi. Ovulum erectum. Involucri fructiferi foliolum intimum 4-5 lin. longum, 6-7 lin. latum, tenuiter hyalino-membranaceum, reticulatim rubrovenium, margine obscure sinuato-trilobum, cæterum obtusissimum et integerrimum, facie undulato-concavum fructum includens, dorso in alas 2 inæquales foliolo ipso textura consimiles excrescens. Foliolum exterius involucri in speciminibus fructiferis deest. Perigonium fructiferum immutatum. Caryopsis 2 lin. longa, trigona, utrinque acuta. Semen caryopsidi conforme, læve et opacum. Albumen farinosum. Embryo excentricus, ratione seminis majusculus, cotyledonibus suborbiculatis planis, radicula supera.

A much stronger and stiffer plant than the very delicate *P. drymarioides*, and remarkable for the large involucres which surround the seed, coloured and veined something like those of a *Bougainvillea*. Each leaf of the involucre, both in this and the *P. drymarioides*, is evidently formed of the union of three, the contiguous margins of which expand into the dorsal wings or crests from whence the generic name is divided, thus assimilating the whole involucre to the usual hexamerous arrangement in other *Eriogoneæ*.

153. ERIOGONUM *parvifolium*, Sm.—Benth. Trans. Soc. Linn. Lond. 17. p. 411.—San Francisco.

154. ERIOGONUM *fasciculatum*, Benth. l. c. p. 411.—San Pedro.

155. ERIOGONUM *latifolium*, Sm.—Benth. l. c. p. 412.—Bodegas.

156. ERIOGONUM *cinereum*, sp. n., suffruticosum, caule ramoso basi foliato, foliis ovatis vel ovato-oblongis supra fuscis subtus albido-cinereis cauleque tomentosis, petiolis basi vix dilatatis nudis, pedunculo nudo elongato apice ramoso, capitulis lateralibus terminalibusve, involucris in capitulo 3-6 sessilibus campanulatis multifloris villosis, bracteolis plumosis demum exsertis, perigonio villosulo.—San Pedro.

Suffrutex habitu *E. oblongifolio* affinis, perigonio villoso facile distinctus. Caules ramosiores, altius foliati. Tomentum breve, undique cinereum, in pagina inferiore foliorum albidum, in pagina superiore et caulibus fuscescens. Folia sæpius in axillis fasciculata, majora pollicaria, obtusa, margine subrevoluta et plus minus undulato-crispa, basi rotundato-cuneata, subtus prominule penninervia, petiolo 2-4 lin. longo. Pedunculus pedalis, apice dichotome ramosus, pleiocephalus. Bracteæ ad ramificationes parvæ, lanceolatæ. Capitula magnitudine *E. oblongifolii*, bracteis paucis minimis suffulta. Involucra 2 lin. longa, anguste campanulata, extus tomentosa, dentibus 5-6 brevibus obtusis inæqualibus. Flores in involucro ultra 20. Pedicelli glabri, involucrum æquantes. Bracteolæ setaceæ, plumosæ, per anthesin involucrum æquantes, demum exsertæ. Perigonium fere 2 lin. longum; laciniæ oblongo-lineares, uninerviæ, obtusæ, margine coloratæ, dorso præsertim exteriores molliter villosæ. Filamenta basi breviter pilosula. Ovarium glaberrimum. Styli tres, divaricati.

A very distinct species, allied in general habit and inflorescence to *E. oblongifolium* and *E. latifolium*, and in the downy flowers and colour of the tomentum to *E. longifolium*.

157. ERIOGONUM *elongatum*, sp. n., perenne? foliis caulinis petiolatis oblongo-lanceolatis supra

arachnoideis subtus albo-lanatis, bracteis brevibus appressis, involucris secus ramos solitariis sessilibus lanatis apice truncatis multifloris.—San Pedro.

Affine *E. dichotomo*. Caulis pars inferior et folia infima mihi desunt. Rami in speciminibus suppetentibus bipedales, stricti, rigidi, basi fasciculato-ramosi, lana arachnoidea demum decidua albicantes. Folia ad ramificationes inferiores bipollicaria, basi in petiolum brevem angustata. Pedunculi seu rami floriferi pedales, semel vel bis furcati. Bracteæ oppositæ vel ternatim verticillatæ, 2 lin. longæ, basi connatæ, lanceolato-subulatæ, rigidæ, appressæ. Involucra in quoque ramulo 5-9, inter se longe distantia, 3 lin. longa, tubuloso-campanulata, extus tomentosa, apice truncata et integra vel obscure et obtusissime 6-dentata. Flores in involucro ultra 30. Pedicelli glabri, graciles, involucro subdimidio longiores. Bracteolæ setaceæ, parce plumosæ, pedicellis breviores. Perigonium glabrum, quam in *E. dichotomo* minus, laciniis cuneato-oblongis. Filamenta basi vix breviter ciliata. Ovarium glaberrimum. Styli tres, divaricati.

158. ERIOGONUM *gracile*, sp. n., annuum, erectum, foliis petiolatis ovatis oblongisve cauleque albo-lanatis, pedunculis gracilibus virgatis dichotome ramosis superne glabris, involucris parvis secus ramos sessilibus solitariis subglabris breviter sexdentatis multifloris.—San Pedro.

Herba gracilis, virgato-ramosissima, semipedalis ad pedalis, lana subarachnoidea in foliis et parte inferiore caulis densa, summitatibus omnino glabris. Folia sub ramis inferioribus fasciculata, semipollicaria, longiuscule petiolata, margine undulato-crispa; ad ramificationes superiores minora, ovata, sessilia. Pedunculi seu rami floriferi tenues, fere filiformes, rigiduli, glabri vel basi laxe et tenuiter lanati. Bracteæ parvæ, lanceolato-subulatæ, appressæ. Involucra vix lineam longa, siccitate nigricantia, dentibus brevibus erectis obtusiusculis. Flores in involucro ultra 20. Pedicelli glabri, exserti. Bracteolæ tenuiter setaceæ, subplumosæ, pedicellis breviores. Perigonium $\frac{3}{4}$ lin. longum, glabrum, laciniis exterioribus late obovatis, interioribus oblongis. Filamenta et ovarium glabra. Styli tres, divaricati.

Allied to *E. vimineum*, but the flowering branches are much more slender, and the involucres and flowers scarcely more than half the size.

159. ERIOGONUM *intricatum*, sp. n., (Plate XXII.) annuum, foliis subradicalibus rosulatis longe petiolatis suborbiculatis viscoso-pubescentibus, pedunculo scapiformi divaricato-ramosissimo glaberrimo, ramulis dense fasciculatis, involucris minimis sessilibus solitariis multifloris, bracteolis obovato-vel cuneato-oblongis.—San Bartolomè.

Folia omnia ad basin caulis conferta, rosulata, pube viscosa non albicante vestita, semipollicem longa et lata, crassiuscula, obtusissima, margine undulato-crispa et subcrenata, petiolo usque ad pollicem longo hirto basi dilatato. Ramus florifer seu pedunculus scapiformis semipedalis usque ad bipedalis, undique glaberrimus, nitidus, siccitate nigricans, basi breviter erectus, dein divaricato-ramosissimus; rami ad quemque nodum numerosissimi, dense verticillato-fasciculati, alii breves subsimplices, alii plus minus elongati, pariter et repetite fasciculato-ramosi. Ramuli ultimi tenues, rigiduli, ad nodos subarticulati. Bracteolæ minutæ, patentes. Involucra ad nodos et secus ramulos ultimos distantia, solitaria, sessilia, $\frac{1}{3}$ lin. longa, campanulata, inæqualiter et obtuse dentata, ultra-12-flora. Pedicelli glabri, involucrum breviter superantes. Bracteolæ obovatæ vel spathulato-oblongæ, exteriores latiores, interiores angustiores, involucrum breviter superantes, apice dorso puberulæ. Perigonium vix $\frac{1}{4}$ lin. longum, laciniis cuneato-oblongis obtusis glabris vix inæqualibus. Stamina perigonio subbreviora, glabra. Ovarium glabrum. Styli tres.

A very remarkable species, differing from all others in the total want of white wool even on the radical leaves, the curious fasciculate ramification, the excessive minuteness of the flowers, and the form of the bracteolæ.

Plate XXII. fig. 1, involucre; fig. 2, separate flower and bractea; fig. 3, portion of the perigon laid open; fig. 4, ovary; fig. 5, fruit enclosed in the persistent perigon; fig. 6, separate fruit; all magnified.

160. RUMEX *crispus*, Linn.—San Pedro.

161. ANTIGONON *leptopus*, Hook. et Arn. Bot. Beech. p. 308. t. 69.—San Lucas.

This curious genus, established by Endlicher, and placed by him next to *Brunnichia*, is in fact closely allied to that genus, although some slight inaccuracies or imperfections in the descriptions published have induced C. A. Meyer, in his arrangement of Polygonaceæ, to doubt even whether it should belong to the same order. The habit and inflorescence, the number and portion of the floral organs, the peculiar insertion of the ovule, and the structure of the seed in all essential points, are the same in *Antigonon* and *Brunnichia*, and characterise, in a marked manner, the small tribe of *Brunnichieæ*. The chief generic distinctions between the two plants are,—1st. The folioles of the perigon in *Brunnichia* are nearly equal, more or less connate usually to about the middle, (though never perhaps so high as figured by Gærtner,) and their midrib is decurrent on the pedicel, one of them very broadly, the four others but slightly; whilst in *Antigonon* the outer folioles are cordate, and very much larger than the inner ones, and all are free nearly to the base and not decurrent. 2nd. The filaments in both genera proceed from a membranous disk or cup, which in *Brunnichia* is entirely adherent to the perigon, in *Antigonon* adherent at the base only and then free, but not so much so as represented in the figure above quoted. 3rd. Both genera have the ovule suspended to a free funiculus, which as the fruit grows, retains its original dimensions, so as to force the seed into an erect position; the seed is large, of a pyramidate oval shape, the embryo slightly excentrical, with large flat cotyledons, and a conspicuous radicle directed to the apex of the fruit, the whole imbedded in a copious mealy albumen, deeply divided by longitudinal furrows; but in *Brunnichia* this albumen is divided to near the middle into about six lobes separated by furrows, to which correspond narrow false dissepiments projecting from the inner surface of the pericarp (as in some species of oak and walnut); whilst in *Antigonon* the lobes of the albumen are deep, numerous, irregular, sinuate and lobed, and closely appressed to each other, resembling in some respects the so called *ruminated* albumens, and the pericarp is perfectly smooth inside.

Chenopodiaceæ.

162. Obione *Barclayana*, sp. n., monoica? procumbens, incana, foliis inferioribus obovatis obtusis, superioribus oblongis acutiusculis, omnibus mucronulatis integerrimis, bracteis demum suborbiculatis indurato-incrassatis margine dentatis extus farinoso-incanis nudis vel cristula duplici minima instructis.—Bay of Magdalena.

Planta tota albido-subfarinosa. Rami elongati, procumbentes. Folia inferiora fere pollicaria, late vel anguste obovata, basi in petiolum longiusculum angustata, superiora minora, angustiora, forma variabilia, suprema vix 3-4 lin. longa, utrinque acuta. Flores in axillis glomerati, masculi in specimine perpauci imperfecti, fœminei in quaque axilla 3-5. Bracteæ fructiferæ vix lineam longæ et latæ, extus farinoso-incanæ et subspongiosæ, intus indurato-cartilagineæ læves, se invicem arcte appressæ et fere ad apicem vel demum omnino coalitæ, margine dentatæ, dente terminali majore, basi angustatæ et integerrimæ, dorso convexæ, uninerviæ et basi nunc cristula vel dente duplici onustæ, nunc nudæ. Pericarpium tenuissimum, hyalinum. Stylus fere ad basin bifidus. Semen verticale, testa brunnea tenui, embryone annulari.

163. Obione *microcarpa*, sp. n., monoica, procumbens vel divaricata, pusilla, incana, foliis ovalibus oblongisve obtusis integerrimis basi vix angustatis, bracteis demum suborbiculatis indurato-incrassatis margine dentatis extus farinoso-incanis nudis vel cristula duplici minima instructis.—San Diego.

Planta vix semipedalis, divaricato-ramosa, junior albido-farinosa, ramis tamen demum denudatis. Folia subsessilia, 2-3 lin. longa, 1-1½ lin. lata, obtusa et rarius mucronulata, uninervia, basi rotundata vel cuneata. Flores in axillis glomerati, masculi plures, fœminei pauci. Perigonium in masculis 5-partitum, laciniis lineari-oblongis. Stamina 5. Bracteæ fœmineæ fructiferæ vix semilineam longæ, cæterum iis *O. Barclayanæ* haud dissimiles. Dentes proportione minores et cristulæ rariores.

The above two species, perfectly distinct from each other, are, however, both of them probably allied to *O. parvifolia* Moq. Tand. Mon. Chenop. p. 73, or *Atriplex parvifolia*, Humb. and Kunth; the *O. Barclayana* comes nearest in the size of the fruit, but both differ in the perfectly entire leaves, and the ripe bracteæ completely adherent to each other in their cartilagineous inner margins, whilst Moquin places the *O. parvifolia* in his first section, with the bracts free in the upper part. Kunth's description is, however, not explicit in this respect.

164. Obione *tetraptera*, sp. n., divaricato-ramosa, canescens, foliis lanceolato-vel oblongo-linearibus obtusis integerrimis, bracteis ovatis apice paucidentatis fructiferis omnino coalitis dorso alis duo quam bracteæ ipsæ multo majoribus instructis.—From the coast of California, probably San Diego.

Rami adsunt sesquipedales, duri, divaricato-ramosi, floribus fœminiis plerisque marcidis fructibusque copiosis, inter quibus flores masculos nullos detexi. Folia majora pollicaria, 1-2 lin. lata, basi breviter angustata. Flores in axillis dense glomerati. Bracteæ floriferæ anguste rhombeæ, acutæ, superne apertæ et subdentatæ, basi coalitæ et longe attenuatæ. Stylus exsertus, ultra medium bifidus. Bracteæ fructiferæ valde auctæ, ovatæ, fere 3 lin. longæ, induratæ, undique clausæ, dorso uninerviæ et ad utrumque latus nervi medii longitudinaliter cristato-alatæ, alis 3-4 lin. latis bractearum apicem longe superantibus membranaceis reticulatis undulato-subcrispis margine dentatis. Semen verticale, maturum tamen non vidi.

This is a remarkable species, and the great expansion of the dorsal wings of the bracteæ gives it a very different appearance from that of the other *Obiones* I am acquainted with; yet, although I have seen neither male flowers nor the perfect seed, there appears no doubt of its belonging to the genus.

LAURACEÆ.

165. OREODAPHNE *californica*, Nees ab Esenb. Syst. Laurin. p. 463.—Most common about the Estrecho de Karquines, also on Angel Island.

A very handsome tree, both bark and leaves are highly aromatic even in the dried state, with nearly the odour of our common Bay-tree (*Laurus nobilis*). The berry is about the size of a damson plum, but the specimens are not in a state to show the size of the cup if any.

EUPHORBIACEÆ.

166. PEDILANTHUS *macrocarpus*, sp. n. (Plate XXIII. A,) ramulis brevibus carnosis articulatis, foliis parvis ovato-lanceolatis carinato-subplanis, capsula maxima coccis bicornutis.—Bay of Magdalena.

Frutex tripedalis, ramosissimus. Ramuli breves, crasso-carnosi, dichotomi, teretes, ad nodos constricti, internodiis 6-9 lin. longis, 2-4 lin. diametro. Folia opposita, sessilia, tenuiter carnosa, 3-4 lin. longa, plana vel leviter carinata, acuta, basi parum angustata. Pedunculi terminales, breves, recurvi. Involucrum pollicare, calceiforme, basi turbinatum, ore contracto obliquo obtuse bilobo, hinc ad medium fissum, ovario e fissura exserto, illinc productum in saccum breviter tricuspidatum, supra usque ad orem involucri triplicatum et lamina auctum lanceolata, biloba, e basi sacci orta, et in plicas arcte appressa, glandulas sex basi intus fovente. Glandulæ in involucro nullæ. Bracteolæ setaceæ, breves, exteriores extra flores masculos basi subconnatæ; interiores circa florem fœmineum paucæ. Flores masculi ultra 30, exteriores involucro breviores, interiores ex ore involucri breviter exserti. Pedicelli glabri, supra medium articulati. Flos fœmineus solitarius, pedicello basi valde incrassato. Stylus superne attenuatus, apice breviter recurvo-trilobus, lobis emarginatis supra stigmatosis. Capsula carnosa, plus pollice diametro, stylo acuminata, coccis singulis deorsum in cornua duo conica productis. Semina globosa.

Plate XXIII. A, fig. 1, involucre cut open, showing the male flowers and the peduncle of the female flower; fig. 2, male flower and bractea; fig. 3, female flower; fig. 4, vertical section of the fruit; fig. 5, transverse section of the fruit; all magnified, except the fruit.

167. EUPHORBIA *californica*, sp. n. (Plate XXIII. B,) fruticosa, nodoso-carnosa, glabra, foliis petiolatis parvis ovatis obtusis integerrimis complicatis, involucri dentibus exterioribus late orbicalatis membranaceis glandula magna depressa, interioribus parvis conniventibus bifidis, capsula glabra lævi.—Bay of Magdalena.

Frutex 2-3-pedalis, ramosissimus, ramulis lignoso-carnosis subaphyllis, ultimis crassis vix pollicaribus. Folia perpauca, carnosula, vix 2 lin. longa. Pedunculus crassus, 1 lin. longus. Involucrum campanulatum, limbo plano 3 lin. diametro, laciniis exterioribus margine membranaceis, interiorum lobis fimbriatis. Flores masculi numerosi. Capsula subcarnosa, 3 lin. diametro. Stylus ad medium sexfidus.

Plate XXIII. B, fig. 1, involucre laid open; fig. 2, male flowers; fig. 3, single male flower and bractea; fig. 4, female flower; fig. 5, seed; all magnified.

168. EUPHORBIA *polycarpa*, sp. n., annua, glaberrima, basi verticillato-ramosa, ramis diffusis dichotome ramosissimis teretibus, foliis sub verticillo cuneato-oblongis, ramorum oppositis oblique obovato-orbiculatis integerrimis basi subcordatis, capitulis parvis pedicellatis, summis fasciculatis, involucri dentibus exterioribus petaloideis integris involucro ipso æquilongis, fructibus lævibus vel ad carpellorum dorsum punctulato-scabris, seminibus lævibus albidis.—Bay of Magdalena.

Rami ad apicem caulis brevissimi, simplices vel ab ipsa basi numerossimi, fasciculato-subverticillati, inæquales, gracillimi, læves, repetite et inæqualiter dichotomi vel ad nodos inferiores subfasciculato-ramosi, usque ad 6-9 poll. longi. Folia sub verticillo perpauca, obtusissima, integerrima, basi angustata, 2-4 lin. longa. Folia ramealia 1-3 lin. longa. Stipulæ parvæ, ovatæ, acutæ, integræ vel apice laceræ, ad folia inferiora obliteratæ. Capitula quam in *E. chamæsyce* minora. Appendices petaloideæ involucri majores albæ vel roseæ, glandula depressa integra; dentes interiores breves, acuti. Capsula vix semilineam longa.

This little plant is near our *E. chamæsyce*, and also probably to *E. callitrichoides*, Humb. et Kunth, but differs in several points from both. The petaloid appendages are much larger and more conspicuous than in *E. chamæsyce*.

169. EUPHORBIA *serpens*, Humb. et Kunth? Nov. Gen. et sp. v. 2. p. 52.—Folia omnia integerrima. Squamæ petaloideæ involucrorum parum conspicuæ, integræ vel obsolete trilobæ. Semina albida, lævia.—San Pedro.

170. EUPHORBIA *leucophylla*, sp. n., herbacea, stipulata, a basi dichotome ramosa, undique albo-lanata, foliis oppositis subsessilibus orbiculato-cordatis argute dentatis, capitulis terminalibus aggregatis, involucri dentibus exterioribus petaloideis latis integris vel crenatis involucro ipso æquilongis, capsula pilosa, seminibus albidis lævibus.—Cape San Lucas.

Herba semipedalis, ut videtur annua. Rami crassiusculi, teretes, pilis mollibus albidis dense lanati. Stipulæ minutæ, ovatæ. Folia 3-4 lin. longa et lata, crassiuscula, basi cordata, margine cartilagineo inæqualiter vel subduplicato-dentata, utrinque vel præsertim in pagina inferiore tomento niveo vestita. Capitula ad apices ramulorum in glomerulum congesta. Involucra turbinata, tomentosa; dentes exteriores petaloidei $\frac{3}{4}$ lin. longi, 1 lin. lati, glandula elliptica integra. Capsulæ quam in *E. pilulifera* majores, pilis laxis vestitæ.

171. EUPHORBIA *Magdalenæ*, sp. n., fruticosa, stipulata, divaricato-ramosa, glaberrima, foliis oppositis petiolatis obovato-oblongis obtusis vel emarginatis integerrimis, capitulis axillaribus alaribusque solitariis parvis, involucri dentibus exterioribus petaloideis obovato-orbicularibus vix involucro brevioribus, capsulis glabris lævibus, seminibus albidis lævibus.—Bay of Magdalena.

Rami teretes cortice albido. Ramuli fere angulo recto divergentes, oppositi vel sæpius abortu solitarii, subtetragoni, rubescentes. Stipulæ breves, latæ, mox obliteratæ. Petioli brevissimi. Folia 3-5 lin. longa, 2-2$\frac{1}{2}$ lin. lata. Pedicelli breves, pauci. Involucra vix semilinea longiora, turbinata, lævia. Squamæ petaloideæ conspicuæ, albæ. Glandulæ parvæ, integræ. Capsula semilineam longa.

There are but very few flowers on the specimens, and several of the involucres are converted by the prick of some insect into red tubular processes, not unlike the calyx of a *Cuphea.*

172. EUPHORBIA *misera*, sp. n., fruticosa, exstipulata, ramis glabris tortuosis, foliis perpaucis obovato-orbiculatis crassiusculis viridibus, capitulis in ramulis nodiformibus 1-2 sessilibus, involucri dentibus exterioribus petaloideis subdentatis glandula sua vix latioribus, capsula majuscula punctato-puberula.—San Diego and San Quentin.

Frutex habitu *Mozinnis* accedens. Rami tortuosi, subaphylli, cortice laxiusculo pallido. Ramuli breves, nodiformes, hinc inde folia ferunt perpauca, 2-4 lin. longa, breviter petiolata, viridia, utrinque minute puberula. Involucra lineam longa; dentes exteriores quinque, squamæformes, orbiculati, margine petaloidei, colorati, basi late glanduliferi; dentes interiores breves, inflexi. Capsulam unicam vidi immaturam, axi jam plus linea longa, styli lobis bipartitis.

173. EUPHORBIA *Hindsiana*, sp. n. (Plate XXIV.) fruticosa, exstipulata, glaberrima, foliis sparsis petiolatis obovato-orbiculatis retusis crassiusculis pallidis penninerviis, cymis terminalibus oligocephalis, involucri dentibus exterioribus amplis dentatis, capsula magna lævi, seminibus obovoideo-globosis albidis foveolatis.—Cape San Lucas.

Frutex ramis crassis subtortuosis divaricatis, junioribus lævibus. Folia ramealia alterna, majora pollicem fere longa et lata, basi subcuneata vel rotundata, crassiuscula, subcarnosa, nervo medio et venis utrinsecus 3-4 subtus immersis et subpurpurascentibus; petiolo 2-3 lin. longo; floralia opposita, similia sed minora. Cymæ foliis breviores, semel bisve irregulariter bifurcæ, sæpius aphyllæ, 4-8-cephalæ, pedicellis ultimis 2-3 lin. longis. Involucrum magnitudine *E. corollatæ*, hemisphæricum; dentes 5 interiores ovati, inflexi; 5 exteriores petaloidei, 1 lin. longi, 1½ lin. lati, plus minus trilobi vel dentati, glandulis majusculis integris. Flores masculi numerosi, bracteis plumosis; fœmineorum styli rami bifidi. Capsula 3 lin. longa. Semina 2 lin. longa, nequaquam angulata, hinc hilo lineari fusco notata.

Plate XXIV. fig. 1, head of flowers; fig. 2, involucre laid open; fig. 3, male flower and bractea; fig. 4, fruit; fig. 5, seed; all magnified.

174. EUPHORBIA *eriantha*, sp. n., herbacea, exstipulata, erecta, subdichotome ramosa, foliis sparsis subpetiolatis linearibus serrulatis integerrimisque superioribus basi discoloribus, capitulis terminalibus aggregatis, involucris incano-tomentosis, dentibus interioribus latis fimbriatis, exterioribus subbrevioribus digitatim 7-11-lobis, capsula cano-tomentosa.—Bay of Magdalena.

Herba stricta, vix pedalis, ramis erectis fastigiatis. Folia caulina pauca, semipollicaria, lineam lata, apice acuta et pauciserrata, vel interdum obtusa vel emarginata et integerrima; basi in petiolum 1-2 lin. longum angustata; floralia plurima, approximata, caulinis longiora longius petiolata et basi albida, cæterum consimilia. Capitula plurima ad apices ramorum subsessilia. Involucrum lineam longum. Styli rami tres, simplices. Capsula 2 lin. longa. Semina nondum matura in sicco foveolata.

175. ACALYPHA *californica*, sp. n., fruticosa, ramulis foliisque novellis tomentoso-puberulis demum glabratis, foliis petiolatis late ovatis subcordatis crenatis, spicis axillaribus solitariis, aliis fœmineis 2-3-floris bibracteatis, aliis masculis vel subandrogynis brevibus ebracteatis.—Bay of Magdalena.

Specimen adest unicum ramosissimum, lignosum, ramulis brevibus teretibus pulveraceo-canescentibus, apicibus junioribus pube subflavicante tomentellis. Stipulæ lanceolato-setaceæ, deciduæ. Folia pollicaria vel paullo longiora, acutiuscula vel obtusa, basi late rotundato-cordata, supra pilis paucis sparsis et subtus ad venas minute hirtella, cæterum glabra, subtus nigro-punctulata, minute pellucido-punctata. Spicæ axillares, fere omnes petiolo breviores. Flores fœminei pauci, uno alterove inter bracteas duo reniformes crenatas 2-3 lin. latas sessili, uno sæpe pedicellato, ebracteato. Calix tripartitus, laciniis brevibus ovato-lanceolatis acutis. Capsula echinato-rugosa. Spicæ masculæ subsessiles, 4 lin. longæ, basi sæpe flore fœmineo ebracteato auctæ.

176. MOZINNA *canescens*, sp. n., (Plate XXV.) foliis petiolatis ovato-subrotundis integris trilobisque utrinque tomento tenuissimo incanis.—Bay of Magdalena.

Frutex ramulis crassis divaricatis, junioribus tomento minuto incanis, ramis cortice albido obtectis. Succus lacteus copiosus e partibus læsis expressus guttas reliquit in sicco atras. Folia 1-1½ poll. longa, longiuscule petiolata, obtusissima, basi cuneata rotundata vel subcordata, margine integerrima undulata vel sinuato-triloba, crassiuscula, subtrinervia et obscure reticulato-venosa; tomentum molliter subvelutinum etsi tenuissimum, in pagina superiore canescens, in inferiore albidum. Flores dioici: masculi in axillis superioribus plures, irregulariter cymoso-corymbosi, cymis tamen vix folia excedentibus. Bracteæ ad ramificationes parvæ. Calyx incanus, 1½-2 lin. longus, 5-partitus, laciniis linearibus obtusis. Corolla urceolata, 3 lin. longa, breviter et obtuse 5-loba, apice extus canescenti-tomentella. Columna staminea basi glandulis quinque oblongis apice capitatis stipata. Antheræ circa decem, irregulariter biseriales, ovatæ, crassæ, didymæ, breviter stipitatæ. Flores fœminei quam masculi rariores. Calyx et corolla maris vel paullo longiores. Ovarium sessile, glandulis quinque brevibus latis retusis circumdatum. Stylus corolla brevior, apice breviter 2-3-lobus, lobis 2-3-fidis, laciniis 2-3 capitato-stigmatosis, cæteris (in specimine unico perfecto) nudis acutis. Fructus calyce persistente suffultus, diametro fere pollicari, axi 6 lin. longa, coccis 2 vel 3, cortice subcarnoso, endocarpio durissimo.

Plate XXV. fig. 1, male flower; fig. 2, calyx; fig. 3, corolla cut open, and stamens; fig. 4, female flower; fig. 5, corolla cut open, and ovary; fig. 6, fruit; fig. 7, fruit with one cell laid open, showing the seed; all magnified, except the fruit.

177. HENDECANDRA *procumbens*, Eschsch.—Hook. et Arn. Bot. Beech. p. 389. t. 91.—From San Francisco to Magdalena Bay, common.

178. SEROPHYTON *lanceolatum*, gen. nov. e tribu *Crotonearum*.—Bay of Magdalena.

CHAR. GEN. Flores monoici. Masculi: calyx 5-partitus, æstivatione valvata. Corollæ petala 5, æstivatione convolutiva. Glandulæ 5, petalis alternæ. Stamina 5-10; filamenta in columnam connata, apice breviter libera, verticillatim subbiseriata. Antheræ biloculares, introrsæ, versatiles. Flores fœminei: calyx 5-partitus. Corollæ petala 5, parva vel rudimentaria. Glandulæ subnullæ. Ovarium sessile, loculis uniovulatis. Styli 3, simplices, hirsuti.—Herbæ erectæ vel adscendentes, pilis longis appressis plus minus vestitæ, pube stellata nulla. Folia alterna, integerrima. Spicæ axillares, flore infimo fœmineo, superioribus pluribus masculis. Bracteæ sub floribus singulis parvæ.

S. lanceolata, adscendens, ramosa, foliis subpetiolatis lanceolatis, spicis folio brevioribus, floris masculi glandulis lanceolatis acutissimis.

Ramus in specimine unico sesquipedalis, adscendens, teres, undique pilis adpressis sericeo-nitentibus obtectus. Folia 1-1½ poll. longa, 4-5 lin. lata, basi rotundata et petiolo brevi subtensa, acuta, integerrima, utrinque viridia at pilis cano-sericeis obtecta, uninervia vel basi subtrinervia. Spicæ in axillis superioribus breviter pedunculatæ, 3-6 lin. longæ. Rhachis flexuosa. Bracteæ oblongæ, patentes, ½ lin. longæ. Flos fœmineus subsessilis. Sepala 2½ lin. longa, lanceolata, acuta, utrinque et præsertim extus piloso-hirta, æqualia, integerrima. Petala sepalis dimidio breviora, linearia vel oblonga. Ovarium disco subgianduloso impositum, villosissimum. Styli tres, filiformes, recurvo-patentes, hirsuti, acutiusculi, versus apicem stigmatosi. Flores masculi 3-4, subsessiles. Sepala 2 lin. longa, lineari-lanceolata. Petala oblongo-lanceolata, basi breviter stipitata, apice acuta, pilis paucis ciliata, sepalis vix breviora. Glandulæ ½ lin. longæ, e basi lata acutissime lanceolatæ. Columna staminea petalis vix brevior, antheris 8-10 breviter stipitatis inæqualiter biseriatis. Capsula pedicello 2-3 lin. longo imposita, sericea, tricocca, axi vix 2 lin. longa.

I have seen but a single specimen, and that not so satisfactory a one as could be wished, of this plant, but it is evidently distinct from any of the genera hitherto enumerated amongst *Crotoneæ*, and has a habit very similar to that of two new Texian species from the late Mr. Drummond's collections, in which also the same generic characters have been verified in excellent specimens. The following specific diagnoses will serve to characterise them.

S. Drummondi, caulibus erectis strictis sericeo-pilosis, foliis sessilibus elliptico-oblongis ad venas pilosis, spicis gracilibus multifloris folio multo longioribus, floris masculi glandulis linearibus glabris.—Texas, Drummond, n. 245 of the 2d collection, and n. 317 of the 3d coll.

S. pilosissimum, caulibus erectis strictis appresse pilosissimis, foliis inferioribus obovatis subpetiolatis, superioribus ovato-lanceolatis omnibus longe pilosissimis, spicis gracilibus multifloris folio multo longioribus, floris masculi glandulis obovato-lanceolatis piloso-hirtis.—Texas, Drummond, n. 263 of the 2d coll. and n. 322 of the 3d coll.

179. EREMOCARPUS *setigerus*, gen. nov. (Plate XXVI.)—San Pedro.

CHAR. GEN. Flores monoici, in dichotomiis caulis fasciculati, masculi plures pedicellati, pedicellis basi subcoalitis, fœminei 1-3, subsessiles. Flores masculi: calyx 5-partitus, æstivatione valvata. Corolla nulla. Stamina 7-10, disco communi centrali setoso imposita; filamenta libera calyce longiora; antheræ adnatæ, oblongæ, biloculares, loculis longitudinaliter dehiscentibus. Flores fœminei: calyx et corolla nulla. Ovarium stellato-pubescens, oblongum, uniloculare. Ovulum unicum, ex apice loculi lateraliter pendulum. Stylus filiformis setosus simplex, apice uncinatus glabrior, summo apice stigmatosus. Capsula obovato-oblonga, bivalvis. Semen nitidum. Albumen carnosum. Radicula supera, linearis. Cotyledones radiculæ vix æquilongi, orbiculato-plani.

Species unica, *E. setigerus*.—*Croton? setigerus*, Hook. Fl. Bor. Amer. v. 2. p. 141.—Herba annua, humilis, graveolens, habitu fere *Crozophoræ*, undique pube stellata copiosa obtecta et setis longis rigidis diaphanis plus minus hispida. Rami divaricati, 2-3-chotome ramosissimi. Folia alterna, vel ad ramificationes gemina vel terna, longiusculo petiolata; lamina pollicaris late ovata, obtusiuscula, subintegerrima, crassiuscula, mollis, subtrinervis, basi cuneata vel rotundata. Glandulæ nullæ. Folia superiora gradatim minora, floralia suprema parva, bracteæformia, omnia tamen longiusculo petiolata. Flores in dichotomiis inferioribus pauciores laxiores, in apicibus ramorum dense fasciculato-cymosi, foliis floralibus circumdati. Pedunculi masculorum communes brevissimi, pedicelli calyce longiores vel breviores. Calycis laciniæ pube stellata rigida copiose obtectæ, lineam longæ, oblongæ, obtusæ. Filamenta in centro floris calyce subduplo longiora, basi setosa, cæterum glabra. Ovaria in fasciculis inferioribus breviter et crasse stipitata, in superioribus omnino sessilia.

This plant is remarkable amongst *Euphorbiaceæ* from the female organ being constantly reduced to a single carpel, in other respects resembling the carpels of which the *Crotoneæ* are composed. It has something the habit of the European *Crozophora tinctoria*, and has, even in the dry state, a very strong disagreeable smell. It was also found by Douglas on the north-west coast, as far as the Columbia river, and from a very imperfect specimen was referred, in the Flora

Boreali-Americana, with doubt to *Croton*, from which more perfect specimens show it to differ in many important particulars.

PLATE XXVI. Fig. 1, fascicle of flowers containing one female and four male flowers; Fig. 2, male flower; Fig. 3, anther; Fig. 4, ovary and style; Fig. 5, fruit; Fig. 6, seed; Fig. 7, section of the seed, showing the albumen and embryo.

180. EUPHORBIACEA?—A shrub found on the coast from San Quentin to the Bay of Magdalena, always close to the sea, with opposite, coriaceous, entire, ovate leaves, and small heads of flowers on very short peduncles, which may possibly belong to the *Euphorbiaceæ*, but the flowers on the specimens found are all male, and only in very young bud.

CELASTRACEÆ.*

181. MAYTENUS *phyllanthoides*, sp. n., glaber, foliis petiolatis obovatis obtusissimis integerrimis basi cuneatis crasso-coriaceis, floribus fasciculatis breviter pedicellatis.—Bay of Magdalena.

Frutex ramis crassis tortuosis, cortice cinereo. Ramuli teretes breves. Folia alterna, majora 10-12 lin. longa, 6-8 lin. lata, basi in petiolum 2 lin. longum angustata, obsolete uninervia vel subpenninervia, sub lente utrinque crebre et minute lepidoto-punctata, inferiora cujusve ramuli interdum ad squamulam minutam reducta. Flores in axillis foliorum, vel ad nodos ramulorum annotinorum plurima, parva, fasciculata, pedicellis singulis unifloris 1-1½ lin. longis. Calyx brevis, cyathiformis, 5-dentatus. Petala patentia, ovata, obtusa, concaviuscula, ½ lin. longa. Discus orbiculato-depressus, margine undulatus. Stamina 5, petalis paullo breviora, inflexa, antheris subglobosis bilocularibus longitudinaliter dehiscentibus. Ovarium disco semi-immersum triloculare. Ovula in loculis solitaria, erecta. Stigmata tria, subsessilia.

JULIFLORÆ.

182—186. SALICES.—There are in the collection specimens of five species of willow, all from San Francisco, and all apparently different from any North American species I am acquainted with; but as they are in leaf only, it is useless to attempt to describe them so as to be afterwards recognised.

187. PLATANUS *californicus*, sp. n., foliis profunde 3-5-lobis, junioribus dense lanatis, lobis acutis integerrimis paucidentatisque, amentis fructiferis stylis elongatis echinatis.—San Francisco.

Stipulæ orbiculatæ, villosæ. Folia juniora dense vestita lana in pagina superiore ferrugineo-flavida mox decidua in pagina inferiore albida diu persistente; adulta 6-7 poll. longa, 7-10 poll. lata, sæpius ultra medium lobata, basi subcordata, supra glabra, subtus plus minus lanata, lana laxa floccosa; lobi ovato-lanceolati, dentibus raris brevissimis. Amenta in racemo 3-4, fructifera quam in *P. occidentali* paullo minora, at stylis persistentibus 2 lin. longis insigniter echinata.

* Omitted above, among *Polypetalæ*, where this order ought to have been placed.

This species was considered by Hooker and Arnott (Bot. Beech. p. 160 and 390) as the same as the *P. occidentalis* from the United States, commonly cultivated in Europe as the occidental plane, but the leaves of the latter, whether wild or cultivated, are but slightly lobed and bordered with large irregular teeth between the lobes, the young leaves are much less woolly, and the styles very short.

188. GARRYA *elliptica*, Dougl.—Lindl. Bot. Reg. t. 1686.—Angel Island.

189. MYRICA *californica*, Cham. Schlecht. Linnæa. v. 6. p. 535.—San Francisco.

190. MYRICA *Gale*, Linn.—The leaves in these specimens are larger, and the growth of the whole branches more vigorous than is usual in the European plant, but I can perceive no other difference.—San Francisco.

191. QUERCUS *agrifolia*, Nee.—Hook. Ic. Pl. t. 377.—San Francisco.

192. QUERCUS *Douglasii*, Hook.? Ic. Pl. t. 383.—San Francisco.—A very imperfect specimen, which may possibly belong rather to the following species.

193. QUERCUS *Hindsii*, sp. n., foliis submembranaceis petiolatis obovato-oblongis basi acutis profunde pinnatifidis supra glabris subtus pallidis glabris puberulisve, lobis obovatis oblongisve obtusis sinnatis, fructibus subsessilibus solitariis paucisve, cupula hemisphærica dense squamosa, squamis ovatis convexis breviter appendiculatis, glandula elongata oblonga subacuminata cupulam 3-4-plo superante obtusa cum umbone parvo conico.—San Francisco.

This oak is near to the *Q. Douglasii*, but the leaves are much deeper divided, especially those of the sterile branches, which are much like the leaves of some varieties of the common hawthorn; and the form of the acorn is very remarkable. It is usually from $1\frac{1}{2}$ to 2 inches long, and scarcely half an inch in diameter in its thickest part. There are some branches without fruit which have the leaves yet more divided, and others with the leaves perfectly smooth underneath, but all are apparently forms of one species.

CONIFERÆ.

194. PINUS *insignis*, Dougl.?—The specimens are without cones, but appear to belong to this species.—Monterey.

GRAMINEÆ.

195. PANICUM *californicum*, sp. n., culmo erecto gracili glabro, foliis angustis acutis extus minute puberulis, panicula stricta angusta, ramis racemiformibus alternis simplicibus, spiculis subgeminis altera longius pedicellata, gluma exteriore minuta, interiore floreque neutro unipaleaceo pilis longis villosissimis, flore hermaphrodito glabro.—Bay of Magdalena.

Habitu primo intuitu *Panico Teneriffæ* accedit, panicula tamen non divaricata. Folia plana, ligula longiuscula acuta. Panicula 2-3-pollicaris, ramulis pollicaribus erectis. Gluma exterior minuta, glabra, interior undique pilis longis mollibus vestita. Palea floris neutri glumæformis, $1\frac{1}{4}$ lin. longa; margine pilis longis mollibus densissime ciliata, dorso glabra. Paleæ floris hermaphroditi cartilagineæ, parum inæquales, acutiusculæ, exterior apice leviter trinervis, interior binervis.

In venturing to add this as a new species to the overgrown, difficult, and confused genus *Panicum*, it is on account of the peculiar aspect given to it by the long hairs of the inner glume and sterile floret, which is only noticed in *P. Teneriffæ*, and two or three South American species evidently different from this one. At the same time, notwithstanding all that has been written on *Gramineæ*, the general works on the order hitherto published are either so incomplete, or so ill digested that it is a matter of the greatest difficulty to determine the species belonging to several of the large genera, or to ascertain whether they are new or not.

196. SPARTINA *leiantha*, sp. n., foliis apice convolutis, racemis circa 8 alternis subremotis strictis, rhachidibus glabris, spiculis imbricatis, glumis lævissimis, inferiore duplo breviore, superiore acuta paleas paullo superante, valvulis dorso nudis.—Bay of Magdalena.

S. *gracili* (Trin. Agrostid. p. 88) similis sed glumarum palearumve carina nec pilosa nec scabra. Racemi $1\frac{1}{2}$-pollicares. Spiculæ 4 lin. longæ, racemorum inferiorum arcte imbricatæ, superiorum subremotæ. Rhachis racemorum dilatata.

The known species of *Spartina* have been so lately and so well described by the late Dr. Trinius, whose decease before having completed his dissertations on *Gramineæ* is so much to be regretted, that I have no hesitation in describing the present one as new.

197. VILFA *virginica*, Pal. de Beauv.—Trin. Agrostid. Vilf. p. 48.—Bay of Magdalena.

198. CENCHRUS *pauciflorus*, sp. n., culmis suberectis, foliis glabris vix scabriusculis, involucris alternis distantibus pilosiusculis sub-10-fidis spiculas subternas superantibus.—Bay of Magdalena.

Affinis C. *echinato*. Folia plerumque angustiora. Spica $1\frac{1}{2}$-2-pollicaris. Spiculæ 8-10, quam in *C. echinato* minores, spinis dorsalibus marginalibusque validis basi dilatatis, et spiculæ (an constanter?) tres nec quinque in quoque involucro.

199. CHLORIS *alba*, Presl?—Kunth. Enum. p. 264.—Bay of Magdalena.—A taller plant than *C. barbata*, with narrower and longer leaves, and the sheaths and stems much less compressed. The spikelets have but one sterile and one perfect flower. The awn of the latter is not quite so long as described by Presl.

200. CHONDROSIUM *polystachium*, sp. n., culmo humili glabro, foliis margine vaginisque pilis paucis ciliatis, spicis 3-5 racemosis secundis falcatis, glumis coloratis, floris hermaphroditi palea superiore breviter biaristata.—Bay of Magdalena.

Gramen cæspitosum, semipedale vel vix pedale. Culmus adscendens. Vaginæ subcompressæ, pilis paucis longis patentibus secus vaginam sparsis, ad orem numerosis onustæ. Ligula brevissime ciliata. Foliorum lamina semipollicaris ad pollicaris, acuta, scabriuscula, pilis paucis ciliata. Racemi numerosi, graciles. Spicæ sæpius 4 vel 5, subsessiles, 4-5 lin. longæ. Rhachis compressa, marginibus minute puberulis. Spiculæ crebræ, imbricato-biseriatæ, vix lineam longæ. Gluma inferior interior parva, hyalina, emarginata, superior exterior purpurascens, apice breviter emarginato-bifida, glabra, nervo dorsali viridi, scabriusculo, in mucronem brevem producto. Flos hermaphroditus unicus, basi dense ciliatus. Palea exterior triloba, laciniis lateralibus ad latus interius aristatis, lacinia intermedia biloba inter lobos aristata; aristæ omnes subæquales gluma subdimidio longiores. Palea interior triloba, exteriore paullo brevior, lacinia media breviter bifida, bicarinata, nervis in aristas breves productis. Stamina 3. Squamellæ minutissimæ, vix conspicuæ. Ovarium obovoideum. Styli plumosi, purpurei. Flores steriles 2, inferior constans ex aristis 3 et paleis 3 brevibus, quarum 2 obovatæ inferiores (vel palea inferior bipartita), tertia superior latissima emarginato-truncata. Flos terminalis breviter stipitatus, constans e palea unica obovata ex aristata.

III.—WESTERN TROPICAL AMERICA,

FROM MEXICO TO GUAYAQUIL.

Different portions of the west coast of intertropical America were so repeatedly visited between the years 1836 and 1839, that we became familiar with its general aspect. There is as much variety and individual force in the character of scenery as in many other objects; and the tropical American has its own, quite distinct from the Asiatic, though probably not to be very satisfactorily expressed. Strictly speaking, intertropical America would include a large portion of Peru, and of which the expedition also had some experience. But to the south of Cape Blanco, in the Bay of Guayaquil, the vegetation is so exceedingly different from what is usually regarded as tropical, that at present, our attention is best confined to that range of country which extends between the Bay of Guayaquil and San Blas, at the entrance of the Gulf of California, or between 2° 30′ S., and 21° 32′ N. L. This extensive tract is far from possessing an uniform vegetation, for that to the north of Panama differs materially from what obtains to the south. Both are, however, excessively tropical; a boundless forest invests the surface nearly every where, and there is a certain uniformity in the physical agents.

The climate is necessarily tropical, but is not every where synchronous in its seasons; at Guayaquil the rains are expected with the new year, but as we ascend the coast to the northward they are gradually later, till at San Blas, on the limits of the tropics, their accession takes place about St. John's day in June. The influence exerted by them over the vegetation is therefore at various times, and between the limits of this tract there will be a difference of nearly six months. The relations of the seasons are those usual within the tropics, with the exception, that in the Bay of Choco, the period of rains is prolonged even to ten or eleven months, and the vegetation is characterised by excessive and rank luxuriance. In the distribution of temperature, we are not prepared to meet, in these latitudes, with any very remarkable diurnal or annual variation, and none such is observable within the limits stated above.

Approaching *Guayaquil* from the south, the first object seen is, not land, but trees, skirting the horizon in broken masses, since the land first-sighted is extremely low; and this is a striking circumstance after an habitual acquaintance with bold and treeless scenery. The land, however, soon becomes elevated and is uniformly covered with forest. Cape Blanco is the southern limit of the Bay, and in the vicinity is Tumbez. These places may be regarded as the limits of that very remarkable climate which stretches over the maritime part of Peru, and is never known to afford a shower of rain. Parallel with this is the absence of thunder and lightning, or electrical disturbances of the atmosphere, and the nearly constant prevalence of a southerly wind; and to this latter Ulloa long since attributed the absence of rain. The transition to a very different state of things is most sudden, and at Guayaquil the rains descend in torrents, the town becomes flooded, and it is not at all unusual to navigate the streets in boats. Vegetation so closely follows climate, that we cannot than be surprised at the sudden change it assumes.

The first favourable impressions are strengthened when the forest is around us. The different habits of the trees, the size and richness of the flowers, and above all, the large and novel seed-vessels, give an exciting freshness to the scene. It may be that a few old acquaintances are recognised, but they have here a new aspect. The pigmy *Jacquinia aurantiaca* of our conservatories is here a forest tree profusely covered with fragrant flowers. The *Mimosa* is no longer a stripling plant but a time-worn tree, venerable from age and long exposed to the vicissitudes of the seasons, and alive with humming birds and gaudy *brujas* or witches. In the forest, in this immediate neighbourhood, there is an absence of certain forms,—thus, ferns are by no means frequent, epiphytic plants are rarely seen, and *Endogenæ* are comparatively rare. The *Bignonias* are particularly handsome, and large species of *Ficus* abound. On the whole, the number of species yielding profit or amusement to the botanist will probably fall beneath his estimate; and during the height of the dry season I have traversed these forests without reaping a single specimen, and witnessed such a scene of desolation in the striped and denuded trees, as I never thought to see within the tropics. The luxuriant vegetation of these latitudes is of short duration, and nearly confined to that period when heat and moisture combine to kindle it. At that time it unquestionably is surpassingly rich.

St. Helena is the northern boundary of the Bay of Guayaquil. In November we found the vegetation very scanty, and though there were patches of shrubs, the land is bolder, but very sandy, everywhere barrenness and aridity presented themselves, and water was scarce even for domestic use. Among the rocks and loose soil on the high table-land of the Point were some magnificent arborescent

Cacti. Some of them were of considerable height, sending numerous branches upwards from a hard solid woody trunk, and these branching again and forming a moderate sized tree.

In the neighbourhood is *Salango,* and here we were surprised at the re-assumed luxuriance. The forest was densely filled with underwood, the trees were loaded with climbers, and *Piper, Passiflora,* and *Cleome,* melastomaceous plants, palms and ferns abounded; sure indications of a climate of excess of heat and moisture. We afterwards learned that in a wide-spread tract of great aridity, within a limited space around Salango, a vegetation characteristic of excessive moisture prevailed. The cause of this was hidden from us, but on a coast where a stream of water is a rarity, the existence of a perennial one was likely to have much weight, though it is most probable that the condition of the vegetation and the unfailing stream were effects of the same cause. Rivers and streams of water are in most cases more the drains than fertilizers of the districts they traverse.

At *Monte Christi* every thing was again burnt up. Not a leaf was to be found on the bushes which covered the sandy soil, and several exceedingly prickly *Cacteæ* made walking unpleasant. Not a bird enlivened the scene. A little verdure was alone visible on the mount whence the town has its name. *Bombax ceiba* grows abundantly, and the softer parts of the wood are given to the horses and mules for fodder, so scarce is their usual food.

Tacames, San Pedro, Tumaco. On entering the northern hemisphere, a great improvement is conspicuous in the vegetation. Every place visited was clothed in a rich and luxuriant vegetation. On all sides is seen a rather dense forest, but of trees not distinguished for their size, and among them the singular *Clusia* abounds, with a sprinkling of palms of *Licuala* and *Caryota.* At Tacames a prominent feature is the great abundance of *Euphorbiaceæ; Hippomane mancinella* was very common, especially as an edging to the forest near the beach; large trees were frequently growing in the immediate vicinity of the houses of the inhabitants, and there can be now no doubt that the wonderful agency formerly attributed to this tree is in great part erroneous. *Orchidaceæ* make their appearance in some force, and there is an interesting mixture of a few shrubby *Compositæ,* with a crowd of common tropical forms.

The *Island of Gorgona* is within the influence of the very moist climate of the Bay of Choco, and the vegetation exhibits a corresponding rank luxuriance, with the exclusion of *Cacteæ,* and the occurrence of arborescent ferns of *Pteris* and *Diplazium,* which latter also make their first appearance on the neighbouring mainland. It would not be easy to convey an overdrawn picture of the excessive luxuriance of the foliage at the places visited, but it is a more profitable field to the observing botanist than to the collector.

Panama received several visits, and its vegetation was seen at different seasons and under very different aspects. The seasons are regularly distributed into wet and dry; in the wet season much rain falls, the atmosphere is loaded with moisture, and feels excessively hot and close from the impeded perspiration. Even the European acknowledges that this is not the period for exertion, and he lingers listlessly among the dense masses of herbaceous and indigenous plants which obstruct the roads and pathways of the forest. The atmosphere is reeking with that peculiar smell which is encountered on entering a hot-house. Very different is the dry season; the atmosphere is now clear, the sun brilliant, and exhilirating to those not too long accustomed to it, but the fugacious vegetation has past away, the avenues of the forest are unencumbered, and *Leguminosæ*, as small trees and shrubs, are in great abundance. Within the tropics, whenever the atmosphere for a lengthened period is conspicuous for its heat and dryness, we miss the arborescent ferns, and scitamineous and musaceous plants, which are usually regarded as the "*sine quâ non*" of tropical vegetation, and instead a prominence is given to arborescent *Leguminosæ*, often with a few *Compositæ*, *Myrtaceæ*, and *Convolvulaceæ*, and a sprinkling of congenial species. Increasing the dryness so as to verge on aridity, these are replaced by *Cacteæ*, growing even as trees with hard woody stems, succulent *Euphorbiaceæ*, and some aloes. There is nothing particularly inviting about such an assemblage, but as this state of climate is constant in some tropical regions, it becomes as strictly a tropical form of vegetation as that which acknowledges the prevalence of *Endogenæ*.

The island of *Taboga* is productive in fruits, and supplies Panama with a considerable quantity. The inhabitants are accustomed to search under the trees after dusk, by the light of torches, for the fruit that has fallen. We here found that errors are very likely to arise from placing too much confidence in vernacular names. Many of the fruits were brought to us under the name "guava," without any second or specific name diagnostic of the fruit meant. And at the same time at other places on the coast this term was applied to fruits not designated as such elsewhere; whilst the fruit known to us as the guava was not uncommon. The isthmus of Panama, if not so stern as to become mountainous, approaches very nearly to it, and such portions as were visited were covered by forest, not always very dense, and with situations of rich and productive soil. From some of the higher lands the views of the vallies around are excessively glowing, the summits of trees crowded together into a rich vesture of green, illumined by a fervent sun, whose brilliant dazzling rays few animated beings venture to brave; yet from beneath the canopy are heard at times sounds various and strange to the traveller. Some of these upland views, of which America furnishes so many, are particularly interesting, and leave a lasting impression. The eye often commands not only a very varied scene, but one which really embraces a very considerable tract of country. This too is greatly varied by the broken surface and irregular direction of the masses of land, whence arise certain conspicuous changes in the vegetation, and these diversified again by the different shadows and lights, which also receive their modifications with the distance. The whole offers a scene which arrests the attention even of the exhausted traveller, and the reminiscences of after times are apt to be rich even to the minute concomitants which attend them. Man seems but a little being when moving through such a wilderness, and I remember that it was on one occasion quite ludicrous to hear the very insignificant shouts our greatest efforts could raise to recall a truant fellow-traveller.

At *Realejo* the accession of the rains is deferred till April. In the vicinity the continuity of the Andes is interrupted, and the surface is flat and with a very trifling general elevation; a few volcanic mountains are spread about. The mahogany forests stretch towards the Pacific, and a few stragglers are found on its shores. Our visits to the *Gulfs of Nicoya* and *Fonseca* were not productive, indeed the sameness of an unbroken but dreary and profitless forest was nowhere more forcibly felt. Many of the upper lands are rather densely clothed with *Pinus occidentalis*. The dry season at *Acapulco* is rich in the great variety of *Bauhinia*; the oaks approach the low lands, and take their lower station at about fifteen hundred feet. A great part of the country is occupied by small forest growth; the summits of the mountain ranges often display bare brown spaces, piled with naked masses of granite. In the elevated lands a different vegetation obtains to what is noticed lower down. *Leguminosæ* abound, and in general different from those of the plains.

San Blas. In the immediate neighbourhood, and covering a large tract of country, an insipid maritime vegetation prevails, attributable in great part to inundations from the sea. A pathway of some miles long at length leads to a more promising scene. The road to Tepic traverses some very fine forest, but when this ascends the hills, the country is more open, and some magnificent views are spread around. Many of the *Mimosa* of the forest furnish specimens of remarkably fine grown timber, and their minutely divided foliage has a very light and airy appearance, and is of a peculiar delicate green; those of the elevated lands are stunted trees. Many instances may here be seen where the *Chamærops palmetto* is closely embraced in the giant arms of the protean figs, and which has received an undue importance from the published figures of Mirbel and Decandolle. A phenomenon of far greater physiological value was seen in a full-grown palmetto, which presented midway up its trunk a fork of two branches of equal dimensions. Subsequently at New Ireland, among a group of the sago-palm, I saw two similar instances. Tepic itself is picturesquely situated in a plain surrounded by an amphitheatre of hills. Not a tree disturbs the uniformity of the surrounding country, but there is much foliage mingled with the buildings, and near at hand is a fine promenade shaded by trees, which travellers have called chestnuts, but which are really figs.—Ed.

The vegetation of this long range of coast includes necessarily a considerable number of species common also to the West Indies, the north coast of South America, and the east coast of Central America, and of these many have long since been published and received into general systematic works. Those species which are peculiar to the western side in general, or to particular stations visited by the Expedition, if already published, must with few exceptions be sought for either in the Nova Genera et Species of Humboldt and Kunth, or amongst Hænke's plants, described partly in Presl's Reliquiæ Hænkeanæ, partly in various detached monographical papers scattered over some of the modern botanical periodicals, or in the later volumes of De Candolle's Prodromus and Kunth's Enumeratio. Several plants also from this region were figured by Cavanilles in his Icones, chiefly from the collections of Nee or of Tafalla, and a few Guayaquil species of the latter collector, have found their way into Ruiz and Pavon's Flora. More recently a small number of Guatemala plants have been published by Bertoloni in his Florula Guatemalensis, or by myself in the Plantæ Hartwegianæ, where a small Guayaquil collection is also described. By these means the more prominent among the species generally diffused over this region are not new, and are therefore here merely mentioned by name. Amongst the species first discovered by the officers of the Sulphur, a few from the Mexican coast have been already published by Hooker and Arnott, in the Supplementary portion of the Botany of Captain Beechey's Voyage. These again I have merely referred to by name, except where better specimens have thrown any additional light upon their characters, or geographical range. The species now first described are chiefly from the more southern portion of the region from Panama to Guayaquil.

RANUNCULACEÆ.

1. CLEMATIS *acapulcensis*, Hook. et Arn. Bot. Beech. p. 410, (sp. n.)—Acapulco.

DILLENIACEÆ.

2. Davila *rugosa*, Poir.—St. Hil. Fl. Bras. Mer. 1. p. 18.—Isthmus of Darien.

3. Curatella *americana*, Linn.—DC. Prod. 1. p. 70.—Bay of Panama.

4. Tetracera *volubilis*, Linn.—DC. Prod. 1. p. 67.—Gulf of Fonseca.

ANONACEÆ.

5. Xylopia *grandiflora*, St. Hil. Fl. Bras. Merid. 1. p. 40.—*X. longifolia*, Alph. DC. Mem. Soc. Gen. 5. p. 210.—Isle of Taboga, in the Bay of Panama. A fine species, not uncommon in Brasilian and Guyana collections, but which does not appear to have been previously found on the west coast of America.

6. Anona *reticulata*, Linn.—DC. Prod. 1. p. 35.—Isle of Puna, near Guayaquil.

MENISPERMACEÆ.

7. Cissampelos *Pareira*, Linn.—DC. Prod. 1. p. 100.—Panama.

8. Cissampelos *Guayaquilensis*, Humb. et Kunth.—DC. Prod. 1. p. 100.—Near Guayaquil.

9. Cocculus *oblongifolius*, DC. Prod. 1. p. 99.—Acapulco.

PAPAVERACEÆ.

10. Argemone *Mexicana*, Linn.—DC. Prod. 1. p. 120.—Common throughout the region.

CAPPARIDACEÆ.

11. Gynandropsis *speciosa*, DC. Prod. 1. p. 238.—Guayaquil.

12. Gynandropsis *trichopus*, sp. n., ramulis pubescentibus demum glabratis, foliolis 5-7 oblongis acuminatis pubescentibus, petiolis elongatis petiolulisque hispido-pilosissimis, toro elongato thecaphoroque brevi quam siliqua glanduloso-puberula brevioribus.—Salango, in Columbia.

Frutex? Rami herbacei, juniores pube brevi subglandulosa demum evanescenti obtecti. Petioli 2-5-pollicares. Foliola fere *G. speciosæ* sed sæpius minora, basi longe angustata et pilis insignia in petiolulo copiosis longis basi incrassatis. Folia floralia bracteæformia, parva, integra, sessilia. Pedicelli pollicares, filiformes, puberuli. Sepala ovata, acute acuminata, membranacea, in sicco rubra. Petala majora calyce duplo longiora. Torus filiformis, 6 lin. longus. Stamina sex. Thecaphorum toro brevius. Siliqua bipollicaris vel paullo longior.

13. CLEOME *polygama*, Linn.—DC. Prod. 1. p. 241.—Guayaquil.

14. CLEOME *pilosa*, sp. n., inermis, pilis sparsis hispidula, foliolis subquinis elliptico-oblongis acuminatis utrinque sparse hispidulis, floralibus parvis ovato-lanceolatis, thecaphoro brevi, siliqua acuminata glabra.—Salango, in Columbia.

Habitus fere *C. roseæ*. Pili sparsi non glutinosi. Foliola majora 2-3-pollicaria, petiolo bipollicari. Pedicelli graciles, glabriusculi, pollicem longi. Sepala vix 1 lin. longa, acutissima. Petala majora 4-5 lin. longa, oblonga, breviter unguiculata. Siliqua matura bipollicaris, thecaphoro 3 lin. longo. Semina rugulosa.

15. CAPPARIS (Cynophalla) *brevipes*, sp. n., glabra, foliis brevissime petiolatis oblongis acuminatis obtusisve basi cordatis, glandula in axillis pezizæforme, racemis terminalibus axillaribusve subcorymbosis paucifloris.—Gulf of Nicoya.

Frutex scandens. Folia coriacea, 2½-3 poll. longa, 1 poll. lata, margine undulata, apice sæpius acuta. Glandula axillaris hinc inde deest. Racemi nonnulli in axillis supremis simplices pauciflori, terminalis interdum ramosus. Sepala ovata, valde imbricata. Petala et genitalia in speciminibus suppetentibus a vermibus exesa. Species videtur *C. heterophyllæ*, Ruiz et Pav. affinis.

16. CAPPARIS (Cynophalla) *Sinclairii*, sp. n. (Plate XXVII.) glabra, foliis lanceolatis muticis coriaceis basi rotundatis breviter petiolatis, glandula in axillis turbinata, racemis axillaribus 4-6-floris folio brevioribus, sepalis orbiculatis corolla dimidio brevioribus, thecaphoro longissimo.—Columbia.

Folia 2-3-pollicaria, viscosissima. Racemi subcorymbosi, pedicellis inferioribus semipollicaribus. Petala 6-7 lin. longa, orbiculata. Stamina numerosissima. Ovarium oblongo-lineare, thecaphoro jam ante anthesin fere 2 poll. longo. Stigma truncatum. Fructus non suppetit.

Plate XXVII. fig. 1, stamen; fig. 2, ovary; fig. 3, the same, cut longitudinally; fig. 4, the same, transverse section; all magnified.

17. CAPPARIS *amygdalina*, Linn.—DC. Prod. 1. p. 250.—Manzanilla Bay.

18. CAPPARIS *scabrida*, Humb. et Kunth.—DC. Prod. 1. p. 251.—Payta, in Columbia.

19. CAPPARIS *crotonoides*, Humb. et Kunth.—DC. Prod. 1. p. 251.—Isle of Puna, in the Bay of Guayaquil.

20. CAPPARIS *avicenniæfolia*, Humb. et Kunth.—DC. Prod. 1. p. 252.—In various places, from Panama to Guayaquil. These specimens are somewhat more downy than those described by Kunth, and the berry is ovoid, or oblong, but in other respects they agree perfectly with the description.

BIXACEÆ.

21. BIXA *orellana*, Linn.—DC. Prod. 1. p. 259.—Mexico to Guayaquil.

CISTACEÆ.

22. HELIANTHEMUM *glomeratum*, Lag. Dun. in DC. Prod. 1. p. 269.—*H. polifolium*, Hook. et Arn. Bot. Beech. p. 410. vix Torr. et. Gr.—Tepic.

This is probably the only species hitherto found in Mexico (exclusive of Texas) or Guatemala.* The two kinds of flowers to be found on the same specimens have been well distinguished by Spach, but they do not always co-exist on the same branch at the same time, nor are they sufficient for generic distinctions, any more than the apetalous flowers which have now been so frequently observed in several *Leguminosæ*, *Malpighiaceæ*, *Violaceæ*, and others. We should therefore refer to *H. glomeratum* both the *Heteromeris Mexicana* and the *Tæniostoma micranthum* of Spach, but the *H. polifolium* of Torrey and Gray from Texas will probably be found to be a constantly distinct species.

SAMYDACEÆ.

23. CASEARIA (Pitumba) *pubiflora*, sp. n., ramulis glabris, foliis oblongis acuminatis serrulatis basi subobliquè cuneatis membranaceis punctatis glabris vel in nervo medio puberulis, pedicellis fasciculatis, floribus decantheris 5-partitis pubescenti-villosis, laciniis calycinis oblongis.—Guayaquil.

Folia tripollicaria vel paullo longiora, crebrè pellucido-punctata, acumine longiusculo acuto. Pedicelli numerosi, in axillis vetustis glomerati, vix 2 lin. longi. Calyces ferè 2½ lin. longi, tomento brevi densè obtecti. Filamenta sterilia subclavata. Ovarium pubescens. Stigma (seu styli apex stigmatosus) subcapitatum.

This species belongs to the section *Pitumba*, as characterised in my account of *Guayana Samydaceæ* in the London Journal of Botany. It agrees in many respects with the descriptions of *C. macrophylla*, Vahl, and of *C. celtidifolia*, Humb. et Kunth, from both of which it differs chiefly in the calyx.

---

* Mr. Skinner has, however, sent from Guatemala an interesting new species of the allied genus *Lechea* which may be thus characterised : *Lechea Skinneri*, humilis, ramosissima, molliter pilosa, foliis linearibus subulatisve sparsis subternisve, floribus distinctè pedicellatis, capsulis latè globosis.—Species *L. minori* affinis at facilè distincta floribus et præsertim capsulis multo majoribus. Habitus humilior, basi ramosior. Folia ramorum sterilium angustiora, pilis longiusculis appressis canescentia. Flores ad apices ramulorum pauci. Pedicelli 1½-2 lin. longi. Sepala interiora concavo-carinata. Petala tria. Stamina (an constanter ?) tria. Styli rami plumoso-multifidi. Capsulæ magnitudine carum *L. Drummondi*, 3-6-spermæ, placentis ut in *L. minore* membranaceo-crustaceis.

POLYGALACEÆ.

24. POLYGALA (Senega) *hebantha*, sp. n., caulibus adscendentibus pubescentibus, foliis subsessilibus ovatis orbiculatisve basi cuneatis membranaceis utrinque parce hirtellis, racemis brevibus, sepalis exterioribus lineari-lanceolatis, 2 anticis approximatis, postico carinato, interioribus obovato-oblongis hirtellis, petalis posticis carinam nudam dorso ciliatam æquantibus, capsula ovali hirsuta.—Gulf of Fonseca.

Caules basi ramosi, vix unquam pedales. Folia inferiora minora late orbiculata, obtusissima, suprema breviter acuminata, rarius acuta. Racemi 1½-2-pollicares, 10-20-flori. Flores minores quam in *P. rivinæfolia*, cæterum iis similes. Capsula hirsutissima et tanquam e statu juniori judicare potes non emarginata, maturam non vidi.

25. POLYGALA *rivinæfolia*, Humb. et Kunth.—DC. Prod. 1. p. 331.—Acapulco.

26. POLYGALA *paniculata*, Linn.—DC. Prod. 1. p. 329.—Guayaquil.

27. SECURIDACA *volubilis*, Linn.—DC. Prod. 1. p. 340.—Panama and the Isle of Taboga.

VIOLACEÆ.

28. ALSODEIA *deflexa*, sp. n., ramulis petiolisque hirtellis mox glabratis, foliis ovali-ellipticis breviter et obtuse acuminatis obtuse dentatis basi rotundatis subobliquis, racemis simplicibus folio brevioribus, pedicellis deflexis, sepalis ovatis acuminatis quam petala glabra dimidio brevioribus, antherarum appendicibus acutis, ovario hispido.—Atacames.

Rami dichotomi, cinerei. Folia 2-4-pollicaria, submembranacea, reticulato-venosissima, inferne angustiora, ima basi obtusa, petiolo 2-3 lin. longo. Racemi bipollicares, hirtelli. Pedicelli 1 lin. longi, arcte deflexi, puberuli. Sepala interiora 1 lin. longa, exteriora paullo breviora, dorso minute puberula, margine ciliata. Petala oblongo-linearia, glabra, apice revoluta. Filamenta brevissima. Antherarum appendices lanceolatæ, petalis paullo breviores. Ovarium dense hispidum. Stylus glaber.

29. SAUVAGESIA *erecta*, Linn.—DC. Prod. 1. p. 315.—Columbia.

LINACEÆ.*

30. LINUM *Schiedeanum*, Cham. et Schl.—Hook. et Arn. Bot. Beech. p. 411.—Tepic.

* The following new species of *Linum*, allied to *L. rigidum* has been sent by Mr. Skinner from Guatemala, within the limits of the present region: *L. guatemalense*, glabrum, caule angulato virgato superne paniculato, foliis alternis lanceolatis vel lineari-lanceolatis acutis, floribus ad apices ramulorum paucis pedicellatis, sepalis lato-ovatis cuspidatis apice glanduloso-ciliatis capsula acutiuscula brevioribus, petalis (luteis) calyce vix triplo longioribus, stylis liberis.—Caules sesquipedales. Folia iis *L. rigidi* latiora, minime pungentia; sepala latiora et inflorescentia parum diversa.

MALVACEÆ.

31. LOPIMIA *malacophylla*, Mart.—DC. Prod. 1. p. 458.—Isthmus of Darien.
32. PAVONIA *typhaleoides*, Humb. et Kunth.—DC. Prod. 1. p. 443.—Guayaquil.
33. PAVONIA *mexicana*, Humb. et Kunth, Nov. Gen. 5. p. 284.—Acapulco.
34. MALVAVISCUS *mollis*, DC. Prod. 1. p. 445.—Gulf of Fonseca.
35. MALVAVISCUS *pilosus*, DC. Prod. 1. p. 445.—Schlecht. Linnæa, 11. p. 359.—Bay of Panama.

These specimens are very similar to the Jamaica ones. The proportion of stellate tomentum and long simple hairs on the pedicels is very variable.

36. MALVAVISCUS *acapulcensis*, Humb. et Kunth ?—Schlecht? Linnæa, 11. p. 360.—Atacames.

37. MALVAVISCUS *brevipes*, sp. n., ramulis petiolisque tomentosis, foliis ovatis leviter cordatis obtusis vel obtuse acuminatis grosse crenato-dentatis rarius obsolete lobatis utrinque sparse stellato-pubescentibus, pedunculis calyce brevioribus subaggregatis, involucello 9-12-phyllo calycem superante.—Nicoya.

Folia 3-5 poll. longa, 2-3 poll. lata, supra tuberculis minutis pilorumque stellulis siccitate canescentia et scabra. Pedunculi tenues, pilosi, longiores vix semipollicares. Flores quam in *M. arboreo* et *M. molli* paullo majores. Involucelli foliola linearia, acuta. Petala minute ciliata.

Some specimens from the Gulf of Fonseca with smaller leaves, and the folioles of the involucre rather shorter and somewhat spathulate, may possibly belong to a distinct species, or perhaps to the *M. concinnus*, Humb. et Kunth, but the materials before me do not enable me to determine them accurately.

38. PARITIUM *tiliaceum*, St. Hil. Fl. Bras. Mer. 1. p. 256.—Columbia and Guayaquil.
39. HIBISCUS (Bombicella) *betulifolius*, Humb. et Kunth.—DC. Prod. 1. p. 452, var. pedunculis abbreviatis.—Isle of Taboga, Bay of Panama.
40. KOSTELETZKYA *sagittata*, Presl.—Benth. Pl. Hartw. p. 114.—Guayaquil.
41. FUGOSIA *cuneata*, sp. n., procumbens, glabra vel junior pilis minutis stellatis canescens, foliis obovatis vel oblongo-cuneatis obtusis integris bifidisve, supremis interdum lanceolatis acutis, pedunculis apice incrassatis, involucelli foliolis minutis setiformibus.—Guayaquil.

Very near to the *Fugosia* (Redoutea) *tripartita*, as described by Kunth, but the leaves, which are about an inch long, are entire or shortly bifid, and not divided into distinct segments.

42. GOSSYPIUM *barbadense*, Linn ?—Tepic, Guayaquil, &c.
43. BASTARDIA *crispa*, St. Hil.—Hook. et Arn. Bot. Beech. p. 412.—Acapulco.
44. BASTARDIA *viscosa*, Humb. et Kunth, Nov. Gen. 5. p. 256.—Acapulco.
45. ABUTILON *reflexum*, Sw.—*Sida reflexa*, Cav.—DC. Prod. 1. p. 469.—Salango, in Columbia.

46. ABUTILON *pedunculare*, Humb. et Kunth? Nov. Gen. 5. p. 273.—The specimen is without flowers, but appears to belong to this species.—Guayaquil.

47. ABUTILON *graveolens*, Wight et Arn. Prod. Fl. Penins. Ind. Or. 1. p. 56.—Panama to Guayaquil.—These specimens do not in the slightest degree differ from East Indian ones.

48. ANODA *hastata*, Cav.—Schlecht. Linnæa 11. p. 214.—Tepic and Acapulco.

49. ANODA *lanceolata*, Hook. et Arn. Bot. Beech. p. 411.—Tepic.

50. WISSADULA *excelsior* Presl.—*Sida excelsior*, Cav.—DC. Prod. 1. p. 468.—Panama.

51. WISSADULA *nudiflora*.—*Sida nudiflora*, Lhér.—DC. Prod. 1. p. 468.—Gulf of Fonseca.

52. SIDA *divergens*, sp. n., fruticosa, ramis tomentosis, foliis amplis late cordato-ovatis acuminatis integerrimis supra minute puberulis subtus cano-tomentosis, panicula ampla laxa subnuda, carpellis quinque, rostris elongatis divergentibus.—Guayaquil.

Frutex parva, ramis teretibus divaricatis. Folia longiuscule petiolata, majora 4-6 poll. longa, ramealia sæpe multo minora, floralia sessilia, infima bipollicaria, suprema ad bracteas minutas reducta. Pedicelli filiformes, elongati. Calyces parvi, laciniis latis obtusis. Petala calyce duplo longiora. Cocci maturitate distincti, subindehiscentes, angulati, angulo interno acuto, externo in rostrum elongatum incurvum bipartibile producto, angulis lateralibus obtusis.

This shrub has very much the habit of the *Wissadulæ*, especially of *W. nudiflora*, but the fruit is that of a true Sida. It was also gathered by Hartweg in the same locality.

53. SIDA *paniculata*, Linn.—DC. Prod. 1. p. 465.—Payta and Guayaquil.

54. SIDA *betonicæfolia*, Balb.—DC. Prod. 1. p. 463.—Gulf of Fonseca.

55. SIDA *Dombeyana*, DC. Prod. 1. p. 463.—Folia juniora utrinque pilosa, adulta fere glabra.—Isle of Puna, near Guayaquil.—Very nearly allied to *S. humilis*.

56. SIDA *glanduligera*, sp. n., foliis petiolatis late cordato-ovatis acuminatis dentatis supra minute stellato-puberulis subtus ramulisque tenuiter canescenti-tomentellis, panicula terminali, floribus breviter pedicellatis confertis, calycibus glanduloso-hirtis, carpellis 5 muticis puberulis.—*S. dumosa*, Hook. et Arn. Bot. Beech. p. 4 2. non Swartz.—Realejo.

Caules elati videntur, teretes, uti folia juniora necnon adultiorum pagina inferior tomento tenui pallido et forte viscidulo vestiti. Petioli 2-3-pollicares. Folia petiolo longiora, basi 5-7-nervia et late leviterque cordata, supra viridia pilis minutis stellatis conspersa. Panicula pyramidata, terminalis, aphylla, floribus secus ramos in cymas breves dispositis. Pedicelli ultimi calycibus breviores, bracteis linearibus brevibus subtensi, uti rami paniculæ, bracteæ et calyces pube stellata pilis rigidulis et glandulis stipitatis vestiti. Calyces fructiferi 3 lin. longi, laciniis latis acute acuminatis. Corolla calyce paullo longior. Carpella *S. dumosæ*.

This plant was considered by the authors of the Botany of Beechey's Voyage as the same as Swartz's *S. dumosa* from Jamaica, but it appears to me to be more downy, the inflorescence different, and the calyxes much larger, which, with the glands and stiff hairs which cover them, give to the panicle something of the appearance of that of some *Rubi*.

57. SIDA *depressa*, sp. n., fruticosa? viscoso-tomentosa, foliis cordato-ovatis crenatis subtus

canescentibus, pedunculis brevissimis, calcycibus viscoso-tomentosis, carpellis 10 pubescentibus angulis exterioribus mucronatis.—Isle of Puna, near Guayaquil.

Habitu *Bastardiæ viscosæ* non dissimilis. Tomentum breve, viscidulum, canescens. Folia 1-1½ poll. longa, petiolo semipollicari. Pedicelli axillares sæpe glomerati, vix lineam longi. Flores magnitudine *S. rhombifoliæ*. Calyx post anthesin auctus et stellato-patens. Fructus depressus, stellato-radians, in coccos vix dehiscentes secedens.

The fruit at first sight resembles that of an *Anoda*, but separates into distinct carpels as in *Sida*. The habit has no resemblance to *Anoda*.

58. SIDA *urens*, Linn.—DC. Prod. 1. p. 465.—Acapulco.

59. SIDA *carpinifolia*, Linn.—DC. Prod. 1. p. 461.—Mexico to Guayaquil.

60. SIDA *rhombifolia*, Linn.—DC. Prod. 1. p. 462, var. carpellis submuticis.—*S. rhomboidea* Roxb.—DC. l. c.—Mexico to Guayaquil.—The *S. Hondensis*, Humb. et Kunth, should also be referred to this species, which varies in having the carpels either quite awnless or with short or long awns, without apparently any means of drawing any line of distinction between the different forms.

61. MALACHRA *humilis*, sp. n., caule hispidissimo, foliis suborbiculatis integris 3-5-lobatisve dentatis basi truncatis supra glabris subtus sparse hispidis, florum capitulis breviter pedunculatis 3-5-floris hispidissimis, foliis floralibus basi cuneatis lobulis setaceis utrinque auctis, laciniis calycinis breviter acuminatis coccis dimidio longioribus.—Guayaquil.

Herba annua, subpedalis, divaricato-ramosa, pilis longis hirsutissima. Folia inferiora fere orbiculata, diametro pollicari, superiora majora, plus minus lobata, lobis latis, medio vix productiore. Pedunculi brevissimi. Bracteæ foliaceæ sæpius tres, inæquales, breviter acuminatæ, basi nervosæ; lobuli utrinque 1-3 prope basin, setacei, hispidi, ciliati, bracteis interioribus similes. Corolla calyce duplo longior. Genitalia et fructus omnino *Malachræ*.

STERCULIACEÆ.

62. PACHIRA *sessilis*, sp. n., glabra, foliolis 5-7 ad apicem petioli sessilibus obovato-oblongis obtusis, calyce integro truncato, tubo stamineo dimidium corollæ æquante.—Isle of Taboga, bay of Panama.

Foliola 3-4 poll. longa vel intermedia semipedalia, basi angustata et omnino sessilia, coriacea, subglaucescentia; petiolus foliolo medio paullo brevior. Pedicelli axillares, crassi, 6-10 lin. longi. Calyx 5 lin. longus, crassus, margine tenui obsoletissime sinuato. Petala fere 4 poll. longa, acutiuscula. Staminum tubi pars integra fere 2 poll. longa. Filamentorum pars superior, antheræ et ovaria in speciminibus suppetentibus omnia a vermibus exesa.

63. ERIODENDRON *anfractuosum* var. caribæum, DC.? Prod. 1. p. 479.—Folia et calyces similia iis speciminium in Antillis nec non in Surinamo lectorum, nisi foliola paullo longiora et angustiora. Flores ita a vermibus destructi ut nil nisi vestigia pauca corollæ supersunt.—Acapulco.

64. HELICTERES *baruensis*, Linn.—DC. Prod. 1. p. 475.—Isle of Taboga, bay of Panama.

65. HELICTERES *guazumæfolia*, Humb. et Kunth.—DC. Prod. 1. p. 476.—Isthmus of Darien.—Probably a smoother variety of *H. baruensis*.

66. HELICTERES *altheæfolia*, Lam. Dict. 3. p. 88.—Acapulco.

BUETTNERIACEÆ.

67. BUETTNERIA *lanceolata*, DC. Prod. 1. p. 487.—Panama.

68. BUETTNERIA *glabrescens*, sp. n., caule aculeato foliisque novellis puberulis mox glabratis, foliis longiuscule petiolatis ovato-lanceolatis acuminatis serratis basi rotundatis vel rarius subcordatis hirtellis glabratisve, pedunculis axillaribus fasciculatis multifloris, calycis laciniis anguste lanceolatis, petalorum appendicibus filiformibus.—Guayaquil.

Folia pleraque 2-3-pollicaria. Pedunculi 6-12 lin. longi, 6-10 flori. Alabastra longe acuminata. Calycis laciniæ 1½ lin. vel paullo longiores. Petala basi angustata, auriculis acutis, appendice longa filiformi apice non incrassata. Fructus aculei longiusculi. Species *B. cordatæ* affinis, sed glabritie et forma foliorum satis distincta videtur.

69. THEOBROMA *Cacao*, Linn.—DC. Prod. 1. p. 484.—Columbia.

70. GUAZUMA *polybotrya*, Cav.—DC. Prod. 1. p. 485.—Manzanilla Bay.

71. WALTHERIA *Americana*, Linn.—DC. Prod. 1. p. 492.—Mexico to Guayaquil.

72. WALTHERIA *ovata*, Cav.—DC. Prod. 1. p. 493.—Guayaquil.

73. MELOCHIA *pyramidata*, Linn.—DC. Prod. 1. p. 490.—Guayaquil.

74. MELOCHIA *tomentosa*, Linn.—DC. Prod. 1. p. 490.—Acapulco.

75. MELOCHIA (Riedleia) *inflata*, DC. Prod. 1. p. 491.—Panama to Guayaquil.

76. MELOCHIA (Riedleia) *nodiflora*, Sw.—DC. Prod. 1. p. 491.—Mexico to Guayaquil.

77. MELOCHIA (Riedleia) *serrata*, Vent.—DC. Prod. 1. p. 492.—Acapulco.

TILIACEÆ.

78. CORCHORUS *tortipes*, St. Hil.? Fl. Bras. Merid. 1. p. 281. t. 55.—Guayaquil.—The specimen is very imperfect, but does not appear to differ from the Brazilian ones.

79. TRIUMFETTA *dumetorum*, Hook. et Arn. Bot. Beech. p. 279. vix Schlecht.—Tepic.—This does not indeed quite agree with Schlechtendahl's description; but the species in this genus are so very variable, that I have much doubt whether this one be new or not.

80. TRIUMFETTA *heterophylla*, Lam.—DC. Prod. 1. p. 506.—Gulf of Fonseca.

81. TRIUMFETTA *rhomboidea*, Jacq.—DC. Prod. 1. p. 507.—Guayaquil.

82. HELIOCARPUS *popayanensis*, Humb. et Kunth.—DC. Prod. 1. p. 503.—Species a *H. Americano* abunde distincta.—Isle of Taboga, Bay of Panama.

83. HASSELTIA *floribunda*, Humb. et Kunth, Nov. Gen. 7. p. 232. t. 651. var. pauciflora.—Isthmus of Darien.

84. MUNTINGIA *Calabura*, Linn.—DC. Prod. 1. p. 514.—Panama to Guayaquil.

85. LUHEA *rufescens*, St. Hil. Fl. Bras. Merid. 1. p. 293. t. 58.—Tiger Island, Gulf of Fonseca and Conchagua, Gulf of Honda.—Precisely similar to the Brasilian and Guayana specimens, and probably the same as *Alegria candida*, Fl. Mex. or *Luhea candida*, Mart.

TERNSTRŒMIACEÆ.

86. COCHLOSPERMUM *hibiscoides*, Humb. et Kunth, Nov. Gen. 7. p. 223.—Isle of Taboga, Bay of Panama, and Isle of Puna, near Guayaquil.

87. TERNSTRŒMIA *clusiæfolia*, Humb. et Kunth?—DC. Prod. 1. p. 524.—Guayaquil.

The American species of *Ternstrœmia* are difficult to distinguish, and the characters derived from the form and size of the leaves and length of the peduncles are variable within limits very difficult to define in descriptions. The present plant agrees very well with Kunth's figure and description, except that the leaves have no black dots underneath, but it is doubtful whether this is a specific distinction, or merely owing to a difference in age, or in the season when gathered.

88. MARILA *macrophylla*, sp. n., foliis oblongis acumine brevissimo glabris, racemis folio brevioribus ferrugineo-tomentellis, stylo ovario vix breviore.—Isle of Gorgona.

Forma foliorum *M. tomentosæ*, Pœpp., sed glaberrima sunt, ultrapedalia, utrinque rotundata et apice in acumen vix 2 lin. longum producta. Racemi vix 6 poll. longi. Flores duplo majores quam in *M. racemosa*. Sepala 5 exteriora angustiora, dorso tomentosa, fere 5 lin. longa. Nec petala nec stamina vidi. Ovarium 3 lin. longum, glabrum, 5-loculare, ovulis numerosissimis. Stylus 2 lin. longum, parte stigmatifera crassa ovoidea 1 lin. longa.

CLUSIACEÆ.

89. CLUSIA *subsessilis*, sp. n., foliis sessilibus obovatis obtusissimis basi angustato-rotundatis, venis valde obliquis crebris utrinque leviter prominulis, pedunculo terminali brevi trichotomo plurifloro, floribus fœmineis bibracteatis 4-sepalis 5-petalis anandris, stigmate (5-?) 6-radiato.—Atacames, not uncommon in Columbia.

Arbor divaricato-ramosa. Folia 3-5 pollicaria, venis a nervo medio minus divergentibus quam in plerisque speciebus. Pedunculus communis terminalis, 3-4 lin. longus, semel vel bis trichotomus, ramis capitulo trifloro terminatis. Flores (in specimine fœmineo) brevissime pedicellati. Sepala orbiculata, coriacea. Petala obovata, 6 lin. longa. Staminum sterilium vestigium nullum detexi. Ovarium globosum, stigmatibus 6 (an tamen constanter?) radiatim dispositis subrotundis, a centro paullulum distantibus.

The flowers of this species are very near to those of the Brazilian *C. criuva*, St. Hil.; the foliage and inflorescence agree pretty well with Kunth's description of *C. multiflora*, but it is evidently distinct from either.

90. TRIPLANDRON *lineatum*, gen. nov. (Plate XXVIII.)—Tumaco and San Pedro in Columbia.

CHAR. GEN. Flores dioici. Masculi: Calyx bibracteatus, 4-sepalus. Corolla 4-petala. Stamina numerosa, triseriata, in massam tetragonam convexam connata, seriei interioris majora; filamenta crassa, angulato-concreta; antheræ terminales, connectivo immersæ, loculis rima oblonga dehiscentibus. Flores fœminei: Calyx et corolla maris. Stamina sterilia in cupulam carnosam tetragonam ovarium cingentem connata. Ovarium tetragono-globosum, stigmata plurima (circa 9) sessilia, radiantia. Ovarii loculi totidem (pluriovulati?).

Species unica. *T. lineatum.* Arbor 20-pedalis. Folia petiolata, opposita, 3-5-pollicaria, ovali-oblonga, utrinque acuta vel rarius apice obtusiuscula, coriacea, percursa venulis crebris parallele divergentibus utrinque prominulis et lineolis tenuibus in sicco purpurascentibus nervo medio subparallelis a basi ad apicem folii extensis. Petiolus 3-8 lin. longus, basi subdilatatus et intus (in glandulam?) incrassatus. Pedunculi ad apices ramorum vel ramulorum brevium axillarium, brevissimi, terni, recurvi. Bracteæ orbiculatæ, 2 lin. longæ. Sepala orbiculata, concava, coriacea, 4 lin. longa. Petala 8-9 lin. longa, patentia, obovato-rotundata, rubra, marginibus reflexis crispis. Stamina marium in serie exteriore circa 20, in intermedia 15-18, in interiore 5-9 duplo fere majora, omnia in massam coalita ovarium abortiens sæpius minimum circumdantem at ab hoc liberam. Staminum sterilium urceolus in flore fœmineo acute tetragonus, ovario brevior. Stigmata inter se distincta et a centro distantia fere *Clusiæ criuvæ*.

Plate XXVIII. fig. 1, mass of stamens, from the male flower; fig. 2, the same, seen from above; fig. 3, nectarium, or abortive staminal mass and ovary of the female flower; fig. 4, the same, seen from above; fig. 5, transverse section of the ovary; all magnified.

91. MAMMEA *Americana*, Linn.—DC. Prod. 1. p. 561.—Isle of Taboga, Bay of Panama.

MARCGRAVIACEÆ.

92. RUYSCHIA *bicolor*, sp. n., (Plate XXIX.) foliis oblongo-vel ovali-ellipticis obtusis aristula decidua mucronatis basi rotundato-cuneatis, bracteæ tripartitæ cruribus oblongo-linearibus obtusis calcare apice discolore clavato brevioribus.—Isle of Gorgona.

Folia 3-4-pollicaria, margine minime revoluta. Pedicelli pollicares. Bracteæ pedicelli et calyces kermesini. Calcar pollicare, apice tumidum, flavidum. Petala intus rubra, extus flavida.

Plate XXIX. fig. 1, bractea and bud; fig. 2, flower expanded; fig. 3, portion of the stamens and corolla; fig. 4, ovary; all magnified.

93. RUYSCHIA? *subsessilis*, sp. n., foliis subsessilibus oblongo-ellipticis obtusis margine recurvis basi truncato-cordatis, racemo abbreviato.—Isthmus of Darien.

Specimen adest unicum, fructiferum. Ramulus crassus, cortice laxo læviusculo. Folia 3-4 poll. longa, 15-18 lin. lata. Pedicelli approximati, fere 2 poll. longi, prope basin cicatrice notati bracteæ delapsæ. Sepala 5, brevia, rotundata. Capsula coriacea, sublignosa, 6 lin. diametro, stigmate 6-7-lobo coronata, intus placenta spongiosa villosa (6-loba?) repleta, obscure pluri-(6-7-?) locularis. Semina in loculis plurima, oblonga, nigra.

TRIGONIACEÆ.

94. TRIGONIA *rugosa*, sp. n., foliis petiolatis ovato-oblongis sublanceolatisve acuminatis basi rotundatis subrugosis supra glabris subtus niveo-tomentosis, floribus secus ramos paucos paniculæ congestis, capsulis ovatis.—Columbia.

Ramuli novelli subflavido-tomentosi, rami lana nivea laxa detergibili vestiti, demum glabrati. Folia 3-5-pollicaria, bullato-rugosa, petiolo 3-4 lin. longo. Flores quam in *T. villosa* multo minores, majores tamen quam in *T. crotonoide*. Sepala extus nivea. Stamina antherifera 5, sterilia 4-5. Glandulæ 2, obtusæ. Capsula latitudine vix duplo longior, in speciminibus 8-9 lin. longa sed nondum matura.

A very distinct species, allied on the one hand to *T. nivea*, and on the other to *T. crotonoides*.

MALPIGHIACEÆ.

95. MALPIGHIA *retusa*, sp. n., foliis brevibus ovatis ellipticisve obtusis vel emarginatis integerrimis utrinque pilis malpighiaceis pubescentibus, umbellis paucifloris, calyce 7-8-glanduloso.—Isle of Puna, near Guayaquil.

Species paucis notis differt a descriptione Jussiæana *M. Galeottianæ*. Rami juniores pilis adpressis sericeis obtecti, subflavicantes, adulti glabrati. Folia majora 9-10 lin. longa, 5-7 lin. lata, omnia obtusa et sæpius emarginata, pilis utrinque sparsis tenuibus medifixis raro simplicibus, in pagina superiore densioribus quam in inferiore; glandulæ nullæ; petiolus 1 lin. longus, dense pubescens; stipulæ minutæ setaceæ. Umbellæ 2-4 floræ. Pedunculi diversorum ordinum adpresso-pilosi, communis brevissimus subnullus, floriferi 1-1½ lin. longi, cum pedicello 1½-2 lin. longo articulati. Bracteæ et bracteolæ minutæ. Calycis laciniæ ovato-lanceolatæ, obtusiusculæ, extus tomentosæ, 2 vel 3 basi biglandulosæ, 3 vel 2 uniglandulosæ. Petala calyce plus duplo longiora, suborbiculata, in floribus tamen examinatis a vermibus partim destructa. Stamina glabra, basi brevissime coalita; antheræ ovato-cordatæ. Ovaria in unicum glabrum coalita, singula dorso obscure costata. Styli ovario longiores, glabri, apice truncato dilatato triquetroque stigmatiferi. Fructus non suppetit.

96. STIGMAPHYLLUM *ellipticum*, Ad. Juss.? Malp. p. 125.—Panama to Guayaquil.

There are a number of specimens in different states which may possibly belong to more than one species, but they are not sufficient to show any distinctive characters which are not very variable in this genus. The Panama specimens (in flower only) agree well with Kunth's description of the foliage and inflorescence, and with Jussieu's notes on the flower. Among those from Guayaquil (in flower also), some are like the Panama ones, others have many-flowered umbels, the middle one sessile, the two lateral pedicellate, and the floral leaves like those of the stem. Others, again, from the Gulf of Fonseca in flower, and from Atacames in fruit, have the same many-flowered inflorescence, but the stem leaves are larger, more pointed, coriaceous, and shining. In all, the flowers appear to be large.

97. STIGMAPHYLLUM *fulgens*, Ad. Juss. Malp. p. 116.—Realejo.

98. HETEROPTERYS *Mathewsana*, Ad. Juss.? Malp. p. 200.—Veragua.

A single specimen with the flowers much injured and without fruit, but agreeing, as far as it goes, with Jussieu's description, except that the leaves are rather smaller.

99. HETEROPTERYS *Beechyana*, Ad. Juss. Malp. p. 221.—Acapulco, also in the Consul's garden at Puna, near Guayaquil.

100. TETRAPTERYS *Acapulcensis*, Humb. et Kunth.—Ad. Juss. Malp. p. 267.—Acapulco.

101. HIRÆA *Barclayana*, sp. n., foliis obovatis obtusissimis basi angustatis cordatis, supra glabriusculis subtus pubescentibus, petiolo biglanduloso bistipulato, umbellis breviter pedunculatis, pedicellis elongatis sericeis, calyce eglanduloso, samaræ alis pilosiusculis lateralibus dorsali cristæformi multoties longioribus.—Libertad in Columbia.

Rami juniores angulato-compressi, pube adpressa densa canescentes, adulti glabriores. Folia 3-5 poll. longa, supra medium 2-2½ poll. lata, apice sæpe emarginata, prope basin contracta et ima basi obtusa plus minus emarginato-cordata, supra glabra vel pilis raris simplicibus conspersa, subtus pallida, pilis simplicibus sparsis vestita, in costa nervisque adpressis et præsertim in costa nonnullis malpighiaceis medifixis admixtis; costa venæque primariæ subtus prominulæ, venulæ transversæ retiformesque parum conspicuæ; petiolus 2-4 lin. longus, tomento denso adpresso canescens, sub apice biglandulosus et supra basin stipulis 2 lineari-subulatis recurvo-patentibus auctus. Umbellæ axillares, pedunculo communi crasso 2-3 lin. longo apice bibracteato 3-umbellifero insidentes. Pedicelli bracteis bracteolisque parvis lanceolatis capitatim congesti, tenues, pollicares uti pedunculi bractea et calyces pube adpressa obtecti. Flores non vidi. Calycis fructiferi laciniæ lato-lanceolatæ videntur, sed partim obliterati sunt. Samaræ sæpius abortu solitariæ, dense pubescentes, dorso cristatæ, crista brevissima undulato-crenata glabra; alæ in utroque latere samaræ semicirculares, ¾ poll. longæ, fere 1½ poll. latæ, tenuiter membranaceæ, pilis simplicibus conspersæ, margine irregulariter crenatæ.

This species differs from *H. crassipes* by the absence of glands on the calyx, and the pubescence of the leaves, from *H. Kunthiana* chiefly by the leaves, which are larger, remarkably obtuse, and neither coriaceous nor shining.

102. GAUDICHAUDIA *Schiedeana*, Ad. Juss. Malp. p. 337.—Acapulco.

SAPINDACEÆ.

103. CARDIOSPERMUM *hispidum*, Humb. et Kunth.—DC.? Prod. 1. p. 602.—Acapulco.

A single specimen without flowers.

104. CARDIOSPERMUM *coluteoides*, Humb. et Kunth.—DC. Prod. 1. p. 602.—Isle of Taboga, Bay of Panama.

This agrees precisely with Kunth's description. The very young fruit is ciliate on the angles with a few long hairs which soon fall off, and the capsule is perfectly smooth long before its maturity. In the common Brazilian form, the capsule is always pubescent all over, as described by Cambessèdes, and rather more pointed.

105. URVILLÆA *Berteriana*, DC.? Prod. 1. p. 602.—Realejo.

106. SERJANIA *brevipes*, sp. n., foliis brevissime petiolatis ternatis, foliolis lato-ovatis subinciso-crenatis mucronatis, lateralibus basi truncato-cordatis, terminali basi late rotundata, petiolulo brevi cuneato-alato, omnibus supra minute hirtellis subtus ramulisque molliter tomentoso-villosis, racemis simplicibus brevibus densis, calyce 5-phyllo.—Columbia and Guayaquil.

Ramuli angulati. Petiolus communis vix unquam semipollicaris, subteres. Foliola lateralia 1-1½-pollicaria, crenaturis apiceque obtusiusculis cum mucrone, subsessilia vel brevissime petiolulata; terminale paullo longius, multo latius, cum petiolulo 2-4 lin. longo continuum. Pedunculus communis folio brevior, rigidus, tomentoso-villosus, apice bicirrhosus. Racemus 1-4-pollicaris, pedunculis secundariis brevissimis 2-4-floris, pedicellis subnullis. Calyx pubescens. Fructus junior tomentoso-pubescens, maturum non vidi.

107. SERJANIA *glabrata*, Humb. et Kunth.—DC. Prod. 1. p. 603.—Salango in Columbia.

108. SERJANIA *racemosa*, Schum.—DC. l. c.—Realejo.

109. SERJANIA *mexicana*, Willd. ?—DC. ? l. c.—Tepic.

110. SERJANIA *paniculata*, Humb. et Kunth?—DC.? l. c.—Acapulco.

111. SERJANIA *lupulina*, Schum?—DC.? Prod. 1. p. 604.—Columbia.

The species of *Serjania* are numerous in tropical America, and variable in the size and form of the leaves, and without good specimens both in flower and fruit it is exceedingly difficult to determine them, especially as so many have been described from very imperfect materials.

112. PAULLINIA *fuscescens*, Humb. et Kunth? Nov. Gen. 5. p. 120.—Isle of Taboga, Bay of Panama.

These specimens, as far as they go, agree with Kunth's description; but like his they are in flower only, and too young to determine the genus, which is more probably *Serjania* than *Paullinia*.

113. PAULLINIA *curassavica*, Linn.—DC. Prod. 1. p. 605.—Tepic and Realejo.

114. PAULLINIA *barbadensis*, Jacq.—DC. l. c.—Atacames in Columbia.

The young capsules are pubescent, but they become smooth or nearly so when ripe. The specimens are quite similar to those from Jamaica, the West Indies, various parts of Brazil, &c.

AMPELIDEÆ.*

115. Cissus *salutaris*, Humb. et Kunth?—DC.? Prod. 1. 630.—Guayaquil.

A single specimen in an imperfect state.

116. Cissus *obtusata*, sp. n., foliis simplicibus obovatis ovatisve obtusissimis vel vix obtuse acuminatis basi angustato-cuneatis 5-nerviis, margine minute et remote dentatis, utrinque ramulisque glabris, umbellæ glabræ ramis 5 bifidis cymosis.—Panama.

Folia 2-3-pollicaria, longiuscule petiolata, basi sæpe inæquilatera, dentibus argutis sæpe obsoletis. Pedunculi petiolo sublongiores, angulato-striati.

There are also very incomplete specimens of another simple-leaved *Cissus* from Columbia, perhaps new, but not in a state to be determined.

GERANIACEÆ.

117. Tropæolum *Moritzianum*, Link. Kl. et Otto, Ic. Rar. p. 41. t. 17.—Guayaquil.

OXALIDACEÆ.

118. Oxalis *Neæi*, DC. Prod. 1. p. 690.—Zucc. Oxal. Nachtr. p. 86.—Acapulco; Tiger Island, Gulf of Fonseca.

119. Oxalis *microcarpa*, sp. n., caulescens, erecta, pubescens, foliolis 3 ovato-vel oblongo-rhombeis obtusiusculis basi cuneatis ciliatis utrinque puberulis subtus glaucis, terminali distante, lateralibus inæquilateris, pedunculis elongato-bifidis multifloris, sepalis acutis capsulas æquantibus.—Columbia.

Herba humilis, vix unquam in speciminibus pedalis, apice more *O. Barrelieri* et affinium alternatim vel fasciculatim foliosa, plus minus pubescens. Stipulæ inconspicuæ. Petioli graciles, pollicares. Foliolum terminale 6-10 lin. longum vel rarius pollicare, lateralia minora, angustiora, in speciminibus vegetioribus fere glabra. Pedunculus 2-3-pollicaris, gracilis, ramis demum ultrapollicaribus simplicibus. Flores breviter pedicellati, 1 lin. longi. Stamina longiora et styli apice pilis paucis barbata. Capsulæ loculi monospermi.

Allied to *O. Barrelieri* and *O. hedysaroides*, but more slender and readily distinguished by the small size of the flowers and especially of the fruit.

---

* There are specimens in the collection of Melia *Azedarach*, Linn., belonging to *Meliaceæ*, and of a species or variety of *Citron*, belonging to *Aurantiaceæ*, which I have omitted as not being indigenous.

SIMARUBACEÆ.

120. QUASSIA *amara*, Linn. fil.—DC. Prod. 1. p. 733.—Manzanilla Bay, Isle of Taboga, Veragua, &c.

CELASTRACEÆ.

121. HIPPOCRATEA *excelsa*, Humb. et Kunth.—DC. Prod. 1. p. 569.—Veragua.

This agrees with Kunth's description, except that I find the stamens and ovaries always three, and not four or five. The young capsules are very broadly obcordate.

122. HIPPOCRATEA *floribunda*, sp. n., foliis ovali-ellipticis oblongisve breviter et obtuse acuminatis integerrimis utrinque ramulis paniculisque glabris, paniculis folio brevioribus repetite trichotome vel umbellatim ramosis, infimis corymbosis, floribus canescentibus.—Isle of Gorgona.

Folia fere *H. excelsæ*, sed constanter integerrima, 2-3½ poll. longa, basi cuneata, petiolo 3 lin. longo. Pedunculi et paniculæ rami acute angulati, glaberrimi. Flores numerosissimi. Sepala brevissima, orbiculata, integra, extus canescentia. Petala oblonga, obtusa, calyce triplo longiora, vix tamen semilineam excedentia, extus canescentia. Stamina tria, intus prope basin disci inserta.

RHAMNACEÆ.

123. ZIZYPHUS *thyrsiflora*, sp. n., glabriuscula, inermis, foliis petiolatis late ovatis obtusis crenatis subintegerrimisve basi subcordatis supra nitidis, cymis pedunculatis in paniculam thyrsoideam vix basi foliatam dispositis, fructu oblongo.—Guayaquil.—Gathered there also by Hartweg, n. 646.

Iconi Vahlianæ *Z. reticulatæ* similis, sed foliis evidentius crenatis oculo nudo glabris, et fructu forma diversa videtur. Arbor est 15-20-pedalis. Ramuli subteretes, glabri, vel vix summo apice in panicula minute puberuli. Folia 2½-3-poll. longa, 2-2½ poll. lata, triplinervia, vel adjectis nervis exterioribus tenuioribus 5-7-nervia, pleraque evidenter crenata, denticulisque inter crenas callosis minutis, supra nitida glaberrima, subtus pilis minutis raris nonnisi ope lente conspicuis conspersa. Petioli 4-6 lin. longi. Paniculæ terminales, 2-4-pollicares, constantes e cymis pluri-vel multi-floris pedunculatis, quarum inferiores ex axillis superioribus natæ, superiores omnino ebracteatæ nec bracteis subtensæ. Flores et partium proportio omnino *Z. reticulatæ*. Drupæ forma et magnitudo fere *Z. vulgaris*.

124. ZIZYPHUS *acuminata*, sp. n., glabra, foliis ovato-lanceolatis acuminatis basi rotundatis remote denticulatis dentibus subtus glanduliferis, cymis axillaribus breviter pedunculatis.—Acapulco.

Ramuli tenues, teretes. Folia 2-2½-poll. longa, 8-10 lin. lata, longiuscule acuminata, dentibus utrinque 1-4 obtusis notata, basi trinervia venisque secus costam mediam utrinque 1-2 prominulis subpenninervia, petiolo 3-5 lin. longo. Inflorescentia et flores parvi fere *Z. vulgaris*. Stamina longitudine calycis. Petala subbreviora, obovato-oblonga, convoluta. Fructus non vidi.

125. GOUANIA *corylifolia* Raddi.—DC. Prod. 2. p. 39.—Columbia.

I can see no difference of specific importance between these specimens and the common Brazilian form, but the genus is at present in so much confusion that it is doubtful whether both may not be referable to some of the older described species. The fruit is acutely three-winged.

ANACARDIACEÆ.

126. RHUS *terebinthifolia*, Schlecht. Linnæa, 5. p. 600.—Tepic.

127. RHUS *macrophylla*, Hook. et Arn. Bot. Beech. p. 413.—Acapulco.

128. MANGIFERA *indica*, Linn.—DC. Prod. 2. p. 63.—Panama, Columbia, Guayaquil.

129. ANACARDIUM *occidentale*, Linn.—DC. Prod. 2. p. 62.—Panama to Guayaquil.

130. RHINOCARPUS *excelsus*, Humb. et Kunth.—Anacardium rhinocarpus. DC. Prod. 2. p. 62.—Columbia.

131. SPONDIAS *purpurea*, Linn.?—DC.? Prod. 2. p. 75.—Guayaquil.

CONNARACEÆ.

132. OMPHALOBII? vel CONNARI? sp.—Isle of Taboga, Bay of Panama.

The specimen is a very indifferent one in fruit only, apparently differing from *Omphalobium Perrottetii* in the smaller size of the folioles, and in the fruit covered with a dense rusty down. The calyx is that of *Omphalobium*, but the specimen is insufficient to determine the genus with certainty.

LEGUMINOSÆ.

133. CROTALARIA *Hookeriana*, Alph. DC. 8. Not. Pl. Rar. Gen. p. 23.—Tepic.

Scarcely different from *C. ovalis* of Pursh.

134. CROTALARIA *buplevrifolia*, Schlecht. Linnæa, 5. p. 575.—Hook. Ic. Pl. t. 382.—Tepic.

135. CROTALARIA *Tepicana*, Hook. et Arn. Bot. Beech. p. 414.—Tepic.

136. CROTALARIA *longirostrata*, Hook. et Arn. Bot. Beech. p. 285 and 414.—Acapulco; and a variety with the leaflets from an inch to an inch and a half long.—Gulf of Fonseca.

137. CROTALARIA *Maypurensis*, Humb. et Kunth.—DC. Prod. 2. p. 132.—*C. Acapulcensis*, Hook. et Arn. Bot. Beech. p. 414.—Acapulco.

138. CROTALARIA *incana*, Linn.*—DC. Prod. 2. p. 132.—Columbia and Guayaquil, Acapulco.

139. MELILOTUS *purviflora*, Desf.—DC. Prod. 2. p. 187.—Guayaquil.

140. INDIGOFERA *anil*, Linn.—DC. Prod. 2. p. 225.—Guayaquil.

141. INDIGOFERA *lespedezioides*, Humb. et Kunth.—DC. Prod. 2. p. 226.—Realejo.

142. DALEA *diffusa*, Moricand, Pl. Amer. p. 8. t. 6.—*D. gracilis*, Hook. et Arn. Bot. Beech. p. 287 and 416.—Acapulco.

143. DALEA *elegans*, Hook. et Arn. in Bot. Misc. 3. p. 183, et Bot. Beech. p. 417.—Tepic.

Although this does not appear to be the same as any of the older described species, it has travelled far with the Spaniards, being certainly the same as the one gathered by Gillies in the Cerro del Morro in the province of S. Luis, S. America, and having been also found at Manilla by Russian navigators and by Cuming.

144. DALEA *elata*, Hook. et Arn. Bot. Beech. p. 416.—Acapulco.

145. TEPHROSIA *toxicaria*, Pers.—DC. Prod. 2. p. 249.—Hook. et Arn. Bot. Beech. p. 416.—Acapulco.

146. TEPHROSIA *leucantha*, Humb. et Kunth.—DC. Prod. 2. p. 252.—Acapulco.

147. TEPHROSIA (Xiphocarpus) *crassifolia*, sp. n., fruticosa, rubiginoso-vel subcanescenti-villosa, foliolis 5-9 ovali-ellipticis utrinque obtusis supra rugoso-pubescentibus subtus rufo-vel subcanescenti-villosis, racemis axillaribus, pedicellis brevissimis subfasciculatis, calycis laciniis setaceo-acuminatis, infimis tubo longioribus, vexillo dense sericeo-villoso, legumine ferrugineo-villoso intus celluloso.—Acapulco.

Rami crassiusculi, subflexuosi, pube densa velutini. Stipulæ lanceolatæ, acutæ, deciduæ, extus villosæ, intus glabræ. Foliorum petiolus communis 1-2-pollicaris. Foliola opposita, inferiora a caule parum distantia, 6-18 lin. longa, superiora majora, terminale 2-3-pollicare, omnia obtusissima, basi rotundata, margine recurva, venis subtus prominentibus. Stipellæ obsoletæ, vel inter villis petiolorum minimæ. Racemi demum 4-6-pollicares. Bracteæ parvæ, stipulis conformes, deciduæ. Flores nunc sessiles, nunc pedicello 1-3 lin. longo stipati. Calycis tubus 1 lin. longus, dentes inferiores paullo longiores, superiores subbreviores basi latiores. Corolla et stamina *T. toxicariæ*.

148. TEPHROSIA *piscatoria*, Pers.—DC. Prod. 2. p. 252.—Realejo.

* The *C. incana* (Hook. et Arn. Bot. Beech. p. 285) from Mexico, but without any precise station, is a distinct species, which may be thus characterized:—

C. eriocarpa, fruticosa, ramulis pubescenti-villosis, stipulis subnullis, foliolis latiuscule oblongis obtusis basi cuneatis supra glabris subtus pubescentibus, racemo elongato multifloro, bracteis setaceo-acuminatis pedicellum subæquantibus, bracteolis minutis, calycibus villosis vexillo pubescente carinaque margine ciliata brevioribus, legumine brevissime stipitato oblongo-cylindraceo dense tomentoso-villoso.—Mexico, *Beechey, Tate*, etc.

Species habitu et floribus *Fruticosis* accedens, legumen *Incanarum*. Ramuli superne striati, pube densa subpatente, in junioribus rufo-vel canescenti-nitente. Petioli demum pollicares. Foliola parum inæqualia, 1½-2-pollicaria. Racemus demum fere pedalis. Flores majusculi. Pedicelli 3-4 lin. longi. Calyces 5 lin. longi, in alabastro acuminati, laciniis lateralibus inter se diu cohærentibus. Vexillum calycem lineis 1-2 excedit. Carina calyci subæqualis, valde incurva, acute rostrata, brevius tamen quam in *C. Maypurensi*, linea dorsali margineque interiore læviter pubescentibus.

149. TEPHROSIA *oroboides*, Humb. et Kunth.—DC. Prod. 2. p. 250.—Gulf of Fonseca.

150. TEPHROSIA *mollis*, Humb. et Kunth.—DC. Prod. 2. p. 250.—Gulf of Fonseca.

This species is closely allied to *T. ochroleuca*. The flowers are smaller; the divisions of the calyx longer; the pod slightly pubescent.

151. TEPHROSIA (Craccoides) *glabrescens*, sp. n., herbacea, glabriuscula, foliolis 5-9 obovatis oblongisve tenuiter membranaceis supra glabris subtus adpresse pilosis glabratisve, racemis laxis folio sublongioribus, calycis puberuli laciniis subulatis superioribus tubo subæquilongis infima paullo longiore alis dimidio breviore, legumine glaberrimo.—Columbia.

T. ochroleucæ affinis, at satis distincta videtur glabritie, foliolis tenuibus, pedicellis duplo longioribus, floribus paullo majoribus.

152. TEPHROSIA (Craccoides) *glandulifera*, sp. n., herbacea, foliolis 11-21 oblongo-ellipticis utrinque præsertim subtus ramisque molliter subsericeo-pubescentibus villosisve, racemis folio multo longioribus laxis, pedunculo pedicellis calycibusque glanduloso-pubescentibus, calycis laciniis subulatis tubo subtriplo longioribus carinam subæquantibus, legumine tenuiter pubescente.—Guayaquil; gathered there also by Hartweg, n. 648.

Habitus et folia fere *T. caribææ*, cui et *T. ochroleucæ* affinis. Foliola 4-5 lin. vel in umbrosis 8-10 lin. longa, basi obliqua parum angustata vel rotundata, apice obtusa cum mucrone. Stipulæ subulato-setaceæ, 2-3 lin. longæ. Stipellæ minutæ, rarius obsoletæ. Racemi cum pedunculo 4-8-pollicares, pube molli cum pilis glanduliferis plus minus intermixta. Flores in racemo 6-10, majores quam in *T. ochroleuca*, minores quam in *T. caribæa*. Pedicelli circa 2 lin. longi. Bracteæ setaceæ, deciduæ. Legumen sessile, leviter incurvum, undique æquilatum vel basi parum angustatum, uti in affinibus obtusum, compressum, lineis transversis depressis inter semina torulosum, intus septatum. Semina quadrata.

153. PISCIDIA *erythrina*, Linn.—DC. Prod. 2. p. 267.—Guayaquil.

154. LONCHOCARPUS *maculatus*, DC. Prod. 2. p. 260.—Nicoya.

155. LONCHOCARPUS, sp., without leaves from Central America, apparently new, but insufficient to describe.

156. ASTRAGALUS *ervoides*, Hook. et Arn. sp. n., Bot. Beech. p. 417.—Tepic.

157. PLANARIUM *latisiliquum*, Desv. Ann. Sc. Nat. Par. 9. p. 411. (Plate XXX.)—Atacames.

When this plant was put into the artist's hands, it was believed to be an entirely new genus of Hedysareæ; it has, however, since been ascertained, with little doubt, to be the same as the one imperfectly described by Desvaux under the above name shortly after the publication of the second volume of De Candolle's Prodromus. As it has never since then been mentioned by any other botanist, and appears to be a scarce plant, there being but a single specimen in the collection before me, I subjoin an amended generic character and description.

CHAR. GEN. Calyx campanulatus, breviter 5-dentatus. Vexillum ovato-orbiculatum, complicatum. Alæ oblongæ, falcatæ. Petala carinalia alis subsimilia, apice dorso connata. Stamina ad medium connata in vaginam postice fissam. Antheræ conformes. Legumen breviter stipitatum, elongatum, planum, sutura utraque ala subcartilaginea marginata, articulis numerosis quadratis indehiscentibus.

P. latisiliquum. Frutex? eglandulosus, ramis subteretibus volubilibus elongatis, junioribus pube brevi molli canescentibus, demum glabris. Stipulæ subfoliaceæ, lanceolatæ, acute acuminatæ, persistentes, 1-2 lin. longæ, liberæ. Folia impari-pinnata. Petiolus communis bipollicaris, tenuis. Foliola 5, opposita cum terminali distante, petiolulata, obovata vel orbicularia, obtusissima cum mucronulo, basi rotundata, 4-8 lin. longa, membranacea, impunctata, utrinque tenuiter puberula, subtus pallida. Racemi axillares, folio multo breviores, pluriflori. Pedicelli 2 lin. longi, ad axillas bractearum stipulis conformium solitarii, ebracteolati. Calyx 2 lin. longus, canescenti-pubescens, dentibus brevissimis latis obtusis subæqualibus. Vexillum semipollicare, basi in unguem brevem latam angustatum, inappendiculatum, supra unguem medio obsolete bigibbosum. Alæ vexillo parum breviores, breviter unguiculatæ, margine postice supra unguem angulatæ, foveolis transversis nullis. Carina alis vix brevior, petalis ultra medium liberis, margine basi ciliatis. Legumen 2-3-pollicare, cum alis 4 lin. latum, glabrum vel pube tenuissima subcanescens, medio utrinque costatum et venis obliquis tenuiter reticulatum, alis fere lineam latis subaveniis, articulis 12-15 monospermis.

Plate XXX. fig. 1, flower; fig. 2, vexillum; fig. 3, one of the alæ; fig. 4, carina; fig. 5, stamens; fig. 6, joint of the pod opened, showing the seed; all magnified.

158. ÆSCHYNOMENE *sensitiva*, Sw.—DC. Prod. 2. p. 320.—Columbia.

159. ÆSCHYNOMENE *glandulosa*, Poir.—DC. Prod. 2. p. 321.—*Æ. hirsuta*, Cham. Schl. Linnæa 5. p. 583.— Hook. et Arn. Bot. Beech. p. 418. an DC?— Realejo.— Foliola ut in *Æ. americana* 2-3-nervia.

160. STYLOSANTHES *humilis*, Humb. et Kunth.—DC. Prod. 2. p. 318. var. angustifolia.—Realejo.

161. DESMODIUM (Chalarium) *plicatum*, Cham. Schlecht. Linnæa 5. p. 585.—Tepic.

162. DESMODIUM (Chalarium) *heterophyllum*, Hook et Arn. Bot. Beech. p. 417.—Realejo.

163. DESMODIUM (Chalarium) *stipulaceum*, DC. Prod. 2. p. 330. var. macrophyllum, foliolis oblongis, usque ad 9 poll. longis.—Central America.

164. DESMODIUM (Chalarium) affine *D. stipulaceo*.—Isle of Taboga, Bay of Panama.—This is probably new, but the specimen is insufficient to describe it.

165. DESMODIUM (Chalarium) *podocarpum*, sp. n., Hook et Arn. Bot. Beech. p. 417. t. 96.—Acapulco.

166. DESMODIUM (Scorpiurus) *scorpiurus*, Desv.—DC. Prod. 2. p. 333.—*D. incanum* β. *supinum*, Hook et Arn. Bot. Beech. p. 417.—Realejo, Puna near Guayaquil.

167. DESMODIUM (Heteroloma) *triflorum*, DC. Prod. 2. p. 334.—Acapulco.

168. DESMODIUM (Heteroloma) *incanum*, DC. Prod. 2. p. 332. — *D. ancistrocarpum*, DC. Prod. 2. p. 331.—*D. diversifolium*, Schlecht. Linnæa, 12. p. 313.—Columbia; and a variety with the lower leaves reduced to one round leaf, possibly a distinct species; Panama.

169. DESMODIUM (Heteroloma) *adscendens*, DC. Prod. 2. p. 332.—Columbia.

170. DESMODIUM (Heteroloma) *axillare*, DC. Prod. 2. p. 333.—*D. reptans*, DC. l. c.—*D. radicans*, Macfad. Fl. Jam.—Columbia, together with a more hairy variety.

171. DESMODIUM (Heteroloma) *Sinclairi*, sp. n., elatum, incumbens?, uncinato-hirsutum, stipulis late lanceolatis acuminatis fusco-membranaceis deciduis, stipellis elongatis, foliolis ovato-

lanceolatis subrhombeis acuminatis utrinque pilis appressis supra raris pubescentibus, bracteis basi latis longe acuminatis ante anthesin comosis, calycis laciniis lanceolatis acuminatis, leguminis articulis 5-8 hirsuto-scabris.—Columbia.

Species *D. Limensi* valde affinis, at planta subscandens videtur, foliola majore (2-4-pollicaria), stipulæ et bracteæ multo majores, longius acuminatæ, et pili caulis ut in *D. uncinato* hamato-prehensiles nec ut in *D. Limensi* molles.

172. DESMODIUM (Nephromeria) *molle* DC.? Prod. 2. p. 332.—*Hedysarum molle*, Vahl? Symb. 2. p. 83. elatum, undique breviter subadhærente-pubescens, stipulis parvis e basi lata striata subulato-acuminatis, foliolis ovato-rhombeis subacuminatis obtusis mucronatis utrinque pubescentibus, racemis paniculatis, floribus minutis, calycis laciniis setaceo-acuminatis suprema bifida, legumine juniore tortuoso pubescente articulo terminali demum plano reniformi membranaceo glabriusculo isthmo angustissimo affixo.—Central America.

173. DESMODIUM (Nephromeria) *Barclayi*, sp. n., caule flexuoso hirtello, stipulis brevibus latis deciduis, foliolis ovato-rhombeis acutiusculis utrinque præsertim subtus puberulis, racemis paniculatis, leguminis stipitati demum glabri articulis 1-2 orbiculato-reniformibus submembranaceis glabris, margine seminali intrusa, isthmis angustissimis.—Central America.

Species, ex diagnosi brevissima Candollei, *D. infracto* affinis, sed hujus leguminis articuli semi-orbiculati discrepant. Specimina nonnisi fructifera adsunt. Ramuli crassiusculi, virides, obtuse angulati. Stipulæ desunt nisi in gemmulis ubi breves sunt, latæ, brevissime acuminatæ, striatæ. Stipellæ parvæ, lanceolatæ, acutissimæ. Petioli 2-3-pollicares. Foliola 2-3-pollicaria, lateralia minora, breviter petiolulata. Racemi in axillis superioribus et ad apices ramorum paniculam formant laxam divaricatam basi foliosam. Pedicelli 2 lin. longi. Bracteæ et flores desunt. Leguminis stipes 2 lin. longus, articuli 6 lin. longi et lati consistentia subchartacea, reticulati; sutura dorsalis tres partes circumferentiæ occupat, seminalis sinu acutangulo profunde intrusa. Semen parvum, ovato-reniforme.

Although the old Linnean *Hedysara* have been broken up by modern botanists into several distinct genera, yet some of these, and especially *Desmodium*, have become so very numerous in species as to require further division into sections. De Candolle had distributed them provisionally according to their native countries, but that is of less convenience in this instance than in many others, as (owing probably to the prehensile nature of the hairs of the pods) the commoner tropical *Desmodia* are so wide spread that it is often difficult to say what is properly their native station. I have attempted to establish sections on the forms of their fruit, which, though in some degree artificial, are the best I have been able to devise. Those above mentioned may be thus characterized.

Scorpiurus. Legumen angustum, elongatum, maturum vix compressum, æquilatum vel ad articulos levissime constrictum, articulis latitudine multo longioribus, æquilateris.

Chalarium. Legumen elongatum, compressum, inter articulos ad utramque suturam valde constrictum, articulis orbiculatis vel ovatis æquilateris vel parum inæquilateris.

Heteroloma. Legumen elongatum pluriarticulatum vel breve 1-2-articulatum, valde compressum, sutura seminali continua, ad alteram suturam inter articulos valde constrictum, articulis semiorbicularibus hinc rectis illinc convexis.

Nephromeria. Legumen plano-compressum, sutura seminali subcontinua ad suturam alteram valde constrictum, articulis magnis reniformibus sæpius membranaceis, sutura seminali cujusve articuli intrusa, altera valde convexa.

174. VICIA *bidentata,* Hook. Bot. Misc. v. 2. p. 215.—Guayaquil.

175. CLITORIA *ternatea,* Linn.—DC. Prod. v. 2. p. 233.—Atacames.

176. CLITORIA *arborescens,* Ait.—DC. Prod. v. 2. p. 235.— C. *Poitæi,* Benth. in Ann. Nat. Hist. 2. p. 234.—Bracteolæ lanceolatæ, acutæ, 3-6 lin. longæ.—Panama.

177. CLITORIA *brachystegia,* sp. n., fruticosa, scandens, elata, glabra, (vel junior puberula?) foliolis ovatis breviter acuminatis amplis subcoriaceis, racemis petiolo brevioribus densifloris, bracteis bracteolisque brevissimis suborbiculatis, calycis late tubulosi glabri dentibus brevibus latis obtusis, vexillo sericeo, ovario villoso.—Guayaquil.

Habitus folia et inflorescentia *C. arborescentis,* sed racemi breviores, flores sessiliores. Calyx vix semipollice longior, dentibus non acuminatis. Bracteolæ latiores quam longæ, vix lineam attingentes.

178. CENTROSEMA *Plumieri,* Benth.—Walp. Repert. v. 1. p. 753.—Gulf of Fonseca; Isle of Taboga; Bay of Panama.

179. CENTROSEMA *angustifolia,* Benth.—Walp. Repert. v. 1. p. 753.—Isle of Taboga; Bay of Panama.

180. CENTROSEMA *Salzmanni,* Benth. in Tayl. Ann. Nat. Hist. 3. p. 436.—*C. virginiana,* Hook. et Arn. Bot. Beech. p. 416. non alior.—Realejo.—Ejusdem var.? *gracilis,* dentibus calycinis superioribus tube paullo brevioribus.—Central America.—Ejusdem var.? *villosum,* foliolis angustioribus, ramulis inflorescentia leguminibusque villosis.—Isle of Taboga.

It is possible that the two latter varieties may, on the examination of a greater number of specimens, turn out to be distinct species, or that the first of the two may be a form of *C. angustifolia.* The Realejo specimens appear to be without doubt of the same species as the Brazilian and Guiana ones I possess, and it is probable that all are mere forms of one very variable plant.

181. CENTROSEMA *hastatum,* Benth.—Walp. Repert. 1. p. 756.—Nicoya.

182. STENOLOBIUM *cæruleum,* Benth. Ann. Mus. Vind. 2. p. 125.— Mexico and Central America.

This is the name under which I had originally published this plant, without perceiving that D. Don had already given it to a Bignoniaceous genus; on that account, I altered mine to *Cyanostremma,* which Hooker and Arnott took up in the Botany of Captain Beechey's Voyage. It appears now, however, that Don's *Stenolobium* is not adopted, and if so the name must be retained for my genus.

183. GLYCINE *oblonga,* ramulis angulatis retrorsum ferrugineo-villosis, foliolis oblongis lanceolatisve rarius ovato-lanceolatis obtusis mucronulatis supra glabris vel sparse pilosis subtus adpresse pilosis, racemis folio longioribus remote multifloris vel inferioribus abbreviatis paucifloris, calycis

rufo-villosi labio superiore bidentato, vexillo calyce dimidio longiore, legumine adpresse piloso.—
Teramnus volubilis, Sw.—DC. Prod. 2. p. 382.—Guayaquil.

Species *G. molli*, W. et Arn. (*Bujaciæ gampsonychiæ*, E. Mey) arcte affinis, sed foliis angustioribus, calycis labio superiore brevius fisso et corolla majore distincta. Folia valde variabilia, nunc vix pollicaria, tenuia, pilis raris, nunc bipollicaria, pilis præsertim in pagina inferiore copiosis ferrugineis. Racemi nunc vix semipollicares, petiolo communi breviores, nunc semipedales. Flores solitarii, gemini vel subfasciculati, remoti. Bracteæ minutæ. Pedicelli $\frac{1}{2}$-$1\frac{1}{2}$ lin. longi. Bracteolæ lanceolatæ, nervoso-striatæ, calyce subtriplo breviores. Calyx vix 2 lin. longus, rufo-villosus, laciniis anguste lanceolatis tubo vix æquilongis, 2 supremis alte connatis. Vexillum 3 lin. longum, obovatum, basi longiuscule in unguem angustatum, inappendiculatum, ecallosum. Alæ vexillum subæquantes, falcato-oblongæ, basi supra unguem obtuse unidentatæ, foveolis transversis nullis, carinæ cohærentes. Carina calycem vix æquans, obtusa, biceps, petalis dorso superne connatis. Ovarium sessile, villosissimum, stylo brevissimo apice capitato-stigmatoso. Legumen sesquipollicare vel paullo longius, forma iis *G. parviflorae* et *mollis* simillimum.

184. GALACTIA *brevistyla*, Schlecht. Linnæa, 12. p. 288.—Habitu *G. Berterianæ*, DC. simillima, sed villosior, flores paullo majores. Legumen undique velutino-villosum.—Central America.

185. DIOCLEA *Guianensis* β, *villosior*, Benth. in Hook. Journ. Bot. 2. p. 60.—Panama.—Ejusdem var. γ *velutina*, major, foliolis sæpe semipedalibus, subtus ramis calycibusque rufo-villosis.—Guayaquil.

186. CANAVALIA *obtusifolia*, DC. Prod. 2. p. 404.—Columbia.

A sea-coast plant within the tropics of both the New and the Old World.

187. CANAVALIA *ensiformis*, DC. Prod. 2. p. 404.—*C. gladiata*, DC. l. c.—*C. brasiliensis*, Mart.—Gulf of Fonseca.

This plant is also frequently sent from Tropical Asia and Africa, but perhaps not always really indigenous.

188. CANAVALIA *multiflora*, Hook. et Arn. Bot. Beech. p. 416.—Tepic.

189, 190. Fragments of an ERYTHRINA from Nicoya, and of a MUCUNA from the Isle of Gorgona.

191. PHASEOLUS *gracilis*, Benth. in Ann. Mus. Vind. 2. p. 141.—Realejo.

192. PHASEOLUS *vulgaris*, Linn.—DC. Prod. 2. p. 392.—Columbia.

193. PHASEOLUS *truxillensis*, Humb. et Kunth.—DC. Prod. 2. p. 391.—Guayaquil.

Varies with the leaves smooth or pubescent.

194. PHASEOLUS (Leptospron) *amplus*, sp. n., caule volubili petiolisque pilosulis demum glabratis, foliolis late ovato-rhombeis acuminatis membranaceis glabris vel ad venas pilosulis, pedunculis petiolo longioribus apice breviter racemiferis, bracteolis parvis ovatis obtusis, calycis glabri late 4-fidi laciniis ciliatis, superiore brevissima emarginata, inferioribus tubo paullo brevioribus ovatis acutis.—Central America.

Habitus *P. membranacei*. Foliola 2-3-pollicaria vel etiam majora, margine subsinuata. Stipulæ parvæ, ovato-oblongæ. Stipellæ minutæ, oblongæ, nervosæ. Pedunculi nunc vix 3 poll. longi, nunc pedales. Flores in racemo pauci. Calyx membranaceus, reticulato-venosus, tubo quam in affinibus latiore, 3 lin. longo, laciniis obscure venosis margine subscariosis. Corolla ampla. Alæ vexillo paullo longiores. Petala omnia (in sicco) transverse rugoso-plicata. Stamen vexillare basi appendice acuto auctum.

195. PHASEOLI sp. *P. micrantho* similis—Tiger Island.—The specimen too imperfect to determine accurately.

196. LABLAB *vulgaris*, Savi.—DC. Prod. 2. p. 401. var. macrocarpus.—Isle of Puna, near Guayaquil.

197. VIGNA *villosa*, Savi.—DC. Prod. 2. p. 401.—*Dolichos mexicanus*, Schlecht. Linnæa, 12. p. 329.—Guayaquil.

198. VIGNA *brachystachys*, sp. n., caule volubili retrorsum hirto, foliolis ovatis acutis pilosiusculis glabratisve, pedunculis folio longioribus apice breviter densifloris, pedicellis inferioribus calyce longioribus, bracteolis oblongo-lanceolatis calyce dimidio brevioribus, calycis late campanulati pilosuli laciniis 3 superioribus ovatis acutis tubo æquilongis, inferiore longiore lineari acuta, carinæ fornicatæ rostro brevi.—Guayaquil.

Caules tenues uti petioli pilis brevibus albidis retrorsis plus minus copiose hirti. Stipulæ erectæ, lanceolatæ, obtusæ, hirtæ, venosæ, 1-1½ lin. longæ. Petioli communes 1½-2-poll. longi. Stipellæ minutæ, oblongæ, obtusæ. Foliola 1-2-pollicaria, basi rotundata, membranacea, pilis in venis raris hispidula vel subglabra. Pedunculi 3-4-pollicares, glabri, apice 6-10-flori. Bracteæ parvæ, deciduæ. Flores quam in *V. villosa* majores. Pedicelli 2 lin. longi. Calyces fere glabri, tubo 1 lin. longo, laciniæ 3 superiores latæ, suprema latissima, infima fere 2 lin. longa, concava. Corolla glabra. Vexillum semipollicare, late rotundatum, basi biauriculatum, biappendiculatum, et supra unguem medio leviter bicallosum. Alæ vexillo subæquilongæ, oblique obovatæ, basi unidentatæ. Carina fornicata, breviter rostrata, alis vix brevior. Stamen vexillare supra basin obscure geniculatum, inappendiculatum. Ovarium villosum. Stylus filiformis, superficie stigmatosa oblonga laterali, infra stigma barbatus. Species *V. villosæ* affinis, sed glabrior, et inflorescentia distincta.

199. VIGNA *oblonga*, sp. n., glabra, foliolis late oblongis ellipticisve obtusis retusis mucronatisve, pedunculis folio longioribus apice breviter paucifloris, pedicellis calyce brevioribus, bracteolis minutis deciduis, calycis late campanulati glabri vel vix puberuli lacinia suprema latissima, lateralibus lanceolatis acutis, infima acutiore tubo æquilonga, carinæ arcuatæ rostro brevi.—Isle of Gorgona.

Tota planta glabra videtur, vel ad apices pedunculorum et in petiolulis pilis paucis onusta. Stipulæ vix semilineam longæ, acutæ. Stipellæ minutissimæ, ovatæ, obtusæ. Petiolus communis cum rhachi vulgo vix pollicaris. Foliola 1-1½ poll. longa, 4-8 lin. lata, trinervia, reticulato-venosa, rigidule membranacea. Pedunculi 3-4-pollicares, crassiusculi, nodis floriferis ad apices paucis approximatis. Flores magnitudine præcedentis. Pedunculi vix linea longiores. Calyx quam in *V. brachystachya* minor. Vexillum et alæ fere ut in illa, carina minus incurva, acuta. Bracteæ et bracteolæ acutæ, calyce quadruplo breviores.

200. VIGNA *carinalis*, sp. n., setis patentibus retrorsisve hispida, stipulis membranaceis nonnullis basi productis, foliolis ovatis obtusis acutisve mucronatis integris vel sinuato-subtrilobis, supra sparse subtus ad venas pilosis, pedunculis folio longioribus apice brevissime paucifloris, bracteolis parvis setaceis, calycis tuboloso-campanulati 5-fidi laciniis setaceo-acuminatis tubo sublongioribus, carinæ fornicatæ rostro elongato valde incurvo obtuso.—Columbia.

Habitu *Phaseolo ovato* et *Vignæ brasiliensi* affinis. Setæ caulis pedunculorum et petiolorum rigidulæ, sæpe fuscescentes. Stipulæ 2-3 lin. longæ, lato-lanceolatæ, obtusiusculæ, membranaceæ, striatæ, pilosæ, basi breviter infra insertionem productæ. Petioli communes cum rhachi circa 2 poll. longi. Stipellæ subulatæ, 1-1½ lin. longæ. Foliola 1½-3-pollicaria, nunc late ovata subrhombea obtusissima, nunc sublanceolato-ovata acuta, rarius lobata, margine ciliata, pilis in pagina superiore longiusculis suberectis, infra pallida. Pedunculus 4-6-pollicaris, basi glabriusculus, superne retrorsum setosus. Nodi floriferi gemini, ad apicem pedunculi approximati, pauciflori. Pedicelli brevissimi. Bracteæ in specimine jam delapsæ, bracteolæ lineam longæ. Calycis tubus 2 lin. longus, fere glaber, laciniæ puberulæ, 2 superiores basi latæ. Corolla 9-10 lin. alta; vexillum reflexum, supra unguem basi acute biauriculatum, inflexo-appendiculatum; alæ oblongæ, subtortuosæ; carina insigniter striata, in cyclum fere integrum curvata.

I have unfortunately only been able to examine a single flower of this very distinct plant, of which there was but one specimen in the collection. The form of the carina is intermediate as it were between that of *Phaseolus* and *Vigna*.

201. RHYNCHOSIA *grandiflora*, Schlecht.—Hook. et Arn. Bot. Beech. p. 287. t. 59.—Tepic.

202. RHYNCHOSIA *minima*, DC. Prod. 2. p. 385.—Panama to Guayaquil.

203. AMERIMNUM *Brownei*, Sw.—DC. Prod. 2. p. 421.—Nicoya, Tumaco.

204. DREPANOCARPUS *microphyllus*, G. F. W. Mey.—DC. Prod. 2. p. 420.—Bay of Panama.

The pod of this species remains unknown, and it is uncertain whether it belongs to *Drepanocarpus* or *Machærium*.

205. MACHÆRIUM *angustifolium*, Vog.—Walp. Rep. 1. p. 794.—Panama.

206. MISCOLOBII,? sp.—Isle of Taboga, under the name of the *Tamarind*; it is certainly, however, not of the same genus as the common *Tamarind*, but a true papilionaceous tree, and apparently a *Miscolobium*. The specimens are not sufficient to describe.

207. PARKINSONIA *aculeata*, Linn.—DC. Prod. 2. p. 486.—Guayaquil.

208. HÆMATOXYLON *campechianum*, Linn.—DC. Prod. 2. p. 485.—Culebra and Realejo, in Central America.

209. CÆSALPINIA *pulcherrima*, Sw.—*Poinciana pulcherrima*, Linn.—DC. Prod. 2. p. 484.—Columbia.

210. CÆSALPINIA *præcox*, Ruiz et Pav.—Hook. et Arn. Bot. Misc. 3. p. 208.—Columbia.

211. CÆSALPINIA (Libidibia) *corymbosa*, sp. n., inermis, glabra vel petiolis superioribus inflorescentiaque puberulis, pinnis 6-8-jugis, foliolis 6-10-jugis ovato-vel oblongo-ellipticis obtusis, panicula densa subcorymbosa, calycis limbi laciniis subpetaloideis, staminibus corollam vix excedentibus, filamentis pilosulis seriei interioris glanduliferis, legumine recto crasso compresso spongioso-coriaceo sub-8-spermo.—Guayaquil.—Gathered there also by Hartweg, n. 117; and on the coast of Peru by Cuming, n. 986.

Arbor 15-20-pedalis, dense foliosa. Folia 4-6-pollicaria, foliola pleraque 3-4-lin. longa, utrinque obtusa, margine subrecurva, venulosa. Stipulæ inconspicuæ (vel delapsæ?). Paniculæ ad apices ramorum foliis superioribus breviores, corymbosæ, multifloræ. Bracteæ membranaceæ, minutæ, cito deciduæ. Pedicelli

2-3 lin. longi, in ramis paniculæ dense racemosi, puberuli, ebracteati. Calyx 3½ lin. longus, glaber, limbo 5-partito tubo suo subduplo longiore, laciniis per anthesin reflexis, 4 superioribus lanceolatis acutis, infima paullo longiore late oblonga obtusa concava. Stamina inter se subæquilonga. Ovarium glabrum. Stylus stamina æquans, apice clavato-incrassatus, apice stigmatoso truncato perforato. Legumen brevissime stipitatum, 3-4 poll. longum, 6-7 lin. latum, crasse carnoso-coriaceum, intus spongiosum, circa semina induratum. Semina oblonga, transversa, in loculis leguminis solitarie nidulantia.

212. CÆSALPINIA *eriostachys*, sp. n., inermis, pinnis 6-8 jugis cum impari, foliolis 15-30 alternis oblongo-rhombeis obtusis valde obliquis supra nitidis subtus minute puberulis, petiolis pubescentibus, racemis laxis simplicibus calycibusque ferrugineo-tomentosis, staminibus corollam æquantibus, filamentis (omnibus?) glanduloso-hirtis.—Nicoya and Cocos Island.

Foliola pleraque 3-4 lin. longa. Racemi 4-6-pollicares. Pedicelli 8-10 lin. longi. Calyces 5 lin., tubo brevissimo, laciniis oblongis, 4 superioribus subæquilongis, inferiore paullo majore concavo. Flores in speciminibus a vermibus fere destructi et petalorum nonnisi fragmenta vidi. Ovarium glabrum. Stylus apice leviter incrassato-clavatus, apice stigmatoso truncato perforato.

213. CASSIA *Brasiliana*, Lam.—Walp. Rep. 1. p. 812.—Panama.

214. CASSIA *viminea*, Linn.—Walp. Rep. 1. p. 814.—*C. undulata*, Benth. in Hook. Journ. Bot. 2. p. 76.—Panama.

215. CASSIA *bacillaris*, Linn.—Walp. Rep. 1. p. 813.—Tumaco.

216. CASSIA *oxyphylla*, Humb. et Kunth.?—Walp. Rep. 1. p. 823.—Central America.

These specimens agree very well with Kunth's description, except in the size of the leaflets. The terminal ones are often four inches long and two inches broad, and nearly æquilateral.

217. CASSIA *bicapsularis*, Linn.—Walp. Rep. 1. p. 815.—Atacames, Guayaquil.

218. CASSIA *occidentalis*, Linn.—Walp. Rep. 1. p. 816.—Panama.

219. CASSIA *alata*, Linn.—Walp. Rep. 1. p. 816.—Columbia.

220. CASSIA *biflora*, Linn.—Walp. Rep. 1. p. 819.—Tiger Island; and a variety, with two or three pair of leaflets, Gulf of Fonseca.

221. CASSIA *picta*, Don.—Walp. Rep. 1. p. 821.—Guayaquil.

222. CASSIA *reticulata*, Willd.—Walp. Rep. 1. p. 822.—*C. strobilacea*, Humb. et Kunth.—Guayaquil.

223. CASSIA *pauciflora*, Humb. et Kunth.—Walp. Rep. 1. p. 829.—*C. punctulata*, Hook. et Arn.? Bot. Beech. p. 420.—Realejo.

224. CASSIA *diphylla*, Lam.—Walp. Rep. 1. p. 831.—Realejo.

225. CASSIA *prostrata*, Humb. et Kunth.—Walp. Rep. 1. p. 833.—Realejo.

226. SWARTZIA *grandiflora*, Willd.—DC. Prod. 2. p. 422.—Acapulco.

227. CASPARIA *subrotundifolia*, Kunth.—*Bauhinia subrotundifolia*, Cav.—DC. Prod. 2. p. 512.—*B. Lunaria*, Hook. et Arn. Bot. Beech. p. 420. non. Cav.—Acapulco.

228. CASPARIA *Pes-capræ*, Kunth.—*Bauhinia Pes-capræ*, Cav.—DC. Prod. 2. p. 512.—Acapulco.

229. CASPARIA *latifolia*, Kunth.—*Bauhinia latifolia*, Cav.—DC. Prod. 2. p. 513.—Acapulco.

230. BAUHINIÆ sp., apparently new, but in fruit only.—Acapulco.

231. BAUHINIA *inermis*, Pers.—DC. Prod. 2. p. 514.—Acapulco; Tepic; Realejo; Fonseca.

232. BAUHINIA *grandiflora*, Juss.—DC. Prod. 2. p. 513.—Guayaquil.

233. SCHNELLA *columbiensis*.—*Bauhinia columbiensis*, Vog.—Walp. Rep. 2. p. 852.—Panama.

234. CRUDYA *acuminata*, sp. n., foliis subsenis oblongis longe acuminatis basi inæqualibus subfalcatis utrinque ramisque glabris, pedicellis abbreviatis, legumine late ovato plano reticulato-rugoso ferrugineo-villoso.—Central America.

Foliola alterna, basi hinc rotundata illinc angustata, terminalia 3-4 poll. longa, supra medium latiora (1½ poll. lata) infra apicem abrupte angustata in cuspidem 6-9 lin. longum obtusum, lateralia gradatim minora. Racemorum rhachis semipedalis. Pedicelli fructiferi 2 lin. longi, crassi. Legumen 2½ poll. longum, fere 2 poll. latum, coriaceum.

A species very distinct from any hitherto published, but nearly allied to an unpublished one long since brought from Cayenne by Martin.*

235. PIPTADENIA (Eupiptadenia) *patens*, sp. n., scandens, ramulis petiolisque pubescentibus aculeatis, pinnis 3-4-jugis, foliolis subtrijugis obovatis glabris vel basi ciliatis, corolla calyce triplo longiore, staminibus corolla dimidio longioribus, ovario brevissime stipitato villoso.—*Inga? patens*, Hook. et Arn. Bot. Beech. p. 419.—Realejo.

Species *P. latifoliæ* valde affinis, differt panicula ampliore, pube in ramulis, petiolis, paniculæque ramis molli, floribus minoribus, staminibus calyceque proportione corollæ brevioribus et ovario brevius stipitato minus villoso. Legumen quod nonnisi junius vidi, jam multo glabrius est quam in *P. latifolia*. Stamina certe decem, nec sub-20, uti mendo quoque a Hook. et Arn. l. c. dicuntur.

Ejusdem var. *macrophylla*, foliolis 1½ poll. longis, 1 poll. latis subglaucis.—Gulf of Fonseca.

236. NEPTUNIA *plena*, Benth.—Walp. Rep. 1. p. 863.—Guayaquil.

237. MIMOSA *floribunda*, Willd.—Walp. Rep. 1. p. 865.—Acapulco to Guayaquil.

238. MIMOSA *pudica*, Linn.—DC. Prod. 2. p. 426.—Panama.

239. MIMOSA (Habbasia § 3 Cæsalpiniæfoliæ) *guatemalensis*, sp. n.—*Inga guatemalensis*, Hook. et Arn. Bot. Beech. p. 419.—Realejo.

240. MIMOSA *asperata*, Linn.—Walp. Rep. 1. p. 878.—Guayaquil.

241. MIMOSA *elliptica*, Benth.—Walp. Rep. 1. p. 878.—Columbia.

242. MIMOSA (Habbasia § 9. Dormientes) *æschynomenes*, sp. n., herbacea? procumbens, inermis, caule petiolisque setoso-hispidis, stipulis ovato-cordatis lanceolatisve acuminatis, pinnis 3-6-jugis, foliolis 10-30-jugis oblongo-linearibus ciliatis glabriusculis, capitulis parvis brevissime pedunculatis, bracteolis lanceolatis ciliato-setosis corollam superantibus, legumine oblongo 1-2-articulato vix obliquo undique setoso.—Realejo.

* *C. oblonga*, foliolis 4-5 oblongis basi parum inæqualibus rectis breviter acuminatis subtus puberulis supra cauleque glabris, pedicellis gracilibus, ovario ferrugineo-villoso.—Cayenne, *Martin*.

Rami teretes, 1-2-pedales, divaricato-ramosi, setis numerosis rigidis hispidi, inter setas puberuli. Aculeos nullos vidi. Stipulæ 2-3 lin. longæ, glabræ, ciliatæ, fuscæ, insigniter striatæ. Petioli communes 1-2 poll. longi. Pinnæ pollice longiores vel inferiores breviores, inter se distantes. Setæ inter pinnas sæpius vix semilineam longæ, basi subdilatatæ. Stipellæ vix conspicuæ. Foliola 2-3 lin. longa, acutiuscula vel obtusa, venosa, basi obliqua, 1-3-nervia. Pedunculi 1-3 lin. longi. Capitula florifera 2-3 lin. diametro, ciliis bracteolarum hispidissima. Calyx minutus. Corolla membranacea, laciniis brevibus pilosulis. Ovarium hirsutissimum. Legumen 2-4 lin. longum, vix 2 lin. latum, acutiusculum.

Very nearly allied to *M. camporum*, and perhaps a mere variety, but it is much more hairy, has no prickles, the stipules are broader and the bracts longer.

243. MIMOSA (Habbasia § 9. Dormientes) *pusilla*, sp. n., herbacea, annua, inermis, caule petiolisque hispidis, stipulis ovatis acutiusculis, pinnis 1-3-jugis, foliolis 6-15-jugis oblongis ciliatis, capitulis breviter pedicellatis parvis paucifloris, bracteolis lato-lanceolatis ciliatis corollas æquantibus, legumine oblongo 1-2-articulato vix oblique undique setoso.—Realejo.

Caules tenues, graciles, 4-6-pollicares. Capitula dimidio fere minora, et tota planta minus hispida quam *M. æschynomenes* cui cæterum affinis est.

244. MIMOSA (Ameria § 4. Acanthocarpæ) *acantholoba*, fruticosa, ramulis puberulis, aculeis sparsis recurvis, stipulis setaceis, pinnis 4-10-jugis, foliolis 15-30-jugis oblongo-linearibus subtus pubescentibus, pedunculis axillaribus folio brevioribus superioribus racemosis, capitulis globosis, bracteis minutis, floribus 4-5-meris 8-10-andris, calycibus corolla quadruplo brevioribus, ovario villoso, legumine membranaceo oblongo vel late lineari-falcato puberulo margine leviter aculeato.—*Acacia acantholoba*, Humb. et Bonpl. in Willd. Spec. 4. p. 1089.—Guayaquil.

245. LEUCÆNA *macrophylla*, sp. n., glabra, pinnis 2-3-jugis, foliolis 2-4-jugis ovatis acuminatis acutis amplis, pedunculis capitulo subbrevioribus fasciculatis in racemos axillares terminalesque dispositis.—Acapulco.

Arbor? Ramuli albidi, verruculosi. Stipulæ breves latæ. Foliorum petioli subteretes, setula terminati, communes 3-4-pollicares, partiales inferiores 1½-2-pollicares, ultimi duplo longiores. Glandulæ elevatæ, demum concavæ, infra pinnas inferiores et foliola ultima plus minus conspicuæ. Pinnæ inter se distantes. Foliola opposita, remota, in pinnis inferioribus sæpius bijuga, in ultimis 3-4-juga, 1½-2-poll. longa, basi oblique angustata, subcoriacea, penninervia et insigniter reticulato-venosa, breviter petiolulata, inferiora sæpius multo minora. Racemi axillares 3-4-pollicares, terminalis pedalis, polycephali. Rhachis crassa, teres. Bracteæ breves, late orbiculatæ, fusco-membranaceæ. Pedunculi in axillis bractearum complures, 2-4 lin. longi, crassi, subangulati. Capitula iis *Acaciæ sphærocephalæ* haud dissimilia, suffulta bracteolis 4 fusco-membranaceis late orbiculatis flore brevioribus. Flores numerosissimi, densissime imbricati. Bracteolæ subulatæ, apice peltatæ, ciliatæ. Calyx tubuloso-campanulatus, membranaceus, ¾ lin. longus, apice hirtellus, brevissime 5-dentatus. Corolla vix calycem excedens. Stamina 10, corolla paullo longiora. Antheræ pilosæ. Legumen ignotum.

246. ACACIA *pellacantha*, Vog.—Walp. Rep. 1. p. 908.—Bay of Caraccas.

247. ACACIA *macracantha*, Humb. et Bonpl.—Walp. Rep. 1. p. 909.—Guayaquil.

248. ACACIA *Hindsii*, sp. n., Benth. in Lond. Journ. Bot. 1. p. 504.—Manzanilla Bay.

249. ACACIA *villosa*, Willd.—Walp. Rep. 1. p. 919.—Manzanilla Bay.

250. LYSILOMA *Schiedeana*, sp. n. (Plate XXXI.), glabra vel ramulis petiolisque minute puberulis, stipulis amplis semicordatis membranaceis, pinnis 6-8-jugis, foliolis multijugis linearibus glabris.—Benth. in Lond. Journ. Bot. 3. p. 83.—Central America.

Ramuli obtuse angulati, faciebus verruculoso-punctulatis, sæpius glaberrimi, rarius uti petioli pilis paucis minutis onusti. Stipulæ 3-6 lin. longæ, basi latissimæ, hinc cordato-auriculatæ, auricula rotundata, apice acutæ vel acuminatæ, membranaceæ, lætevirentes. Petioli communes 3-5-pollicares, partiales subbipollicares. Glandulæ elevatæ infra pinnas inferiores et inter pinnas 1-3 ultimas, nonunquam etiam minutæ inter foliola ultima. Foliola 20-30-juga, obliqua, obtusiuscula, 2-3 lin. longa, vix ¾ lin. lata, uninervia, subglaucescentia. Pedunculi 1-1½-pollicares, solitarii (vel fasciculati?) vel in ramulos 2-3-cephalos bracteatos abeuntes, glabri vel minute puberuli, supra medium bracteis 1-2 parvis alternis stipulis subsimillibus vel oblongis instructi. Capitula globosa, staminibus neglectis 4 lin. diametro. Bracteolæ obovato-cuneatæ, corolla breviores. Flores sessiles. Calyx 1 lin. longus, 5-dentatus. Corolla calyce dimidio longior, 5-fida, extus puberula. Stamina 15-20, corolla subtriplo longiora, parte connata vix corolla breviore et ab ea soluta. Ovarium sessile glabrum. Legumen (immaturum) 5-poll. longum, 8-9 lin. latum, stipite semipollicari, apice longiuscule cuspidatum.

Plate XXXI. fig. 1, flower; fig. 2, staminal sheath with one stamen; fig. 3, anther; fig. 4, pollen mass; fig. 5, ovary; all magnified.

251. CALLIANDRA *portoricensis*, Benth. in Lond. Journ. Bot. 3. p. 99.—Columbia.

252. CALLIANDRA *grandiflora*, Benth. l. c. p. 111.—Tepic.

253. PITHECOLOBIUM *macrostachyum*, Benth. l. c. p. 198.—Manzanilla Bay.

254. PITHECOLOBIUM *oblongum*, Benth. l. c. p. 198.—Gulf of Fonseca.

255. PITHECOLOBIUM *dulce*, Benth. l. c. p. 199.—Conchagua.

256. PITHECOLOBIUM *candidum*, Benth. l. c. p. 201.—Guayaquil.

257. PITHECOLOBIUM *multiflorum*, Benth. l. c. p. 221.—Guayaquil.

CHRYSOBALANACEÆ.

258. CHRYSOBALANUS *Icaco*, Linn.—DC. Prod. 2. p. 525.—Realejo, Panama, Columbia.

259. HIRTELLA *americana*, Aubl.—H. *racemosa*, Lam.—DC. Prod. 2. p. 529.—Central America, in various places.

260. LICANIA (Eulicania) *hypoleuca*, sp. n., (Plate XXXII.) foliis ovatis acuminatis tenuiter coriaceis, subtus incanis, panicula ampla, florum glomerulis longiuscule pedicellatis, calyce breviter 5-fido ramisque paniculæ incanis.—Veragua.

Foliorum forma et inflorescentia *L. floribundi*. Ramuli subcanescentes, tenues. Folia breviter petiolata, tripollicaria, supra siccitate nigricantia vix nitentia, subtus penninervia, reticulato-venosa et incana vel juniora nivea. Racemi in axillis superioribus et in apicibus ramorum foliis longiores, divaricato-ramosi, paniculam formant amplam foliatam, ramulis 2-4-pollicaribus. Pedicelli vel rami ultimi 2-4 lin. longi, apice cymosocapitati, 3-7-flori. Flores quam in *L. incana* minores. Calyx ovatus, dentibus ovatis tubo dimidio brevioribus, intus pubescens. Corolla nulla. Stamina fertilia 2 vel 3, brevia. Fructus obovoideo-pyriformis, basi valde attenuatus, semipollicaris, rufo-tomentellus.

Plate XXXII. fig. 1, calyx; fig. 2, the same cut open, showing the stamens and style; fig. 3, style with the ovary cut open; fig. 4, fruit, longitudinal section; fig. 5, seed, longitudinal section; all magnified except the fruit.

COMBRETACEÆ.

261. CONOCARPUS *erectus*, Jacq.—DC. Prod. 3. p. 16.—Puna near Guayaquil.

262. LAGUNCULARIA *racemosa*, Gærtn.—DC. Prod. 3. p. 17.—Columbia.

263. COMBRETUM *farinosum*, Humb. et Kunth.—DC. Prod. 3. p. 19.—Manzanilla Bay, Realejo, Nicoya.

264. COMBRETUM *argenteum*, Bertol.—Walp. Rep. 2. p. 65.—*C. erianthum*, Benth. Pl. Hartw. p. 73.—Tiger Island, Gulf of Fonseca.

265. COMBRETUM *mexicanum*, Humb. et Bonpl.—DC. Prod. 3. p. 19.—San Blas, Manzanilla Bay.

RHIZOPHOREÆ.

266. RHIZOPHORA *Mangle*, Linn.—DC. Prod. 3. p. 32.—Guayaquil.

267. RHIZOPHORA *racemosa*, G. F. W. Mey.—DC. Prod. 3. p. 32.—Realejo.

These two species appear to me to be perfectly distinct.

ONAGRACEÆ.

268. ŒNOTHERA *rosea*, Ait.—DC. Prod. 3. p. 51.—Guayaquil.

269. JUSSIÆA *peploides*, Humb. et Kunth.—DC. Prod. 3. p. 53.—Tepic.

270. JUSSIÆA *peruviana*, Linn.—DC. Prod. 3. p. 53.—Variat floribus tetrameris pentamerisque. *J. macrocarpa*, Humb. et Kunth.—DC. l. c. p. 57.—Guayaquil and Payta. I have it also from Lima.

271. JUSSIÆA *linifolia*, Vahl.—DC. Prod. 3. p. 55.—Columbia.

272. JUSSIÆA *octofila*, DC. Prod. 3. p. 57.—*J. hirta*, Hook. et Arn. Bot. Beech. p. 421. vix Vahl.—Tepic and Panama to Guayaquil.

273. JUSSIÆA *calycina*, Presl.? ex Walp. Repert. 2. p. 73.—Forma *J. villosæ* valde affinis, at distincta videtur imprimis ramis basi lignosis.—Guayaquil.

274. SEMEIANDRA *grandiflora*, Hook. et Arn. Bot. Beech. p. 291 et 422, t. 59.—Tepic.

275. DIPLANDRA *lopezioides*, Hook. et Arn. Bot. Beech. p. 292 et 422. t. 60.—Tepic.
276. LOPEZIA *hirsuta*, Jacq.—DC. Prod. 3. p. 62.—Tepic.

LYTHRACEÆ.

277. HEIMIA *salicifolia*, Link. et Otto.—DC. Prod. 3. p. 89.—Tepic.
278. LYTHRUM *maritimum*, Humb. et Kunth.—DC. Prod. 3. p. 82.—Guayaquil.
279. CUPHEA *Melvilla*, Lindl.—DC. Prod. 3. p. 84.—Guayaquil.
280. CUPHEA *Llavea*, La Llav. et Lex.—DC. Prod. 3. p. 85.—Tepic.
281. CUPHEA *floribunda*, Hook. et Arn. Bot. Beech. p. 289 et 423.—Tepic.
282. CUPHEA *bracteata*, Hook. et Arn. l. c.—Tepic.
283. CUPHEA *Balsamona*, Cham. Schlecht.—Walp. Rep. 2. p. 107.—Salango and Guayaquil.
284. DODECAS *Surinamensis*, Linn.—DC. Prod. 3. p. 91.—Pateo in Columbia.
285. ADENARIA *purpurata*, Humb. et Kunth.—DC. Prod. 3. p. 92.—Guayaquil.

MELASTOMACEÆ.

286. CHÆTOGASTRA *Havanensis*, DC.? Prod. 3. p. 132.—Isle of Tumaco, Bay of Panama.
287. CHÆTOGASTRA *ferruginea*, Hook. et Arn. Bot. Beech. p. 423.—Realejo.
288. HEERIA *cupheoides*, sp. n., (Plate XXXIII.) herbacea, pumila, caule tetragono ad angulos setuloso vel glabro, foliis petiolatis ovatis oblongisve acutis integerrimis trinerviis supra sparse pilosis subtus puberulis, floribus sessilibus in axillis superioribus solitariis tetrameris.—Panama.

Herba tenera, erecta, ramosa, semipedalis vel paullo altior. Folia 9-10 lin. vel vix pollicem longa, acutiuscula, basi rotundata vel cuneata, petiolo 2-3 lin. longo; pili sparsi, in pagina superiore longiusculi, in inferiore breves; venæ transversales subtus conspicuæ. Flores in axillis superioribus alternatim solitarii, axilla altera cujusve paris foliorum sterili. Pedicelli brevissimi vel subnulli. Bracteæ nullæ. Calyx florifer 2 lin. longus, fructifer 4 lin., tubulosus, parum obliquus, 8-costatus, costis dorso setosis; laciniæ 4, lanceolato-subulatæ, pectinato-ciliatæ, tubo breviores, setulo ad apicem costæ intermediæ cæteris majore. Petala calyces paullo superantia, ovato-elliptica, apice truncata et dorso aristulata. Stamina majora 4, petalis alterna, anthera ovata, connectivo elongato basi ultra insertionem in appendiculas 2 breves subclavatos producto; 4 minora petalis opposita, anthera parva ovato oblonga (cassa?), connectivo brevissimo biauriculato. Stylus apice clavatus, 4-sulcus, intra sulcos et medio stigmatosus. Ovarium apice sub-8-setosum. Capsula oblonga, 4-locularis, 4-valvis, cum calyce mediantibus nervis dorsalibus connexa. Semina numerosa, cochleata, granulato-rugosa.

Plate XXXIII. fig. 1, bud; fig. 2, flower cut open, showing the style and a portion of the petals and stamens; fig. 3, fertile stamen; fig. 4, sterile stamen; fig. 5, apex of the style; fig. 6, section of the fruit; fig. 7, seed; all magnified.

289. SPENNERA *aquatica*, Mart.—DC. Prod. 3. p. 116.—San Pedro in Columbia.
290. HETERONOMA *diversifolium*, DC. Prod. 3. p. 122.—Salango.

291. HETERONOMA *mexicanum.*—*Heterocentron mexicanum*, Hook. et Arn. Bot. Beech. p. 290, 423.—The genus *Heterocentron* appears to come entirely within *Heteronoma*, as characterised by Alph. DC. 5. Not. Pl. Rar. Jard. Gen. p. 10.—Tepic.

292. BERTOLONIA *hirsuta*, sp. n., caule humili erecto hirsuto, foliis inæqualibus petiolatis ovatis basi rotundatis subcordatisve utrinque setoso-hispidis 5-nerviis, floribus in racemo elongato simplici subsessilibus numerosis.—Guayaquil.

Caulis in specimine unico 2 poll. altus, racemo tripollicari. Folia immaculata, alterum cujusve paris 2½ poll. longum, alterum dimidio minus. Racemus fere a basi florifer, hispidus. Calyx truncatus, brevissime 5-dentatus, setoso-hispidus. Cætera fere *B. maculatæ*.

293. BLAKEA *glabrescens*, sp. n., ramulis foliorumque juniorum nervis rufo-puberulis demum glabratis, foliis ovalibus breviter et abrupte acuminatis 5-nerviis, pedunculis solitariis geminisve petiolum æquantibus, bracteis calyce duplo longioribus, calycis limbo 6-lobo.—Atacames and Isle of Gorgona.

Arbor elegans. Folia 3-5-pollicaria, longiuscule petiolata, lætevirentia. Bracteæ ovatæ, striatæ, ferrugineæ, 9-10 lin. longæ. Calycis laciniæ acutæ, tubo parum breviores. Flores pallide rosei.

294. TOCOCA *acuminata*, sp. n., ramulis setosis, foliis parum inæqualibus amplis oblongis utrinque longe angustatis crenulatis 3-5-nerviis supra sparse subtus ad venas setosis, petiolis brevibus vesiculosis, thyrso brevi, calycibus setosis, margine truncato minute dentato.—Columbia and Isle of Gorgona.

Folia majora pedalia, altero cujusve paris altero vix quarta parte breviore, acumine longo acuto. Petioli 6-15 lin. longi, e maxima parte in vesicam oblongam dilatati. Thyrsus 2-3-pollicaris, terminalis. Flores pentameri.

295. CLIDEMIA *rubra*, Mart.—*Sagræa sessilifolia*, DC. Prod. 3. p. 170.—Acapulco.

296. CLIDEMIA *crenata*, DC. Prod. 3. p. 157.—Panama and Columbia.

297. CLIDEMIA *lacera*, DC. Prod. 3. p. 164.—Tumaco.

298. CLIDEMIA *cyanocarpa*, sp. n., ramulis teretibus, petiolis nervisque foliorum tomento pulveraceo ferrugineis, foliis cujusve paris valde inæqualibus ovatis breviter acuminatis subintegerrimis ciliatis quintuplinerviis supra sparse setosis subtus præter venas glabris, pedunculis brevissimis axillaribus cymosis, pedicellis calyce multo longioribus, floribus parvis, calycibus setoso-hispidis brevissime 5-dentatis, bacca depresso-globosa.—Tumaco.

Pluribus notis cum descriptione *C. diversifoliæ* convenit, attamen specifice diversa videtur. Ramuli pro foliorum magnitudine tenues; pubes pulveracea in junioribus densa demum evanescit. Folium cujusve paris alterum 6-8 poll. longum, petiolo pollicari, alterum a dimidio ad quadruplo minus, petiolatum vel rarius subsessile, omnia membranacea, supra nitidula. Cymæ quam petiolus folii majoris sæpius breviores; pedunculus communis, et interdum ramuli, brevissimi; pedicelli 3-4 lin. longi. Flores parvi *Tschudyæ*. Calycis laciniæ breves, acutæ. Petala oblonga, obtusa. Fructus ut in affinibus cœrulescens.

299. CLIDEMIA *fenestrata*, sp. n., ramulis petiolisque dense tomentosis, foliis cujusve paris inæqualibus petiolatis late ovatis acuminatis margine crenulatis ciliatisque basi subcordatis 7-9-nerviis, supra pustulatis setoso-hispidissimis subtus tomentosis elevato-venosis, paniculis paucifloris terminalibus mox axillaribus, floribus in ramulis 1-3 sessilibus, calycis tubo ovoideo, limbo breviter 5-dentato, petalis obtusiusculis.—Cocos Island.

Tomentum ramulorum dense et breve. Folia majora 4-8 poll. longa, petiolo 1-3-pollicare, alterum cujusve paris altero dimidio vel triplo minus, omnia subtus canescenti-tomentosa et venis valde elevatis eleganter fenestrata, et pustulis, in pagina superiore elevatis in inferiore foveolato-depressis, quasi punctata. Paniculæ bipollicares, parum ramosæ, novellæ terminales sed ramulus in axilla folii majoris mox evolvitur et panicula jam ante anthesin axillaris videtur folio minore subtensa. Flores magnitudine fere *C. surinamensis* cui hæc species affinis quidem sed characteribus datis satis diversa videtur.

300. CLIDEMIA *barbinervis*, sp. n., ramis petiolisque villis longis rufis simplicibus ramosisque dense vestitis, foliis parum inæqualibus breve petiolatis ovali-ellipticis suboblongisve acuminatis basi rotundato-cordatis subintegerrimis 5-nerviis supra setosis subtus ad venas rufo-barbatis, panicula thyrsoidea terminali setoso-hispidissima, floribus capitato-congestis, calycis hispidissimi dentibus breviter subulatis.—Tumaco, Guayaquil.

Folia cujusve paris vulgo fere æqualia, alterum altero rarius subdimidio minus; majora 9-10 poll. longa, ramealia 4-5-pollicaria; setæ paginæ superioris numerosæ, at non e pustula ortæ. Panicula 2-3-pollicaris, ramis paucis, ramulis capitulum ferentibus multiflorum, setis dense obtectum. Flores pentameri, in capitulo sessiles, bractea ovata subtensi. Calycis laciniæ minutæ. Petala obovato-oblonga, obtusa, tubo calycino æquilonga. Filamenta petalis sublongiora. Antheræ lineares.

301. CLIDEMIA *polyandra*, sp. n., (Plate XXXIV.) ramis petiolisque gianduloso-pilosis et rufo-pubescentibus, foliis vix disparibus petiolatis amplis late cordato-ovatis acuminatis crenulatis 7-9-nerviis utrinque viscido-puberulis, panicula brevi lata, floribus 7-9-meris polyandris, calycis dentibus latis acutis.—Columbia.

Ramuli ut in *Tococis* alternatim compressi, uti petioli pedunculi et costæ foliorum pilis glanduliferis rufo-hirsuti, pube brevi substellata rufescente intermixta. Folia 8-10 poll. longa, crenis inæqualibus. Panicula fere *Tococæ*, cui hæc species etiam floribus affinis, et fere æquo jure huic vel *Clidemiæ* referenda. Calycis tubus ovoideus, limbus cyathiformis, 7-9-dentatus. Petala 7-9, obovata, obtusa. Stamina circa 30; antheræ lineares, apice uniporosæ, basi brevissime bituberculatæ. Ovarium calycis tubo omnino adnatum, carnosum, 7-9-loculare, apice paucisetum (vel nudum?). Stylus subulatus apice clavatus, obtusus, tenuiter stigmatosus. Fructus baccatus.

The habit of this plant not being decidedly that of either of the allied genera *Miconia*, *Tococa*, and *Clidemia*, I had at first considered it as a new genus characterised by the indefinite stamens in an order in which the definite stamens had been considered as one of the essential characters, but the same multiplication of stamina has now been observed in a true *Miconia* (*M. polyandra*, Gardn.) and in several *Conostegiæ*, and proves in no case to be of generic but only of specific value. I have, therefore, referred the present species to *Clidemia*, which, amongst several closely allied and indeed barely distinct genera, it approaches the nearest.

Plate XXXIV. fig. 1, flower expanded seen from above; fig. 2, calyx and style; fig. 3, anther; fig. 4, ovary and style, vertical section: fig. 5, transverse section of ovary; all magnified.

302. OXYMERIS *macrophylla*, sp. n., ramulis compressiusculis vel obtuse tetragonis, novellis lana subsquamosa mox derasa rufescentibus, foliis amplis obovatis breviter acuminatis basi longe angustatis 5-nerviis pulchre venosis glabris vel subtus ad venas sublanatis, paniculis axillaribus sessilibus divaricato-ramosis rufo-tomentosis.—Cocos Island.

Ramuli crassi, post indumentum delapsum læves, virides. Petioli 1-2-pollicares. Folia cujusve paris inæqualia, majora sesquipedalia, margine denticulata, membranaceo-chartacea, supra viridia, subtus pallidiora, juniora lana subsquamosa uti ramuli et petioli conspersa, mox glabrata, venis regularibus subtus prominentibus, inter venas plus minus pellucido-punctata. Paniculæ subtripollicares, in axillis solitariæ sed a basi ipsa divaricato-ramosæ; ramuli rufo-tomentosi, bis, ter quaterve trichotomi, divaricatissimi, ultimi flores paucos parvos sessiles gerentes. Calycis tubus subglobosus, costatus, breviter rufo-tomentosus, demum sæpe glabrescens. Flos pentamerus. Petala parva, lato-lanceolata, acutissima. Antheræ apice poro lato dehiscentes, basi in appendiculam brevissimam hirtellam productæ. Stylus apice capitato-stigmatosus. Bacca calyci omnino adnata, 5-locularis.

303. MICONIA *guayaquilensis*, Don.—DC. Prod. 3. p. 186.—A single specimen with the young branches more compressed and the leaves larger than described by Bonpland (seven inches to a foot long), but probably the same species.—Guayaquil.

304. MICONIA *attenuata*, DC. Prod. 3. p. 186.—The specimens are in fruit only, but in that state precisely resemble several Guiana specimens of the species.—Cocos Island.

305. CREMANIUM *compressum*, sp. n., ramulis compressis petiolis paniculisque tomento brevissimo ferrugineis, foliis petiolatis ovatis breviter acuminatis denticulatis 5-nerviis supra glabris subtus tomento brevissimo substellato aureo-fulvis, panicula divaricata, floribus parvis numerosis pentameris.—Veragua.

Arbor elata. Rami et folia fere *Miconiæ Schomburgkii*. Panicula gracilior, ramosior, flores dimidio minores et antheræ *Cremanii*. Ramuli crassiusculi, sub folia dilatato-compressi et petioli dorso decurrente subcostati. Petioli pollicares, crassiusculi. Folia 5-6 poll. longa, acumine brevi acuto, margine minute et irregulariter denticulata, basi rotundata et integerrima. Panicula semipedalis, pyramidata, gracilis, bis terve opposite ramosa, ramulis ultimis cymiferis, cymarum ramulis subscorpioideis 3-7-floris. Bracteæ minutæ. Calyces sessiles, sesquilineam longi, fulvo-tomentosi, costati, dentibus brevissimis obtusis. Petala obtusa, parva. Antheræ apice poro vel fere rima duplici dehiscentes. Ovarium in fundo calycis breve, 3-5-loculare. Stylus apice peltato-dilatatus supra stigmatosus.

306. CONOSTEGIA *xalapensis*, DC. Prod. 3. p. 175.—Acapulco.

307. CONOSTEGIA *lasiopoda*, sp. n., ramulis obtuse tetragonis, novellis petiolisque barbato-hirtis demum glabris, foliis petiolatis ovali-ellipticis oblongisve acuminatis subdenticulatis basi longe angustatis 3-5-nerviis supra glabris subtus ad venas ferrugineo-scabris, panicula brevi pauciflora, bracteis lanceolatis, alabastro basi obtuso apice acute acuminato aspero.—Cocos Island.

Pubes scabro-ferruginea in ramulis petiolis nervisque paginæ inferioris foliorum et panicula plus minus densa, pilis longis præsertim in petiolis intermixta. Folia semipedalia, præter nervum tenuem marginalem trinervia. Panicula fere 4-pollicaris. Flores majusculi, in specimine a me viso plerique a vermibus exesa.

308. CONOSTEGIA *polyandra*, sp. n., (Plate XXXV.) ramulis novellis paniculaque pube ferruginea brevissima pulveraceo-lepidotis demum glabris, foliis breviter petiolatis ovalibus obtusis vel vix acuminatis basi rotundatis integerrimis denticulatisve 5-nerviis viridibus supra scabriusculis subtus glabris, panicula pyramidata, alabastro acute acuminato, staminibus indefinitis.—Columbia.

Tota planta sublutescenti-viridis, partes juniores pulveraceæ, ramuli et foliorum pagina superior punctata scabra, cæterum glabra. Petioli 2-3 lin. longa. Folia 2-4-pollicaria. Panicula pedunculata, 3-4-pollicaris. Bracteæ parvæ, lineares. Flores magnitudine fere *Diplochitæ Fothergillæ*. Alabastra basi turbinata, apice longiuscule attenuato-conica. Calycis tubus brevis, obscure costatus, limbus integer, circumscisse deciduus. Petala 5 vel 6, obovata. Bacca globosa, glabra, calycis tubo arcte adnata, loculis 7-8. Semina numerosa, obovoideo-cuneata. Stamina vulgo circa 30.

Plate XXXV. fig. 1, bud, showing the dehiscence of the calyx; fig. 2, flower expanded; fig. 3, bud deprived of its petals, showing the arrangement of the stamens; fig. 4, vertical section of the flower; fig. 5, stamen; fig. 6, transverse section of fruit; fig. 7, seed. Figs. 1 and 2 natural size, the remainder magnified.

MEMECYLACEÆ.

309. MOURIRIA *parvifolia*, sp. n., (Plate XXXVI.) foliis sessilibus ovatis vel ovato-lanceolatis acutis basi cordatis, pedicellis solitariis geminisve axillaribus bracteatis calyce brevioribus, calycis laciniis acutis reflexis, ovario uniloculari.—Bay of Honda, Veragua.

Frutex glaberrimus. Rami tenues, teretes, ramosissimi. Folia arcte sessilia, sesquipollicaria, subcoriacea, costa subtus prominenti, venulis vix conspicuis, punctis crebris nonnisi in folio juniore pellucidis. Squamulæ ad basin ramulorum juniorum et pedunculorum 2, parvæ, acutæ, rigidulæ. Pedunculi 1½-2 lin. longi, bractea lanceolato-subulata medio instructi. Flores quam in cæteris speciebus multo minores. Calyx per anthesin campanulatus, parte libera longa, limbi laciniæ ovato-lanceolatæ, (coloratæ?), demum reflexo-patentes. Petala angusta, acutissima, lacinias calycinas superantia. Stamina 10. Filamenta petalis duplo longiora. Antheræ oblongæ, loculis apice rima brevi dehiscentibus, connectivo crasso calcarato. Stylus stamina æquans, filiformis, superne attenuatus, summo apice truncatus et tenuiter stigmatosus. Ovarium in fundo calycis erectus, perfecte unilocularis. Placenta centralis e fundo ovarii elevata ad tertiam partem cavitatis attingens, infra apicem ovulifera. Ovula 6 vel 8, supra basin lateraliter affixa, oblonga, erecta. Fructus junior intra calycis basin grossificatum inclusus, calyce igitur urceolato. Bacca matura (quam ipse non vidi) teste Hindsio atropurpurea, sapore dulcidulo grato. Semen unicum, testa ossea.

This species has certainly the unilocular ovarium originally attributed to the genus by Jussieu and others, whereas in *M. pusa*, and all the Brazilian ones which I have examined, it is completely two or more celled, as described by Gardner.

Plate XXXVI. fig. 1, flower; fig. 2, stamen; fig. 3, calyx and ovary cut longitudinally; fig. 4, ovary, longitudinal section; fig. 5, ovary, transverse section.

MYRTACEÆ.

310. PSIDIUM *pyriferum*, Linn.—DC. Prod. 3. p. 233.— San Pedro, in Columbia, and Guayaquil.

311. CAMPOMANESIA *crassifolia*, sp. n., (Plate XXXVII.) glabra, foliis ovatis vel ovali-ellipticis breviter acuminatis basi obtusis crassis coriaceis nitidis venis obscuris, pedunculis unifloris brevibus inferioribus aggregatis, bacca depresso-globosa calyce coronata 1-5-loculari.—Isle of Gorgona.

Habitu *C. glabræ* (Benth. in Hook. Journ. Bot. 2, p. 319) simillima, sed differre videtur imprimis foliis majoribus (4-5 poll. longis 2-2½ poll. latis) crassioribus, venis multo obscurioribus fere obsoletis. Flores non suppetunt. Bacca magna, depresso-globosa, abortu 1-4-locularis vel rarius 5-locularis, siccitate dura, inter loculos sulcis profundis extus notata et partibilis, coronata calycis limbo persistente breviter et obtuse 5-lobo. Semina in loculis solitaria, placentæ centrali mediante hilo lato circulariter affixa, magna, ovoidea (axi 5-6 lin. longo); testa dura cornea vel sublignosa; cotyledones crassi, fere recti, subhemisphærici, carnosi, sese arcte appressi at non conferruminati; radicula basilaris brevissima; plumula parva sed conspicua.

The above description of the seed is very different from that which is usually, after Lindley (Collect. Bot. sub n. 16.), given to *Campomanesia*, and is much nearer to that of *Eugenia*, yet it is probable that this plant is a congener to the *C. cornifolia*, Humb. et Kunth, *C. glabra*, Benth., and to the *C. hirsuta* and *laurifolia*, Gardn. Whether, however, they are or are not referable to the true *Campomanesia* of Ruiz and Pavon must remain doubtful; for Ruiz and Pavon's description, and Lindley's, are so totally at variance with each other, both as to the leaf and the fruit, that they must have been taken from different plants, and it is well known that Pavon's labels, in the different collections he disposed of, were in several instances misplaced.

Plate XXXVII. fig. 1, fruit, transverse section, natural size; fig. 2, seed; fig. 3, embryo; fig. 4, the same, with one cotyledon cut off, showing the plumula; fig. 2 to 4, slightly magnified.

312. EUGENIA *pacifica*, sp. n., glabra vel ramulis costisque foliorum vix puberulis, foliis breviter petiolatis ovatis subacuminatis basi cuneatis subcoriaceis supra nitidulis, pedunculis brevissimis axillaribus pauciferis, fructu oblongo glabro.—Cocos Island.

Habitus et folia fere *Coffeæ arabicæ*, sed ab *E. coffeæfolia* diversa foliis vix 4 poll. longis, 2 poll. latis, et bacca olivæformi 4-5 lin. longa. Semen unicum, embryone homogeneo intus vesiculis glandulosis prope marginem instructo.

313. EUGENIA *guayaquilensis*, DC. Prod. 3. p. 275.—Panama.

314. EUGENIA *sericiflora*, sp. n., ramulis junioribus inflorescentiaque sericeis, foliis oblongo-lanceolatis acuminatis basi angustatis subcoriaceis utrinque pilis tenuibus appressis pubescentibus, racemis laxis folio brevioribus, bracteis lanceolato-subulatis calycis tubo longioribus, calycis sericei laciniis orbiculatis, petalis ciliatis.—Isle of Taboga, Bay of Panama; gathered also by Cuming, n. 1137.

Ramuli tenues, superne compressi. Folia 3 poll. longa, 7-10 lin. lata, apice in acumen longum acutum mucronatum producta, basi in petiolum brevem angustata, margine subrecurva, pellucido-punctata, venis supra vix conspicuis, primariis subtus prominulis; pili breves albidi in pagina superiore crebri, in inferiore rariores. Pedunculi in axillis solitarii vel gemini, subbipollicares; pedicelli oppositi vel rarius alterni, divaricati, solitarii vel gemini, semipollicares, apice uniflori. Bracteæ sub pedicellis et bracteolæ sub flore fusco-membranaceæ, 1-2 lin. longæ, sericeæ, e basi latiuscula setaceæ. Calycis tubus parvus, turbinato-globosus, laciniæ limbi inæquales, orbiculatæ, obtusæ, maxima 1¼ lin., minimæ vix 1 lin. longæ. Petala fere 3 lin. longa. Stamina numerosa. Ovarium ante anthesin vix complete biloculare, ovulis in quoque loculo circa 8.

315. MYRCIA *acuminata*, DC. Prod. 3. p. 256.—Veragua.

316. MYRCIA *aromatica*, Schlecht? Linnæa, 13. p. 415.—Isle of Taboga, Bay of Panama.

Species *M. splendenti* affinis. Folia angustiora, acumine minus abrupto. Paniculæ latiores, ramosiores. In omnibus cum descriptione Schlechtendalii convenit, nisi paniculis vix bipollicaribus. Ovarium complete biloculare, ovulis in quoque loculo 2, prope basin affixis.

317. GUSTAVIA *angustifolia*, sp. n., foliis anguste oblongis acuminatis apice remote serrulatis basi longe angustatis sessilibus, florum fasciculis terminalibus, calycibus integris petalisque 6-7 extus tomentoso-puberulis.—Columbia.

Ramuli crassiusculi, cortice albido. Folia suppetunt pedalia et sesquipedalia, superne 2-4 poll. lata, basi longe angustata, membranacea, utrinque viridia et pube minuta rara scabriuscula, obscure pellucido-punctata, costa venisque subtus prominulis. Pedicelli complures ad apicem rami congesti, pollicares, tomentoso-puberuli. Bracteæ sub pedicellis 4-5 lin. longæ, lato-lanceolatæ, acutæ, subcartilagineæ. Bracteolæ supra medium pedicelli 2, minutæ. Petala sæpius 6, vix pollicaria, exteriora ovata, interiora oblonga, omnia obtusa.

CUCURBITACEÆ.

318. BRYONIA *attenuata*, Hook. et Arn. Bot. Beech. p. 424.—Acapulco.

319. MOMORDICA? *quinquefida*, Hook et Arn. l. c.—Acapulco.

320. MOMORDICA? sp., with male flowers only.—Guayaquil.

321. APODANTHERA *gracilis*, sp. n., caule tenui puberulo vel glabrato, foliis profunde cordatis acuminatis integris vel obscure 3-5-angulato-lobatis margine subciliatis, supra glabriusculis punctulatis, subtus pilosiusculis, floribus longe pedunculatis, masculis paucis racemoso-corymbosis, fœmineis solitariis, fructibus ovato-globosis glabris.—Isle of Taboga, Salango.

Folia bipollicaria, acumine longiusculo. Pedunculi masculi et fœminei ex iisdem axillis gracillimi, petiolo longiores. Flores masculi ad apicem pedunculi pauci, breviter pedicellati. Calyx tubulosus, extus puberulus, breviter 5-dentatus. Petala lata, acutiuscula, integerrima, brevissime ciliato-puberula. Stamina medio tubo inserta mediantibus filamentis tribus brevissimis et sic revera triadelphica; antheræ oblongæ, omnes inter se læviter cohærentes. Discus cupuliformis in fundo calycis. Calyx floris fœminei latius tubulosus, subcampanulatus. Petala quam in mare latiora. Discus cupuliformis similis nisi duplo major. Stylus brevis, crassus, in lobos 3 stigmatosos acutos non fimbriatos divisus. Ovarium junius uniloculare? mox placentis hinc inde intromissis spurie septatum; ovula pauca, parietibus sine ordine affixa. Pepo, in speciminibus nondum maturus, fere globosus.

I am unacquainted with the *A. Mathewsi* named but not described by Arnott, and therefore am unable to say whether this be the same species, though it is undoubtedly a congener. The genus ought, perhaps, to be considered only as a section of *Melothria*, and, in general appearance, the present plant closely resembles the Brazilian *M. fluminensis*, Gardn.; my specimens of the latter are too imperfect to show the structure of the flower.

322. CYCLANTHERA *leptostachya*, sp. n., glabra, caule gracillimo, foliis pedatim 7-9-sectis, segmentis petiolulatis oblongo-lanceolatis grosse dentatis extimis brevioribus subincisis, racemo masculo longissimo gracili corymbulis remotis, flore fœmineo longe pedunculato.—Salango.

Rami quam in *C. pedata* multo graciliores. Petioli 1½-2 poll. longi. Segmenta majora 2-3 poll. longa, 6-9 lin. lata, quam in *C. pedata* tenuiora, minus dentata. Racemi masculi semipedales vel longiores, floribus parvis in racemulos breves subcorymbosos secus rhachin communem dispositis. Pedunculus foemineus petiolo longior. Calyx in mare corollae omnino adnatus; corolla stellato-patens, laciniis ovato-triangularibus acutis; anthera circa marginem connectivi peltato-disciformis confluentes. Floris foeminei nec calycem nec corollam vidi. Ovarium jam parum auctum ovoideum, dense echinatum, apice obliquum et in stylum brevem incurvum desinens; intus placenta parietali longe intromissa incomplete biloculare. Ovula circa tria.

323. RYTIDOSTYLES *gracilis*, Hook. et Arn. Bot. Beech. p. 424. t. 97.—Folia inferiora longe petiolata, angulato-sublobata.—Realejo, Gulf of Fonseca, Panama.

PAPAYACEÆ.

324. CARICA *Papaya*, Linn.—Walp. Rep. 2. p. 205.—Realejo, Columbia.

325. CARICA *peltata*, Hook. et Arn. Bot. Beech. p. 425. t. 98.—Realejo.

326. CARICA *cauliflora*, Jacq?—Willd.? Spec. 4. p. 815.—Puna, near Guayaquil.—The leaves are wanting.

PASSIFLORACEÆ.

327. PASSIFLORA *littoralis*, Humb. et Kunth.—DC. Prod. 3. p. 323.—Guayaquil.

328. PASSIFLORA *suberosa*, Linn.—DC. Prod. 3. p. 325.—Guayaquil.

329. PASSIFLORA *biflora*, Linn.—DC. Prod. 3. p. 326.—Variat foliis basi rotundatis vel subcordatis, pedicellis solitariis vel geminis.—Panama.

330. PASSIFLORA *rubra*, Linn.—DC. Prod. 3. p. 325.—Panama.

331. PASSIFLORA *quadrangularis*, Linn.—DC. Prod. 3. p. 328.—Puna, near Guayaquil.

332. PASSIFLORA *foetida*, Cav.—DC. Prod. 3. p. 331.—Guayaquil.

333. TACSONIA *laevis*, sp. n., glaberrima, stipulis late semi-cordato-reniformibus mucronatis, foliis trilobis basi subpeltatis, lobis ovatis obtusis integerrimis intermedio productiore, lateralibus divaricatis, sinubus 2-3-glandulosis, petioli glandulis circa 4-stipitatis, bracteis ovato-oblongis integerrimis liberis, calycis laciniis tubo parum longioribus.—Guayaquil; gathered also by Hartweg, n. 662.

Ex omni parte glabra et saepius plus minus glauca. Stipulae 6-9 lin. longae, 6 lin. latae, falcato-dimidiatae, interdum fere orbiculares. Petioli pollicares, tenues, glandulis supra medium per paria dispositis rarius obsoletis. Folia 5-nervia, lobus intermedius 2 poll. (a petiolo) longus, laterales pollicares, ab intermedio ultra medium soluti, sinubus latiusculis. Pedunculi solitarii, bipollicares. Bracteae a calyce parum distantes, semipollicares vel paullo minores, obtusae, mucronulatae. Calycis tubus pollicaris, viridis, glaber; laciniae latolanceolatae, obtusiusculae, dorso breviter aristulatae, 14-15 lin. longae, extus linea dorsali virides, margine intusque coloratae. Petala lacinias calycinas subaequantia, undique colorata (rubra?) Corona exterior pluriserialis, filamentosa, filamentis exterioribus 1-2 lin. longis, interioribus minimis; corona intermedia ad basin tubi brevis, cyathiformis, brevissime lacera; interior vaginaeformis, conica, apice truncata, tubo stamineo arcte appressa, 2½ lin. longa.

Allied to *T. reflexiflora*, Cav., but apparently distinct.

334. TACSONIA *sanguinea*, DC. Prod. 3. p. 334.—Common in woods near Panama; gathered also by Cuming, n. 1122.

LOASACEÆ.

335. LOASA *chelidoniifolia*, sp. n., divaricato-ramosa, scabro-puberula, foliis pinnatim 3-7-sectis, segmentis ovatis inciso-dentatis basi oblique subcordatis, inferioribus subpetiolatis, terminali maximo subpinnatifido, pedunculis extra-axillaribus, calycis tubo setosissimo, laciniis lato-ovatis foliaceis, petalis calyce vix duplo longioribus.—Atacames.

Very near *L. triphylla* and *L. papaverifolia*, and only differs from Kunth's description of the latter species by the much larger leaves with broader segments, the stems and peduncles not setose, and the lobes of the calyx scarcely acute.

336. GRONOVIA *scandens*, Linn.—Hook. et Arn. Bot. Beech. p. 426. t. 97, B.—Tepic.

BEGONIACEÆ.

337. BEGONIA *humilis*, Dryand.—Walp. Rep. 2. p. 215.—Atacames.

338. BEGONIA *filipes*, sp. n., annua, caule gracili glabro, foliis longiuscule petiolatis oblique semicordatis ovato-oblongis triplicatim ciliato-serratis tenuibus sparse setulosis, pedunculis tenuibus subtrifloris, floribus minimis, capsulæ ala altera ipsa capsula multo latiore, duabus angustis.—Isle of Taboga, Bay of Panama.

B. humili affinis; petioli inferiores multo longiores, et capsulæ ala major 4 lin. lata, transverse oblonga, nec omnes anguste rotundatæ.

339. BEGONIÆ, sp. n., affinis *B. hydrocotylæfoliæ*.—Equador.—The specimens are insufficient for description.

TURNERACEÆ.

340. TURNERA *ulmifolia*, Linn.—DC. Prod. 3. p. 346.—*T. cuneiformis*, Hook. et Arn. Bot. Beech. p. 426, non Juss.—A very pretty low shrub on the top of the sandy beach, Atacames, Realejo.

341. TURNERA *Hindsiana*, sp. n., foliis ovato-oblongis acuminatis serratis basi angustatis eglandulosis glabriusculis, racemulis axillaribus brevibus paucifloris, capsulis globosis tuberculosis.—Guayaquil.

Simillima *T. salicifoliæ*, differt foliis latioribus plerisque 3 poll. longis, 1½ poll. latis, racemulis simplicibus paucifloris, pedunculo communi brevissimo, pedicellis 3 lin. longis infra medium minute bracteolatis et capsulæ tuberculis evidentioribus.

PORTULACEÆ.

342. PORTULACA *oleracea*, Linn.—DC. Prod. 3. p. 353.—Guayaquil.

ARALIACEÆ.

343. SCIODAPHYLLUM *sphærocoma*, sp. n., foliis digitatis, foliolis 7-11 longe petiolulatis amplis oblongis abrupte acuminatis utrinque glabris, umbellulis longe racemosis, racemis pubescentibus in comam amplam subglobosam approximatis.—Isle of Gorgona.

Arbor, inflorescentia ampla globosa insignis. Foliola maxima pedalia vel longiora, circa 5 poll. lata, petiolulo 5-pollicari, acumine pollicari, margine undulata, basi obtusa, costa media venisque primariis utrinsecus 7-9 valde prominentibus, venulis crebris reticulatis; foliola lateralia paullo minora. Racemi pedales, rhache rigida angulata, pube brevi ferruginea. Pedunculi numerosi, tenues, rigiduli, divaricati, 3-4 lin. longi, umbellula 10-12-flora terminati. Pedicelli 1 lin. longi. Calycis dentes 5, minutissimi. Petala connata in corollam parvam, ovato-conicam, obtusiusculam, calyptratim deciduam. Stamina 5, filamentis longiusculis. Styli 5, in columnam conicam coaliti. Ovarium 5-loculare.

LORANTHACEÆ.

344. VISCUM *Kunthianum*, DC. Prod. 4. p. 283.—Gulf of Nicoya, Guayaquil.

The Nicoya specimens are more robust than those from Guayaquil, but they appear to belong to the same species.

345. VISCUM *tomentosum*, DC. Prod. 4. p. 670.—Nicoya.

Species dioica. Spicæ masculæ $1\frac{1}{2}$-2 poll. longæ, interrupte 6-10-articulatæ, floribus in quoque articulo numerosis multiseriatis densissime imbricatis. Spicæ fœmineæ 4-5-articulatæ; baccæ in quoque articulo circa 6, globosæ, velutinæ.

346. LORANTHUS (Euloranthus?) *inconspicuus*, sp. n., ramosissimus, ramulis ancipitibus demum vix teretibus, foliis parvis obovato-oblongis obtusis basi angustatis obscure trinervibus, floribus minimis in axillis sessilibus congestis.—San Blas.

Ramuli, præsertim sub nodis, compresso-dilatati, cinerascentes. Folia 6-10 lin. longa, basi longiuscule angustata at vix petiolata. Flores in axillis gemini vel terni, bracteis 3-4 ovatis minutis margine fimbriatis suffulti. Specimina tamen suppetentia omnia jam deflorata, nec petala nec stamina vidi, et semel tantum stylum observavi semilineam longum, ex ovario vix $\frac{1}{4}$ lin. longo.

347. LORANTHUS *Schiedeanus*, Schlecht.—Hook. et Arn. Bot. Beech. p. 426.—San Blas.

348. LORANTHUS (Oscillatoria) *rhynchanthus*, sp. n., glaber, ramulis acute tetragonis, foliis oppositis ovato-lanceolatis falcatis basi angustatis vix petiolatis crasso-coriaceis subaveniis, corymbis terminalibus trichotomis, bractea cyathiformi sub floribus singulis, alabastro oblique rostrato, petalis

sex linearibus acutis.—*L. calyculatus*, Hook. et Arn. Bot. Beech. p. 294. non DC.—Tiger Island.

Similis *L. calyculato* DC., sed rami tetragoni, folia majora, sæpe 4-5-pollicaria, corymbi ampliores, et flores ante anthesin longius acuminato-rostrati.

349. LORANTHUS (Oscillatoria) *obovatus*, sp. n., glaber, scabriusculus, ramis subteretibus dichotomis verticillatisve, foliis subsessilibus obovatis obtusis basi rotundatis cuneatisve venosis, pedunculis opposite ramosis terminalibus tenuiter puberulis, ramis trifloris floribus pedicellatis, bractea cupuliformi ovario paullo breviore, corollæ sesquipollicaris obtusæ vix puberulæ petalis sex linearibus.—Common on several trees, especially Mimoseæ, near Guayaquil.

Folia 1-2 poll. longa, ½-1 poll. lata, subcoriacea, venis pinnato-reticulatis parum prominentibus. Pedunculi nunc ad apices ramorum solitarii, ramulis per paria distantibus 3-4 lin. longis, pedicellis 2-3 lin. longis; nunc in axillis superioribus vel ad apices ramorum complures, breves, ramulorum paribus approximatis, pedicellis abbreviatis.

RUBIACEÆ.

350. POSOQUERIA *decora*, DC. Prod. v. 4. p. 375.—Isle of Gorgona.

Frutex glaberrimus, ramulis junioribus tetragonis demum teretibus. Folia petiolata, late ovata, 6-8 poll. longa, 4-6 poll. lata, brevissime acuminata, margine subundulata, basi rotundata, coriacea, supra nitida, costa media venisque primariis subtus magis quam in affinibus prominentibus. Petioli 6-10 lin. longi. Stipulæ late ovatæ, obtusæ, 8-12 lin. longæ, coriaceo-foliaceæ. Corymbus 12-16-florus, terminalis, pedunculatus, pedunculo tamen foliis superioribus breviore. Pedicelli floriferi 3-4 lin. longi, post anthesin elongati. Calyx 2 lin. longus, tubo adnato turbinato, limbo brevissime et obtusissime 5-dentato. Corollæ tubus rectus, 5-6-pollicaris, gracilis, summo apice paullo dilatatus; limbus in alabastro obliquus, hinc gibbus, obtusus; laciniæ 7-8 lin. longæ, oblongæ. Styli lobi lineares.

Although the geographical station of De Candolle's plant (French Guiana) be so distant, his character agrees perfectly with our specimens. They also answer as to foliage with Kunth's description of *Tocoyena macrophylla*, but the flowers of our plant are not racemose, and are decidedly those of a *Posoqueria*.

351. RANDIA (Oxyceras) *glomerata*, sp. n., ramulis glabris apice bispinosis, foliis subsessilibus obovatis glaberrimis basi cuneatis, floribus ad apices ramulorum sessilibus pluribus congestis, corollæ parvæ fauce pilosa.—Atacames.

Frutex affinis *R. latifoliæ*, sed folia et flores minora. Ramuli breves, crassi. Spinæ divergentes, conicæ. Folia in ramulis floriferis abbreviatis fasciculata, semipollicaria vel paullo longiora, supra nitida, ramulorum sterilium non vidi. Flores magnitudine *Ribesios grossulariæ*, 3-5 ad apices ramulorum brevissimorum sessiles. Calycis tubus minutus, limbus cyathiformi-campanulatus, brevissime 5-dentatus. Corolla alba, tubo 1½ lin. longe; laciniæ lanceolatæ, acuminatæ, 1½ lin. longæ, crassiusculæ, æstivatione valvata vel levissime imbricata, intus dense pilosæ. Antheræ lineares, e tubo breviter exsertæ. Stylus corolla longior, apice bilobus.

352. BERTIERA *angustifolia*, sp. n., foliis oblongis acuminatis, venis ramulisque villosis, stipulis

connatis in vaginam hinc fissam apice bidentatam, fructibus parvis sessilibus striatis basi hirtellis calycis dentibus minutis coronatis.—Cocos Island.

Habitus et flores *B. Guianensis*, sed stipularum forma foliis angustis necnon fructibus parvis primo intuitu distincta. Ramuli, foliorum venæ paginæ inferioris, stipulæ et thyrsus pilis substrigosis villosa uti in cæteris speciebus Americanis. Stipulæ semipollicares, rufo-membranaceæ, angustæ, uno latere usque ad medium altero fere ad apicem connatæ. Folia brevissime petiolata, 4-5-pollicaria, longe et acute acuminata, basi parum angustata, obtusa, supra undique et subtus nonnisi ad venas glabra, punctis irregularibus crebris obscure pellucido-punctata. Thyrsus terminalis, breviter pedunculatus, 2-3-pollicaris. Flores quam in *B. Guianensi* paullo minores, minus villosi, tubo gracili, limbo campanulato, laciniis aristato-acuminatis. Fructus globosus, striatus, dimidio minor quam in *B. Guianensi*, demum fere glaber. Dentes calycini quam in affinibus multo minores. Semina *B. Guianensis*.

353. BUENA *macrocarpa*, sp. n., (Plate XXXVIII.) foliis late ovalibus ellipticisve venosis obscuris, floribus 3-5-nis sessilibus, calycis limbo quam ovarium multo breviore, corollæ pentameræ laciniis ovali-oblongis obtusis.—Isle of Gorgona.

Arbor speciosa, glabra. Ramuli crassiusculi, juniores subcarnosi. Folia ovali-elliptica, obtusa, basi cuneata et in petiolum 6-9-linearem anguste decurrentia, 3-4 poll. longa, 2-3 poll. lata, crassiuscula, atrovirentia, nec nitentia; venæ utrinque 7-10, parallelæ, a costa media divergentes multo magis quam in *B. triflora* et *B. latifolia* prominentes. Stipulæ membranaceo-foliaceæ, 4-6 lin. longæ. Flores ad apices ramulorum subsessiles. Bracteæ in speciminibus desunt, verosimiliter delapsæ. Calycis limbus vix 1½ lin. longus, breviter 5-dentatus, cito deciduus. Ovarium semipollicare. Corollæ albidæ tubus bipollicaris, limbi laciniæ 8-9 lin. longæ, æstivatione imbricata. Filamenta brevissima versus apicem tubi. Antheræ lineares, fere omnino inclusæ. Stylus apice breviter exsertus, in lacinias 2 oblongas intus stigmatiferas dilatatus. Capsula 3-4-pollicaris, sublignosa, teres, demum septicide bipartibilis, loculis intus dehiscentibus. Semina numerosissima, ala angustissima infra longe producta lineari-subulata subdentata, supra bipartita, laciniis longe lineari-subulatis subdentatis.

This species differs from both of Ruiz and Pavon's by the obtuse corollas, from *B. triflora* and *B. latifolia* by the distinctly veined and not shining leaves, smaller flowers, and short limb of the calyx. The pod is of the shape of that of the closely allied genus *Hillia*, but the seed is different. The Brazilian *Buenæ* figured by Pohl and by Endlicher do not belong to the genus.

Plate XXXVIII. fig. 1, flower cut open;* fig. 2, transverse section of the ovary; fig. 3, portion of one half of the capsule, the outer coating or pericarp having decayed away; fig. 4, seed: all magnified.

354. EXOSTEMMA (Pseudostemma) *occidentale*, sp. n., glabrum, foliis amplis obovato-oblongis cuspidatis basi longe angustatis, paniculis brevibus laxe pyramidatis, calycis limbo subintegerrimo, corollæ intus extusque glaberrimæ laciniis tubo paullo longioribus, stigmate bilobo.—Isle of Gorgona.

Frutex elata. Ramuli teretes. Folia longiuscule petiolata, 8-10 poll. longa, supra medium 3-3½ poll. lata, acumine longo angusto superata, punctis sparsis pellucidis notata. Stipulæ a specimine jam delapsæ. Panicula terminalis, breviter pedunculata, subquadripollicaris, laxe trichotoma, pauciflora. Bracteæ ad ramificationes parvæ, ovato-lanceolatæ. Calycis tubus 2 lin. longus, oblongus; limbus cyathiformis, brevis, integer vel obscure

---

* By a mistake in the drawing the whole of the corolla is shown, and only half of the ovary and calyx.

5-angulatus. Corolla crassiuscula, in alabastro pentagona; tubus 2½ lin. longus; limbi laciniæ 3 lin. longæ, oblongæ, acutiusculæ, æstivatione valvatæ, per anthesin patentes. Stamina ad faucem inserta; filamenta brevissima, pubescentia; antheræ oblongo-lineares. Ovarium carnosum, biloculare. Placentæ lineares, ovulis numerosissimis dense imbricatis. Stylus e tubo corollæ exsertus, apice breviter bilobus, in lobis stigmatosus. Fructus non vidi.

355. LASIONEMA *glabrescens*, sp. n., ramulis subcompressis glabriusculis, foliis petiolatis obovali-oblongis acuminatis supra glabris subtus ad axillas venarum barbatis junioribus ad venas sericeis demum glabris, paniculis pedunculatis compactis, corollæ extus glabræ tubo obscure pentagono limbi laciniis supra tomentellis.—Nicoya.

Frutex, ramulis junioribus pube minuta mox evanida rufescentibus. Folia ad apices ramorum approximata, 3-4-pollicaria, in petiolum 3-6 lin. longum insidentia, apice in acumen breve obtusum producta, basi angustata, rigide membranacea, supra demum nitidula. Stipulæ oblongo-ellipticæ vel obovali-oblongæ, obtusissimæ, 5-8 lin. longæ, cito deciduæ. Paniculæ ad apicem pedunculi 2-3-pollicaris densæ, subcorymbosæ. Bracteæ minimæ, acutæ. Flores sessiles. Calyx 1½ lin. longus, limbo brevissime 5-dentato. Corollæ tubus 3½ lin. longus; limbi laciniæ breves, latæ, obtusæ, patentissimæ, supra tenuiter tomentellæ, æstivatione imbricatæ. Stamina medio tubo inserta; filamenta villosa, apice e tubo breviter exserta; antheræ ovatæ. Stylus filiformis, inclusus, apice breviter bifidus stigmatosus. Capsulam non vidi, in ovario tamen deflorato vix aucto semina numerosissima linearia, apice et basi membranacea.

356. MANETTIA *cuspidata*, Bert.—DC. Prod. v. 4. p. 363.—Panama.

357. BOUVARDIA *linearis*, Humb. et Kunth.—Hook. et Arn. Bot. Beech. p. 427.—Tepic.

358. BOUVARDIA *scabra*, Hook. et Arn. Bot. Beech. p. 427.—Tepic.

359. CALYCOPHYLLUM *candidissimum*, DC. Prod. v. 4. p. 367.—Variat floribus tetrameris.—Conchagua, Gulf of Honda, and Gulf of Fonseca.

360. CONDAMINEA *corymbosa*, DC. Prod. v. 4. p. 402.—Veragua.

361. LINDENIA *rivalis*, Benth. Pl. Hartw. p. 84.—Hook. Ic. Pl. t. 476.—Mexican coast.

362. PENTAGONIA *macrophylla*, gen. nov. e tribu *Rondeletiearum* (Plate XXXIX.)—Panama.

CHAR. GEN. Calycis limbus infundibuliformis, 5-fidus, lobis amplis persistentibus. Corolla infundibuliformis, tubo elongato; limbus 5-partitus, laciniis æstivatione valvatis; alabastrum apice acute pentagono-subalatum. Stamina infra medium tubi inserta; filamenta filiformia; antheræ lineares, inclusæ. Discus epigynus cupuliformis. Stylus filiformis, lobis obovatis concavis intus stigmatosis. Capsula bilocularis. Semina numerosa, angulata.

Ramulorum apices tantum adsunt crassæ, subtetragonæ. Stipulæ sesquipollicares vel longiores, utrinque solitariæ, lanceolatæ, acuminatæ, crassæ. Folia 1-2-pedalia, ovalia vel ovali-oblonga, apice obtuse angustata, margine subundulata, basi longiuscule angustata, crassiuscula, glaberrima, costa media venisque primariis divergentibus subtus prominentibus; petiolus 1-2-pollicaris, canaliculatus. Corymbi in axillis superioribus brevissime pedunculati, floribus in corymbo numerosis sessilibus confertis. Bracteæ ovatæ, obtusæ, concavæ, exteriores 9 lin. longæ. Calyx pollicaris, basi extus candicans, laciniis crassis ovatis margine tenuibus coloratis, intus ad faucem ad sinus loborum pilis paucis brevibus glandulosis munitus. Corolla extus glabra vel parce pilosula, intus ad insertionem staminum tomentosa et in limbo pilosula; tubus calyce dimidio longior, limbi laciniæ ovatæ, marginibus ante anthesin valde prominentibus. Capsulas nonnisi juniores vidi, in his semina more

Rondeletiearum arcte appressa nec imbricata. Textura foliorum stipularum et florum intus insigniter albo-filamentosa.

Plate XXXIX. fig. 1, flower, nat. size; fig. 2, corolla cut open; fig. 3, longitudinal section of ovary and calyx, with the style; fig. 4, transverse section of ovary: the three last magnified.

363. HEDYOTIS (Ericotis) *thymifolia*, Ruiz et Pav.—*Anotis thymifolia*, DC. Prod. v. 4. p. 432.—Huamantango.

364. ISERTIA *coccinea*, Vahl.—DC. Prod. v. 4. p. 437. var. foliis longe petiolatis, thyrso abbreviato, nec aliter a forma Guianensi distinguenda videtur.—Columbia.

365. SCHRADERA *stellata*, sp. n., (Plate XL.) foliis oblongo-ellipticis acuminatis, pedunculo solitario terminali, involucro brevi lobato, calycis limbo truncato integerrimo, corollæ laciniis 5 linearibus, ovario biloculari.—Isle of Gorgona.

Rami crassi, cortice lævi, medulla copiosa farcti; ramuli juniores acute tetragoni. Folia breviter petiolata, 3-5-pollicaria, apice longiuscula acuminata, venis parallelis juxta marginem confluentibus. Stipulæ breves in vaginam brevem sublobatam deciduam connatæ. Pedunculi communes vix pollicares. Capitulum circa 6-florum, suffultum involucro brevissimo, per anthesin irregulariter sinuato-lobato, deflexo. Calyx 6 lin. longus, basi ampla ovario adherens, apice parum contractus, ore transverse truncato integerrimo vel obscure sinuato. Corolla alba, intus extusque glabra, tubo tereti calycem æquante; laciniæ stellato-patentes, circa 10 lin. longæ, acutæ, basi incrassatæ, æstivatione imbricata. Antheræ 5, lineares, inclusæ, filamentis brevibus in medio tubo affixis. Ovarium biloculare, carnosum, disco epigyno pulviniformi medio depresso; ovula in loculis numerosa, placentæ carnosæ immersa. Stylus filiformis, subexsertus, apice bilobus, lobis oblongis crasso-compressiusculis acutiusculis intus et margine stigmatiferis. Bacca calycis limbo coronata, bilocularis. Semina ovato-compressa, testa dura fragili minute rugulosa, albumine carnosa, embryone recto.

Plate XL. fig. 1, flower, nat. size; fig. 2, corolla, cut open; fig. 3, stamen; fig. 4, ovary, longitudinal section with the style; fig. 5, ovary, transverse section: figs. 2 to 5 magnified.

366. HAMELIA *patens*, Jacq.—DC. Prod. v. 4. p. 441.—Realejo, Panama, Gulf of Fonseca.

367. GUETTARDA *conferta*, sp. n., foliis ovatis acuminatis basi acutis utrinque hirsutis, stipulis latis petiolum subæquantibus, cymis subsessilibus, calycis limbo brevi obsolete lobato, corollæ sericeo-hirtæ laciniis crispis.—Cocos Island.

Affinis *G. hirsutæ*. Pili ferruginei in ramulis petiolis pedunculis venisque foliorum primariis densi, in venulis transversis rariores. Folia 4-6-pollicaria, utrinque longiuscule acuminata, venis primariis utrinsecus 10-12 subtus prominentibus. Stipulæ late obovatæ, mucronato-acutæ, fusco-membranaceæ, dorso basi hirsutæ, cæterum glabræ, subsemipollicares. Pedunculi communes per anthesin subnulli, fructiferi 2-4 lin. longi, ramis recurvis demum pollicaribus. Flores sessiles, parvi (4 lin. longi). Calyx brevis, breviter et inæqualiter 3-4-dentatus. Corollæ limbi lobi 4, breves, obtusi, margine crispi. Drupa ovato-tetragona, 2 lin. longa, hirsuta, calycis limbo minimo coronata, putamine osseo, 4-loculari.

368. CHIOCOCCA *racemosa*, Jacq.—DC. Prod. v. 4. p. 482.—Tumaco and Atacames.

369. PSYCHOTRIA *viridis*, Ruiz et Pav.—DC. Prod. v. 4. p. 506.—Salango.

370. PSYCHOTRIA *micrantha*, Humb. et Kunth.—DC. Prod. v. 3. p. 507.—Tumaco.

In some specimens the leaves are longer and narrower than those figured and described by Kunth, and the panicle more slender, but they all appear to belong to one species.

371. PSYCHOTRIA *justicioides*, Schlecht. Linnæa, v. 9. p. 596.—Columbia.

372. PSYCHOTRIA *conferta*, sp. n., glabra vel vix apice puberula, stipulis utrinque binis lanceolatis, foliis petiolatis ovali-ellipticis acuminatis basi acute angustatis, panicula parva corymbosa, floribus numerosis confertis, bracteis minutis, corolla minute puberula intus ad faucem villosa, laciniis tubo longioribus.—Columbia.

Specimina siccitate nigrescunt. Ramuli obtuse tetragoni, sub inflorescentia leviter pubescentes, cæterum glabri. Folia longiuscule petiolata, 4-6-pollicaria vel interdum longiora, acumine longo acuto et basi in petiolum longiuscule angustata, costa media et venis primariis utrinsecus circa 10 prominulis, utrinque viridia, glabra. Stipulæ rufo-membranaceæ, acutissimæ, 2 lin. longæ. Pedunculus terminalis, foliis brevior. Panicula trichotoma, in corymbum parvum contracta. Bracteæ sub corymbo 1-1½ lin. longæ, aristato-acuminatæ, cæteræ vix conspicuæ. Flores breviter pedicellati. Calycis tubus ovoideus, limbus brevis, inæqualiter 5-fidus. Corollæ extus puberulæ tubus brevissimus; faux intus villosa; limbi 5-partiti laciniæ tubo duplo longiores, apice non cornutæ. Antheræ 5, lineares. Styli lobi longiuscule lineares.

373. PSYCHOTRIA *acuminata*, sp. n., glabra, foliis petiolatis ovalibus oblongisve longe acuminatis basi acutis membranaceis subtus ad axillas minute hirtellis, stipulis brevissime vaginantibus truncatis utrinque bidentatis, panicula parva breviter pedunculata ovata, corollæ glabræ intus ad faucem pilosulæ laciniis tubo brevioribus.—Isle of Gorgona, and Columbian coast.

Frutex orgyalis. Rami subteretes, dichotomi; ramuli sub foliis compressi vel ancipites. Stipularum vagina vix conspicua, dentibus utrinque 2 inter se distantibus subulatis semilineam longis. Folia 3-5 poll. longa, latitudine varia, in acumen longum acutum apice producta, basi breviter acutata, petiolo 2-4 lin. longo; venæ primariæ utrinsecus 6-8 vel interdum numerosiores, axillis minute foveolato-hirtis. Panicula irregulariter ramosa vel subtrichotoma, laxiuscula, pollicaris vel paullo longior, pedunculo vix pollicari. Bracteæ inconspicuæ. Calycis limbus truncatus, obscure dentatus. Corolla ochroleuca, glaberrima nisi ad faucem pilis paucis hirtella, tubo gracili sesquilineari. Stamina in speciminibus exserta.

Nearly allied to *P. bahiensis* DC., but the leaves are thinner, more abruptly acuminate, with rather longer petioles, the panicles more compact, the flowers smaller, &c. The leaves in the Columbian specimens are narrower than in those from Gorgona, and again, Hartweg gathered on the Magdalena a form with broader leaves than either.

374. PSYCHOTRIA *fimbriata*, Benth. in Hook. Journ. Bot. v. 3. p. 226.—Columbia.

375. PALICOUREA? *parviflora*, sp. n., caule tereti glabro, foliis ternatim verticillatis oblongis acuminatis supra glabriusculis subtus pubescentibus, stipulis distinctis lanceolatis acuminatis petiolo longioribus, panicula brevi stricta racemiformi, pedunculis brevibus 1-3-floris.—Island off the coast of Veragua.

Ramuli subherbacei, læves, internodiis elongatis sub foliis more Acanthacearum siccitate constrictis. Folia 4-6-pollicaria, medio 1½ poll. lata, costa media venisque primariis utrinsecus 10-12 subtus prominentibus villosulis, pube in pagina inferiore inter venas brevissima; pagina superior scabriuscula, vel interdum pilis paucis præsertim secus costam hirtella. Stipulæ semipollicares, setaceo-acuminatæ, fusco-membranaceæ, ciliolatæ.

Panicula vix pedunculata, contracta, 2-3-pollicaris, axi communi triquetro ferrugineo-pubescente. Ramuli et pedicelli brevissimi. Calycis limbus brevissime et obscure 5-dentatus. Corolla glabriuscula, vix tamen perfectam vidi. Ovarium more generis biloculare, ovulis solitariis erectis.

This plant must be very near to the *P. triphylla* DC., differing in the downy under side of the leaves and the broader stipules. It is doubtful, however, whether both species should not rather be referred to *Psychotria*, the fully-formed corolla not being known in either.

376. PALICOUREA *Guianensis*, Aubl?—DC.? Prod. 4. p. 530.—Isle of Gorgona.—The flowers are rather smaller than in my Guiana specimens, but I can detect no other difference.*

377. CEPHÆLIS *tomentosa*, Willd.—DC. Prod. v. 4. p. 533.—Isle of Gorgona.

378. CEPHALANTHUS *occidentalis* var. *brachypodus*, DC. Prod. v. 4. p. 538.—Manzanilla Bay.

379. DIODIA *crassifolia*, sp. n., glaberrima, diffusa, radicans, foliis linearibus lanceolatisque crassiusculis, vaginis amplis longe multisectis, floribus in axillis subsolitariis, fructibus ovali-oblongis calycis laciniis 4-6 inæqualibus lanceolatis coronatis.—San Blas.

Ramuli crassiusculi, stipularum vaginis fere omnino obtecti. Folia subsesquipollicaria, sessilia, acuta, rigida, supra lævia, margine recurva, costa media subtus valde prominente, cæterum enervia. Stipularum vagina 2 lin. vel paullo longior. Setæ utrinque 6-8, vaginam æquantes. Flores non vidi. Calyces fructiferi vaginam breviter superant; laciniæ limbi foliacei, rigidi, valde inæquales, longiores 2 lin. longæ.

380. DIODIA *setigera*, DC. Prod. v. 4. p. 563.—Isle of Taboga, Bay of Panama.

381. SPERMACOCE *tenuior*, Linn.—DC. Prod. v. 4. p. 552.—Common from Mexico to Guayaquil.

382. SPERMACOCE (Borreria) *parviflora*, Mey.—DC. Prod. v. 4. p. 544.—Gulf of Fonseca.

This species appears to have a wide range and to vary considerably in the smoothness or roughness of its leaves, and in the proportionate length of the teeth of the calyx, which are sometimes nearly equal, sometimes two are much shorter than the two others. It is probable that *Spermacoce prostrata*, Aubl., is the same plant, nor can I see any constant character to separate *Borreria ramisparsa*, DC.

The genus *Borreria*, as already observed by Hooker and Arnott, and others, cannot indeed be separated from *Spermacoce* by any tangible characters, and the membranous fruited *Diodiæ* are also too closely allied to it; but it does appear that the fruit, as well as the habit of De Candolle's section *Eudiodia* are sufficiently marked to maintain it as a distinct genus.

383. MITRACARPIUM *villosum*, Cham. Schl.—DC. Prod. v. 4. p. 572.—Folia ovali-vel oblongo-lanceolata, paullo angustiora quam in speciminibus Mexicanis Galeottianis; corolla dentes calycinos non excedit.—Guascuma, in Columbia.

---

* There are also specimens in the collection of *Coffea Arabica* from Columbia, probably cultivated.

384. MITRACARPIUM *Schizangium*, DC.—Hook. et Arn. Bot. Beech. p. 429. t. 99 A.—Tepic.

385. MITRACARPIUM *pallidum*, Hook. et Arn. Bot. Beech. p. 430. (sp. n.)—Realejo.

386. CRUSEA *parviflora*, Hook. et Arn. Bot. Beech. p. 430. t. 99 C. (sp. n.)—Acapulco.

387. CRUSEA *subalata*, Hook. et Arn. Bot. Beech. p. 431. (sp. n.)—Tepic.

388. CRUSEA *lucida*, sp. n., caule tetragono subalato glabro, foliis late lanceolatis glabris nitidis margine scabris, capitulis terminalibus involucratis, calycis laciniis subulatis rigidis corollæ tubum æquantibus.—Southern Mexico.

Ramulus adest sesquipedalis, decumbens, glaber, nitidus, angulis acutissimis subalatis lævibus. Folia subsessilia, pollicaria, acuta, marginibus subtus revolutis et pilis brevissimis serrulato-scabris, supra viridia nitentia, subtus pallidiora, costa media prominente, venis obscuris. Ramuli et folia juniora in axillis fasciculata. Stipulæ e vagina brevi utrinque plurisetæ, setis ciliatis rigidis. Pedunculus terminalis, fere 5-pollicaris, capitulo majusculo coronatus. Folia floralia caulinis similia, sed paullo latiora, interiora minora. Flores numerosi, sessiles, bracteis intermixti setaceis setisque stipulinis similibus sed evidentius ciliatis. Calycis tubus linearis, superne bigibbosus, gibbis (ovarii loculos continentibus) oblongis; laciniæ limbi subulati, basi parum dilatati et leviter ciliati, rigidi, 2 lineas parum excedentes. Corollæ tubus tenuis, extus puberulus, 2 lin. longus; limbi laciniæ oblongo-lineares, apice piliferæ. Stamina longiuscule exserta. Stylus laciniis corollinis brevior.

VALERIANACEÆ.

389. ASTREPHIA *Mexicana*, Hook. et Arn. Bot. Beech. p. 432.—Tepic.

COMPOSITÆ.

390. VERNONIA *scorpioides*, Pers.—DC. Prod. v. 5. p. 41.—Columbia.

391. VERNONIA *lanceolaris*, DC.—Hook. et Arn. Bot. Beech. p. 432.—Realejo; Isle of Taboga, Bay of Panama; Libertad, in Columbia.

392. VERNONIA *Sinclairii*, sp. n., fruticosa?, ramis pubescentibus, foliis subsessilibus oblongis remote serratis supra scabris subtus pubescentibus, panicula composita divaricata subcorymbosa, pedicellis plerisque elongatis, capitulis ovoideis 9-10-floris, involucri squamis glabriusculis mucronatis, exterioribus lanceolatis, interioribus linearibus, corollis glabris, achænio multicostato pubescente, pappo seriei exterioris brevi paleaceo.—San Blas and Tepic.

Affinis videtur *V. liatroidi*. Ramorum summitates quæ solæ adsunt, teretes, striatæ, pube subferruginea. Folia 2-2½ poll. longa, 6-9 lin. lata, venoso-rugosa, supra scaberrima, pube subtus brevi subintricata pallida. Paniculæ rami primarii in axillis foliorum caulinis similium orti, cæterum inflorescentia aphylla vel hinc inde bractea parva foliacea instructa. Pedunculi inferiores secus ramos elongati, 1-3-cephali; superiores breviores, capitulis subcongestis. Involucra 4 lin. longa; squamæ pluriseriatim imbricatæ, in parte tecta scariosæ, apice purpurascentes, dorso glabræ vel minute puberulæ, margine tenuissime sublanatæ, exteriores acutæ, interiores obtusæ cum mucrone brevissimo. Pappus albus, rigidus, involucro dimidio longior.

393. DISTREPTUS *spicatus*, Cass.—DC. Prod. v. 5. p. 87.—Realejo; Tiger Island, Gulf of Fonseca.

394. LAGASCEA *rubra*, Humb. et Kunth?—DC.? Prod. v. 5. p. 92.—A poor specimen scarcely sufficient to determine.—Tepic.

395. LAGASCEA *suaveolens*, Humb. et Kunth.—DC. Prod. v. 5. p. 92.—*L. latifolia*, DC.? l. c.—Hook. et Arn. Bot. Beech. p. 432.—Tepic.

396. LAGASCEA *angustifolia*, DC. Prod. v. 5. p. 92.—Tepic.

397. PECTIS *taliscana*, Hook. et Arn. Bot. Beech. p. 296.—Realejo.

398. PECTIS *arenaria*, sp. n., prostrata, glabra, foliis linearibus margine revolutis utrinque basi 3-4-ciliatis crebre et minute pellucido-punctatis, pedunculis folio brevioribus pauci-bracteatis, involucri squamis 5-6 valde imbricatis, ligulis 5-6, floribus disci circa 15, pappi disci setis 10-20 valde inæqualibus nonnullis basi dilatatis, radii setis paucioribus.—Sands of the sea coast, Acapulco; Conchagua; Puna, near Guayaquil.

Caules in arena prostrati, crassi, uni-pluri-pedales, ramulos emittentes plurimos breves dense foliatos. Folia opposita, subconnata, fere pollicaria, crassiuscula, ciliis baseos latitudine folii longioribus. Pedunculi vix pollicares, monocephali, bracteis paucis setaceis rigidis. Involucrum cylindraceum, 4-5 lin. longum, squamis acutis latis magis quam in affinibus lateraliter imbricatis. Ligulæ involucro fere duplo longiores; flores disci squamas paullulum superant. Achænia fere 3 lin. longa, angulata, glabra. Pappi setæ longiores achænio breviores, aliæ multo minores, ex eorum numero 4-5 sæpius basi dilatatæ, cæteræ subulatæ, scabridæ.

A much coarser plant than most species, with larger heads of flowers, and growing in the dark sand of the beach, at a temperature of 128°. It was gathered in the same situation by Galeotti, and is his No. 2063.

399. SINCLAIRIA *discolor*, Hook. et Arn. Bot. Beech. p. 433.—Hook. Ic. Pl. t. 451. (gen. nov.)—Realejo.

400. PIQUERIA *trinervis*, Cav.—DC. Prod. v. 5. p. 104.—Tepic.

401. PIQUERIA *densiflora*, sp. n., glabra, foliis ovatis vel ovato-lanceolatis acuminatis grosse dentatis, capitulis 4-floris in ramulis paniculæ subnudæ confertis numerosis, involucri squamis obtusiusculis.—Isle of Puna, near Guayaquil.

Rami lignosi, ramulis teretibus glabris lucidis, et ex specimine sicco scandentes videntur. Folia 2-2⅓-pollicaria, acute acuminata, dentibus seu crenis paucis inæqualibus notata, basi acute cuneata, membranacea, glabra, trinervia, venulis subpellucidis, petiolo gracili 3-6 lin. longo; superiora angustiora, integriora. Panicula leviter glutinosa, pyramidata, opposite ramosa, capitulis ad apices ramorum in glomerulos polycephalos subsessiles confertis. Involucrum 1 lin. longum, squamis 4 subæqualibus oblongis, apice ciliolatis obtusis, dorso leviter glutinosis, adjectis sæpe 1-2 minoribus exterioribus. Corollæ involucrum superantes, tubo tenui extus glanduloso-puberulo basi dilatato, fauce glabra campanulata, limbo profunde 5-fido. Antheræ apice appendiculatæ. Styli rami subclavati. Achænia glabra, angulata, areola lata cartilaginea coronata.

402. ISOCARPHA *divaricata*, sp. n., (Plate XLI.) pubescens, caule divaricato-dichotomo, foliis alternis vel imis oppositis petiolatis oblongis lanceolatisve integerrimis trinervibus, petiolis basi nudis, capitulis pedicellatis ovoideis, involucri squamis lanceolatis acutiusculis ciliato-pubescentibus, achænio glaberrimo.—Isle of Puna, near Guayaquil.

Herba ut videtur annua, pedalis vel altior, ramis alternis elongatis gracilibus teretibus nunc puberulis nunc molliter villosis. Folia inferiora 1½-2-pollicaria, longiuscule petiolata, obtusiuscula, utrinque pube minuta mollia, minute pellucido-punctata; superiora minora, angustiora. Capitula ad apices ramulorum ultimorum 2-3, breviter pedicellata, 2½ lin. longa, forma fere *Spilanthis*. Involucrum turbinatum, squamis subbiserialibus paucis pallide virescentibus, pube molli subviscosa. Receptaculum elongato-conicum. Paleæ concavæ, corollis vix breviores, apice ciliatæ, exteriores squamis involucri subsimiles, interiores lineari-spathulatæ, hyalinæ. Corollæ tubus tenuis, basi dilatatus et deorsum pilosus; faux elongata, tubo duplo amplior, glabra; dentes limbi breves, patentes. Antheræ inclusæ, apice ovato-appendiculatæ. Styli rami obtusiusculi, exserti, hispiduli. Achænia tetragona, nigra, glabra, omnino calva.

The genus *Isocarpha*, to which this plant belongs, is rather that established by Lessing, in the Linnæa, v. 5. p. 141, than the original *Isocarpha* of Brown, founded on the *I. oppositifolia*. It is true that Lessing afterwards considered his as the same as Brown's, and as differing from *Calydermos* by the style, that of *Eupatoriaceæ*, and that De Candolle, following him in this opinion, has placed *Isocarpha* of Brown among *Eupatoriaceæ*, but has copied Brown's description of the style, altering only the phraseology to suit the general views adopted by him: "Styli rami elongati, extus convexi, hispiduli, acuti," a character accurately taken from *I. oppositifolia*, Br., but not applicable to the *I. echioides*, Less., where the branches of the style are described and figured as obtuse, nor yet conformable to the general form of the style in *Eupatoriaceæ*. It is probable that, on a further investigation, the present species, with three or four unpublished Brazilian ones, and the *I. echioides*, Less. (with which I am unacquainted), will be found to be true *Eupatoriaceæ*, whilst the *I. oppositifolia*, Br., appears to be strictly congener with the *Dunantia achyranthes*, DC., admirably figured in the 4th vol. of Delessert's Icones, and to be nearly allied to *Spilanthes*. With regard to the names to be respectively adopted for the two genera, it would occasion less confusion were Lessing's to retain that of *Isocarpha*, and were the *I. oppositifolia* to be transferred to *Dunantia*; but this would perhaps be too contrary to the rules of priority to be adopted. I refrain, however, for the present from establishing any further the separation, as I have no opportunity of examining three of the four species enumerated in the Prodromus.

Plate XLI. fig. 1, head of flowers, vertical section; fig. 2, scale of the receptacle; fig. 3, flower; fig. 4, upper part of the style; fig. 5, achænium; fig. 6, the same cut across: all magnified.

403. CŒLESTINA *corymbosa*, DC. Prod. v. 5. p. 108.—San Blas and Tepic.—A species apparently well distinguished from *C. ageratoides*, with which some botanists unite it.

404. CŒLESTINA *petiolata*, Hook. et Arn. Bot. Beech. p. 433. (sp. n.)—Realejo.

405. AGERATUM *conysoides*, Linn.—DC. Prod. v. 5. p. 108.—Columbia.

406. ADENOSTEMMA *Swartzii*, Less.—DC. Prod. v. 5. p. 110.—Folia inferiora sæpe semi-pedalia, 4-5-poll. lata.—Salango.

407. STEVIA *elliptica*, Hook. et Arn. Bot. Beech. p. 434. (sp. n.)—Tepic, Acapulco.

408. STEVIA *Hænkeana*, DC.? Prod. v. 5. p. 122. var.? inflorescentia laxiore, pappo longiore 10-12-aristato; an *S. suboctoaristata*, Lag.?—Huamantango.

409. DECACHÆTA *Hænkeana*, DC. Prod. v. 5. p. 133.—Tepic.

410. HEBECLINIUM *tepicanum*, Hook. et Arn. Bot. Beech. p. 434. (sp. n.)—Tepic.

411. EUPATORIUM *sericeum*, Humb. et Kunth?—DC.? Prod. v. 5. p. 142.—Leaves smaller, and fewer florets in each head than as described by Kunth, but the specimen, which is young, and scarcely yet in flower, agrees in other respects.—Puna, near Guayaquil.

412. EUPATORIUM *odoratum*, Linn.—DC. Prod. v. 5. p. 143.—Columbia.—Also a variety with elongated involucres, and whitish, almost shining scales, from Central America.

413. EUPATORIUM *conysoides*, Vahl.—DC. Prod. v. 5. p. 143.—San Blas, Nicoya, Gulf of Fonseca.

414. EUPATORIUM *ovaliflorum*, Hook. et Arn. Bot. Beech. p. 297.—Tepic.

415. EUPATORIUM (Imbricata) *compactum*, sp. n., fruticosum, ramis obtuse hexagonis superne viscido-puberulis glabratisve, foliis oppositis petiolatis ovato vel oblongo-lanceolatis acutis vix crenulatis basi rotundatis coriaceis supra bullato-rugosis glabris subtus dense cano-tomentosis, corymbo compacto foliis breviore, capitulis circa 35-floris, involucri ovati squamis pluriseriatim imbricatis laxis acutis ciliolatis extus glutinosis vix puberis.—Huamantango.

Pluribus notis cum *E. discolori* convenit, sed folia valde rugosa, et flores in capitulo numerosiores; affine etiam *E. salviæfolio*, sed folia in hoc argute serrato-dentata, et flores infra 30. Folia in specimine 4 poll. longa, 1½ poll. lata, juniora margine revoluta, adulta versus apicem minute crenulata vel subintegerrima, more *E. glutinosi* penninervia reticulato-venosa et bullato-rugosa, basi tamen nec cordata ut in *E. glutinoso* nec angustata ut in *E. discolori;* tomentum paginæ inferioris densum, sordide albidum. Petioli 3-4 lin. longi. Corymbus subsessilis, 2½ poll. diametro, ramis infimis oppositis, cæteris alternis, ultimis pedicellisque brevissimis. Bracteæ ad ramificationes lineari-lanceolatæ, parvæ. Capitula circa 5 lin. longa. Squamæ seriebus circa 7 imbricatæ, laxiusculæ, omnes acutæ, margine scarioso-ciliolatæ, dorso glutinosæ, exteriores breves ovatæ, interiores elongatæ lineares. Corollæ (in specimine vix apertæ) involucrum æquantes, basi parum attenuatæ, iis *E. glutinosi* similes.

416. EUPATORIUM (Imbricata) *Barclayanum*, sp. n., fruticosum? glabrum, ramis obtuse sexangularibus, foliis oppositis subpetiolatis ovatis vel ovato-oblongis obtusissimis integerrimis vel obscure calloso-denticulatis basi rotundatis rigidis reticulatis subtus punctulatis, paniculæ subcorymbosæ ramis oppositis, capitulis subsessilibus circa 35-floris, involucri squamis 3-4-seriatis imbricatis linearibus striatulis plerisque acutis ciliatis dorso-puberulis.—Isle of Taboga, Bay of Panama.

Plura cum diagnosi *E. dodoneæfoliæ* DC. conveniunt. Ramus adest rigidus, sesquipedalis, simplex, in siccitate leviter scaber, in vivo verisimiliter viscosus. Internodia foliis longiora. Petioli 1-2 lin. longi, semi-amplexicaules. Folia 2-2½ poll. longa, 12-15 lin. lata, subcoriacea, penninervia, nervis reteque venarum subtus prominentibus, punctæ glandulosæ parvæ in pagina inferiore sparsæ. Paniculæ rami omnes oppositi, infimi per paria distantes, apice dense corymbosi, oligocephali; superiores in corymbum dispositi; bracteæ ad ramificationes parvæ. Capitula subsessilia, ovoidea, 3 lin. longa, squamellis in pedicello brevi paucis parvis suffulta. Squamæ striatæ, puberulæ, margine præsertim interiores subscariosæ, omnes acutæ vel præsertim intermediæ obtusiusculæ, exteriores brevissimæ, interiores flores subæquantes. Corollæ tenues in faucem paullo ampliatæ. Stylus basi leviter bulbosus, at glaber nec ut in *Brickelliis* pilosus, rami elongati, obtusi, non clavati. Achænia (immatura) ad angulos ciliata.

417. EUPATORIUM *Neæanum*, DC. Prod. v. 5. p. 160.—San Blas and Tepic.

418. EUPATORIUM *Schiedeanum*, DC. Prod. v. 5. p. 159.—*E. multinervium*, Benth. Pl. Hartw. p. 76.—Species valde variabilis cui etiam verosimiliter referendum, *E. ageratifolium*, var. β. *Texense*, Torr. et Gr. Fl. N. Amer. v. 2. p. 90.—Realejo.

419. EUPATORIUM *paniculatum*, Schrad.—DC. Prod. v. 5. p. 167.—Nicoya, Gulf of Fonseca.

420. EUPATORIUM (Subimbricata) *dissectum*, sp. n., herbaceum, caule gracili dichotomo pubescente, foliis oppositis bi-tri-pinnatim sectis, segmentis parvis ovato-lanceolatis acutis incisis membranaceis, pedunculis monocephalis elongatis terminalibus vel in dichotomiis geminis, capitulis multifloris, involucri squamis pauciseriatis angustis acutissimis glabris.—*Phania? dissecta*, Hook. et Arn. Bot. Beech. p. 434.—Acapulco.

The true *Phania* of De Candolle, admirably figured in the 4th vol. of Delessert's Icones, is a very different plant from the present one, partaking, perhaps, rather more of the character of the *Senecionideæ Helenieæ* than of the *Eupatoriaceæ*. I have already suggested (above, p. 21.) that the *Phania urenæfolia*, Hook. et Arn., belongs probably to the new genus which I have there described as *Helogyne*, a name which had however been already taken up by Nuttall for a very different plant, and which must now therefore be altered, as has most probably been done by Endlicher, in the Fourth Supplement to his Genera now in the press. The present plant, referred by Hooker and Arnott with doubt to *Phania*, appears to me to have all the characters of *Eupatorium*, having the involucre, receptacle, flowers, and achænia of many of the section *subimbricata*. The hairs of the pappus are, it is true, rather fewer and more rigid than is usual in that genus, but yet they are not definite in number as in *Ageratum* and *Stevia*. There are also several instances of dissected leaves in *Eupatorium*.

421. MIKANIA *Guaco*, Humb. et Bonpl.—DC. Prod. v. 5. p. 193.—Isthmus of Darien.

422. MIKANIA *tamoides*, DC. Prod. v. 5. p. 197 ?—Perfectly smooth, with small dense corymbs, as described by De Candolle, but the leaves not so acuminate. It is, however, very difficult to ascertain the limits of the species in this group.—Central America.

423. MIKANIA *gonoclada*, DC. Prod. v. 5. p. 199.—Columbia.

424. MIKANIA *angularis*, Humb. et Kunth.—DC. Prod. v. 5. p. 202.—Tumaco.

425. TRIPOLIUM *subulatum*, Nees.—DC. Prod. v. 5. p. 254.—This is the small-flowered form, probably the same as the one described by Lessing, from the Sandwich Islands, and, perhaps, different from the *Aster divaricatus*, Torr. et Gr. Fl. N. Amer. 2. p. 163; but it would be difficult

to clear up the confusion which prevails over this species and its allies, without good sets of specimens from various localities.—Peyta, in Columbia.

426. ERIGERON *velutipes*, Hook. et Arn. Bot. Beech. p. 434. (sp. n.)—San Blas to Tepic.

427. CONYSA *apurensis*, Humb. et Kunth.—DC. Prod. v. 5. p. 380. var. hispidior, foliis majoribus, inferioribus longe petiolatis obovatis grosse dentatis, cætera omnia uti a Kunthio descripta.—Central America.

428. BACCHARIS *rhexioides*, Humb. et Kunth.—DC. Prod. v. 5. p. 399.—Answers well to De Candolle's character, and to Kunth's description, and agrees with specimens from other parts of South America, but very unlike any *Rhexia* I am acquainted with.—Columbia.

429. BACCHARIS *cinerea*, DC. Prod. v. 5. p. 400.—The specimens (both male and female) are more rigid, and the heads of flowers more numerous and crowded than is usual in Brasilian ones, but I cannot perceive any specific difference.—Guayaquil.

430. BACCHARIS *spartea*, sp. n., suffruticosa? glabra, ramis virgatis striatis, foliis subsessilibus oblongo-linearibus obtusis mucronulatis integerrimis subtrinervibus, capitulis fœmineis multifloris ad apices ramulorum paniculæ pyramidatæ foliosæ sessilibus, involucri campanulati squamis margine scarioso-fimbriatis, exterioribus ovatis obtusis, interioribus oblongis acutiusculis, receptaculo paleato.—Huamantango.

Specimina quæ adsunt omnia fœminea. Ramuli (vel caules?) parum ramosi, sesquipedales, paucifoliati, iis *Genistæ tinctoriæ* subsimiles, superne subviscosi. Folia sparsa, majora pollicem longa, 1½-2 lin. lata, apice rotundata, mucronulo minuto, basi angustata et nonnulla subpetiolata, subcoriacea, utrinque viridia, costa media subtus prominula, lateralibus utrinque sæpius obscuris, venis vix conspicuis; folia floralia in panicula caulinis subconformia at multo minora. Panicula pyramidata vel subcorymbosa, vix semipedalis, polycephala. Capitula ad apices ramulorum 2-6, congesta, vix 2⅓ lin. longa. Involucri squamæ pluriseriatim imbricatæ, exteriores breves latæ appressæ, interiores gradatim longiores, seriei intimæ apice patentes, omnes margine scariosæ, medio dorso virides. Receptaculum planum. Paleæ deciduæ, angustæ, scariosæ, pappo paullo breviores. Flores numerosi (ultra 30). Corollæ filiformes, truncatæ, pappo breviores. Styli rami angusti, acuti, planiusculi. Ovarium glabrum. Achænia non vidi.

The *Baccharides* with paleate receptacles have been generally distinguished, by C. H. Schultz, under the name of *Achyrobaccharis*, but, as far as hitherto known, this character appears much too indefinite, and too little accompanied by any other difference to warrant the separation.

431. ECLIPTA *erecta*, Linn.—DC. Prod. v. 5. p. 490.—Guayaquil.

432. CLIBADIUM *acuminatum*, sp. n., scabro-pubescens, foliis petiolatis ovatis longe acuminatis duplicato-serratis basi cuneatis subtriplinervibus, panicula subcorymbosa, capitulis ovatis, floribus fœmineis circa 5 biserialibus, achæniis vix apice minute puberulis, masculis circa 3, ovarii rudimento apice piloso.—Cocos Island.

Rami subteretes, minute scabro-pubescentes. Folia 6 poll. longa, 3 poll. lata, petiolo 1-1½-pollicari, utrinque pilis minutis scaberrima, penninervia, sed nervi 2 cæteris sæpius validiores. Panicula laxa, ramis divaricatis. Capitula in genere parva, vix 2 lin. longa, extus minute scabro-puberula. Squamæ lato-ovatæ, concavæ, striatæ, valde imbricatæ, exteriores 2-3 steriles, interiores 5 paleæformes, latæ, biseriales, flores fœmineos in axillis foventes. Flores fœminei vix paleas superantes; ovarium obovato-compressum, apice minute glanduloso-puberulum; corolla tubulosa, extus glandulosa, inæqualiter tridentata; styli rami glabri, obtusiusculi, recurvi; achænia matura late obovata, obcompressa, apice vix minute puberula, calva. Flores masculi 3-4, in disco epaleaceo sessiles; ovarium breve, abortiens, apice longiuscule villosum, corolla extus glandulosa, tubo brevissimo, fauce ampla tubuloso-campanulata quinquedentata; filamenta complanata; antheræ subliberæ, basi brevissime sagittatæ, apice ovato-appendiculatæ; stylus simplex, puberulus.

This answers to De Candolle's short character of *C. havaneuse*, as to the foliage, but the female flowers, few as they are, are certainly not in a single row, and the achænia are not villous.

433. BALTIMORA *recta*, Linn.—*Fougerouxia recta*, DC. Prod. v. 5. p. 510.—Central America.

434. MELAMPODIUM *tenellum*, Hook. et Arn. Bot. Beech. p. 299. — Acapulco.—Ejusdem var. *flaccidum*, caule elongato foliisque majoribus vix strigillosis.—Tepic.

435. AMBROSIA *artemisiæfolia*, Linn.—DC. Prod. v. 5. p. 526.—Guayaquil.

436. ZINNIA *angustifolia*, Humb. et Kunth.—DC. Prod. v. 5. p. 536.—Tepic, Realejo.

437. WEDELIA *paludosa*, DC. Prod. v. 5. p. 538.—Mundiche, in Columbia, Guayaquil.—A very variable plant in the form of its leaves.

438. WEDELIA *populifolia*, Hook. et Arn. Bot. Beech. p. 435. (sp. n.)—Realejo.

439. WEDELIA *acapulcensis*, Humb. et Kunth.—DC. Prod. v. 5. p. 542.—Columbia.

440. WEDELIA *grandiflora*, sp. n., caule herbaceo? elato pilis longis hispido, foliis petiolatis ovatis acuminatis serrato-crenatis triplinervibus supra hispido-scabris subtus pubescenti-pilosis, pedunculis terminalibus solitariis, involucri squamis exterioribus late ovatis acuminatis foliaceis hispidis, interioribus late oblongis membranaceis, ligulis 12-15 bidentatis, achæniis subtetragono-compressis angulis 2 acutissimis apice emarginatis calyculatis.—Guayaquil.

Ramuli herbacei, 1-1½-pedales, pilis longis albis mollibus præsertim apice hirsuti. Folia pleraque 3 poll. longa, 2 poll. lata, helianthoidea, basi truncato-cuneata et in petiolum brevem alatum decurrentia. Pedunculi in dichotomiis et apicibus ramorum 2-3-pollicares, pilosi. Capitulum hemisphæricum, quam in *W. helianthoidi* majus. Involucri squamæ exteriores 5, semipollicem longæ, interiores iis subæquilongæ, paucæ, fere scariosæ. Ligulæ 9-10 lin. longæ, bidentatæ, tubo brevi; styli rami subulati. Flores disci numerosi; antheræ exsertæ; stylus inclusus, ramis appendice subulato hirsuto terminatis.—Ejusdem var.? *macrophylla*, in eodem loco lecta, caule foliisque supra hispidis, capitulis paullo minoribus, involucri squamis exterioribus angustioribus. An species propria?

441. WEDELIÆ, sp. *W. helianthoidi* subsimilis.—Peyta, in Columbia.—The specimens too young to determine.

442. WEDELIÆ? v. VIGUIERÆ? sp.—Cocos Island.—The specimens in too imperfect a state to determine.

443. WEDELIA? *strigosa*, Hook. et Arn. Bot. Beech. p. 435. (sp. n.)—Acapulco.

444. WEDELIA? *cordata*, Hook. et Arn. l. c. (sp. n.)—Realejo.

445. WEDELIA? *subflexuosa*, Hook. et Arn. l. c. (sp. n.)—Realejo.

The plants belonging to the *Helianthoid* genera with a calyculate pappus are very difficult to determine; the distinction between the female rays of *Wedelia*, and the neuter ones of *Gymnopsis, Anomostephium, Viguiera*, &c., is perhaps not constant in some species, nor ever very consonant with habit. Thus the three last-mentioned species, published by Hooker and Arnott as *Wedeliæ*, appear to me to have the ray always neutral or sterile. The achænia of *W. strigosa* are not yet ripe, but seem to refer the plant either to *Oyedæa* or to the section of *Viguiera* with a nearly flat receptacle (very different in habit from the *Viguieræ* with a conical receptacle); the *W. subflexuosa* has the habit as well as the achænium and pappus of *Gymnopsis rudbeckioides*, DC.; and the *W. cordata* is also very near that plant, but the specimens are too young to determine accurately.

446. MELANTHERA *deltoidea*, Reichb.—DC. Prod. v. 5. p. 545.—Columbia.

447. MELANTHERA *oxylepis*, DC.? l. c.—Species colore pallido et rete venarum insignis. Variat foliis ovatis integris vel hastato-trilobis.—Realejo, Gulf of Fonseca.

448. GYMNOPSIS (Aldama) *divaricata*, sp. n. herbacea, divaricato-ramosa, strigoso-pubescens, foliis inferioribus oppositis petiolatis ovatis vel ovato-lanceolatis grosse dentatis basi cuneatis 5-nervibus superioribus alternis lanceolatis, involucri squamis uniseriatis ovato-lanceolatis acuminatis foliaceis strigosis, receptaculi paleis achænia glaberrima arcte involventibus obovatis obtusis corrugatis, pappo coroniformi minutissimo.—Gulf of Fonseca.

Herba 1-1½-pedalis, ramis oppositis vel dichotomis, divaricato-adscendentibus. Folia inferiora bipollicaria, superiora minora, subrugosa, viridia, pilis crebris appressis rigidis præsertim subtus canescentia. Flores fere *G. uniserialis*. Involucri squamæ subsemipollicares, laxæ, latitudine variæ. Ligulæ 5-6, ovario parvo nudo, tubo elongato, lamina obovata vel oblonga, obtusa, subintegra, lutea. Paleæ receptaculi virides, villosulæ, demum achænia disci undique involventes et clausæ, achænio arcte appressæ et subcohærentes, basi lateraliter affixæ, nec acuminatæ nec cucullatæ. Flores disci longe tubulosi, hirtelli. Styli rami appendice longa hirtella superati. Achænia obovoideo-pyriformia, apice umbonata. Pappus vix conspicuus, e palea brevissime protrudens.

This species with the *G. dentata*, DC., *G. Schiedeana*, DC., and *G. uniserialis*, Hook., to which it is nearly allied, cannot surely be congeners to the *Gymnoloma* of Humb. and Kunth, with which they have been united under the common name of *Gymnopsis*. The remarkable manner in which the fertile achænia of the disk are enclosed in the paleæ of the receptacle, like those of the ray flowers in *Melampodium*, seems fully to warrant the retaining for them Llave and Lexarsa's generic name, *Aldama*.

449. TITHONIA *angustifolia*, Hook. et Arn. Bot. Beech. p. 435. (sp. n.)—Tepic.

450. TITHONIA *tagetiflora*, Desf.—DC. Prod. v. 5. p. 584.—Realejo, Acapulco.

451. HELIANTHUS *annuus*, Linn.—DC. Prod. v. 5. p. 585.—Isle of Puna, near Guayaquil.

452. BIDENS *tereticaulis*, DC. Prod. v. 5. p. 598, var. foliorum segmentis minus acuminatis, cæterum speciminibus Mexicanis simillima.—Columbia.

453. BIDENS *leucantha*, Willd.—DC. Prod. v. 5. p. 598.—Tepic.

454. BIDENS *hispida*, Humb. et Kunth.—DC. Prod. v. 5. p. 599.—Peyta, in Columbia.

455. COSMOS *caudatus*, Humb. et Kunth.—DC. Prod. v. 5. p. 606.—*Bidens bipinnata*, Hook. et Arn. Bot. Beech. p. 436. non Linn.—Various stations, from Tepic to Guayaquil.

456. COSMOS *carvifolius*, sp. n., glaber, foliis bipinnatipartitis lobis capillaceo-linearibus integerrimis, involucri squamis exterioribus circa 8 lanceolatis acutis quam interiores brevioribus, achæniis glabris lævibus longiuscule rostratis 5-aristatis.—Tepic.

In omnibus cum descriptione Kunthii *C. parviflori* convenit, nisi achæniis longius rostratis ad angulos non scabridis et aristis in omnibus quos vidi capitulis semper quinque nec tres.

457. LIPOCHÆTE *macrocephala*, Hook. et Arn. Bot. Beech. p. 436. (sp. n.)—Acapulco.

458. LIPOCHÆTE *umbellata*, DC. Prod. v. 5. p. 610.—Tepic.

459. DUNANTIA *achyranthes*, DC. Prod. v. 5. p. 627.—Deless. Ic. Sel. v. 4. t. 37.—Gulf of Fonseca.

The style of this plant, very well represented in the figure quoted, as well as that of *Isocarpha oppositifolia*, Br. (which I have above shown to be a congener), and of some other *Senecionidæ*, is, strictly speaking, nearer that of *Vernoniaceæ*, and shows the difficulty of relying on the style alone for the distinction of these tribes. In both tribes the sterile summit of the branches is hispid, and neither club-shaped as in *Eupatoriaceæ*, nor (except in a few *Senecionidæ*) broad or flattened as in *Astereæ*. In *Vernoniaceæ* the hairs usually extend on the outside, much below the end of the stigmatic leaves, and even below the fork of the style, without any sudden difference in the length of the hairs, and the sterile part is always long and pointed; in the greater number of *Senecionidæ*, on the contrary, the branches of the style are usually entirely smooth up to the end of the stigmatic lines, and are there either truncate, with the sterile part reduced to a tuft of hairs, or terminated by a conical or elongated and pointed sterile part, with the hairs at its base longer than the others; but there are many *Vernoniaceæ* where the stigmatic portion of the branches is nearly or even perfectly smooth, and there are several *Senecionidæ*, like *Dunantia*, in which the long hairs at the base of the sterile portion are wanting, and the stigmatic part is not wholly smooth on the outside. In such cases other characters must be resorted to for the distinction of these two large groups, which are, generally speaking, natural, and would be still more so if the opposite-leaved radiate, *Vernoniaceæ* (*Pectideæ* and *Liabeæ*), could be transferred to *Senecionidæ*.

460. SALMEA *angustifolia*, sp. n., foliis oblongo-lanceolatis utrinque angustatis acutis cauleque scaberrimis, corollis rectiusculis, aristis æqualibus.—Mexican coast.

Frutex, ramulis teretibus pube brevi albida scabris. Folia subsessilia, 3 poll. longa, medio 6-9 lin. lata, margine recurva, penninervia, rugosa, utrinque pube brevi scaberrima. Capitula ad apices ramorum pauca, breviter pedunculata, quam in *S. curviflora* paullo majora. Involucri squamæ perpaucæ, ovatæ, breves. Receptaculum elongato-conicum. Paleæ floribus breviores, ovatæ, acuminatæ, complicatæ, crassiusculæ, margine membranaceæ, exteriores apice squarrosæ. Corollæ omnes tubulosæ, tubo brevissimo hispido, fauce elongato vix latiore glabriusculo, limbo 5-dentato. Stamina subinclusa; filamenta complanata; antheræ basi truncatæ, appendice apicis brevi ovata mucronata. Styli rami exserti, complanati, apice subtruncati et cono brevi superati. Achænia lateraliter compressa, obovata, plana, emarginata, ad angulos ciliata et summo apice subalata; aristæ breves, ciliatæ.

461. SYNEDRELLA *nodiflora*, Gærtn.—DC. Prod. v. 5. p. 629.—Panama to Guayaquil.

462. TAGETES *microglossa*, sp. n., erecta, elata, alterne ramosa, foliis inferioribus oppositis superioribus alternis pinnatisectis, segmentis 5-8-jugis lineari-lanceolatis acute serratis, infimis paucis setaceo-divisis, pedunculis elongatis apice incrassatis monocephalis, involucris tubulosis 4-5-dentatis sub-20-floris, ligulis paucis minimis.—Salango.

Affinis *T. glanduliferæ*. Rami elongati, laterales capitula superant. Folia forma fere *T. patulæ*, 2-3-pollicaria; segmenta subdistantia, 6-12 lin. longa, acuta et acute serrata, basi angustata, glandulis sparsis mediocribus; segmenta infima cauli approximata, parva, in lacinias paucas capillaceas fissa. Pedunculi ad apices ramorum pauci, erecti, tripollicares. Capitula per anthesin 5-6 lin. longa; involucra fructifera 7-8 lin. longa, maculis linearibus notata, dentibus obtusiusculis. Achænia nigra. Pappi palearum una flores disci subæquans acutissima, cæteræ connatæ in paleam unicam dimidio breviorem obtusam vel emarginatam.

463. TAGETES *multiseta*, DC. Prod. v. 5. p. 645.—Tepic.

464. POROPHYLLUM *viridiflorum*, DC.? Prod. v. 5. p. 648.—Hook. et Arn. Bot. Beech. p. 436. non Benth. Pl. Hartw. p. 20. (quod species nova est.)—San Blas to Tepic.

465. OXYPAPPUS *scaber*, gen. nov. *Heleniearum*, (Plate XLII.)—*Chrysopsis scabra*, Hook. et Arn. Bot. Beech. p. 434.—San Blas to Tepic.

CHAR. GEN. Capitula heterogama, radiata. Involucri squamæ uniseriales, acutæ, æquales. Receptaculum convexum, nudum. Flores radii pistilligeri (an fertiles?), lamina oblonga tridentata. Flores disci tubulosi, 5-dentati. Styli rami filiformes, acutiusculi, vix hirtelli. Antheræ ecaudatæ. Achænia linearia. Pappi aristæ 3-5, scabrellæ, basi paleaceo-dilatatæ.

O. scabra. Herba annua, erecta, 1-1½-pedalis, basi hispida, superne pube brevi glandulosa scabriuscula. Caulis tenuis, striatus, rigidulus, superne laxe corymbosus, ramis elongatis gracilibus. Folia infima ad basin caulis subrosulata, oblonga, 1½-2-pollicaria, basi angustata, margine grosse dentata vel subintegerrima; caulina remota, inferiora opposita, lanceolata, basi angustata, margine integerrima vel paucidentata vel basi utrinque lobulo lineari aucta; suprema alterna, parva, linearia, obtusa, integerrima. Capitula parvula, in apicibus ramulorum solitaria. Involucrum hemisphæricum, squamis 1¼ lin. longis, dorso viridibus scabro-pubescentibus, margine submembranaceis. Flores subglabri, lutei: radii tubus gracilis, lamina 2 lin. longa; disci involucro vix longiores, basi tenuiter tubulosi, versus medium abrupte dilatati in faucem tubulosam, tubo vero duplo ampliorem, dentibus limbi brevibus. Stamina vix exserta, appendice lanceolata. Styli rami breviter exserti, recurvi. Achænia vix lineam longa, nigri, pilis paucis minutis conspersa. Pappi aristæ achænio sublongiores, æquales, in radio sapius tres, in disco quinque.

Hooker and Arnott, in describing this plant from the present collection as a *Chrysopsis*, expressed, at the same time, their opinion that it would hereafter be found to belong to some other genus; but, although certainly not a *Chrysopsis*, it does not appear to agree with the character of any other known genus, but to form a new one in that group of *Heleniæ* called by Torrey and Gray the *Eugaillardiæ*. The form of the style is not, it is true, decidedly that of either of the four first great divisions of *Compositæ*, for the branches are not so flat as in *Astereæ*, there is no tuft of hairs at the base of the sterile portion as in most *Senecionideæ*, the branches are not obtuse as in *Eupatoriaceæ*, nor so hairy as in *Vernoniaceæ*; we must therefore be guided by the secondary characters derived from the combination of the opposite leaves, yellow flower, paleaceous pappus, &c., in fixing its place amongst *Senecionidæ* of the tribe *Heleniæ*. In this tribe the nearest affinities of *Oxypappus* are on the one hand with *Palafoxia*, on the other with *Hymenoxys*, but it is abundantly distinct from both. I have borrowed the generic name from a sectional one, once proposed by De Candolle for a species of *Hymenoxys*, now unoccupied, as that plant is adopted as a genus (by Fischer and Meyer) under Nuttall's name of *Ptilomeris*.

Plate XLII. fig. 1, head of flowers, vertical section; fig. 2, flower of the ray; fig. 3, flower of the disk; fig. 4, summit of the style; fig. 5, achænium of the ray; fig. 6, achænium of the disk: all magnified.

466. PERITYLE *microglossa*, sp. n., achæniis margine dense ciliatis apice tenuiter biaristatis inter aristas breviter subsquamoso-ciliatis.—Realejo.

Herba habitu *P. californicæ* similis sed robustior; pubes brevior, rarior; folia majora; pedunculi breviores. Ligulæ paucæ, parvæ, obovatæ, orbiculatæ, tricrenatæ. Achænia margine calloso dense ciliato cincta. Pappi aristæ breves, latitudinem achænii vix æquantes; squamellæ intermediæ ciliæformes, vix dilatatæ. Styli rami læviter compressi, acuti, hirtelli.

This second species, nearly allied to the Californian one described and figured above (p. 23, pl. xv.), does not throw any further light on the affinities of the genus. The style (represented in the plate with rather too broad branches) brings it nearer to *Astereæ* than to *Senecionidæ*, but the leaves are opposite and the aspect of the plant not unlike that of *Galinsoga*. It may, therefore, be better placed among the *Euheleniæ* than at the end of *Astereæ*.

467. GALINSOGA (Vargasia) *hispida*, sp. n., herbacea, decumbens, ramosa, piloso-hispida, foliis petiolatis ovatis grosse dentatis 3-5-nerviis, pedunculis in apicibus ramorum paucis brevibus monocephalis, floribus disci pappo duplo longioribus.—Peyta, in Columbia, Guayaquil; gathered also by Cuming at Lima (n. 1028).

Herba rudis, laxe opposite ramosa, 1-1½-pedalis. Pili longi, albi, rigidi, in ramulis junioribus copiosi, in ramis foliisque rariores, sparsi. Folia longiuscule petiolata, 1½-2 poll. longa, 1-1½ poll. lata, breviter et obtuse acuminata, superne grosse et obtuse dentata, basi late cuneata, integerrima, membranacea, nervis primariis prominentibus, rete venarum parum conspicua. Capitula in ramo 3-5, in corymbum foliis breviorem disposita, 2 lin. longa. Pedunculi 2-4 lin. longi, hirsuti, ebracteati. Involucrum campanulatum, squamis 3 vel 4 suborbiculatis striatis glabris vel basi dorso puberulis, adjecta altera exteriore angustiore hirsuta. Receptaculum convexum, paleis exterioribus 6-8 late oblongis per paria cum squamis involucri et achænia radii deciduis, interioribus paucis angustioribus. Flores radii 3 vel 4, inter involucri squamas et paleas exteriores arcte inclusi; tubus tenuis hirsutus; ligula exserta, lata, concava, purpurascens, triloba, lobo medio ovato, lateralibus latissimis valde obliquis. Flores disci involucro æquilongi, tubo brevi hirtello, fauce elongata, limbo 5-dentato. Stamina corollam vix æquantia, non nigricantia, basi brevissime sagittata. Stylus inclusus, ramis inappendiculatis. Achænia radii subcompressa, pappi squamis circa 20 achænio brevioribus linearibus lanceolatis vel oblongis acuminatis ciliato-laceris. Achænia disci obscure angulata, basi attenuata, nigra, pilis paucis brevibus hirtella; pappus illo radii similis, sed e squamellis latioribus constans.

The genus *Vargasia*, DC., with all the habit of the common *Galinsoga*, only differs in the pappus of the ray being reduced to smaller and narrower scales than those of the disk, a distinction so slight as scarcely to warrant the separation, the more so as there is much doubt whether the original *Vargasia caracasana*, DC., is not a mere variety of the common *Galinsoga parviflora*. The plant now described is certainly distinct as to species, and if the supposed generic character be retained as sectional, it would belong to *Vargasia*, but as in *G. parviflora* the breadth of the scales of the pappus is variable. Both sections are remarkable from each achænium of the ray being inclosed between the subtending scale of the involucre, and the two paleæ of the receptacle next above it, which form a kind of envelope, falling off with the achænium at its maturity.

468. TRIDAX *procumbens*, Linn.—DC. Prod. v. 5. p. 679.—Gulf of Fonseca.

469. CALEA *prunifolio*, Humb. et Kunth.—DC. Prod. v. 5. p. 672.—Guayaquil.

470. GNAPHALIUM *luteo-album*, Linn.—DC. Prod. v. 6. p. 230.—Mexican coast.

471. NEUROLÆNA *lobata*, Br.—DC. Prod. v. 6. p. 292.—Various places along the Columbian coast.

472. GYNOXIS *Hænkei*, DC. Prod. v. 6. p. 326.—Panama to Guayaquil.

This plant varies much in pubescence and in the number of flower-heads, some branches of the same specimen being, as well as the leaves, quite smooth, whilst others are more or less downy. The flower-heads are arranged from two to six or eight in axillary or terminal corymbs, they are always much larger than those of *G. cordifolia*, and the teeth of the leaves are much smaller. It is probable that *G. Berlandieri* is a mere form of the same species.

473. GYNOXIS *Sinclairi*, sp. n., suffruticosa, scandens, foliis alternis breviter petiolatis lato-ovatis acutis dentatis basi subcordatis, supra scabrellis, subtus cauleque pubescenti-hirtis, capitulis 3-6 multifloris, involucri squamis interioribus circa 20 discum æquantibus, exterioribus plurimis filiformibus.—Columbia.

Rami angulato-striati pube rufescente demum fere evanida. Folia ramorum primarium 2-3 poll. longa, 2 poll. lata, sæpius grosse dentata, basi auriculis latis rotundatis cordata, supra subbullata, subtus reticulata, pube rufescente; ramulorum floralium minora, angustiora, denticulata, basi rotundata. Corymbi axillares vel terminales, laxe 3-6-cephali. Pedunculi 1-1½-pollicares, bracteolis setaceis onusti. Involucra 4 lin. longa, squamis linearibus acuminatissimis dorso scabro-puberulis, exterioribus sæpius numerosis setaceis. Ligulæ circa 15, vix 3 lin. longæ. Styli rami appendice acutissima superati. Achænia compressiuscula, præsertim ad margines puberulo-hirta, apice in discum expansa.

474. GYNOXYS *scabra*, sp. n., scandens, foliis alternis petiolatis late ovatis acuminatis subdentatis basi cordatis utrinque cauleque scabro-hirtis, capitulis numerosis multifloris in paniculas axillares ovatas confertis, involucri campanulati squamis circa 15, accessoriis perpaucis.—Guayaquil.

Rami tenuiter striati. Folia 2-3 poll. longa, 1½-2 poll. lata, subbullata, utrinque præsertim in pagina inferiore scabra, margine irregulariter plus minus denticulata. Paniculæ densæ vix folio longiores. Capitula magnitudine *G. cordifoliæ* vel paullo minora, pedicellis brevissimis. Involucri squamæ 3 lin. longæ, dorso scabræ, apice uncinato-acuminatæ, disco paullo breviores. Ligulæ 12-15, 3 lin. longæ. Styli rami appendice acutissima superati. Ovaria glabriuscula, apice in discum expansa. Achænia non vidi.

475. CACALIA *cirsiifolia*, Hook. et Arn. Bot. Beech. p. 436. (sp. n.)—Achænia angulata, pubescentia.—Tepic.

476. CIRSIUM *cernuum*, Lag. ?—DC. Prod. v. 6. p. 639.—Hook. et Arn. Bot. Beech. p. 437.—The external scales are ciliate with prickles, not entire as they are described by De Candolle, and as they really appear to be in Vera Cruz specimens. It was upon this ground chiefly that I formerly considered the present plant as a distinct species which I described as *C. heterolepis*, (Pl. Hartw. p. 87); but I doubt much whether it be not a mere variety of *C. cernuum*.—Tepic.

477. LYCOSERIS (Diazeuxis) *latifolia*, (*Diazeuxis latifolia*, Don.—DC. Prod. v. 7. p. 22.—Less. Syn. Comp. p. 97) ramis striatis arachnoideo-lanatis mox glabratis, foliis late lanceolatis triplinervibus supra glabris subtus niveo-lanatis, involucris glabris vel vix arachnoideo-lanatis, squamis appressis vel exterioribus vix patentibus acutis, pappi setis 20-30.—Realejo, Isle of Taboga, Bay of Panama; gathered also by Cuming, near Panama (n. 1161).

The plants retained by De Candolle and Lessing in *Lycoseris*, are now ascertained to be usually, if not always, diœcious; there remains therefore no character to distinguish *Diazeuxis* but the venation of the leaves, the habit being the same in both, and they should therefore only be considered as sections. The flower-heads in this the most common species are considerably larger than in the two following.

478. LYCOSERIS (Diazeuxis) *bracteata*, sp. n., ramis striatis arachnoideo-lanatis mox glabratis, foliis lato-lanceolatis tri-quintuplinervibus supra glabris subtus niveo-tomentosis, involucris lanatis, squamis appressis lanceolatis longe acuminatis, pappo 10-15-seto.—Guayaquil.

Habitus et folia *L. latifoliæ*. Capitula (mascula) minora, radio incluso pollicem diametro, bractea foliacea sæpissime suffulta. Involucri squamæ angustiores, longius acuminatæ, exteriores radium brevem subæquantes. Corollæ *L. latifoliæ*. Pappi paleæ setiformes, parum inæquales, majores leviter complanatæ, minute serrulato-hirtæ, apice acutæ non penicillatæ. Capitula fœminea non visa.

479. LYCOSERIS (Diazeuxis) *squarrosa*, sp. n., ramis striatis subnudis, foliis lato-lanceolatis, 3-5-plinervibus supra glabris subtus tenuiter albo-lanatis viridibusque, involucris glabris squamis

lanceolatis exterioribus reflexo-patentibus, pappo multipaleaceo. — Nicoya, Gulf of Fonseca, Panama.

Folia quam in *L. latifolia* tenuiora, minus lanata, longius acuminata, pariter integerrima vel denticulis distantibus notata. Capitula speciosa, late campanulata, mascula absque radio pollicem diametro, ligulis numerosis fere 5 lin. longis. Involucrum viride squamis fere omnibus apice patentibus vel reflexis. Flores cæterum *L. latifoliæ*. Ligulæ minute 2-3-dentatæ. Pappi paleæ setiformes, parum inæquales, majores subcomplanatæ, apice omnes acutiusculæ nec penicillatæ. Capitula fœminea non visa.

480. ACOURTIA *formosa*, Don.—DC. Prod. v. 7. p. 66.—Hook. et Arn. Bot. Beech. p. 437.—*Trixis latifolia*, Hook. et Arn. l. c. p. 300.—Acapulco.

481. ACOURTIÆ, sp.?—*Cacalia sessilifolia*, Hook. et Arn. Bot. Beech. p. 436.—The anthers have certainly short tails, and the lobes of the corolla are revolute and apparently bilabiate. The habit combined with these characters show that the plant is allied to *Acourtia* or *Trixis*, but the flowers are so much injured by insects that I am unable to ascertain the genus with accuracy.—Tepic.

482. TRIXIS *frutescens*, Br.—DC. Prod. v. 7. p. 68.—Tepic, Gulf of Fonseca.

483. TRIXIS *obvallata*, Hook. et Arn. Bot. Beech. p. 300. t. 65.—Acapulco.

484. PICROSIA *longifolia*, Don.—DC. Prod. v. 7. p. 251.—Pappus sordidus. — Peyta in Columbia, Guayaquil.

LOBELIACEÆ.

485. CENTROPOGON *Surinamensis*, Presl.—A. DC. Prod. v. 7. p. 345.—Columbia.

486. LOBELIA *laxiflora*, Humb. et Kunth.—A. DC. Prod. v. 7. p. 383.—Realejo.

To this belong *L. lanceolata* and *L. angulato-dentata*, Hook. et Arn. Bot. Beech. p. 301. *L. ovalifolia*, Hook. et Arn. l. c. p. 300, is intermediate between the above forms (all broad leaved), and *L. rigidula*, Humb. et Kunth, which in the *Prodromus* has been considered (and probably with good reason) to belong to the same species, although with some hesitation, as it is given both as a synonym to *L. laxiflora*, and as a substantive species. The narrow-leaved variety, which is the *Siphocampylus bicolor* of our gardens, is in this respect constant, but still probably a mere variety of a very variable plant.

ERICACEÆ.

487. GAULTHERIA *odorata*, Humb. et Kunth., β. *mexicana*, DC. Prod. v. 7. p. 595.—Realejo.

Myrsineae.

488. Myrsine *erythroxyloides*, sp. n., foliis petiolatis oblongo-ellipticis integerrimis obtusis basi cuneatis coriaceis glabris margine subrecurvis, paniculis 6-12-floris, pedicellis flore multo longioribus, calycis laciniis subciliatis, corollæ lobis valvatis calyce dimidio longioribus.—Huamantango.

Ramuli juniores angulati, demum teretes. Folia 2-3 poll. longa, 12-15 lin. lata, supra venulis crebris tenuiter percursa, subtus in sicco rufescentia sed glabra, punctis minutis nigris obscuris paucis non pellucidis; petioli 4-5 lin. longi. Fasciculi florum ad apicem stipitis crassi bracteis ovatis imbricatis obtecti subumbellati. Pedicelli 2-3 lin. longi; flores vix lineam longi. Calycis lobi acutiusculi, glanduloso-maculati. Corolla profunde 5-fida, laciniis oblongis crassiusculis. Stamina corolla breviora; filamenta complanata; antheræ filamento paullo longiores, oblongæ. Stylus brevis, pulviniformis, apice breviter sublobatus (fere undique stigmatosus?). Ovula 3 vel 4.

489. Ardisia *cuspidata*, sp. n., foliis obovato-oblongis abrupte acuminatis integerrimis basi angustatis utrinque glabris, panicula terminali pyramidata glabra, pedicellis fructu longioribus, calycis laciniis ovatis.—Cocos Island.

Specimina fructifera omnino glabra excepta pube tenuissima parca rufescente ad apices ramulorum inque gemma terminali. Petioli 2-3-lineares. Folia circa 3 poll. longa, 1-1½ poll. lata, acumine 3-6 lin. longo obtuso vel acutiusculo terminata, margine interdum obscure undulata, subtus punctis parvis nigris non pellucidis conspersa. Panicula bipollicaris, supra folium supremum fere sessilis, glaberrim; aramuli divaricati apice breviter racemiferi. Pedicelli 2 lin. longi. Calycis segmenta 5, obtusiuscula, glanduloso-maculata. Bacca parva (vix 1½ lin. diametro) globosa, undique in sicco corrugata, glandulosa. Stylus subulatus, acutus.

490. Jacquinia *armillaris*, Jacq.—A. DC. Prod. v. 8. p. 149.—Nicoya.

491. Jacquinia *pubescens*, Kunth.—A. DC. Prod. v. 8. p. 150.—Guayaquil.

492. Jacquinia *macrocarpa*, Cav.—A. DC. Prod. v. 8. p. 150.—Acapulco.

Sapotaceae.

493. Chrysophyllum *Cainito*, Linn.—A. DC. Prod. v. 8. p. 157.—Isle of Taboga, Bay of Panama.

Oleaceae.*

494. Linociera *compacta*, Br.—DC. Prod. v. 8. p. 296.—Isle of Gorgona.

---

* There are two *Jasmineæ* in the collection, *Jasminum Sambac* and *J. grandiflorum*, but evidently both of them cultivated.

Apocynaceae.

495. Thevetia *neriifolia*, Juss.—A. DC. Prod. v. 8. p. 343.—Acapulco; Isle of Taboga, Bay of Panama.

496. Thevetia *plumeriæfolia*, sp. n., (Plate XLIII.) glaberrima, foliis obovali-vel cuneato-oblongis brevissime acuminatis basi angustatis, venis transversalibus costæ perpendicularibus prominulis, cymis folio brevioribus paucifloris, bracteis sepalisque ovatis acutis tubo corollæ plus duplo brevioribus.—Gulf of Fonseca.

Ramuli crassiusculi, teretes, uti tota planta glaberrimi, cicatricibus foliorum delapsorum parvis basi notati. Folia alterna vel sparsa, vix semipedalia, sesquipollicem lata, apice rotundata cum acumine brevissimo vel obsoleto, basi longiuscule angustata in petiolum tenuem 6-8 lin. longum, supra nitidula, subtus pallida; costa media subtus valde prominens, venæ primariæ numerosæ, parallelæ, apice in nervum submarginalem conniventes. Gemmulæ in axillis parvæ, squamæformes, ciliato-laceræ. Ramuli floriferi (in speciminibus) apice bifurcati, cyma in bifurcatione dichotoma, 5-6-flora, pedunculo communi angulato 6 lin. longo, pedicellis 6-18 lin. longis. Bracteæ crassiusculæ ad ramificationes et sub pedicellis 2-3 lin. longæ, undulatæ. Calyx 5-partitus, segmentis ovatis 4-5 lin. longis undulatis verruculosis at glabris, basi intus multiglandulosis. Corollæ tubus fere pollicaris, medio parum attenuatus, apice leviter campanulato-dilatatus, limbi lobi ampli, æstivatione sinistrorsum contorti, tubo longiores, extus intusque uti tubus glaberrimi. Squamæ ad faucem parvæ, villosissimæ. Filamenta supra medium tubi inserta, brevia, complanata, pilis rigidulis hyalinis reflexo-patentibus densissime hispida. Antheræ lanceolatæ, connectivo acuto acuminatæ, loculis basi obtusis. Nectarium ovario longius, crassum, obtusum, apice obtuse 5-lobum, lobis cum calycis segmentis alternantibus. Ovarium bilobum, lobis singulis unilocularibus, ovulis in loculo binis superpositis. Stylus apice in discum annulatum dilatatus, sub disco lobis 5 parvis lanceolatis acutis erectis auctus, stigmate in medio disco conico bilobo.

Plate XLIII. Fig. 1, Calyx with the calycine glands and nectary; Fig. 2,* portion of the corolla, cut open, showing the stamens; Fig. 3, stamen, front view; Fig. 4, stamen and scale, side view; Fig. 5, section of the ovary; Fig. 6, style; all more or less magnified.

497. Vallesia *dichotoma*, Ruiz. et Pav.—A. DC. Prod. v. 8. p. 349.—Punta Santa Elena in Columbia.

The Californian plant referred to above, p. 33, as the *V. dichotoma*, is the *V. glabra*, Cav., but, as well as the *V. chiococcoides*, appears to me to be but a variety of *V. dichotoma*, which I have also from South Brazil, and often assumes in South America the form described by Cavanilles. The radicle is certainly inferior, as described by Kunth.

498. Stemmadenia *glabra*, gen. nov., (Plate XLIV.) glaberrima, foliis subsessilibus obovatis breviter acuminatis basi obtusis, corollæ tubo calyce paullo longiore.—Gulf of Fonseca.

Char. Gen. Calyx 5-partitus, segmentis valde imbricatis, interioribus obovatis, exterioribus ovatis brevioribus bracteis 2 consimilibus minoribus suffultis. Glandulæ numerosissimæ, intra calycem verticillatæ. Corolla ampla, infundibuliformi-campanulata, laciniis sinistrorsum contortis; faux plicis 5 longitudinalibus aucta. Stamina tubo inserta; filamenta brevia, crassiuscula; antheræ

---

* The corolla was, by mistake, omitted to be reversed on the stone, and appears in the plate twisted from left to right, instead of from right to left.

sagittatæ, acutæ, circa stigma arcte conniventes. Nectarium breve crassiusculum (5-lobum?). Ovaria 2, distincta. Placentæ in quoque loculo duæ, suturæ utrinque affixæ. Ovula numerosissima, amphitropa. Stylus apice appendice umbraculiformi reflexo lobato coronatus, stigmate pulvinato breviter bilobo. Frutices vel arbores, ramulis apice bifurcatis vel dichotomis. Folia opposita. Racemi breves, pauciflori, in bifurcatione ramulorum vel in axillis superioribus solitarii. Corollæ magnæ, speciosæ, albæ vel flavæ. Genus *Odontadeniæ* affine.

S. glabra. Rami juniores compressi, mox teretes, apice bifurcati. Folia 5-6 poll. longa, 2½-3 poll. lata, acumine brevi acutiusculo terminata, basi obtusa, membranacea, utrinque viridia, subtus pallidiora, costa media venisque primariis utrinsecus 12-16 subtus prominulis, eglandulosa, petiolis 2-4 lin. longis margine angusta subconnexis. Racemi in bifurcatione ramorum foliis breviores 3-5-flori. Pedicelli inferiores 4-6 lin. longi, superiores brevissimi, singuli bractea minuta squamæformi subtensi. Bracteæ 2 et sepala 5 gradatim accrescentia a bractea exteriore subfoliacea appressa vix 3 lin. longa, in sepala interiora 2 vel 3 subæqualia, valde imbricata, fere pollicaria, apice obtusa truncata membranacea. Corollæ sub-3-pollicares, extra calycem in faucem ample campanulatam dilatata, lobis latis rotundatis. Glandulæ calycis ultra 100, breves, lineares in verticillum densum circa corollam dispositæ. Nectarium breve, annulare, uti in speciebus sequentibus lobatum videtur, lobis brevibus latis (3 vel 5?). Ovaria a basi distincta.

Plate XLIV. fig. 1, corolla cut open; fig. 2, anther; fig. 3, pistil; fig. 4, ovary, vertical section; fig. 5, ovary, transverse section.

499. STEMMADENIA *pubescens*, sp. n., foliis brevissime petiolatis obovatis breviter acuminatis supra glabris subtus ad venas pubescenti-hirtis, corollæ tubo calyce paullo longiore.—*Bignonia? obovata,* Hook. et Arn. Bot. Beech. p. 439.*—Realejo.

Vix differt a *S. glabra* nisi pube in pagina inferiore præsertim ad venas copiosa e pilis brevibus simplicibus erectis composita. Folia etiam subpetiolata et corollæ paullo minores videntur.

500. STEMMADENIA *mollis*, sp. n., foliis brevissime petiolatis obovato-oblongis basi angustatis supra puberulis subtus inflorescentiaque molliter tomentoso-pubescentibus, corollæ tubo longiuscule exserto.—Guayaquil.

Rami teretes, dichotomi, ramulis junioribus angulatis pubescentibus. Folia 4-5 poll. longa, 1½-2 poll. lata. Racemi foliis subbreviores, oppositi. Calyx *S. obovatæ,* sed segmenta exteriora et bracteæ extus pubescentia. Corolla tripollicaris vel longior, tubo quam in præcedentibus longiore et minus abrupte ampliato. Glandulæ, nectarium et ovarium omnino *S. glabræ.*

The size and form of the flowers in the above three species are those of a *Cerbera* or a *Thevetia*, from both of which, however, they widely differ in the calycine glands, and from the latter in the ovary; in many points also there is a considerable degree of affinity with *Odontadenia*, but that genus again has not the remarkable calyx and glands of *Stemmadenia*. A fourth species of the genus allied to *S. mollis*, with the same structure and pubescence, but longer petioles, and some other points of difference, has been gathered by Galeotti (n. 1632), and

---

* A portion of the seed vessel and seeds of a *Pithecoctenium*, probably *P. muricatum*, had been by mistake laid by Dr. Sinclair into the same sheet with the specimens of this plant, and had misled the authors of the Botany of Captain Beechey's voyage and induced them to refer the plant doubtfully to *Bignonia*.

Linden (n. 385), near Vera Cruz, and is said to have yellow flowers. Linden's n. 330 from Teapa in South Mexico with white flowers appears to be a sixth species quite smooth with a very long tube to the corolla, but I have not had an opportunity of examining its structure.

501. PLUMERIA *rubra*, Linn.—A. DC. Prod. v. 8. p. 390.—Guayaquil.

502. VINCA *rosea*, Linn.—A. DC. Prod. v. 8. p. 382.—Realejo.

503. HÆMADICTYON *tomentellum*, sp. n., foliis ovato-oblongis brevissime acuminatis basi cordatis supra glabris vel minute hirtellis subtus brevissime et molliter glaucescenti-tomentosis, lobis calycinis lanceolatis acuminatis vix basi hirtellis corollæ tubo 2-3-plo brevioribus, corollæ fauce annulari, appendicibus tubi antherisque vix exsertis.—Guayaquil, gathered also by Hartweg, n. 670.

Rami volubiles, angulati, glabri vel brevissime glauco-tomentelli. Folia breviter petiolata, 2-3-pollicaria, supra pilis brevissimis sparsis scabrella, subtus tomento molli et denso etsi brevissimo obtecta, penninervia, venis lateralibus parum conspicuis. Racemi axillares, folio breviores. Pedunculi vix petiolo longiores, angulati, minute hirtelli. Flores conferti, pedicellis calyce brevioribus. Calyces 5-6 lin. longi, laciniis inæqualibus acuminatis, basi interne glandula brevi lata auctis. Corollæ tubus pollicaris, superne constrictior, limbi laciniæ amplæ patentes; corona faucis callosa, latiuscula; appendices lineari-lanceolatæ, acutæ, extra faucem brevissime prominulæ. Stamina medio tubo inserta; filamenta filiformia; antheræ connatæ, sagittatæ, basi biaristatæ, apice aristato-acuminatæ, extra faucem brevissime prominulæ. Nectarii squamæ crassæ, latæ, ovatæ, ovario ipso paullo breviores, liberæ sed arcte approximatæ. Stylus filiformis, sub stigmate membrana lobata reflexa indusiatus; stigma obtusum. Folliculi 4-6 poll. longi, conniventes, triquetri, coriacei, extus tomentelli. Semina oblonga, triquetra, apice in collum brevem attenuata, coma longa copiosa. Albumen parcum. Embryo linearis, cotyledonibus oblongis radicula longioribus.

This agrees very nearly with Kunth's description of his *Prestonia glabrata* (*Hæmadictyon glabratum*, A. DC. Prod. v. 8. p. 427) gathered by Humboldt in the same locality, but the leaves are constantly clothed underneath with a close soft down, so that even if it prove to be a mere variety, it cannot well retain the specific name of *glabratum*.

504. ECHITES *biflora*, Jacq.—A. DC. Prod. v. 8. p. 450.—Var. calycis segmentis fere 6 lin. longis.—Salt marshes, Mundiche, Columbia.

505. ECHITES *trifida*, Jacq.—A. DC. Prod. v. 8. p. 454.—Calycis lobi potius ovati quam oblongi, cætera conveniunt.—Tiger Island, Gulf of Fonseca.

506. ECHITES *trifida*, var.? major, caule sub nodiis tenuiter tomentellis.—Central America.

Flos adest unicus, quam in præcedente paullo major. Glandulæ calycis irregulares. Folliculi ultrapedales vix torulosi. Semina anguste fusiformia, coma rufa.

507. ECHITES *hirtiflora*, A. DC. Prod. v. 8. p. 456.—Columbia; gathered also by Hartweg near Guayaquil, n. 669.

Folia breviter petiolata basi profunde auriculato-cordata, juniora supra villosa. Corollæ pilis paucis longiusculis villosæ, uti descriptæ sunt in *E. microcalyce*. Cætera omnia conveniunt.

Asclepiadaceæ.

508. Sarcostemma *cumanense*, Humb. et Kunth.—Dcsne. in DC. Prod. v. 8. p. 539.—Columbia.

509. Sarcostemma *bilobum*, Hook. et Arn. Bot. Beech. p. 438.—This is not taken up by Decaisne, but comes very near to his *S. cynanchoides* (in DC. Prod. v. 8. p. 540), if it be not the same.—Acapulco.

510. Asclepias *curassavica*, Linn.—Dcsne. in DC. Prod. v. 8. p. 566.—*A. incarnata*, Hook. et Arn. Bot. Beech. p. 438. non Linn.—Mexico to Guayaquil.

511. Asclepias *longicornu*, Benth.—Dcsne. in DC. Prod. v. 8. p. 570.—Realejo.

512. Blepharodon *mucronatum*, Dcsne. in DC. Prod. v. 8. p. 603.—Guayaquil.—I can find no difference between these specimens and those from Vera Cruz gathered by Galeotti and Linden and described by Decaisne.

Gentianaceæ.

513. Gyrandra *speciosa*, sp. n., (Plate XLV.), caule diffuso vel adscendente ramosissimo acute tetragono, calycis profunde 5-fidi laciniis tubum corollæ æquantibus superantibusve, corollæ lobis acutiusculis, antheris filamento gracili sublongioribus.—*Erythræa macrantha*, β *major*, Hook. et Arn. Bot. Beech. p. 438.—Tepic.

Planta glaberrima, ut videtur perennis, semipedalis usque ad sesquipedalis, habitu *Chironiæ*. Rami alterni, graciles, angulis fere alatis, apice laxe et dichotome 1-5-flori. Folia 4-8 lin. longa, raro lineam lata, acutissima, margine scabriuscula, basi non angustata, superiora parva setacea. Internodia inferiora semipollicaria, superiora fere pollicaria. Pedicelli ultimi 6-10 longi. Calyx 3 lin. longus, laciniis carinatis angustis acutis vix ad quartam partem connatis. Corollæ (roseæ?) primum florentis tubus laciniis calycinis multo brevior, in corolla emarcida persistente elongatur et lacinias calycinas tandem æquat vel superat, limbus rotatus, 5-partitus, lobis ovato-lanceolatis acutiusculis fere 7 lin. longis, 2½-3 lin. latis. Antheræ luteæ, loculis absque connectivo connatis, demum gyris 4-5 tortæ. Stylus stamina superans; stigma late bilamellatum.

I have had some doubts whether this beautiful plant might not be either identical with, or a slight variety of, the *G. chironioides* described by Grisebach, (DC. Prod. v. 9, p. 44), but that accurate botanist states expressly that the stem is nearly terete, and the anthers shorter than the filaments. The calyx of our plant is usually not divided to the base, and the lobes of the corolla more pointed than described by Grisebach. The variety *a latifolia* of Hooker and Arnott's *Erythræa macrantha* is a different plant. In the flower I examined the anthers were much injured, but they were evidently much shorter and less twisted, and appeared to have the cells less closely combined. At the same time the very short tube and large limb of the corolla give the flower much more resemblance to that of a *Gyrandra* than of an *Erythræa*.

Plate XLV. fig. 1, calyx; fig. 2, portion of the corolla cut open; fig. 3, anther from an unexpanded flower; fig. 4, anther from a fading flower; fig. 5, pistil; fig. 6, summit of the style; fig. 7, ovary, longitudinal section; fig. 8, ovary, transverse section; all magnified.

514. EUSTOMA *exaltatum*, Griseb. in DC. Prod. v. 9. p. 51.—Island off the coast of Veragua.

515. ERYTHRÆA *setacea*, sp. n., caule erecto gracillimo ramoso paucifloro, foliis radicalibus minimis obovatis caulinis remotis lineari-setaceis, floribus longe pedicellatis, corollæ tubo calyce subbreviore lobis elliptico-oblongis obtusis, stylo apice brevissime bifido lobis cuneatis crasse stigmatosis, capsula uniloculari.—Acapulco.

Herba annua, 2-6-pollicaris, ramis filiformibus 4-angulatis, oppositis vel dichotomis. Folia radicalia rosulata, vix 2 lin. longa, caulina remota, angustissima, 3-6 lin. longa. Pedicelli ultimi pollicares. Calyx 5-partitus, rarius 4-partitus, segmentis carinatis, basi anguste lanceolatis, apice setaceis. Corollæ tubus 2 lin. longus, laciniæ limbi tubo æquilongæ. Stamina infra faucem inserta, e tubo exserta; antheræ oblongæ, demum tortæ, filamento breviores, loculis distinctis, connectivo tenuissimo vix distincto. Styli lobi recurvi obtusi fere a basi stigmatosi. Capsula calycem subæquans, oblonga, valvularum marginibus placentiferis vix introflexis. Semina numerosa, minuta.

516. COUTOUBEA *densiflora*, Mart.—Griseb. in DC. Prod. v. 9. p. 66.—Isle of Taboga, Bay of Panama.

517. HALENIA *multiflora*, Benth.—Griseb. in DC. Prod. v. 9. p. 130.—Tepic.

518. LIMNANTHEMUM *Humboldtianum* β *parviflorum*, Griseb. in DC. Prod. v. 9. p. 140.—Columbia.

BIGNONIACEÆ.

519. BIGNONIA *patellifera*, Schlecht.—DC. Prod. v. 9. p. 149.—Var. fere glabra, cæterum speciminibus prope Veracruz lectis simillima.—Conchagua.

520. BIGNONIA *sarmentosa*, Bertol. ?—DC. ? Prod. v. 9. p. 155.—Foliola quam in *B. equinoctiali* majora, latiora, subtus ad axillas venarum sæpe foveolata: flores breviores.—Realejo to Guayaquil.—Ejusdem var. *hirtella*, foliorum venis subtus ciliato-hirtis.—Realejo.

521. BIGNONIA *alliacea*, Lam. ?—DC. ? Prod. v. 9. p. 148.—Atacames, Isle of Gorgona, Guayaquil.

Specimina Caribæis simillima ramis exceptis qui subteretes nec tetragoni. Folia et flores omnino eadem. Capsula (vix matura) pedalis, 7 lin. lata, plana, valvulis septo parallelis medio nervo longitudinali prominente percursis. Semina superiora inferioribus incumbentia. Tota planta (et in sicco capsula et semina insigniter) allium redolet.

522. BIGNONIA *longiflora*, Cav.—DC. Prod. v. 9. p. 159.—Very common about Guayaquil. It varies considerably in the shape of the leaflets. The corolla, when fully developed, is often three

inches long. The pod is six to eight inches long, about five lines broad, with the seeds in single rows.

523. BIGNONIA *Sinclairi*, sp. n., scandens, glabra, vel superne tenuissime pulveraceo-tomentosa, foliis conjugatis, foliolis ellipticis vix acuminatis basi rotundato-cuneatis penninervibus crebre reticulato-venosis subcoriaceis, petiolo petiolulis æquilongo, panicula terminali laxa pyramidata, calyce subcoriaceo truncato demum repando, corolla extus tomentosa.—Panama, gathered also by Cuming, n. 1179.

Rami teretes, glabri vel juniores pube minutissima pulveracea nonnisi sub lente conspicua conspersi. Petioli et petioluli 6-12 lin. longi, auriculis foliolisve ad basin nullis; cirrhi elongati simplices vel sæpius nulli. Foliola 3-6 poll. longa, 1½-3 poll. lata, subcoriacea, venis primariis secus costam mediam utrinque 5-6, subtus minute lepidoto-punctata vel glabra. Panicula semipedalis vel longior, ramis oppositis laxe dichotomis. Bracteæ minutissimæ vel nullæ. Calyx cupuliformis, coriaceus, extus pulveraceus, margine sæpius irregulariter et obtusissime 5-crenatus vel sublobatus, rarius integerrimus. Corolla extus tomento brevi sublepidoto vestita; tubus pollicaris vel paullo longior, superne parum ampliatus, ima basi (infra staminum insertionem) extus glaber, intus ad originem staminum pubescens; limbi lobi lati, rotundati, non ciliati. Stamina inclusa, didyna, cum rudimento quinti. Antherarum loculi lineares, divergentes. Discus hypogynus crassus, pulviniformis. Ovarium oblongum, tomentosum. Stylus apice spathulato-dilatatus, bilamellatus, lamellis intus stigmatosis. Ovula in utroque latere cujusve placentæ uniserialia. Species valde affinis *B. rupestri* Gardn. et præsertim *B. elongatæ*, Vahl. Calyx quam in hac brevior, foliola angustiora.

524 to 526. BIGNONIA, three species, two from Guayaquil, and one from Manzanilla Bay, all apparently new, but the specimens insufficient for accurate description.

527. AMPHILOPHIUM *paniculatum*, Humb. et Kunth.—DC. Prod. v. 9. p. 193.—Gulf of Fonseca.

528. PITHECOCTENIUM *panamense*, sp. n., ramis glabris, foliis digitatis, foliolis 4-5 petiolulatis ovali-vel oblongo-ellipticis acuminatis subtus minute nigro-punctatis et tenuissime lepidotis glabratisve, racemis folio brevioribus, calycibus truncatis.—Panama, gathered also by Cuming, n. 1110.

Rami albidi, striati, ad nodos leviter compressi, cæterum subteretes. Folia opposita, petiolo communi 2-3-pollicari, versus apicem sæpius minute canescenti-tomentello; petioluli 6-10 lin. longi. Foliola inæqualia, majora 3-5 poll. longa, 1½-2 poll. lata, acumine longo obtuso, basi rotundata vel cuneata, utrinque viridia et oculo nudo glabra, sub lente tamen pubes minuta sparsa sublepidota sæpe apparet in pagina inferiore quæ etiam punctis nigris sparsis crebris conspersa. Racemi 2-3-pollicares, axillares, more generis canescentes. Bracteæ minutissimæ, subnullæ. Calyx late campanulatus, canescens, crassiusculus, ore truncato membranaceo extus minute 5-dentato. Corolla sesquipollicaris vel paullo longior, glabra, tubo superne parum ampliato basi contracto et ad originem faucis intus pubescente, limbi lobis latis integris. Stamina ad originem faucis inserta, didyna, corolla breviora, cum rudimento quinti; antheræ glabræ, loculis divaricatis. Discus hypogynus crassus. Ovarium ovato-oblongum, minute et densissime muriculatum. Stylus apice spathulato-dilatatus, bilamellatus, lamellis intus stigmatosis.

529. PITHECOCTENIUM *muricatum*, DC. Prod. v. 9. p. 194.—Realejo.—There are only loose pods in the collection, but they appear to be those of this species.

530. TABEBUIA *cordata*, sp. n., scandens, ramulis compressiusculis puberulis, foliis conjugato-bifoliolatis plerisque cirrhiferis, foliolis ovatis acuminatis basi cordatis subcoriaceis glabris, racemis axillaribus laxis.—Isthmus of Darien.

Ramuli levissime striati, nequaquam angulati, pube brevissima sparsa subglandulosa. Petioli communes 2-3-pollicares, minute puberuli, plerique cirrho elongato simplici vel apice trifido terminati; petioluli 1-1½-pollicares. Foliola 3-4 poll. longa, circa 2 poll. lata, crassiuscule membranacea vel subcoriacea, venis subtus prominentibus reticulatis. Racemi in specimine folio breviores, 6-12-flori, rhachi flexuosa subglabra, bracteis minutis. Pedicelli 3-4 lin. longi, flexuoso-reflexi vel divaricati. Calyx 5 lin. longus, tubuloso-campanulatus, versus basin leviter canescens, apice submembranaceus, irregulariter fissus in labia duo quorum alterum latum obtusum, alterum bifidum lobis latis obtusis. Corolla sesquipollicaris, glabra, tubo basi tenui, mox in faucem campanulatam ampliato, lobis 5 latis rotundatis. Stamina ad basin faucis inserta, corolla breviora, didynama absque rudimento quinti; antherarum loculi divaricati glabri. Discus hypogynus pulviniformis, latus. Ovarium oblongum glaberrimum. Stylus apice spathulato-dilatatus, bilamellatus, lamellis acutis intus stigmatosis.

The specimens from Surinam, n. 334 of Hostmann's collection, appear to belong to the same species, although the leaves are less cordate.

531. TABEBUIA *rosea*, DC.? Prod. v. 9. p. 215.—Rami crassi et inflorescentia *T. fluviatilis*; foliola multo majora, crasso-coriacea, subtus lepidoto-punctata, glaucescentia. Corollæ amplæ, similis iis *Tecomæ speciosæ*, quæ verosimiliter cum pluribus *Tecomis* digitatifoliis, congener est *Tabebuiæ fluviatilis*.—Nicoya.

532. TECOMA *Gaudichaudi*, DC. Prod. v. 9. p. 223.—Guayaquil.

533. TECOMA *stans*, Juss.—DC. Prod. v. 9. p. 224.—Acapulco, Panama.

534. CRESCENTIA *cuneifolia*, Gardn.—DC. Prod. v. 9. p. 246.—Columbia, probably cultivated. The specimens agree in every respect with those described by Gardner, from Brazil, where also it is cultivated only.

535. CRESCENTIA *obovata*, sp. n., (Plate XLVI.) glabra, foliis alternis obovatis coriaceis, calyce tubuloso bifido superne extus impresse glandulifero, corollæ limbo suberecto crenato vix lobato.— Isle of Gorgona, and island off the coast of Veragua.

Frutex elata. Rami crassiusculi, teretes vel primum obtuse angulati, cortice albido, ad basin innovationum squamulis numerosis brevibus acutis persistentibus instructi. Folia semipedalia, 3-4 poll. lata, brevissime acuminata, basi cuneata, subsessilia vel brevissime petiolata, crasso-coriacea, nitidula, costa media venisque primariis utrinsecus 10-12 subtus prominentibus. Pedicelli ad apices ramulorum 1-3 (vel plures?), sesquipollicares, erecti. Flores nutantes. Calyx 1¼ poll. longus, tubulosus, supra medium dilatatus, ante anthesin clavatus et clausus, per anthesin usque ad medium (vel rarius hinc fere ad basin) in labia duo patentia fissus, coriaceus, glaber sed supra medium præsertim in labio inferiore glandulis numerosis impressis notatus eas *Adenocalymnæ* fere referentibus. Corolla 2½-pollicaris, glabra, tubo elongato superne ampliato, limbo campanulato rarius breviter lobato, sed (in floribus suppetentibus) crenis numerosis excisa. Stamina corolla breviora, didynama cum rudimento quinti. Antherarum loculi lineari-oblongi, divergentes. Discus hypogynus, crassus, pulviniformis. Ovarium oblongum, obtusum, bisulcatum, uniloculare, placentis 2 tenuibus parietalibus multiovulatis. Stylus apice clavatus, concavus, brevissime bilobus, intus stigmatosus.

This fine species differs somewhat from other *Crescentiæ* in the form both of the calyx and corolla, but not sufficiently so to warrant the establishing it as a distinct species, especially as the calyx appears to be sometimes divided nearly to the base, as in other *Crescentiæ*, and the stamens and ovary are precisely the same.

Plate XLVI. fig. 1, portion of the corolla, cut open; fig. 2, ovary and style; fig. 3, summit of the style; fig. 4, ovary, transverse section.

Gesneriaceæ.

536. Gesneria *spicata*, Humb. et Kunth.—DC. Prod. v. 7. p. 531.—Nicoya.

537. Gesneria *rhynchocarpa*, sp. n., caule herbaceo elato tomentoso-hirsuto, foliis ternatim verticillatis oppositisve breviter petiolatis ovatis acuminatis basi inæqualiter rotundatis cuneatisve supra hirsutis subtus tomentosis, pedicellis in quaque axilla subgeminis petiolo longioribus, calycis lobis triangularibus acutis, corolla tubulosa parum ventricosa villosissima lobis brevissimis, capsulæ rostro incurvo truncato.—Isthmus of Darien, Columbia.

Rami vel caules adsunt sesquipedales, fere a basi floriferi. Folia inferiora 3-4 poll. longa, 1½-2 poll. lata, crassiuscula, leviter crenata, penninervia, petiolo 3-4 lin. longo, superiora floralia gradatim decrescentia, summa vix calyces superantia. Pedicelli in verticillo vulgo 6, 2 in quaque axilla, pedunculo communi subnullo, singuli 4-6 lin. longi, tomentoso-hirsuti. Calyces campanulati, 3 lin. longi, lobis parte integra subbrevioribus. Corolla 10-11 lin. longa, parum incurva, basi et apice paullulum contracta, lobis 5 brevissimis latis retusis subpatentibus, 2 superioribus tamen paullo longioribus et altius connatis. Glandulæ perigynæ 5 ovato-lanceolatæ, obtusæ vel truncatæ. Stamina inclusa, glabra, antheris connatis; quinti rudimentum parvum. Ovarii pars libera conica, recta, apice truncata, villosa. Stylus basi pubescens, apice bilamellatus, lobis intus stigmatosis. Capsula calyce parum aucto semi-inclusa, parte libera valde incurva, valvulis medio placentiferis. Species affinis *G. tubiflorœ*, Cav., sed in hac laciniæ calycis angustæ dicuntur et corolla longior.

538. Gesneria *petiolaris*, sp. n., caule herbaceo erecto tomentoso, foliis oppositis ternatimque verticillatis, inferioribus longe petiolatis ovali-oblongis vix acuminatis basi cuneatis vel angustatis crassis utrinque tomentosis, floralibus parvis, pedicellis numerosis in axillis fasciculatis, verticillis remotis vel supremis approximatis racemosis subsecundis, calycis lobis triangularibus acutis, corolla tubulosa villosa superne ampliata, limbi lobis ovatis patentibus, capsulæ rostro incurvo truncato.—Island off the coast of Veragua.

Caules pedales vel paullo altiores, obtuse tetragoni, tomento brevi tenui sæpe rubescentes. Folia radicalia petiolo suo breviora, caulina inferiora 3-4-pollicaria, apice acutiuscula vel vix obtusa, crenata, basi integerrima et plus minus angustata, supra viridia vix tomentosa, subtus densius tomentosa sæpe rubentia, petiolo 1-2 poll. longo; floralia in pare vel verticillo infimo subconformia, cætera multo minora, summa bracteæformia. Pedicelli in axillis foliorum floralium nunc 1-2 nunc 6-10, inæquales, longiores semipollicares. Calyx 2 lin. longus vel fructifer paullo major, laciniis latis acutis tubo suo æquilongis. Corolla 9-10 lin. longa, basi constricta, supra medium ventricosa, ad faucem parum contracta, lobis linea paullo longioribus. Stamina glabra, corolla breviora, cum rudimento quinti. Glandulæ et stylus *G. rhynchocarpœ*; capsula pariter sed sæpius brevius incurvo-rostrata.

539. Gesneria *incurva*, sp. n., herbacea, erecta, hirsuta, foliis petiolatis subfalcato-ovatis oblongisve acuminatis crenatis basi valde inæqualiter angustatis supra hirsutis subtus dense tomentosis, pedicellis 1-3-nis folio florali parum brevioribus, calycis lobis lanceolatis acutis, corolla tubulosa incurva vix ampliata ore 5-crenato, capsulæ rostro vix calyce longiore leviter incurvo.—Isle of Gorgona.

Herba vix pedalis videtur, undique dense hirsuta. Folia inferiora 2-4 poll. longa, crassa, crenata, supra dense hispida, subtus molliter tomentosa et ad venas hispida, floralia decrescentia, omnia petiolata, petiolis inferioribus 6-10 lin. longis. Pedicelli pollicares. Calyces per anthesin 3 lin. longi, lobis tubo suo paullo brevioribus; fructiferi aucti, basi acuti. Corolla pollicaris vel paullo longior, coccinea, hirsuta, margine breviter et late 5-crenata. Stamina, glandulæ et stylus præcedentium. Capsula fere 6 lin. longa, pars exserta fere recta, parte adhærente brevior.

540. GESNERIA *Deppeana*, Cham. et Schl.—DC. Prod. v. 7. p. 528.—Tepic.

541. DIASTEMA *racemifera*, gen. nov.—Salango.

CHAR. GEN. Calyx basi breviter adnatus, limbo 5-partito. Corollæ tubus subæqualis, exsertus, declinatus; limbus obliquus, patens, 5-fidus.—Stamina 4, didynama, cum rudimento quinti; antheræ liberæ, subrotundæ. Glandulæ perigynæ 5. Stylus apice bilamellatus, lobis membranaceis intus stigmatosis. Capsula unilocularis, valvulis 2 medio placentiferis. Semina numerosa.

Herba tenera, flaccida, semipedalis vel vix pedalis, ramis paucis divaricatis villosulis. Folia opposita, longiuscule petiolata, ovata, obtusa, crenata, basi rotundata vel angustata, 2-3-pollicaria, tenuiter membranacea, supra hispida, subtus pallidiora, glabra vel ad venas villosula. Racemi in axillis superioribus solitarii vel terminales, folio sæpius breviores. Pedicelli oppositi, filiformes, 6-10 lin. longi, singuli bractea ovata sessili $1\frac{1}{2}$-2 lin. longa subtensi. Calyx $1\frac{1}{2}$ lin. longus, viridis, fere glaber, lobis ovatis vel oblongis obtusiusculis parte integra adnata longioribus. Corolla semipollicaris, leviter pilosula. Stamina inclusa, antheris parvis globosis. Glandulæ perigynæ inter se æquales, lineares, ovario longiores. Capsula calyce brevior, basi adnata. Semina numerosissima, minuta (albumine parco?), in speciminibus nondum matura.

The free stamens of this plant indicate an affinity with *Achimenes*, and the form of the corolla is not unlike that of some of the small-flowered species of that genus, but the tube is neither gibbous nor spurred at the base, and the five equal perigynous glands are more prominent even than in *Gesneria* and *Gloxinia*. It is not improbable, however, that the *Achimenes erinoides*, DC., and *A. comifera*, DC., may be congeners of our plant.

POLEMONIACEÆ.

542. LŒSELIA *coccinea*, G. Don.—Benth. in DC. Prod. v. 9. p. 318.—Tepic.

543. LŒSELIA *glandulosa*, G. Don.—Benth. l. c. p. 319.—Tepic.

544. LŒSELIA *involucrata*, G. Don.—Benth. l. c.—Realejo and Acapulco.

545. LŒSELIA *amplectens*, Benth. l. c. p. 320.—Tepic.

546. CANTUA *buxifolia*, Lam.—Benth. l. c. p. 321.—Huamantango.

547. COBÆA *macrostema*, Pav.—Benth. l. c. p. 322.—Atacames.

Convolvulaceæ.

The plants of this order appear to be very numerous in tropical America, but owing to the early period of the day at which their flowers close, and the difficulty of drying them well, the comparatively few specimens brought home by collectors are usually very unsatisfactory. The leaves, moreover, vary much in form in different parts of the same plant, and the genera into which the known species are distributed are for the most part established upon purely technical characters, having often little or no relation to the habit of the plants. I have therefore refrained from describing several species of which the specimens are not very satisfactory, although I have been unable to refer them to any of those contained in De Candolle's Prodromus, and have only established as new those of which the collection contains good specimens affording decided characters by which they differ from all others with which I am acquainted, as well as from the specific characters given by Choisy.

548. ARGYREIA? *oblonga*, sp. n., volubilis, ramis lignosis, novellis angulatis tomentosis, foliis elliptico-oblongis vel rarius ovatis basi obtusis supra pilosulis subtus nervosis ad venas tomentosis, pedunculis brevibus, corymbis confertis tomentosis, sepalis coriaceis ovatis obtusis tomentosis, corolla infundibuliformi-tubulosa glabra vel apice tomentella.—Tepic.

Frutex alte scandens? Folia 2-4 poll. longa, 1-1½ poll. lata, acuminata vel obtusa, basi nec cordata nec angustata, omnia quæ vidi integra, supra pilis minutis conspersa, subtus prominente penninervia et transversim venulosa; petiolo tenui 6-10 lin. longo. Pedunculi crassi, uti pedicelli et calyces tomento denso albido-flavicante obtecti. Inflorescentia bipollicaris, corymboso-multiflora. Bracteæ parvæ, lineares. Sepala subsemipollicaria, inter se subæqualia, intus glabra sæpe rubescentia. Corolla sesquipollicaris vel paullo longior, basi contracta, superne in faucem elongatam ampliata, limbo (patente?) 5-angulato. Alabastrum apice leviter tomentosum. Antheræ 4 lin. longæ. Ovarium carnosum, biloculare, 4-ovulatum.

Although I have not seen the fruit of this plant, the ovary is so thick and fleshy as to leave little doubt of its belonging to the tribe of the *Argyreiæ*, and the ovary is certainly bilocular; I have therefore ventured to place it in *Argyreia*, although Choisy has no American species of that genus. The habit is that of some of the Asiatic species, and Choisy himself suspects that one or two of the American plants placed by him doubtfully in *Rivea* may prove to belong rather to *Argyreia*.

549. QUAMOCLIT *coccinea*, Chois. in DC. Prod. v. 9. p. 335.—Tiger Island, Gulf of Fonseca, Guayaquil.

550. QUAMOCLIT *hederæfolia*, Chois. l. c. p. 336.—Columbia.

551. QUAMOCLIT *vulgaris*, Chois. l. c.—Mexico to Guayaquil.

552. CALONYCTION *speciosum*, Chois. in DC. Prod. v. 9. p. 345.—Isle of Taboga, Bay of Panama.

Very few of the American specimens which I have examined come precisely within Choisy's character of this very variable species. The three outer sepals are usually shorter in their dilated portion than the inner ones, and terminated by very long points, whilst the inner ones are longer without any points at all, or scarcely any. The peduncles are sometimes indeed "longissimi," but often also very short. The character of the genus is very obscure, as both *Exogonium* and *Ipomœa* are made to include species with hypocrateriform corollæ and exserted stamens.

553. BATATAS? *crassicaulis*, sp. n., caule erecto elato fistuloso glabro, foliis amplis late cordato-lanceolatis glabris, corymbo laxo multifloro minute canescenti-tomentello, sepalis orbiculatis obtusis extus tomentellis, corolla infundibuliformi-campanulata extus minute tomentella.—Guayaquil.

Caulis summitates adsunt pedales, non volubiles, glabri, læviusculi. Folia 6-10 poll. longa, 2-4 poll. lata, longiuscule acuminata, margine integra vel sinuata, basi auriculis rotundatis cordata vel angulato-subhastata membranacea, utrinque glabra, petiolo 2-4 poll. longo. Calyx 2-3 lin. longus, sepalis margine tenuibus glabris dorso canescenti-tomentellis, exterioribus paullo brevioribus. Corollæ tubus supra ovarium leviter constrictus, mox in faucem elongatum ampliatus, limbo campanulato 5-angulato. Stamina inclusa. Styli lobi stigmatosi subglobosi. Ovarium non carnosum, supra medium 4-loculare, basi biloculare.

This plant may be equally well placed in *Ipomœa*, but it is unlike any species described. A transverse section of the ovary, if taken above the middle, shows four distinct and complete cells, if below the middle, two cells only, without any trace of the additional dissepiments.

554. BATATAS *acetosæfolia*, Chois. in DC. Prod. v. 9. p. 358.—Guayaquil.

These specimens have both the leaves and flowers smaller than usual, but appear to belong to the species. The *Ipomœa longifolia* (Benth. Pl. Hartw. p. 16) referred here by Choisy, differs essentially in foliage, flowers, and ovary, being a true Ipomœa with a two-celled ovary, a calyx 8 or 9 lines long, and a corolla full four inches diameter.

555. BATATAS *paniculata*, Chois. in DC. Prod. v. 9. p. 339.—Ovarium dissepimentis basi incompletis sub-4-loculare.—Guayaquil.

556. BATATAS *pentaphylla*, Chois. l. c.—Guayaquil.

557. BATATAS *quinquefolia*, Chois. l. c.—Tepic, Realejo, Guayaquil.

558. PHARBITIS *hispida*, Chois. in DC. Prod. v. 9. p. 341.—Guayaquil.

559. PHARBITIS *heterosepala*, sp. n., volubilis, caule pilis adpressis retrorsis pubescente, foliis latis cordatis acuminatis glabris vel vix puberulis, pedunculis folio brevioribus confertim 3-5-floris,

sepalis lanceolatis acuminatis exterioribus multo majoribus adpresse pilosulis.—Mundiche in Columbia.

Affinis *P. hispidæ*, sed glabrior, pili quæ adsunt omnes breves, adpressi, nec unquam patentes. Pedicelli brevissimi ad apicem pedunculi 1-3-pollicaris. Sepala exteriora 6-9 lin. longa, interioribus majora et 2-3-plo-latiora. Corolla speciosa, tripollicaris. Ovarium triloculare, loculis biovulatis.

560. PHARBITIS *Nil*, Chois. in DC. Prod. v. 9. p. 343.—Realejo.

561. IPOMÆA *urbica*, Chois. in DC. Prod. v. 9. p. 349.—Guayaquil.

Distinguished by Choisy from *I. pes-capræ* chiefly by the venation of the leaves, which, however, is scarcely constant.

562. IPOMÆA *codonantha*, Benth. Pl. Hartw. p. 120.—Pedunculi et pedicelli sæpe 4-alati. Species ab omnibus in Prodromo enumeratis distincta videtur.—Guayaquil.

563. IPOMÆA *brachypoda*, sp. n., glabra vel pilis longis hispida, volubilis, foliis petiolatis profunde cordatis longe acuminatis integris vel basi late sinuatis angulatis trilobisve membranaceis, pedunculis plerisque petiolo brevioribus confertim 3-10-floris, sepalis longe linearibus lanceolatisve acutis, corolla glabra, capsula glabra, seminibus puberulis.—Acapulco; Isle of Taboga, Bay of Panama; Columbia.

Habitus fere *Pharbitidis hispidæ*, sed ovarium repetite observatum constanter biloculare vidi; affinis etiam *Ipomææ trichocarpæ* sed pluribus notis distincta. Caules tenues, volubilis, uti petioli nunc glabri, nunc sæpius pilis longis patentibus vel subretrorsis hispidi. Petioli 6-18 lin. longi. Folia 2-3 poll. longa, sæpius longe et acute acuminata, auriculis baseos latis rotundatis rarius angulatis, viridia, tenuiter membranacea, glabra vel juniora pilosa præsertim in pagina superiore. Pedunculi raro semipollicares, inferiores confertim cymoso-6-10-flori, superiores sæpe 1-3-flori. Bracteæ lineares, cæterum sepalis subsimiles. Sepala 6-9 lin. longa, viridia, acuta, apice glabra, basi pilis longis hirsutissima vel omnino glabra, exteriora interioribus paullo latiora. Corollæ forma eadem videtur ac in *Pharbitide hispida* sed minor. Capsula subcoriacea, glabra, 4-valvis. Semina pilis minutis sparsis puberula, magnitudine eorum *Pharbitidis hispidæ*.

564. IPOMÆA *pedicellaris*, sp. n., volubilis, glabra vel rarius superne puberula, foliis late cordatis acute acuminatis membranaceis, pedicellis pedunculo 1-3-floro longioribus, sepalis ovatis obtusis subæqualibus glabris, corolla speciosa longe campanulata glabra, capsula glabra.—Acapulco; Tiger Island, Gulf of Fonseca.

Habitu et foliis ad *I. rubrocœruleam* accedit. Folia latiora, breviter et late cordata. Pedunculi semipollicares vel rarius pollicares. Pedicelli vulgo sesquipollicares, post anthesin incrassati. Sepala 3 lin. longa, margine scariosa. Corolla fere 3-pollicaris, tubo extra calycem abrupte ampliato in faucem elongatam superne campanulatam. Alabastrum junius extus apice tomentellum. Ovarium 2-loculare; loculis 2-ovulatis.

565 to 570. IPOMÆÆ, sp., six, three from Mexico, one from Central America, and two from Columbia, which I have been unable to refer to any of those enumerated in the Prodromus, but which, owing to the insufficiency of the specimens, cannot be satisfactorily described as new.

571. IPOMÆA *cymosa*, Rœm. et Schult.—Chois. in DC. Prod. v. 9. p. 371.—*Convolvulus densiflorus*, Hook. et Arn. Bot. Beech. p. 303.—Mexico to Guayaquil.

The specimens are generally, but not always, more pubescent than the East Indian ones, but I can find no other difference in foliage, flower, or seed. It varies much in the breadth of the leaves and the number of flowers in the cyme, but it is readily known by the peculiar brown colour and texture of the sepals when dry. It is surprising that Choisy should not have met with it from America, as I have it from the West Indies and Guiana, as well as from tropical Africa. It has not the slightest resemblance with *I. tyrianthina*, to which Choisy refers the *Conv. densiflorus*.

572. IPOMÆA *microsepala*, sp. n., caule volubili tenui glabro vel longe patentim piloso, foliis cordatis acuminatis auriculis baseos rotundatis membranaceis glabris opacis, pedunculis tenuibus vulgo folia superantibus laxe plurifloris, sepalis parvis oblongis obtusis mucronatisve, corolla basi longiuscule attenuata superne campanulata glabra.—Acapulco; some specimens from Tumaco in fruit only, appear also to be the same species.

Habitu accedit ad *Quamoclit coccineam*. Folia 1-2-pollicaria, acumine longo vel brevi obtuso vel rarius acuto, non pellucida, petiolo tenui pollicari vel paullo longiore. Pedunculi graciles, glabri, 1½-3-pollicares; flores in cyma 8-12, nunc 1-3, breviter pedicellati. Bracteæ parvæ, lineares. Sepala subæqualia, vix linea longiora, margine subscariosa. Corolla fere pollicaris, in sicco lutea videtur, an alba? Ovarium 2-loculare, 4-ovulatum et stigma *Ipomœæ*. Capsula globosa, glabra, 2 lin. diametro, calyce patente suffulta, ei *Quamoclit coccineæ* similis sed bilocularis sub-4-valvis.

573. IPOMÆA *oocarpa*, sp. n., volubilis, gracilis, glabra, foliis breviter petiolatis cordatis acuminatis pellucido-punctatis, pedunculis 1-3-floris folio longioribus ramulisque glutinosis, sepalis ovatis obtusis, corolla basi longiuscule attenuata superne campanulata glabra, capsula ovata glabra calyce multo longiore.—Guayaquil.

Ramuli graciles, fere filiformes, juniores uti pedunculi et petioli glutinosi. Petioli 1-3 lin. longi. Folia 1-1½-pollicaria, forma iis *I. microsepalæ* similia, punctis parvis oblongis pellucidis conspersa. Pedunculi tenues, riguduli, 2-3-pollicares, apice 1-3-flori, pedicello primum florente brevissimo, post anthesin incrassato recurvo, 1-2 tardioribus elongatis tenuibus. Sepala parum inæqualia, exteriora 1½ lin. interiora 2 lin. longa, margine subscariosa, in fructu paullo aucta, latiora. Corolla pollicaris, ex sicco purpurea vel rubra videtur. Genitalia corolla paullo breviora. Stylus et ovarium *Ipomœæ*. Capsula 4-5 lin. longa, 4-valvis, glabra, abortu sæpius 1-2-sperma.

574. IPOMÆA *puncticulata*, sp. n., caule volubili gracili glabro, foliis petiolatis cordatis vel hastatis acuminatis supra glabris vel brevissime glanduloso-puberulis minute pellucido-punctatis subtus lepidoto-glaucescentibus, pedunculis 1-3-floris, sepalis ovatis obtusis, corolla basi longiuscule attenuata superne campanulata.—Mexico.

Habitus, calyces et corolla *I. oocarpæ*; pedicelli breviores, et foliis facile distinguenda.

The three last species have at first sight considerable resemblance to each other in foliage, in the small size of the calyx, and the shape of the corolla, but are perfectly distinct from each other, especially in the dotting of the leaves, and the two first in the capsules. I do not know of any species nearly allied to them, and amongst the descriptions in the Prodromus none appear to come near to them except perhaps the *I. aristolochiæfolia*.

575. IPOMÆA *trifida*, Don.?—Chois.? in DC. Prod. v. 9. p. 383.—Acapulco, Realejo, Panama.

Variat glabra, pubescens, vel hirsuta; foliis integris cordato-ovatis lanceolato-sagittatis vel profunde trilobis. Sepala subscariosa nec herbacea, setaceo-acuminata vel acuta, dorso hirsuta vel rarius glabra. Corolla 15-18 lin. longa.

576. IPOMÆA *evolvuloides*, Moric.—Chois. in DC. Prod. v. 9. p. 373.—Acapulco.

These specimens agree perfectly with Blanchet and Gardner's Brazilian, Schomburgh's Guiana, and Linden's Mexican ones. The corolla as well as the habit of the plant are much more those of a *Jacquemontia* than of an *Ipomæa*, and the stigmatic branches of the style are not quite so globose as they usually are in the latter genus.

577. JACQUEMONTIA *pycnocephala*, sp. n., volubilis, undique dense tomentoso-hirsuta, foliis plerisque cordiformibus, pedunculis apice capitato-multifloris, bracteis late cordato-ovatis, sepalis exterioribus ovatis acuminatis, interioribus multo minoribus, corolla calyce vix duplo longiore.—Acapulco.

Rami teretes, dense vestiti pilis mollibus patentibus in ramulis novellis velutinis. Folia vulgo 1-2-pollicaria, acute acuminata, margine integra vel undulata, basi auriculis latis rotundatis cordata, crassiuscula, utrinque molliter velutina, petiolo 3-8 lin. longo. Pedunculi nunc abbreviati, vix petiolo longiores, nunc rarius fere 4 poll. longi, velutino-villosi, capitulum ferentes hemisphæricum dense imbricatum. Bracteæ exteriores late cordato-ovatæ, acuminatæ, foliaceæ, tomento velutino vestitæ, 4-6 lin. longæ, 4-8 lin. latæ, interiores angustiores. Pedicelli brevissimi. Sepala exteriora 3-4 lin. longa, ovata, acuminata, basi cuneata vel angustata, interiora 2-3 minora, quorum intimum vulgo membranaceum acutum vix 1½ lin. longum. Corolla 7 lin. longa, campanulata, glabra, lobis acutis. Stamina corolla breviora. Styli lobi stigmatosi crassiusculi, oblongi, iis *J. violaceæ* simillimi.

This species differs from the downy form of *J. violacea* by the remarkable bracts which, instead of being smaller than the outer sepals, are very much broader and larger, as in some of the capitate *Ipomææ*; and also by the ferruginous down which covers both surfaces of the leaves more densely even than in the *J. ferruginea*.

578. JACQUEMONTIA *violacea*, Chois. in DC. Prod. v. 9. p. 397 var.—A very imperfect specimen.—Panama.

579. JACQUEMONTIA *corymbulosa*, sp. n., volubilis, undique ferrugineo-tomentosa, foliis breviter petiolatis cordato-ovatis acuminatis, pedunculis elongatis apice cymoso-multifloris, bracteis minimis setaceis, sepalis parum inæqualibus ovatis vel ovato-lanceolatis acuminato-acutis corolla pluries brevioribus.—Guayaquil.

Caules et folia fere *Convolvuli nodiflori*. Rami teretes, pube brevissima densa vix demum derasa tomentosi. Folia in aliis speciminibus vix pollicaria, superiora minora, petiolo 1-3 lin. longo; in aliis fere bipollicaria, petiolo 6 lin. longo, omnia utrinque molliter tomentosa. Pedunculi 2-5 poll. longi, floribus sæpius numerosissimis in cymam densam confertis. Bracteæ majores vix lineam longæ, tenuissimæ. Pedicelli per anthesin breves, fructiferi 1-3 lin. longi. Calyces tomentoso-pubescentes, 1½-2 lin. longi, vel sepala externa rarissime fere 3 lin. longa. Corolla late campanulata, semipollicaris, cœrulea. Capsula calycem vix æquans, glabra, quadrivalvis.

580. Convolvulus *nodiflorus*, Lam.—Chois. in DC. Prod. v. 9. p. 414.—Guayaquil.

581. Evolvulus *nummularius*, Linn.—Chois. in DC. Prod. v. 9. p. 445. var. parvifolia.—Acapulco.

582. Evolvulus *glabriusculus*, Chois. in DC. Prod. v. 9. p. 448. var. altera foliis iis *E. nummularii* simillimis, 6-9 lin. longis, pedunculis folia æquantibus vel duplo longioribus; altera *heterophylla*, foliis aliis *E. nummularii*, aliis ovatis acutis ultrapollicaribus.—Guayaquil, both varieties.

583. Evolvulus *linifolius*, Linn.—Chois. in DC. Prod. v. 9. p. 449.—Tepic.

584. Cuscuta *laxiflora*, sp. n., caule filiformi, pedunculis brevissimis, pedicellis calyce sæpius longioribus, calyce pentagono lobis latis obtusis parte integra brevioribus, corolla urceolata calyce vix duplo longiore lobis oblongis obtusis recurvo-patentibus, squamis laceris? stylis apice globoso-stigmatosis corolla paullo brevioribus.—Acapulco, on a *Tephrosia*, and on a *Composita*.

Flores sæpius in racemo brevissimo umbellæformi subsessiles, 4 ad 10. Pedicelli filiformes, inæquales, 2-3 lin. longi. Calyx laxus, per anthesin $1\frac{1}{4}$ lin., in fructu 2 lin. longus. Corolla 2 lin. longa. Affinis videtur *C. intermediæ*, Chois., sed calyx descripto laxior, major, lobis non imbricatis, pedicelli longiores, pedunculus communis sæpius nullus.

585. Cuscuta *globulosa*, sp. n., caule filiformi, floribus glomerato-racemosis vel corymbosis brevissime pedicellatis subglobosis, calyce laxiusculo campanulato lobis latissimis obtusis imbricatis parti integræ æquilongis, corolla vix calycem excedente lobis brevissimis latis obtusis, squamis alte fimbriatis, stylis apice late peltato-stigmatiferis subexsertis.—Acapulco.

Tota siccitate nigrescit. Glomerulæ florum oblongæ vel subglobosæ. Pedicelli raro lineam longi, squamis nullis intermixtis. Calyx linea paullo longior, lobis conniventibus. Corolla superne constricta, lobis patulis. Squamæ latæ, ultra medium exciso-fimbriatæ.

586. Cuscuta *congesta*, sp. n., caule filiformi, florum glomerulis densis ovatis subramosis squamellis intermixtis, calyce ovato lobis parte integra brevioribus latis obtusis, corolla calycem vix superante intus squamata, lobis brevissimis latis obtusis, squamis integris, stylis apice globoso-stigmatosis subexsertis.—Acapulco.

Flores in glomerulo numerosi, sessilis vel breviter pedicellati, vix lineam longi. Squamæ ovatæ, obtusæ, integerrimæ vel vix obscure denticulatæ.

BORAGINEÆ.

587. Varronia *calyptrata*, DC. Prod. v. 9. p. 469.—Tiger Islands, Gulf of Fonseca; it is also n. 1305 of Cuming's Central American collection.

588. Varronia *rotundifolia*, Alph. DC. Prod. v. 9. p. 469.—Columbia, Guayaquil; also n 1174 of Cuming.

589. Cordia *gerascanthus*, Jacq. β. *subcanescens*, DC. Prod. v. 9. p. 472.—Acapulco; Isle o Gorgona.—These specimens correspond with the common West Indian ones in every respect excep

that the flowers are rather smaller. The Acapulco plant mentioned in the Botany of Beechey's Voyage, p. 304, is rather the *C. tinifolia*.

590. CORDIA *ferruginea*, Rœm. et Schult.—DC. Prod. v. 9. p. 488.—Tepic.

591. CORDIA *peruviana*, β. *mexicana*, DC. Prod. v. 9. p. 491.—Panama.

592. CORDIA (*Myxæ spicæformes*) *hispida*, sp. n., ramulis petiolis pedunculisque pilis longis rigidis hirsutissimis, foliis lanceolatis utrinque acuminatis supra scaberrimis subtus ad venas hispidis, spicis elongatis gracilibus, calyce glabriusculo tubo corollæ paullo breviore.—Gulf of Fonseca.

Pili, e tuberculo orti, longiores et rigidiores quam in omnibus hujus sectionis mihi notis speciebus, in ramis petiolis pedunculis costis paginæ inferioris foliorum et etiam in foliis novellis superne copiosi. Folia pleraque 3-4 poll. longa, 6-12 lin. lata, irregulariter serrata basi longe angustata et interdum usque ad articulationem petioli decurrentia, adulta supra pilis derasis et tuberculis persistentibus scaberrima, subtus inter costas viridia, glabriuscula, minutissime glandulosa-puncticulata. Spicæ in pedunculo bipollicari 2-3-poll. longæ. Calyx ante anthesin globosus, florens campanulatus, irregulariter 4-5-fidus. Corollæ tubus 1½ lin. longus, superne paullo latior, limbus patens 5-fidus, lobis tubo brevioribus ovatis, fauce nuda vel parce pilosa. Stamina e tubo vix exserta.

This and the two preceding species belong to a numerous group often confounded in herbaria under the name of *Varronia curassavica*, and comprised in De Candolle's *Myxæ spicæformes;* they are often very difficult to distinguish, and probably several of the published ones are but varieties of each other; the *C. hispida* now described appears, however, to differ from them all in the long stiff hairs with which it is covered. In other respects it comes nearest to *C. Pœppigii*.

593. CORDIA (Myxæ subcapitatæ) *microcephala*, Willd.? in Rœm. Schult. Syst. v. 4. p. 465, undique strigoso-scabra, foliis petiolatis ovato-lanceolatis utrinque longe angustatis grosse serratis, pedunculis folio brevioribus, spicis ovato-globosis parvis, calyce subgloboso strigoso corolla vix breviore, staminibus corollam æquantibus.—Gulf of Fonseca.

Nomen Willdenowii optime convenit, et diagnosis nimis brevis non discrepat. Rami adsunt sesquipedales, dichotome ramosi, undique uti foliorum pagina utraque pedunculi et calyces pilis strigosis adpressis scabri. Folia 2½-3 poll. longa, 9-12 lin. lata, acute acuminata et basi in petiolum longe angustata. Capitula fere globosa, pauciflora, vix 3 lin. lata. Calyces 5-fidi, lobis seu dentibus triangularibus obtusiusculis muticis. Corolla subcampanulata, calycem vix excedens, breviter 5-fida, ad faucem intus pilosa.

594. CORDIA *guayaquilensis*, Humb. et Kunth.—DC. Prod. v. 9. p. 496.—*C. polyantha*, Benth. pl. Hartw. p. 121.—Guayaquil.

595. CORDIA *Bonplandii*, Rœm. et Schult.?—DC.? Prod. v. 9. p. 497.—Atacames.

596. CORDIA *dasycephala*, Humb. et Kunth.—DC. Prod. v. 9. p. 497.—Columbia.

597. TOURNEFORTIA *hirsutissima*, Linn.—DC. Prod. v. 9. p. 517.—Realejo, Manzanilla Bay.

598. TOURNEFORTIA *lævigata*, Linn.—DC. Prod. v. 9. p. 519.—Panama, Atacames.

599. TOURNEFORTIA (*Pittonia*) *calycina*, sp. n., scabro-puberula vel demum glabrata, foliis breviter petiolatis ovatis oblongisve subacuminatis basi longe angustatis membranaceis, pedunculis

sub-4-stachyis, floribus confertis, calycis segmentis lineari-spathulatis obtusis corollæ tubum subæquantibus, corollæ lobis obtusis, fructu subgloboso glabro.—Acapulco.

Species calyce ab omnibus distincta. Ramuli subteretes, scabro-puberuli. Folia 3-6 poll. longa, 1-2 poll. lata, utrinque viridia, supra scaberrima, subtus ad venas scabra, cæterum glabra. Pedunculi terminales, 2-4-pollicares, apice sæpius bis bifidi, ramis scorpioideis 1-1½-poll. longis a basi confertim floriferis. Flores brevissime pedicellati. Calyx usque ad basin fissus, segmentis viridibus fere 3 lin. longis. Corolla extus glabra vel leviter puberula; tubus medio parum inflatus, ibidem intus staminifer; lobi undulato-plicati, obtusissimi vel emarginati. Ovarium glabrum. Stylus brevis, stigmate brevi conico. Fructus globosus, magnitudine seminis *Lathyri odorati*, integer.

600. TOURNEFORTIA *leptostachya*, sp. n., scandens, junior puberula, demum glabrescens, foliis oblongis obtusis vel acutis basi in petiolum brevem angustatis, cymis breviter pedunculatis dichotomis, spicis gracilibus remotifloris, calycis lobis acutis corollæ tubo subtriplo brevioribus, corollæ lobis obtusissimis emarginativse, fructu pubescente.—Huamantango.

Habitus et forma corollæ fere *T. fuliginosæ*, sed spicæ et flores multo minores. Ramuli novelli uti inflorescentia ferrugineo-puberuli. Folia quæ adsunt 2-3-pollicaria, rigide membranacea. Pedunculi laxe 5-7-stachyi, spicis vix pollicaribus. Flores omnes remoti; calyx vix ½ lin., corollæ tubus fere 1½ lin. longi, limbus patens, undulato-plicatus, tubo paullo brevior. Ovarium et fructus junior hirsuta. Stylus subnullus. Stigma elongato-conicum, ovario pluries longius. Fructus subinteger videtur, sed vix grossificatum vidi.

601. TOURNEFORTIA *obtusiflora*, sp. n., ramis pubescentibus, novellis subferrugineis, foliis petiolatis oblongis acutis acuminatisve basi angustatis supra tenuiter strigosis subtus pubescenti-hirtis tomentosisve, pedunculis terminalibus dichotomis 4-8-stachyis, calycibus strigoso-hirtis, corollæ tubo breviter exserto, limbi lobis brevissimis obtusissimis vel emarginatis, fructu glabro.—Guayaquil.

Rami lignosi, adulti teretes; ramuli novelli angulati, pilis brevibus dense hirsuti. Folia 2-3 poll. longa, 1 poll. lata, vel in ramis vegetioribus duplo majora, integerrima, interdum bullulata, infra nunc viridia parce hirsuta, nunc pube densa molliori canescentia. Pedunculi communes breves. Spicæ 1-1½-pollicares. Flores sessiles. Calycis lobi angusti, acuti. Corollæ tubus linea brevior, fere glaber, limbus latus subreflexus undulato-plicatus, brevissime et late 5-lobus, lobis emarginatis obtusissimis. Stylus supra ovarium brevissimus; stigma conicum, ovario styloque longius, e corolla tamen non exsertum. Fructus parvus, depresso-globosus, glaber, integerrimus.

602. TOURNEFORTIA *rufipila*, sp. n., ramis sparse rufo-hirtis et brevissime tomentoso-canescentibus, foliis breviter petiolatis elliptico-oblongis lanceolatisve utrinque longe angustatis supra sparse hirtis subtus tomentoso-pubescentibus ad venas hirtis, cyma rufo-hirta 5-7-stachya, floribus approximatis, calycis lobis subulato-acuminatis corollæ tubo paullo brevioribus, corollæ lobis ovatis obtusiusculis, fructu depresso-globoso subintegro glabro.—Salango.

Ramuli, pedunculi, petioli et foliorum pagina inferior vestiti pube brevissima canescente vel rufescente, pilis intermixtis longiusculis patentibus. Folia 3-5 poll. longa, 1-1½ poll. lata, pilis paginæ superioris rufis strigosis vel suberectis. Pedunculi 1-2-pollicares. Spicæ multifloræ, 1-1½ pollicares. Calycis lobi e basi ovata in acumen subulatum producti. Corollæ tubus extus pubescens, 1½ lin. longus, lobi breves, marginibus inflexis. Stamina vix tubo breviora. Ovarium pubescens. Stylus ovario longius, stigmate ovato conico subintegro. Fructus parvus, medio leviter depressus at vix lobatus, rugulosus. An eadem ac *T. cuspidata*, Humb. et Kunth? cujus flores et fructus ignota sunt.

603. TOURNEFORTIA *velutina*, Humb. et Kunth.—DC. Prod. v. 9. p. 524.—Acapulco.

604. TOURNEFORTIA, sp. n.? foliis subsessilibus bullato-rugosis scaberrimis, calycis lobis subulatis Corollæ in specimine destructæ.—Huamantango.

605. HELIOTROPIUM *curassavicum*, Linn.—DC. Prod. v. 9. p. 538.—Columbia.

606. HELIOTROPIUM *corymbosum*, Ruiz. et Pav.—DC. l. c.—These specimens agree perfectly with those cultivated as *H. grandiflorum*, but in both the calycine lobes are ovate, terminating in a short point.—Guayaquil.

607. HELIOPHYTUM *parviflorum*, DC. Prod. v. 9. p. 553.—Mexico to Guayaquil.

608. HELIOPHYTUM *indicum*, DC. Prod. v. 9. p. 556.—Mexico to Guayaquil.

609. LITHOSPERMUM, sp.—Apparently new, but the specimens imperfect, and cannot be well characterized till the remainder of the *Boragineæ* shall have been published in De Candolle's Prodromus.—Tepic.

HYDROLEACEÆ.

610. HYDROLEA *spinosa*, Linn.—Chois. Hydrol. p. 16.—Tepic, Acapulco, Panama.

611. WIGANDIA *Kunthii*, Chois. Hydrol. p. 22.—Manzanilla Bay.

612. WIGANDIA *scorpioides*, Chois. Hydrol. p. 23.—Realejo.

SOLANACEÆ.

613. NICANDRA *physalodes*, Gærtn.—Walp. Rep. 3. p. 22.—Guayaquil.

614. PHYSALIS *Linkiana*, Nees.—Walp. Rep. 3. p. 25.—Gulf of Fonseca.

615. WITHERINGIA *montana*, Dun.—Walp. Rep. 3. p. 32., var. uniflora, angustifolia, a varietate vulgatiore *arenaria*, Dun., verosimiliter specifice distincta.—Guayaquil.

616. WITHERINGIA *phyllantha*, Dun.—Walp. Rep. 3. p. 32.—Guayaquil.

617. CAPSICUM *frutescens*, Willd.—Walp. Rep. 3. p. 34.—San Blas, Guayaquil.

618. CAPSICUM *longum*, DC.—Walp. Rep. 3. p. 35.—Gulf of Fonseca.

619. SOLANUM *nigrum*, Linn.—Walp. Rep. 3. p. 47.—Guayaquil.

620. SOLANUM *verbascifolium*, Linn.—Walp. Rep. 3. p. 53.—Guayaquil.

621. SOLANUM *diphyllum*, Linn.—Walp. Rep. 3. p. 59.—Guayaquil.

622. SOLANUM, sp. præcedenti affine, floribus in specimine destructis.—Atacames.

623. SOLANUM (Micracantha) *flexicaule*, sp. n., undique pilis stellatis ferrugineo-villosum, ramis flexuosis, foliis geminis elliptico-oblongis integerrimis sinuatisve, costa utrinque aculeata, racemis folio brevioribus, pedicellis hirsutissimis subinermibus, calycibus crebre aculeatis.—Guayaquil.

Caulis in speciminibus scandens videtur, lignosus. Ramuli teretes, flexuosi, undique pilis stellatis rigidulis ferrugineis tecti et aculeis sparsis brevibus recurvis armati. Folia gemina, alterum 2-3 poll. longum, 6-9 lin. latum, apice et basi angustatum, alterum sæpius brevius, obtusius at non angustius, omnia crassiuscula, margine nunc integerrima nunc sæpius leviter et obtusissime sinuata; pagina superior pilis densis stellatis rigidulis scabro-hirta, inferior pilis pariter stellatis sed longioribus mollioribus tomentosa; venæ subtus prominentes; costa media subtus aculeis numerosis parvis recurvis, supra aculeis rarioribus acicularibus armata. Racemi laterales pollicares, a medio floriferi. Pedunculi ferrugineo-hispidi; pedicelli vix 2 lin. longi, pariter hispidi et interdum aculeis paucis acicularibus armati. Calycis tubus per anthesin brevis, aculeis rectis parvis mox increscentibus, lobi 1-1¼ lin. longi, lanceolati, dense ferrugineo-hispidi. Corolla profunde 5-partita, lobis lanceolato-linearibus, extus stellato-tomentosis, 5-6 lin. longis. Antheræ corollam subæquantes, superne attenuatæ. Ovarium hirsutum, biloculare. Baccam non vidi. Species affinis videtur *S. aturensi* et *S. volubili*.

624. SOLANUM *scabrum*, Vahl.—Walp. Rep. 3. p. 72.—Variat foliis omnibus integris vel plerisque profunde sinuato-lobatis.—Panama, gathered also by Cuming, n. 1134.

625. SOLANUM *torvum*, Sw.—Walp. Rep. 3. p. 78.—Mexico to Guayaquil.

626-629.—SOLANUM, four species; two from Panama, and two from Columbia, all belonging apparently to the *torvum* section, but in too imperfect a state to be determined accurately in this overgrown genus.

630. LYCOPERSICUM *peruvianum*, Mill.—Walp. Rep. 3. p. 100.—Guayaquil.

631. LYCOPERSICUM *esculentum*, Mill.—Walp. Rep. 3. p. 101.—Tepic.

632. THINOGETON *maritimum*, gen. nov. *Solanacearum* baccatarum.—Sandy beech, Columbia.

CHAR. GEN. Calyx 5-dentatus. Corolla infundibuliformi-campanulata, limbo vix patente, plicato, 5-angulato. Stamina 5 inæqualia, inclusa, infra medium corollæ inserta; antheræ erectæ, oblongæ, biloculares, loculis longitudinaliter dehiscentibus. Ovarium biloculare. Stylus apice spathulato-dilatatus, margine crassiuscule stigmatosus. Bacca calyce aucto membranaceo inclusa, bilocularis, cortice membranaceo, pulpa tenui. Semina plurima, suborbiculata, compressa, rugosa. Embryo valde curvatus.

T. maritimum. Herba in arena prostrata, pedalis vel longior, ramosa, viscoso-pubescens, carnosula. Folia alterna, longiuscule petiolata, lanceolata vel oblonga ½-1-pollicaria, sinuato-lobata vel grosse dentata, basi angustata, crassiuscula. Pedicelli solitarii vel gemini, laterales vel ad apices ramorum unilateraliter racemosi, 2-4 lin. longi, ebracteati. Calyx 3 lin. longus, viscoso-pubescens, dentibus angustis acuminatis tubo suo brevioribus; fructifer 5 lin. longus, subinflatus. Corolla 15-16 lin. longa, tubus intra calycem tenuis, dein gradatim ampliatus more *Convolvuli* vel *Ipomœæ* in faucem campanulatam. Bacca 4 lin. longa, obtusa.

The specimens of this plant are covered with particles of sand adhering to them as in *Abroniæ*, *Nolanæ*, and other maritime plants from the same coast. The genus approaches, in some respects, to *Jaborosa*, but is readily distinguished both by the calyx and corolla.

633. LYCIUM *salsum*, Ruiz et Pav.—Walp. Rep. 3. p. 108.—Guayaquil.

634. ACNISTUS *arborescens*, Schlecht.—Walp. Rep. 3. p. 112.—Columbia.

635. DATURA *Stramonium*, Linn.—Walp. Rep. 3. p. 16.—Mexico to Guayaquil.

636. CESTRUM *Parqui*, Lher.—Walp. Rep. 3. p. 119.—Tepic.

637. CESTRUM sp.—A very imperfect specimen, from Panama.

SCROPHULARIACEÆ.

638. LEPTOGLOSSIS *schwenckioides*, gen. nov. e tribu *Salpiglossidearum*.—Huamantango.

CHAR. GEN. Calyx 5-dentatus. Corollæ tubus elongatus, apice subgibbus, faux non dilatata, limbi obliqui patentis laciniæ 5, subæquales, breves, latæ, integræ, æstivatione imbricatæ subplicatæ, posticæ exteriores. Stamina didynama; antheræ biloculares, loculis divaricatis latis demum explicato-planis confluentibus; staminum posticorum dimidio minores. Stylus apice petaloideo-dilatatus, lamina orbiculari supra tenuiter stigmatosa. Capsula membrancea, valvulis dissepimentum membranaceum parallelum nudantibus demum bifidis. Placentæ dissepimento adnatæ. Semina numerosa, subangulata.—Huamantango.

L. schwenckioides. Herba erecta, ramosa, undique viscido-puberula. Folia alterna, sessilia, 6-9 lin. longa, lanceolata vel lineari-lanceolata, acuta, integerrima, uninervia, utrinque viridia, superiora decrescentia. Panicula terminalis, oblonga, semipedalis. Flores ad apices ramulorum conferti, irregulariter et sæpius simpliciter cymosi, subsessiles vel pedicello calyce breviori ebracteato. Calyx sub anthesi 1½ lin., fructifer 2 lin. longus tubuloso-campanulatus, viscido-puberulus, venis 5 latis viridibus inter venas membranaceus, dentibus 5 acutis tubo suo multo brevioribus. Corollæ tubus 8-9 lin. longus, tenuis, membranaceus; limbus 3-4 lin. latus. Capsula calycem subæquans, ovata, acutiuscula. Semina nondum matura, sed forma iis Schwenkiæ similia et verosimiliter embryo pariter leviter incurva.

This genus is in some measure intermediate between *Schwenckia* and *Browallia*, but well characterized by the form of the corolla and by the stamens. It belongs to the *Salpiglossideæ*, one of the three suborders into which I have divided the *Scrophulariaceæ*, in the manuscript prepared for the tenth volume of De Candolle's Prodromus. This suborder is characterized by the inflorescence, which like that of the capsular *Solanaceæ*, is always some modification of a terminal centrifugal simple or compound cyme, and by the æstivation of the corolla which is a combination of the plicate, and imbricato-bilabiate, approaching more or less to the one or to the other in different genera.

639. BROWALLIA *demissa*, Linn.—Walp. Rep. 3. p. 236.—Salango, Guayaquil.

640. BROWALLIA *peduncularis*, sp. n., viscoso-pubescens, foliis ovatis vel ovato-oblongis sessilibus vel inferioribus petiolatis utrinque scabro-hirtis, floribus paucis axillaribus vel laxe racemosis, pedunculis calyce pluries longioribus, calycis viscosissimi laciniis oblongis tubo longioribus.—Huamantango; it is also Mathew's, n. 512, from Purrochuca.

Tota rigidior quam *B. demissa*. Folia pollicaria vel superiora minora. Rami floriferi viscosi. Flores majusculi et calyces fere *B. viscosæ* cui etiam scabritie affinis, sed pedunculi 1-3-pollicares nec calyce breviores et folia minora.

641. BROWALLIA *abbreviata*, sp. n., superne viscoso-pubescens vel demum glabrata, foliis ovatis vel ovato-oblongis glabriusculis, floribus racemosis, pedicellis calyce subbrevioribus, calycis campanulati laciniis ovato-oblongis tubo æquilongis.—Huamantango; it is also Mathew's, n. 712, from Purrochuca, and Cuming's, n. 1078, from Lima.

Species affinis *B. grandifloræ* et forte ejus varietas, sed distincta videtur imprimis calyce brevi lato.

642. GALVESIA *limensis*, Domb. β *grandiflora*, Benth. in DC. Prod. n. 10 ined., foliis calycibusque acutioribus, corolla kermesina 9 lin. longa.—Mante, in Columbia.

643. RUSSELIA *sarmentosa*, Jacq.—Walp. Rep. 3. p. 251.—Very abundant, from Tepic to Panama.

644. RUSSELIA *rotundifolia*, Cav.—Walp. Rep. 3. p. 252.—San Blas, Acapulco.

645. STEMODIA (Adenosma), *pusilla*, sp. n., humilis, annua, villosula, foliis petiolatis ovatis crenatis, pedicellis calyce longioribus, segmentis calycinis anguste linearibus tubo corollæ brevioribus.—Tepic.

Specimen unicum 4-pollicare, ramosum, fere a basi florens. Pubes brevis viscidula pilis longiusculis albidis præsertim in caule mixta. Ramuli graciles, subfiliformes, adscendentes vel erecti. Petioli tenues, 2 lin. longi, basi non dilatati. Folia 2-4 lin. longa, obtusa, grosse paucicrenata, basi obtusa vel cuneata, superiora minora angustiora. Pedicelli axillares, filiformes, 3-4 lin. longi. Calyces 1½ lin. longi, segmentis 4 inferioribus angustissimis, supremo paullo majore, superne subdilatato. Bracteæ vel desunt vel minutæ, setaceæ. Corolla 3-3½ lin. longa, ei *S. parvifloræ* similis. Stamina et stylus eadem. Capsula calycem subæquans, acuminata, bipartibilis; valvulæ integræ, marginibus involutis placentas demum segregatas nudantibus. Semina numerosa minuta, obovoidea.

A very distinct species, allied to *S. foliosa* and to *S. viscosa* in the structure of the flower and fruit, but totally different in habit and foliage.

646. STEMODIA *durantifolia*, Sw.—Walp. Rep. 3. p. 269.—Guayaquil.

647. HERPESTES *Monnieria*, Humb. et Kunth.—Walp. Rep. 3. p. 282.—Manzanilla Bay.

648. CAPRARIA *biflora*, Linn.—Walp. Rep. 3. p. 263.—Tepic.

649. CAPRARIA *peruviana*, Feuill.—*Xuaresia biflora*, Ruiz. et Pav.—Walp. Rep. 3. p. 264.—Guayaquil.

650. SCOPARIA *dulcis*, Linn.—Walp. Rep. 3. p. 331.—Guayaquil.

651. BUDDLEIA *americana*, Linn.—Walp. Rep. 3. p. 325.—Salango.

652. BUCHNERA *pilosa*, Benth. in DC. Prod. v. 10. ined.—*B. elongata*, β *pilosa*, Schlecht. Linnæa, v. 8. p. 245.—Realejo.

653. BUCHNERA *elongata*, Sw.—Walp. Rep. 3. p. 301.—Tepic.

654. BUCHNERA *lavandulacea*, Cham. Schlecht.—Walp. Rep. 3. p. 304.—Isle of Taboga, Bay of Panama.

655. LAMOUROUXIA *viscosa*, Humb. et Kunth.—Walp. Rep. 3. p. 398.—Acapulco.

656. LAMOUROUXIA *cordata*, Cham. Schlecht.—Walp. Rep. 3. p. 398.—Acapulco.

657. LAMOUROUXIA *multifida*, Humb. et Kunth.—Walp. Rep. 3. p. 398.—Tepic.

ACANTHACEÆ.

The specimens belonging to this natural order have been submitted to Professor Nees von Esenbeck of Breslau, who has kindly determined them, and transmitted to me the following names and characters of the new species.

658. MENDOZIA *puberula*, Mart.—Salango.

659. ELYTRARIA *apargiæfolia*, Nees ab E.—Gulf of Fonseca.

660. ELYTRARIA *ramosa*, Humb. et Kunth.—Acapulco.

661. SCLEROCALYX *mexicanus*, Nees ab E., gen. nov.—Acapulco.

CHAR. GEN. Calyx grandis, coriaceus, basi brevi spatio tubulosus, profunde quinquefidus, laciniis æqualibus extus canaliculatis, æstivatione quinquangularis, laciniis lateris interioris superficie valvatim conjunctis. Corolla crassiuscula, tubulosa, extus tomentosa, limbo 5-fido regulari laciniis planis. Stamina 4; antheræ bilocellatæ, cordato-oblongæ, locellis parallelis muticis margine nudis. Ovarium ovatum, biloculare, loculis biovulatis; stylus filiformis; stigma oblique rostratum sive unilabiatum, basi superne impressum. Fructus latet. Inflorescentia: pedunculi versus apicem caulis axillares, oppositi, solitarii vel gemini, apice trifidi foliisque bractealibus caulinis similibus at minoribus præditi. Pedunculi partiales firmi, infra apicem bibracteati, uni-triflori. Bracteæ partiales parvæ.—Herba Mexicana, erecta. Genus *Trichantheræ* et *Macrostegiæ* accedens, differt ab hac calycis æqualis et crassi æstivatione et antheris, ab illa calyce longo nec imbricato antherisque haud ciliatis.

S. Mexicanus. Caulis erectus, ramosus, pluripedalis, obtuse tetragonus, grosse lenticellatus, dense at subtiliter tomentosus, sicuti et petioli, inflorescentia et calyces. Folia caulis 7-8 poll. longa, 3 poll. lata, ovato-elliptica, basi acuta in petiolum pollicarem desinentia, apice cuspidato-acuminata cuspide obtusiusculo, integerrima, supra subtusque (præsertim in costis) puberula. Pedunculi folio breviores, rigidi, erecti. Folia floralia 1-1½ poll. longa, oblonga, petiolata. Pedunculi proprii patentes, longitudine petioli folii floralis. Bracteolæ infra apicem duæ, aliis spathulatæ aliis lineares, tomentosæ. Calyx pollicaris, laciniis lanceolatis acutiusculis utrinque tomentosis. Corollam explicatam non vidi (*albam* describit schedula adjecta). Stamina quod ad antheras, si pilos demis, *Tricantheræ* similia. Ovarium annulo lato cinctum, biloculare, quadriovulatum.

662. SCORODOXYLUM *terminale*, Nees ab E., sp. n., suffruticosum, caule basi repente adscendente tetragono apicem versus laxe pubescente, foliis oblongo-ovalibus acuminatis basi acutis repando-crenatis tenuibus glabris costis subtus strigosis, thyrso terminali sessili parvo, bracteis calycisque laciniis subulatis scabris, capsula a medio superne 6-8-sperma.—Atacames.

Quod ad inflorescentiam haud absimile est *Stemonacantho Humboldtiano*, sed reliqua sunt hujus generis. Caulis anguli acutiusculi sunt. Folia inferiora cum petiolo semipollicari 6-7 poll. longa, 2-2¼ poll. lata, obiter repando-crenata. Thyrsus, caulem terminans, adjecto folio 4-pollicari, vix pollicaris est, floribus arcte contiguis, quasi glomeratis, plerisque sessilibus bracteis parvis interstinctis. Corolla 8 lin. longa, anguste infundibuliformis, coccinea, limbo regulari, laciniis ovalibus retusis. Stamina inclusa. Capsula 5 lin. longa, basi valde angusta, a medio ovalis et juxta originem septi 6-sperma.

663. APHRAGMIA *Haenkei*, Nees ab E.—*Ruellia albicaulis*, Bertero, var. α et β.—Central America; Acapulco.

664. APHRAGMIA *rotundifolia*, Nees ab E., sp. n., ramis teretibus glanduloso-pubescentibus, foliis ovatis obtusis integerrimis viscoso-pubescentibus, pedunculis axillaribus dichotomis, bracteis subrotundis; capsulæ loculis mono-vel dispermis.—Guayaquil.

A. viscida differt ramis teretibus, foliis minoribus obtusis, pedunculis crassioribus, bracteis subrotundis floribusque minoribus.

665. APHELANDRA *pectinata*, Herb. Willd.—Acapulco; Nicoya; Isle of Taboga, Bay of Panama; Gulf of Fonseca; Isthmus of Darien.—Ejusdem var. *macra*, Nees ab E.—Columbia.

666. APHELANDRA *Sinclairiana*, Nees ab E., sp. n., (Plate XLVII.) fruticosa, foliis oblongo-lanceolatis apice et basi acuminatis et in petiolum longum attenuatis utrinque præsertim in costis cauleque hirsutis, spicis terminalibus fastigiatis, bracteis ovalibus integerrimis sericeo-pubescentibus calyce longioribus, infimis patulis acuminatis, reliquis imbricatis ventricosis obtusissimis, laciniis calycinis chartaceis lanceolatis acutis subtilissime velutinis, corolla ringente, labio superiore bidentato, inferioris lacinia media ovato-lanceolata acuminata, lateralibus brevissimis obtusis labio superiori accretis.—Panama, Isthmus of Darien.

Differt ab *A. Schiedeana*, Schl., hirsutie insigni et abii corollæ inferioris longe alia figura; ab *A. Hartwegiana* recedit bracteis majoribus (licet minoribus quam in *A. Schiedeana*) calyces obtegentibus nec iis brevioribus, magisque pubescentibus. Folia pedalia, 2-2⅓ poll. lata, pilosa, costis hirsutis. Spicæ in summo caule 3-5, semipedales, cylindricæ. Bracteæ infimæ herbaceæ, acuminatæ, steriles, tunc aliquot coloratæ atque acutæ; reliquæ cunctæ coloratæ et obtusæ. Corolla coccinea, bipollicaris.

Plate XLVII. fig. 1, calyx; fig. 2, corolla cut open; fig. 3, ovary and base of style; fig. 4, summit of the style; fig. 5, longitudinal section of the ovary.

667. DIPTERACANTHUS *foetidus*, Nees ab E.—*Ruellia foetida*, Humb. et Kunth.—Acapulco.

668. BARLERIA *micans* (Nees ab E.), suffruticosa, inermis; foliis oblongo-lanceolatis utrinque attenuatis cauleque strigosis, spica terminali imbricata subcylindrica, bractea calycisque laciniis majoribus ovatis brevi-cuspidatis dentato-ciliatis, lacinia inferiore bifida, floribus subdiandris.—*Eranthemum cristatum*, herb. Willd. R. et Sch. S. Veg. Mant. 1. p. 153.—*Justicia serrata*, Humb. in herb. Willd. l. c.;—*Justicia oxyphylla*, herb. DC.—Isle of Taboga, Bay of Panama; Isthmus of Darien.

669. BARLERIA *discolor*, Nees ab E., sp. n., suffruticosa, inermis, foliis ovalibus vel ovali-oblongis acutis in petiolum cuneatim desinentibus cauleque strigosis subtus argenteo-albicantibus, spica terminali ovata imbricata, bractea calycisque laciniis majoribus rhombeo-ovalibus acuminatis dentato-ciliatis, lacinia inferiore bifida, floribus diandris.—Nicoya.

Similis *B. micanti*, differt autem non modo notis adlatis, sed etiam calycibus bracteisque cyaneis dentibus paucioribus circa margines (laciniæ superioris 6-7, inferioris 3-4 a medio ad apicem) magisque patentibus præditis, corollaque (læte violacea) paullo majore, limbo magis patulo magisque inæquali. Folia inferiora 8½-9 poll. longa, 3-3½ poll. lata, cuspidato-acuta; omnia subtus plus minus argenteo-nitentia, qui color neutiquam ab integumento quadam oritur, nam pili plantæ ut in *B. micante* flavescentes sunt.

670. LEPTOSTACHYA *Martiana*, Nees ab E., spicis simplicibus ramosisve umbellatis folium æquantibus in paniculam terminalem magis compositam transeuntibus, foliis subsessilibus ovato-lanceolatis subcordatis apice attenuatis, rhachi paniculæ terminalis hirsuta glandulosave, antheris muticis.—Var. caule foliisque glabris, paniculæ rhachi hinc inde hirsuta.—Guayaquil.

671. LEPTOSTACHYA *crinita*, Nees ab E., sp. n., spicis subsimplicibus umbellatis folio duplo brevioribus in paniculam terminalem parvam transeuntibus, foliis ovali-oblongis acumine obtuso basi in petiolum longum cuneatim attenuatis, caule basi repente glabro articulis panicularibus patenti-pilosis, antheris muticis.—Columbia.

Differt a *L. parviflora* foliis latioribus (4-4¼ poll. longis, et 1¼ poll. fere latis) basi elongato-cuneiformibus, apice minus attenuatis, articulis infra et intra paniculam pilis patentissimis vestitis, et antheris muticis.

672. ORTHOTACTUS *oblongus*, Nees ab E., sp. n., herbaceus, spicis axillaribus e foliorum superiorum angulis folio brevioribus, bracteis rhombeo-ovatis acuminatis venosis ciliatis, foliis oblongis in acumen obtusiusculum longe attenuatis basi acute in petiolum brevem desinentibus glabriusculis, caule geniculato basi radicante apicem versus incano et ad genicula compresso, corollæ labio superiori bifido, inferioris laciniis ovalibus obtusis puberulis.—Columbia.

Propinquus est *Orthotacto nemoroso*, at differt bracteis fere glabris angustioribus basique magis cuneatis, tum spicis axillaribus alternis, nec una primitus terminali accedente subinde et altera laterali. Folia tenuia, flaccida; inferiora 7-8 poll. longa, 2 poll. lata; superiora 4-5 poll. longa, 1½ poll. fere lata.

673. ERANTHEMUM *cordatum*, Nees ab E., sp. n., foliis ovali-oblongis in acumen obtusum attenuatis basi anguste cordatis subrepandis glabris (tenuibus), spica terminali simplici rhachi cauleque superne puberulis, floribus glomeratim simpliciterve oppositis approximatis, bracteis subulatis brevissimis, corollæ tubo calyce subglanduloso multo longiore, limbo brevi.—Atacames.

Folia valde tenuia, inferiora (cum petiolo angusto 1-1¼ poll. longo) 9 poll. longa, 3 poll. lata, basi rotundata et ad petioli insertionem emarginata, nonnihil inæqualia, læte viridia, utrinque lineolata. Corolla pollicaris, angusta, laciniis limbi obtusis (oblongis) vix trilinearibus. Stamina duo, exserta; sterilia nulla. Capsula virescens, 7 lin. longa, tetrasperma, ungue longo.

674. TETRAMERIUM *polystachyum*, Nees ab E., gen. nov.—*Justiciæ*, sp. Auct.—Tiger Island, Gulf of Fonseca.

CHAR. GEN.—Calyx parvus, quadrifidus, laciniis æqualibus, bracteolatus. Corolla tubuloso-infundibuliformis, profunde et inæqualiter quadrifida, laciniis angustis, altera lacinia magis ad alterum latus conversa. Stamina duo, prope a faucibus inserta; antherarum locelli paralleli, contigui, basi mutici. Stigma obtusum. Capsula bivalvis, bilocularis, basi brevi spatio compressa et unguiculata, commissura valvularum plana, apicem versus depressa, dorso valvularum angusto plano, tetrasperma. Dissepimentum maturo fructu a dorso valvularum earumque parietibus basi solutum brevi spatio, quoad retinacula ei inserta sunt, unci ad instar reflectitur. Semina discoidea, papillosa, retinaculis acutis suffulta. Inflorescentia: spicæ in ramulis axillaribus terminales, bracteatæ, quadrifariæ. Flores sub singula bractea 2-3, sessiles. Bracteæ latæ, herbaceæ. Bracteolæ laciniis calycinis similes. Corolla parva, tenera, pallida.—Fruticuli Mexicani et insularum Indiæ occidentalis, ramosi, polystachyi, foliis mediocribus petiolatis, bracteis plus minus ciliatis.

T. polystachyum, caule ramosissimo petiolisque patenti-hirsutis, foliis ovatis basi obtusis apice attenuatis, spicis in ramulis brevibus axillaribus oppositis terminalibus, bracteis oblongo-ovalibus mucronatis.—Frutex 1-2-pedalis, dense ramosus, patenti-hirsutus, incanus, infra genicula alternatim compressus; rami inferius genuflexi. Folia (ramorum) inferiora, cum petiolo 4-5 lin. longo angusto hirsuto, 1½-2 poll. longa et 6-8 lin. ad basin lata, hinc apicem versus attenuata, apice obtusiusculo, ciliata, subrepanda, tenuia, ramis costalibus 4-5 subtus hirtis; folia superiora et bractealia infra spicas minora, magis lanceolata. Spicæ cum ramulo suo folio breviores, ovales, foliorum rami summo pari suffultæ. Bracteæ 4 lin. longæ, obtusæ cum mucrone, dorso et margine hirsutæ, tri-vel obscure 5-nerves, flavo-virides. Bracteolæ calyce longiores, lanceolatæ, ciliatæ (3 lin. longæ). Calycis quadrifidi laciniæ subulatæ, ciliatæ, 1 lin. longæ. Corolla 6 lin. longa, pallida, tubo gracili, limbi laciniis lanceolato-linearibus obtusis patentibus, una remotiori. Stamina parum exserta, antheris linearibus basi parum inæqualibus. Ovarium ovale. Fructum non observavi.

675. TETRAMERIUM *nervosum*, Nees ab. E., sp. n., (Plate XLVIII.), caule ramose bifariam piloso, foliis ovatis acuminatis longe petiolatis supra parce pilosis (nec lineolatis), spicis in ramulis brevibus axillaribus alternis adscendentibus tetragonis, bracteis arcte incumbentibus ovatis mucronato-acutis villosis ciliatisque venoso-quinquenervibus.—Puna, near Guayaquil.*

Caulis et rami graciles, laxi, ad genicula compresso-tetragoni, cortice brunneo confertim griseo-punctato. Folia cum petiolo ¾-½ poll. longo hirto 2½-2¾ poll. longa, circa basin 10-12 lin. lata, hinc attenuata, basi obtusa, supra raris pilis conspersa, subtus ad costas et in margine scabra, ramis costalibus 5 debilibus. Spicæ ratione ramorum crassæ, sæpe incurvæ, 1-1¼ poll. longæ. Bracteæ virides, basi brevi spatio contractæ et pallidæ, longis villis ciliatæ, 4 lin. longæ, 3 lin. latæ. Calyx cum bracteolis lin. 1 longus, laciniis lanceolato-subulatis mollibus longe ciliatis haud ad basin divisis. Corolla 5-6 lin. longa, laciniis linearibus? (incompletis in nostro specimine.) Capsula bilinearis, pubescens, pallida. Semina matura fusca, grosse tuberculata. Tertia hujus generis species est *T. racemulosum* (*Justicia racemulosa*, Wikstr.)

Plate XLVIII. fig. 1, bud; fig. 2, stamen; fig. 3, ovary; fig. 4, summit of the style; fig. 5, capsule; fig. 6, seed; fig. 7, embryo; fig. 8, bud of *T. polystachyum*: fig. 9, expanded flowers of *T. polystachyum*; all magnified.

676. HENRYA *insularis*,† Nees ab. E., gen. nov. (Plate XLIX.)—Island off the coast of Veragua.

CHAR. GEN.—Flores in capitulo unifloro, bracteis involucralibus duabus altero margine connatis altero liberis et igitur rima apiceque bidente dehiscentibus inclusa, dispositi. Calyx quinquepartitus, parvus, æqualis. Corolla bilabiata, labio superiore latiore usque ad medium bifido, inferiore bipartito laciniis spathulatis.‡ Stamina duo; antheræ bilocellatæ, muticæ, locellis parallelis contiguis apice æqualibus basi inæqualibus. Stylus longus, filiformis, apice contortus; stigma compressum, obtusum. Capsula ab inferiori parte compressa valvularum commissura plano-contigua asperma, apicem versus incomplete bilocularis disperma, dissepimento angusto basi cum retinaculo suo uncinato obtuso brevi spatio solubili uncinatim reflexo. Semina plano-convexa, dorso setosa, ventre pubescenti-scabra. Inflorescentia: involucra in ramis oppositis cauleque terminali spicata,

---

* Amongst the specimens not seen by Professor Nees are some of a narrower leaved variety from Tepic.

† Amatus Henry, instituti lithographici academici Bonnensis Possessor, Academiæ Leopoldino-Carolinæ Cæsareæ Naturæ Curiosorum Bibliothecarius, tum dissertationibus suis de gemmarum plantarum structura tum stylo artificiosissimo de scientia nostra ut qui maxime meritur est. (N. ab E.)

‡ In the *H. insularis*, I find rather a quadrifid corolla, the lobes all spathulate, nearly equal in length, and entire, the upper one rather broader and the style blunt, but shortly two-lobed at the apex (G. Bentham).

opposita, bracteis parvis suffulta.—Frutices Americæ meridionalis, ramis elongatis involucrisque glanduloso-pilosis, foliis ovatis ovalibusve petiolatis subhirsutis minus glandulosis, spicis longis, involucris distantibus, bracteis involucro multo minoribus ovato-subrotundis mucronatis. Genus intermedium inter *Hypoestem* et *Dicliptera*, et maxime id quidem insigne eo, quod involucrum bivalve *Dicliptera* hic veluti in utriculum oblongum apice bidentatum coalescit, neque vera eum ab omni latere, sed ab altero margine tantum clausum, ab altera parte vero discretis marginibus rima apertum.

H. insularis, involucris acutis, caule inferne tereti superne tetragono.—Foliorum lamina 4 poll. longa, utrinque acuta, integerrima, pilosa, nitida, viridis, costis senis parum prominulis; petiolus pollicaris, piloso-glandulosus. Racemi circiter tripollicares, laterales oppositi arcu incurvi. Involucra 4¼ lin. longa, obconoidea, apice bidentata, pubescenti-glandulosa. Calyx vix lin. 1 longus. Corolla tenera, infundibuliformis, 3 lin. longa. Stamina limbum 1¼-2 lin. longum æquantia, erecta. Stylus longior. Capsula 3 lin. longa, straminea, glabra. Seminum setæ dorsales statu humido strictæ, in sicco corrugatæ, laxæ, lanam referentes; constant singulæ e pluribus cellis elongatis conjunctis, in quibus hinc inde fibræ spiralis vestigia vidisse puto; cellulæ interiores obscuriores sunt quam reliquæ. In superficie setarum sub inde denticuli prominent.

Plate XLIX; fig. 1, involucre; fig. 2, flower; fig. 3, corolla cut open; fig. 4, ovary; fig. 5, summit of the style; fig. 6, capsule; fig. 7, seed; fig. 8, embryo; all magnified.

677. HENRYA *Barclayana*, Nees ab E., sp. n., involucris obtusis, caule quadriquetro.—Manzanilla Bay.

Folia brevi-petiolata. Involucra densissime pubescenti-glandulosa, apice obtusa, scil. foliolis conjunctis haud mucronatis sed apice rotundatis.

678. BLECHUM *Linnæi*, Nees ab E.—Panama to Guayaquil.

679. DICLIPTERA *multiflora*, Humb. et Kunth.—Guayaquil.

680. DICLIPTERA *confinis*, Nees ab E., sp. n., caule sexangulari glabro novello sparsim piloso, foliis oblongis acuminatis basi acutis longe petiolatis utrinque lineolatis glabris, florum umbellis sessilibus in spicam terminalem foliosam transeuntibus, bracteis late ovatis cuspidato-acuminatis glabris ciliatis trinervibus nervis lateralibus trifidis.—Guayaquil.

Differt a *D. peruviana* caule fere glabro nec nisi pilis raris adsperso, foliisque angustioribus et bracteis, præter harum cilia, fere omnino glabris. An var. ?

681. DICLIPTERA *unguiculata*, Nees ab E., sp. n., caule geniculato obsolete angulato apicem versus pubescentia brevi reversa scabro, foliis ovatis utrinque acutis longe petiolatis lineolatis margine hispido-scabris, florum umbellis sessilibus axillaribus vel in spicas axillares terminalemque compactis, bracteis inæqualibus scabris ciliatis trinervibus, superiori suborbiculari aristato-cuspidata basi longe cuneiformi, inferiori duplo minore spathulato-lineari truncata aristato-cuspidata.—Guayaquil.

Caulis videtur procumbens et diffusus; valde est geniculatim flexus, inferne glaber et fere teres. Folia cum petiolo semipollicari 2-3 poll. longa, 1-1¼ poll. lata, acumine arguto prædita et basi etiam acuta. Bracteæ basi luteæ, subtilissime pubescenti-scabræ, mucrone longo setaceo cuspidatæ, ciliatæ; superior 5 lin. longa, inferior 3 lin. et ea arcte incumbens. An eadem ac *D. pilosa* H. et Kunth.? repugnant autem "bracteæ villosæ," et in descriptione: "tres, quarum laterales lineari-subulatæ," missa omnino bractea inferiore, quæ singulari sua structura oculos effugere nequibat.

LABIATÆ.

682. HYPTIS *capitata*, Jacq.—Benth. Lab. p. 104.—Acapulco.

683. HYPTIS (Cephalohyptis) *florida*, sp. n., herbacea, erecta, glabriuscula, foliis petiolatis ovatis vel ovato-lanceolatis acuminatis obtusiusculis irregulariter crenatis basi cuneatis, pedunculis capitulo demum subgloboso dense multifloro longioribus, bracteis numerosis oblongo-lanceolatis obtusis coloratis exterioribus capitulo longioribus, receptaculo vix pilosulo, calycis florentis tubuloso-campanulati dentibus e basi lanceolata subulatis rigidis hirtellis tubo suo longioribus.— Guayaquil.

Affinis *H. involucratæ*, *H. capitatæ*, et. *H. radiatæ*, a priore foliis, ab his bracteis amplis et dentibus calycinis abunde distincta. Caules elati videntur, tetragoni, ad nodos ciliati, cæterum glabri. Folia bipollicaria utrinque viridia, subtus pallidiora, undique glabra, petiolo 6-12 lin. longo interdum minute ciliolato. Folia superiora angustiora, floralia lanceolata, omnia tamen petiolata. Capitula pauca in racemum laxum disposita, pedunculis bipollicaribus. Bracteæ exteriores 6-8 lin. longæ, primum patentes, dein reflexæ. Receptaculum dilatatum, concavum. Calycis tubus hirtellus, sub anthesi abbreviatus, dein elongatus, limbus campanulatus, submembranaceus, dentibus basi breviter lanceolatis in setam rigidam $1\frac{1}{2}$ lin. longam productis. Corollæ tubus dentes calycinos æquans, labium superius breve, lobis latis rotundatis, labium inferius longius, lobis lateralibus late lanceolatis, intermedia longiore abrupte deflexo orbiculato-concavo subsaccato. Carpidia lævia, ovoidea, in specimine nondum matura.

684. HYPTIS *rhytidea*, Benth. Pl. Hartw. p. 21.—Tepic.

685. HYPTIS *polystachya*, Humb. et Kunth.—Benth. Lab. p. 119.—Tepic.

686. HYPTIS *spicata*, Poit.—Benth. Lab. p. 120.—Tepic.

687. HYPTIS *melissoides*, Humb. et Kunth.—Benth. Lab. p. 123. — Var. petiolis longioribus, pedunculis fasciculatis.—Guayaquil.

688. HYPTIS *suaveolens*, Poit.—Benth. Lab. p. 124.—Realejo.

689. HYPTIS *pectinata*, Poit.—Benth. Lab. p. 127.—Panama to Guayaquil.

690. HYPTIS *stellulata*, Benth. Lab. p. 129.—Acapulco.

691. HYPTIS *verticillata*, Jacq.—Benth. Lab. p. 130.—Panama, Columbia.

692. SALVIA *occidentalis*, Sw.—Benth. Lab. p. 244.—Tepic; Tiger Island, Gulf of Fonseca.

693. SALVIA (Microsphace) *privoides*, sp. n., herbacea, caule hispido, foliis breviter petiolatis ovatis acutiusculis basi cuneatis supra hispidis subtus ferrugineo-vel albido-villosis, floralibus bracteæformibus ovatis acuminatis persistentibus, racemis elongatis basi subramosis, verticillastris 2-6-floris remotis, floribus minutis, calycis tubulosi hispidi subglandulosi labio superiore integro lobisque inferioris setaceo-mucronatis, corolla calyce paullo longiore, connectivis postice membranaceo-dilatatis obtusis connatis, styli lobo superiore acuto, inferiore breviore orbiculato-reniformi.— Gulf of Fonseca.

Habitu *S. occidentali* affinis, sed rigidior et undique hispida. Rami crassi, tetragoni, pilis subreversis undique canescenti-hirti. Folia 1-2-pollicaria, inferiora in petiolum brevem angustata, ovata vel rhombea, supra medium serrato-crenata, rugosa; superiora minora, basi latiora; summa basi rotundato-truncata. Racemi 3-6-pollicares. Bracteæ (seu folia floralia) ovato-lanceolatæ, setaceo-acuminatæ, erectæ, 1 vel vix 2 lin. longæ. Calyx sub anthesi 1½ lin. longus, fructifer 3 lin., pilis rigidis hispidus aliis glanduliferis intermixtis. Corolla ei *S. occidentalis* similis. Stylus glaber, lobo inferiore latissimo. Carpidia ovoidea, humectata extus gelatinosa; albumen nullum; cotyledones ovato-cordatæ; radicula brevis, recta, ad hilum spectans.

694. SALVIA (Calosphace, Micranthæ) *orbicularis*, sp. n., fruticosa, humilis, pubescens, foliis petiolatis orbiculatis crenatis basi late subcordatis utrinque puberulis glabratisque, racemis simplicibus, verticillastris sexfloris longiusculis, calycis hirti subglandulosi labio superiore integro inferiorisque lobis vix mucronulatis, corolla calyce subdimidio longiore, connectivis postice subclavatis connatis, styli glabri lobo superiore brevi acuto, inferiore longiore oblongo-spathulato obtuso.—Panama.

Fruticulus tortuoso-ramosus. Rami herbacei, adscendentes, vix semipedales, pilis brevibus subreversis canescentes. Folia pleraque ½ poll. longa et lata, supra glabriuscula vel sparse puberula, subtus pallidiora præsertim ad venas puberula, crebre at minute punctata. Racemi 2-3-pollicares. Bracteæ (seu folia floralia) parvæ, lanceolatæ, acuminatæ, hispidæ, deciduæ. Pedicelli breves. Flores fere *S. micranthæ*. Calyx florens vix 2 lin. longus, fructifer fere 3 lin. Corolla 3 lin. longa, cœrulea, glabra; labium superius abbreviatum, truncatum; inferius patens, lobo medio lato emarginato. Genitalia breviter e labio superiore exserta. Carpidia humectata extus dense gelatinosa. Embryo *S. privoidis*. Species *S. micranthæ* proxima, sed imprimis caule frutescente, racemo densiore aliisque notis dignoscenda.

695. SALVIA (Calosphace, Brachyanthæ) *prasiifolia*, sp. n., suffruticosa? ramis gracilibus herbaceis bifariam puberulis, foliis petiolatis ovatis acutis subinciso-serratis basi rotundato-truncatis cuneatisve membranaceis glabriusculis ciliatis, racemis brevibus, verticillastris sub-6-floris, calyce membranacei piloso-hispidi labio superiore lato integro, inferioris lobis mucronato-acutis, corolla calyce duplo longiore tubo superne ventricoso labio superiore erecto villoso inferiore lato patente, styli superne pilosuli lobis acutis, superiore elongato.—Tepic.

Specimina adsunt sesquipedalia, divaricato-ramosa, herbacea, sed rami videntur plantæ basi lignosæ. Folia distantia, tenuia, 1-1½-pollicaria, grosse et profunde serrata, basi integerrima, supra glabra, subtus interdum ad venas pilosula, margine ciliata, punctis in pagina inferiore minutissimis vix conspicuis. Racemi pauciflori, subtripollicares vel in ramulis lateralibus brevissimi. Bracteæ (seu folia floralia) parvæ, deciduæ. Calyx florens 2⅓ lin. longus, fructifer 3-4 lin. Corollæ cœruleæ tubus infra faucem ampliatus, ad faucem contractus; galea concava, integra, obtusa, 2 lin. longa; labium inferius paullo longior, lobo medio latissimo emarginato.

Allied to *S. gracilis* and *S. membranacea*, but easily known by the deep teeth of the leaves, something like those of *Elsholtzia incisa*.

696. SALVIA *membranacea*, var. β., *acuminata*, Benth. Lab. p. 259.—Guayaquil.

697. SALVIA *Cruikshanksii*, Benth. Lab. p. 261.—Huamantango.

698. SALVIA *scorodonia*, Poit.—Benth. Lab. p. 264, var. foliis subsessilibus brevibus.—Manzanilla Bay; Tepic.

699. SALVIA (Calosphace, Brachyanthæ) *thyrsiflora*, sp. n., fruticosa? ramis pubescentibus, foliis petiolatis ovato-lanceolatis obtusis basi rotundatis rugosissimis subtus albo-tomentosis, floralibus

parvis deciduis, cymis evolutis laxæ dichotomis in thyrsum terminalem dispositis, calycis glanduloso-pubescentis labio superiore integro lobisque inferioris acutiusculis, corolla calyce vix duplo longiore, stylo antice barbato, lobo superiore longo tenui, inferiore a latere compresso incurvo acuto.—Tepic.

Affinis *S. scorodoniæ*, foliis fere *S. inconspicuæ*, sed ab omnibus inflorescentia distincta. Rami adsunt sesquipedales, obtuse tetragoni, pube brevi subreversa canescentes. Folia pollicaria, 4-5 lin. lata, supra rugosissima et rigide puberula, margine crenata, subtus pube implexa densa vestita, superiora decrescentia, distantia. Thyrsus 3-6-pollicaris, simplex vel basi ramosus, multiflorus. Cymæ omnes (in hac sola specie inter omnes Calosphaceis a me cognitis) pedicellatæ, laxe dichotomæ, inferiores in pedunculo semipollicari circa 20-floræ, superiores brevius pedunculatæ pauciforæ. Pedunculi, rami et calyces pube glanduloso-viscosa et pilis nonnullis patentibus vestiti. Calyx vix 3 lin. longus, fructifer paullo auctus, herbaceus, tubulosus, striatus, superne parum dilatatus, lobis brevibus latis. Corollæ (cœruleæ?) tubus ventricosus, vix exsertus, ad faucem contractus; galea erecta, obtusa, pubescens; labium inferius patens, lobo medio obcordato. Antheræ galea breviores; connectiva postice parum dilatata, obtusa, connata. Stylus sæpius breviter exsertus, lobo superiore tenui acutissimo revoluto, inferiore cartilagineo verticaliter dilatato incurvo-patente acuto.

700. SALVIA *lasiocephala*, Hook. et Arn. Bot. Beech. p. 306.—Tepic.

701. SALVIA (Calosphace, Membranaceæ) *elsholtzioides*, sp. n., (Plate L.) herbacea, erecta, caule adpresse pilosulo, foliis longe petiolatis ovatis basi rotundato-truncatis cuneatisve membranaceis pilosulis, verticillastris hemisphærico-capitatis multifloris inferioribus remotis supremis approximatis, foliis floralibus reniformibus membranaceis calyces æquantibus, calycis membranacei tubulosi labiis post anthesin clausis, superiori lobisque inferioris lanceolatis acutis, corolla vix calycem superante, connectivis postice triangulari-dilatatis, styli lobo superiore elongato acuto inferiore brevissimo orbiculato-reniformi.—Realejo, Gulf of Fonseca.

Affinis *S. buplevroidi* et *S. lasiocephalæ*. Caulis sesquipedalis, virgato-ramosus, pilis arcte adpressis parvis. Petioli graciles, pilosi. Folia 1-2-pollicaria, obtusa vel acuminata, crenata, membranacea, supra sparse et subtus ad venas pilosula. Verticillastri dense multiflori, ad unum latus dejecti, demum semipollicem diametro, bracteis membranaceis suffulti, illos *Elsholtziæ cristatæ* quodammodo simulant. Bracteæ (seu folia floralia) orbiculato-reniformes, membranaceæ, reticulato-venosæ, margine ciliatæ. Calyx $1\frac{1}{2}$ vel demum vix 2 lin. longus, basi glaber, superne a tergo compressus, hispidus, lobis 3 subæqualibus in labia duo dispositis. Corolla tenerrima, glabra; labium superius galeatum, breve, obtusum; inferius longius, patens, lobo medio obcordato. Stylus glaber, subexsertus. Carpidia obcompressa, suborbiculata, non gelatinosa.

Plate L. fig. 1. calyx; fig. 2. corolla; fig. 3. stamens; fig. 4. ovary and style; all magnified.

VERBENACEÆ.

702. PRIVA *lappulacea*, Pers. Syn. 2. p. 139.—Guayaquil.

703. STACHYTARPHETA *dichotoma*, Humb. et Kunth.—Walp. Rep. 4. p. 5.—Acapulco.

704. VERBENA *veronicæfolia*, Humb. et Kunth.—Walp. Rep. 4. p. 20.—An eadem ac. *V. caroliniana*, Linn.?—Tepic.

705. VERBENA *littoralis*, Humb. et Kunth, Nov. Gen. et Sp. 2. p. 276. t. 137.—Guayaquil.

706. VERBENA *littoralis*, var.? glabrior, foliis hinc inde trifidis grosse et obtusiuscule incisodentatis. An species propria? Folia *V. menthæfoliæ*, Benth. Pl. Hartw. p. 21. sed flores parvi *V. littoralis*.—Peita.

707. VERBENA *fasciculata*, sp. n., suffruticosa? adscendens, ramosa, hirsutissima, foliis 3-5-partitis, segmentis lanceolatis linearibusve integerrimis vel 3-5-fidis, spicis sessilibus vel breviter pedunculatis densis, bracteis lanceolato-subulatis calyces æquantibus, calycis hirti costati dentibus setaceis, corollæ tubo exserto.—Huamantango.

Affinis *V. Aubletiæ*, sed hirsutior et folia diversa. Caulis basi lignosus videtur, decumbens, ramis adscendentibus vel erectis ½-1-pedalibus. Folia arcte sessilia, usque ad basin dissecta et sic quasi verticillata, juniora in axillis fasciculata; segmenta majora 1½-2-pollicaria, 2 lin. lata, alia minora et multo angustiora, omnia acuta. Calyces et bracteæ *V. Aubletiæ*, sed spica brevior et corollæ minores, tubo calycem parum excedente. Antherarum loculi distincti, latiusculi. Styli lobus superior brevissimus, crasse pulvinato-stigmatosus, inferior brevis sed pulvinum superans, incurvo-acutus, nudus. Carpidia oblonga, maturitate sponte secedentia, externe rete elevata venarum rugosa. Seminum testa tenuissima, membranacea; albumen parcissimum, sed non omnino deesse videtur.

Cuming's n. 954, from the coast of Peru, appears to be the same plant, with rather blunter lobes to the leaves.

708. LIPPIA *nodiflora*, Rich.—Walp. Rep. 4. p. 49.—Guayaquil.

There are several varieties of this plant in the collection, some of which may turn out to be distinct species, but the characters upon which the several species of *Lippia* and *Lantana* are made to rest are at present so vague and uncertain, that it is exceedingly difficult to determine them, and even the number of genera into which the very numerous species should be distributed must remain very doubtful until the whole shall have been worked up systematically. This task has, it is understood, been undertaken by Professor Schauer, for De Candolle's Prodromus. In the mean time, I have considered the three genera *Lippia*, *Lantana*, and *Camara* as distinguished by the fruit, as stated in Taylor's Ann. Nat. Hist., v. 2, p. 446, 447.

709. LIPPIA *asperifolia*, Rich. ex Hook. et Arn. Bot. Beech. p. 442.—*Lantana lippioides*, Hook. et Arn. Bot. Beech. p. 305.—Manzanilla Bay; Realejo.

710. LIPPIA *geminata*, Humb. et Kunth ex Hook. et Arn. Bot. Beech. p. 442.—Realejo.

711. LIPPIA *cardiostegia*, sp. n., strigoso-puberula, foliis ovatis serrato-crenatis basi cuneatis utrinque scaberrimis, pedunculis in axillis pluribus folio brevioribus, bracteis cordatis acuminatis, exterioribus flores superantibus, calyce obcompresso bifido bicarinato, carinis pilosis.—Gulf of Fonseca.

Frutex videtur, ramis elongatis tenuibus, pube parca strigosa scabris. Folia 2-3 poll. longa, 1-1½ poll. lata, acuta vel obtusa, crenaturis obtusis vel acutatis, basi breviter vel longius angustata, membranacea, parum rugosa, utrinque viridia et scaberrima, pilis brevissimis rigidis in pagina superiore e tuberculis ortis, in inferiore præsertim secus venas dispositis. Pedunculi in axillis sæpius gemini, graciles, longitudine varii, rarius tamen pollicem excedentes. Capitula subglobosa vel demum parum elongata, circa 4 lin. diametro.

Bracteæ imbricatæ, apice patentes, late cordatæ, acuminato-acutiusculæ, membranaceæ, puberulæ, exteriores 2 lin. longæ, interiores paullo minores. Calyx per anthesin ⅔ lin. longus, lobis divergentibus acutiusculis raro bidentatis, carinis dorso longiuscule et dense pilosis, demum bipartitus, undique puberulus. Corollæ infundibuliformis tubus glabriusculus, 1½ lin. longus, superne paullo ampliatus, limbus patens, obliquus, 4-fidus, tubo multo brevior, extus apiceque intus puberulus. Fructus late obovoideus, obcompressus, glaber, exsuccus (?), sponte bipartibilis.

712. LIPPIA *myriocephala*, Cham. Schl.—Walp. Rep. 4. p. 52.—Consul's garden at Puna, near Guayaquil.

This is the same form as Galeotti's Vera Cruz specimens, n. 775. The specimens referred to this species by Hooker and Arnott, Bot. Beech., p. 305, belong to a very distinct and probably unpublished species.

713. LANTANA *salviæfolia*, Jacq.?—Walp.? Rep. 4. p. 64.—Consul's garden, Puna, near Guayaquil.

714. LANTANA, near *L. trifolia*, Linn. and *L. celtidifolia*, Humb. et Kunth, but less hairy with larger bracts.—Realejo.

715. CAMARA *vulgaris*.—*Lantana camara*, Linn.—Acapulco, Realejo.

716. CAMARA *tiliæfolia*.—*Lantana tiliæfolia*, Cham. Schl. Linnæa, 7. p. 122.—Guayaquil.

717, 718. CAMARA, sp. from Tepic, and another from the Gulf of Fonseca, neither in a state to determine accurately.

719. DURANTA *Plumieri*, Jacq.—Walp. Rep. 4. p. 79.—Tumaco, Salango, Atacames.—Several varieties, especially as to the form of the leaf, but the specimens mostly very much injured.

720. CITHAREXYLUM, near *C. spinosum*, Humb. et Kunth, but in a very bad state.—San Pedro.

721. ÆGIPHILA *glomerata*, sp. n., undique tomentoso-villosa, foliis ovatis longe acuminatis basi rotundatis, cymis in capitula confertis in axillis superioribus subsessilibus, calyce obovoideo apice breviter fisso quam corolla paullo breviore.—Salango.

Rami teretes vel ad nodos compressi, pube subferruginea dense vestiti. Folia breviter petiolata, 8-10 poll. longa, subcaudato-acuminata, integerrima, infra medium 3-3½ poll. lata, utrinque molliter villosa, superiora minora angustiora densius lanato-villosa. Pedunculi axillares, oppositi, 1-2 lin. longi; cymæ multifloræ capitula formant subglobosa. Bracteæ subulatæ, calyces æquantes vel exteriores longiores. Calyces in cyma subsessiles, 2-2½ lin. longi, basi contracti, superne inflati, dense villosi, apice in dentes 2-4 irregulariter et breviter fissi. Corolla vix calycem excedens, infundibuliformis, tubo brevi intus extusque tomentoso, limbo campanulato glabro semi-4-fido, lobis oblongis obtusis, æstivatione valde imbricatis, uno exteriore. Stamina breviter exserta (?) glabra; antheræ majusculæ oblongæ. Stylus staminibus brevior semibifidus. Ovarium minutum, glabrum. Ovula in ovariis paucis a vermibus non læsis imperfecta fuerunt.

722. HOSTA *longifolia*, Humb. et Kunth?—Walp.? Rep. 4. p. 81.—Folia 6-8 poll. longa, 2-4 poll. lata. Panicula interdum pedalis, minute cano-tomentella nec hirsuta ut in *H. grandifolia*, Schlecht.—Tumaco, Salango.

723. VITEX *gigantea*, Humb. et Kunth.—Walp. Rep. 4. p. 85.—Folia juniora supra sparse

pilosula. *V. cymosa*, Bertol. vix ab hac differre videtur, nec longe distat *V. cujabensis* Mart, tomento densiore in pagina inferiore vestita.—Guayaquil.

724. VITEX *lasiophylla*, sp. n., ramulis ferrugineo-villosis, foliolis subternis oblongis obtusis utrinque molliter villosis lateralibus minoribus nunc minimis vel nullis, cymis axillaribus dichotomis villosis folio brevioribus.—*V. mollis*, Hook. et Arn. Bot. Beech., p. 305, non Humb. et Kunth.—Manzanilla Bay.

Frutex? Ramuli juniores pube densa ferruginea obtecti, annotini glabrati. Petioli subpollicares. Foliola subsessilia, terminale 2-3 poll. longum, vix pollicem latum vel sæpius angustius, basi rotundatum vel breviter cuneatum, subcoriaceum, etiam vetustius villosum, nec unquam glabratum vel nitidum, lateralia nunc dimidio breviora, nunc vix 2-3 lin. longa vel plane nulla. Pedunculi petiolo subæquilongi, bis terve divaricato-ramosi, uti rami et calyces molliter villosi. Bracteæ parvæ. Pedicelli brevissimi. Calyces per anthesin linea paullo longiores, truncati, minute 5-dentati, fructiferi aucti, cyathiformes. Corolla in specimine imperfecto calyce subtriplo longior videtur.

725. AVICENNIA *Meyeri*, Miq. Linnæa, 18. p. 264.—Guatemala to Guayaquil, not uncommon, always in salt water.—Probably a mere narrow-leaved variety of *A. tomentosa*; yet the several forms of this plant are said to differ much in stature and aspect, and require further examination as to flowers and fruit, generally very imperfect in the specimens preserved in herbaria.

LENTIBULARIEÆ.*

726. UTRICULARIA *aphylla*, Ruiz et Pav.—A. DC. Prod. 8. p. 17.—Guayaquil.

727. PINGUICULA *lilacina*, Cham. Schlecht.—A. DC. Prod. 8. p. 31.—Realejo.

PLUMBAGINEÆ.

728. PLUMBAGO *scandens*, Linn.—Mexico to Guayaquil.

NYCTAGINEÆ.

729. MIRABILIS *jalapa*, Linn.—Realejo.

730. BOLDOA *lanceolata*, Lag.—Rœm. Schult. Syst. 1. p. 522.—*Salpianthus arenarius*, Humb. et Bonpl. Pl. Æq. 1. p. 153. t. 44.—Acapulco.

731. BOLDOA *ovatifolia*, Lag. ex charactere nimis brevi in Rœm. Schult. Syst. 1. p. 522.—Folia ampla, late cordato-ovata. Flores vix lineam longi, glomerati, glomerulis paniculatis.—Tepic.

732. BOERHAAVIA *polymorpha*, A. Rich.—supra p. 43.—Guayaquil, Huamantango.

---

* Omitted above, p. 123.

This common American form is the one described by Miquel, Linnæa, 18, p. 244, under the name of *B. surinamensis*. We have it from numerous localities, extending from the Southern United States and Mexico to Brazil and Peru, and the species, including probably *B. erecta* and *B. decumbens* of Linnæus, appears to extend over the islands of the Pacific, perhaps even to East India. It is generally smooth, or nearly so, with the exception of a few long hairs on the margins of the leaves; the panicle has very numerous slender branches; the flowers are solitary, or three or four together on very short pedicels; the fruit angular, turbinate, from a line to a line and a half in length, and very variable in the degree of glandular pubescence; the perigon red, campanulate, and small, and very different in this respect from that of *B. scandens*, *B. repanda*, and *B. littoralis*, in which it is infundibuliform, with rather a long tube. The bractes in *Boerhaavia* are not more decidedly collected into an involucre than in *Pisonia*, although on account of a supposed difference in this respect, the two genera are placed by Endlicher and others in different subdivisions of the order *Nyctagineæ*.

733. BOERHAAVIA *viscosa*, Lag.—Vahl. Enum. 1. p. 288.—Guayaquil.

This is very near to *B. polymorpha*, but the leaves are broader and more blunt, the whole plant thickly clothed with a viscid down, and the flowers crowded into a few dense heads.

AMARANTHACEÆ.

734. IRESINE *celosioides*, Linn. var. *eriophylla*, foliis inferioribus novellisque subtus dense albo-lanatis, caule basi tomentello. Folia superiora, panicula et flores omnino formæ vulgatioris.—Realejo.—Ejusdem var. glabra.—Tiger Island, Gulf of Fonseca.

735. IRESINE *interrupta*, sp. n., foliis lanceolatis acutis cauleque glabris, paniculæ ramis divaricatis, spicis secus ramulos ultimos subsessilibus parvis ovato-globosis.—Tepic, Acapulco.

Rami elongati, graciles, læves. Folia 2-3-pollicaria, vix semipollicem lata, superiora multo minora, basi rotundato-cuneata, petiolata. Panicula ampla, bis terve ramosa, glabra vel rarissime puberula. Spiculæ 1 lin. vel vix 1½ lin. longæ, sessiles vel breviter pedicellatæ, floribus 6-12 parvis arcte sessilibus. Bracteæ 3, perigonio duplo breviores. Perigonium vix semilineam longum, pilis paucis longis laxissimis sublanatum. Filamenta 5, libera, additis inter filamenta squamulis 5 brevibus latis hyalinis. Ovarii rudimentum effœtum. Flores fœmineos non vidi.

736. HEBANTHE? *parviflora*, sp. n., foliis ovali-oblongis acuminatis novellis pubescentibus demum cauleque glabris, panicula floribunda pubescente, cupulæ stamineæ lobulis sterilibus 5 brevissimis rotundatis.

Habitu *Hebanthi paniculatæ et Iresini grandifloræ*, Hook. simillima et vix nisi floribus parvis et cupula staminifera differt. Folia 2-3 poll. longa, pollicem lata, petiolata, basi cuneata, crassiuscula, inferiora omnino glabra, ramealia et juniora in specimine minora, subtus præsertim pilis appressis pubescentia. Panicula ampla, gracilis, foliata; rami primarii oppositi, superiores sæpe ad utrumque latus gemini vel terni, longior scilicet ad axillam brevioris insertus, nec verticillati. Bracteæ minutæ, uti ramuli pubescentes. Flores secus ramulos ultimos 3-6 lin. longos spicatim dispositi, sessiles, subdissiti, lineam longi. Bracteæ 3, ovatæ, perigonio dimidio breviores. Perigonii laciniæ glabræ, exceptis pilis exterioribus e basi perigonii ortis, qui per anthesin flore breviores sunt, in fructu tamen perigonium longe superant. Filamenta fertilia perigonio breviora, non ciliata, oriuntur e crenis cupulæ ovarium æquantis. Ovarium depresso-globosum, basi attenuatum. Stylus (vel si mavis stigma) brevissimus, capitato-bilobus, crassiuscule stigmatosus.

The characters derived from the stamens would place this plant nearer *Tromsdorffia* than *Hebanthe*, but the habit is totally different. I should have considered it as the same as *Iresine grandiflora*, Hook. Ic. Pl. t. 102, but that the stamens are there figured as entirely without intermediate lobes. There is little doubt, however, but that the latter plant should also be included in *Hebanthe*, as the flowers are hermaphrodite, not diœcious as in *Iresine*.

737. GOMPHRENA *globosa*, Linn.—Guayaquil, but, perhaps, not really wild.

738. GOMPHRENA *decumbens*, Jacq.—*G. celosioides*, Mart.—Realejo.

739. BRANDESIA *pycnantha*, sp. n., foliis lanceolatis acuminatis cauleque pilosulis vel demum glabratis, capitulis compositis dense corymbosis, corymbis paniculatis, bracteis acutis, perigonio laxe piloso.—*Brandesiæ*, sp. n., Hook. et Arn. Bot. Beech. p. 308.—Acapulco.

Planta ex speciminibus scandere videtur. Rami herbacei, teretes vel obtuse tetragoni. Folia 2-4 poll. longa, 6-12 lin. lata, utrinque viridia, pilis brevibus raro omnino evanescentibus conspersa. Paniculæ rami divaricati, apice corymboso-polycephali, capitulis albidis floribusque quam in *B. porrigente* majoribus. Bracteæ breves, latæ, acutæ sed non aristatæ. Perigonii segmenta subæqualia, late oblongo-lanceolata, concava, acuta, extus pilis longis laxis at vix implexis vestita. Staminum tubus brevis; filamenta sterilia dilatata, apice fimbriata, quam fertilia paullo longiora. Stylus brevis, apice capitato-stigmatosus.

740. BRANDESIA *pubiflora*, sp. n., foliis ovatis acutis utrinque cauleque molliter pubescentibus, capitulis ovato-globosis pedunculatis sessilibusque solitariis vel subaggregatis, bracteis lanceolatis acutis, perigonii segmentis hirtis.—Guayaquil.

Caulis decumbens videtur, uti folia pilis subappressis mollibus vestitus. Folia breviter petiolata, 1-2 poll. longa, 6-12 lin. lata, summa proportione angustiora, omnia utrinque acuta. Capitula iis *Gomphrenæ decumbentis* minora et pleraque subglobosa, alia ad nodos in pedunculo sesquipollicari solitaria, alia ad basin pedunculi sessilia vel in pedunculo subramoso aggregata vel interrupte sessilia, omnia in sicco alba. Bracteæ perigonio subtriplo breviores. Perigonii segmenta lanceolata, acuta, 2½ vel demum fere 3 lin. longa, extus pilis brevibus mollibus hirta. Tubus stamineus ovarium æquans; filamenta sterilia angusta, apice fimbriata; fertilia multo breviora. Stylus brevis, apice capitato-stigmatosus.

741. BRANDESIA *pubiflora*, var? *glomerata*, pube tenuiore, foliis ovatis lanceolatisve 2-3-pollicaribus, capitulis sæpius aggregato-sessilibus, in sicco flavicantibus. An species propria?—Guayaquil.

742. BUCHOLTZIA *frutescens*, Mart.—Panama to Guayaquil.

743. ACHYRANTHES *aspera*, Linn.—Tepic; Guayaquil. Probably introduced.

744. AMARANTHUS *spinosus*, Linn.—Guayaquil.

745. AMARANTHUS *retroflexus*, Linn.—Guayaquil.

746. AMARANTHUS *scariosus*, sp. n., (Plate LI.), foliis ovatis longe petiolatis, glomerulis plerisque spicatis, spicis superioribus paniculatis, bracteis aristatis perigonium superantibus, staminibus 5, stylis 3-4, perigonio fœmineo cum fructu deciduo urceolato basi indurato, segmentis apice scarioso-dilatatis patentibus obovatis emarginatis.—Tiger Island, Gulf of Fonseca; gathered also in Guatemala, by Friedrichsthal.

Habitus et inflorescentia *A. retroflexi*. Folia pleraque angustiora et acutiora. Bracteæ scariosæ, 1½-2 lin. longæ, costa viridi in aristam subpungentem excurrente. Florum dispositio, stamina, styli (hi tamen interdum 4) et utriculus *A. retroflexi*. Perigonii masculi segmenta 5, oblonga, obtusiuscula, costa vix conspicua undique hyalina; fœminei segmenta superne multo patentiora quam in *A. retroflexo* et valde dilatata, basi in fructu incrassata, et utriculum includens cum illo sub forma urceoli deciduum, segmentis singulis a medio ad apicem hyalinis scariosis costa virescente tenui percursis.

Plate LI. fig. 1. fasciculus of three flowers, two female and one male; fig. 2. male flower opened; fig. 3. female flower opened; fig. 4. perigon in fruit; fig. 5. achænium; fig. 6. seed; fig. 7. embryo; all magnified.

747. AMARANTHUS *urceolatus*, sp. n., foliis ovatis oblongisve longe petiolatis, cymulis axillaribus summis simpliciter subspicatis, bracteis calyce brevioribus vix mucronatis, staminibus 5, stylis 3, perigonio fœmineo cum fructu deciduo urceolato basi indurato, segmentis spathulatis apice scarioso-dilatatis patentibus.—Guayaquil.

Habitus, folia et inflorescentia *A. polygonoidis*. Bracteæ parvæ, acutæ. Flores et fructus fere *A. scariosi*, sed minores. Perigonii masculi segmenta oblonga, mucronata, hyalina; fœminei fructiferi segmenta tria exteriora apice orbiculato-spathulata basi valde angustata, duo interiora apice subsimilia a basi tamen dilatata; omnium lamina viridi-venulosa, margine integro vel subcrenulato.

748. CHAMISSOA *altissima*, Sw.—Tepic.

749. CELOSIA *cristata*, Linn.—Guayaquil.

750. CELOSIA *paniculata*, Linn.—Guayaquil.

751. CELOSIA *nitida*, Vahl? Symb. 2. p. 44.—*A. C. paniculata* parum diversa floribus majoribus paucioribus, bracteis ovatis acutis nec lanceolatis, perigonii foliolis latioribus.—Between San Blas and Tepic.

PHYTOLACCACEÆ.

752. RIVINA *humilis*, Linn.—Realejo.

753. MOHLANA *secunda*, Mart.—*Rivina secunda*, Ruiz. et Pav.—*Rivina inæqualis*, Hook. Ic. Pl. t. 130.—Salango.

754. PETIVERIA *alliacea*, Linn.—Mexico to Guayaquil.

The number of hooks to the fruit is, in these specimens, constantly two on each side. In Schomburgk's Guiana specimens, the number is usually three on each side, but occasionally one is deficient, which would lead to the supposition that *P. hexaglochin*, Fisch and Mey., founded on no other character, may not be a good species.

755. PHYTOLACCA *octandra*, Linn.—Tepic; Manzanilla Bay.

CHENOPODIACEÆ.

756. CRYPTOCARPUS *pyriformis*, Humb. et Kunth, Nov. Gen. et Sp. 2. p. 188. t. 124.—Common on the skirts of the forest near Guayaquil.—Kunth states that Bonpland observed a third species of this genus near Guayaquil. The specimens, however, brought by collectors from that neighbourhood appear all to agree perfectly with the character and figure of *C. pyriformis*.

757. CHENOPODIUM *murale*, Linn.—Guayaquil.

758. AMBRINA *ambrosioides*, Moc. Chenopod. p. 39.—Guayaquil.

POLYGONACEÆ.

759. POLYGONUM *acre*, Humb. et Kunth, Nov. Gen. et Sp. v. 2. p. 179.—Mexico to Guayaquil.

760. POLYGONUM *persicarioides*, Humb. et Kunth, l. c.—Guayaquil.

761. COCCOLOBA *acuminata*, Humb. et Kunth, l. c. v. 2. p. 176.—Isthmus of Darien.

762. COCCOLOBA *leptostachya*, sp. n., glabra, foliis ovalibus obovatisve obtuse et brevissime acuminatis basi oblique rotundatis coriaceis, racemis elongatis laxis, floribus subternis, bracteis minimis, bacca coronata (?)—Libertad, in Columbia.

Ramuli lignosi, tortuosi, cortice pallido. Vaginæ laxæ, 3-4 lin. longæ, submembranaceæ, in sicco brunneæ, juniores sub lente minute tomentellæ, mox glabratæ, oblique truncatæ, hinc breviter fissæ, illinc juniores breviter acuminatæ et subciliatæ, acumine mox obliterato. Petioli 5-6 lin. longi. Folia 3-4 poll. longa, 2-2½ poll. lata, glabra at non nitida, tenuiter coriacea, venis primariis secus costam utrinque 4-6 subtus prominulis et rete venularum ramosissimo in pagina inferiore eleganter conspicuo. Racemus adest unicus, 8-pollicaris, terminalis, gracilis, fere a basi florifer. Pedicelli vix semilineam longi bracteas duplo superant. Perigonium per anthesin 1 lin. longum, tubo carnoso ovarium circumdante; limbus patens, 5-partitus, laciniis subrotundis tubo paullo longioribus, duabus exterioribus paullo minoribus. Stylus brevis, trifidus, lobis subulatis brevibus apice incrassato-stigmatosis. Stamina 7 vel 8; antherarum loculi discreti. Perigonii tubus per maturationem increscit et ovario adhæret; laciniæ ad apicem ovarii diu persistunt, forte in fructu maturo a me non viso deperiunt.

763. CAMPDERIA *floribunda*, gen. nov. (Plate LII.)—Tiger Island, Gulf of Fonseca.

CHAR. GEN. Flores hermaphroditi (fere Coccolobæ). Perigonium sub-5-partitum, tubo brevissimo, laciniis subæqualibus. Stamina 8. Styli 3. Achænium triquetrum, carpophoro carnoso impositum; perigonii fructiferi tubus immutatus, limbi laciniæ auctæ, siccæ, achænium includentes.—Frutex (vel arbor?) habitu *Coccolobæ*.

C. floribunda. Specimina suppetentia undique glabra. Ramuli leviter striati, cortice cinereo. Vaginæ 2-4 lin. longæ, oblique truncatæ, integerrimæ, glabræ, membranaceæ, in sicco brunneæ. Petioli vagina breviores vel paullo longiores. Folia alterna, obovali-oblonga, 3-5 poll. longa, 1-2 poll. lata, obtusa, infra medium inæqualiter angustata, basi oblique obtusa et interdum emarginata vel brevissime peltata, coriacea, rete venularum utrinque prominulo. Racemi 3-5-pollicares, a basi densiflori. Bracteæ scariosæ, obtusæ, 1-1½ lin. longæ. Perigonium per anthesin 1 lin. longum, laciniis orbiculatis patentibus. Stamina perigonio breviora; filamenta basi brevissime connata, disco staminifero cum basi perigonii adnato; antherarum loculi discreti. Styli apice capitato-stigmatosi. Achænium immaturum tantum vidi triquetrum, crustaceum, albidum, inclusum intra perigonii limbum jam duplo auctum at consistentia vix mutatum, tubo cum carpophoro crasso carnoso connato.

This plant, when in flower, is certainly very much like a true *Coccoloba*, but the fruit, unripe as it is in the specimens gathered, has certainly not the essential character of that of *Coccoloba*, the adherence to a fleshy perigonium. I have, therefore, been under the necessity of establishing it as a new genus, which I have great pleasure in dedicating to the author of a monograph of *Rumex*, with some observations on other *Polygoneæ*, published at Montpellier in 1819. Of the two genera which have been already intended to be named after him, one proved to be the *Vellosia* of Vandelli, the other is the *Kundmannia* of Scopoli.

Plate LII. fig. 1. perigon opened, showing the stamens; fig. 2. ovary; fig. 3. young fruit, enclosed in the perigon; fig. 4. the same, with the perigon opened out; fig. 5. section of the young fruit; fig. 6. arrangement of the parts of the flower; all magnified.

764. TRIPLARIS *Cumingiana*, Fisch. et Mey. in C. A. Mey. Bemerk. Polyg. p. 14.—The under surface of the leaves is less pubescent, the axils of the veins more frequently bearded, and the inner segments of the perigon rather longer than in Cuming's plant, but it appears to be the same species.—Columbia.

765. PODOPTERUS *mexicanus*, Humb. et Bonpl. Pl. Æq. 2. p. 89. t. 107.—Manzanilla Bay.

766. ANTIGONON *leptopus*, Hook. et Arn. Bot. Beech. p. 308.—Supra, p. 47.—San Blas.

OLACACEÆ.

767. XIMENIA *americana*, Linn.—Veragua.

SANTALACEÆ.

768. QUINCHAMALIUM *chilense*, Lam.—Huamantango.

LAURACEÆ.

769. NECTANDRA (Porostema) *glabrescens*, sp. n., foliis elliptico-oblongis sublanceolatisve acuminatis basi acutis venoso-costatis, junioribus subtus puberulis axillis venarum barbatis, adultis glabris, paniculis axillaribus folio subbrevioribus ramis 2-3-chotomis, ramulis novellis floribusque canescenti-puberulis, filamentis staminum exteriorum subnullis, bacca globosa?—*Ocotea salicifolia*, Hook. et Arn. Bot. Beech. p. 309. vix Humb. et Kunth.—San Blas, Realejo, Acapulco; and a narrow-leaved variety from Tepic.

Arbor 30-40-pedalis. Ramuli juniores angulati, pube brevissima pulveraceo-canescentes, demum teretes glabrati. Folia forma varia, nunc 7-8 poll. longa, 2½ poll. lata, nunc 5-6 poll. longa, 1-1½ poll. lata, vel superiora minora et proportione angustiora, juniora subtus pube brevi in costa evidentiore conspersa, et in axillis saltem inferioribus venarum costalium barbata, adulta utrinque sæpius glabrata, opaca vel rarius nitidula, concoloria; venæ costales prominentes utrinque 5-8, pleræque simplices, prope marginem in rete evanescentes. Paniculæ in axillis superioribus dispositi, a dimidium ad duas tertias folii attingunt, pleræque a medio ad apicem floriferæ, ramulis alternis brevibus divaricatis cymoso-5-15-floris. Perigonium rotatum, 4 lin. diametro, laciniis late obovatis parum inæqualibus crassiusculis. Antheræ perigonio multo breviores, exteriores 6 reniformes, fere sessiles, locellis prope basin in arcum dispositis; stamina tertii ordinis duplo longiora, filamento distincto crasso prædita. Glandulæ majusculæ, distinctæ. Staminodia quarti ordinis oblonga, obtusa. Fructus pedicellus semipollicaris; cupula truncata fere 3 lin. diametro; bacca unica adest, pressione deformata, sed globosa videtur, magnitudine *Cerasi* minoris.

This agrees in many respects with *N. sanguinea*, *N. japurensis*, and *N. turbacensis*, but the anthers are different in shape from those described by Nees of either of the two first species, and the glands are not confluent as they are said to be in *N. turbacensis;* the staminodia are also more distinct, and the berry appears to be globular. The *Nectandræ* are, however, many of them so much alike, as to make it very difficult to characterise them in words.

PROTEACEÆ.

770. RHOPALA *complicata*, Humb. et Kunth, Nov. Gen. et Sp. 2. p. 153. t. 119, scarcely differing from *R. montana*, Br.—A small tree growing on a very stony mountain in the Isle of Taboga, Bay of Panama.

EUPHORBIACEÆ.

771. POINSETTIA *pulcherrima*, Grah, in Bot. Mag. t. 3493.—Central America.
772. EUPHORBIA *dioica*, Humb. et Kunth, Nov. Gen. et Sp. 2. p. 53. var.—San Blas to Tepic.

This plant differs from Kunth's description, in that it is certainly monœcious, not diœcious, as observed by Klotzsch (Lond. Journ. Bot. 2, p. 42), but the involucra are generally aggregate as described by Kunth, not solitary as stated by Klotzsch, and in these specimens they are smaller, with very much smaller coloured lobes than in Schomburgk's specimens. The species, though variable, and very common from the Southern United States and Mexico to Brazil, appears to be constantly distinct from all the European and Asiatic species allied to *E. chamæsyce*, but is probably the same as *E. depressa*, Torrey, and if so, the latter name might be substituted for the erroneous one of *dioica*.

773. EUPHORBIA (Aggregatæ, Procumbentes, Stipulatæ), *anceps*, sp. n., suffruticosa, procumbens, ramis compressis bifariam villosis, foliis sessilibus semicordatis oblongo-rhombeis crenulatis, capitulis axillaribus densis folio brevioribus, involucri compressi dentibus 2 parvis, 2 appendiciformibus semicordatis erectis intus glanduliferis.—*E. ocymoides*, Hook. et Arn. Bot. Beech. p. 310. non Linn.—Realejo.

Caules e basi lignosa ramosissima 4-6-pollicares vel paullo longiores, parum ramosi, ramis valde compressis, faciebus striatis, angulis pilis patentibus insigniter villosis. Stipulæ utrinque geminæ, subulatæ. Folia opposita, 4-6 lin. longa, 2-3 lin. lata, valde obliqua, crassiuscula, obtusa vel rarius oblique acutiuscula, obscure 2-3-nervia. Spicæ in axillis superioribus solitariæ, vel (rhachi basi ramosa) fasciculatæ, oblongæ vel subglobosæ, sæpius foliis 2 parvis suffultæ. Bracteæ intra spicam membranaceæ, lanceolatæ vel subovatæ, involucri dentibus breviores, cum involucris imbricatæ, margine longe ciliato-fimbriatæ, rarius herbaceæ involucra superantes. Involucra in axillis bractearum solitaria, subsessilia, magnitudine *E. piluliferæ*, pilosula, compressa; dentes 2 brevissimi subulati; appendices laterales involucro ipso longiores, longitudine tamen variæ, erecte et arcte appositæ, ita ut appendicem simulant unicam cordiformem obtusam medio biglandulosam. Bracteolæ intra involucrum parvæ, setaceæ. Pedicelli sæpius glabri. Capsula undique pilosa vel hinc glabra. Styli subulati, apice breviter bifidi. Semina foveolata. Cæterum variat caulis faciebus foliisque glabris vel pubescentibus, spicis magis minusve pilosis, bracteis in spica omnibus membranaceis brevibus vel foliaceis majoribus (spicis tunc iis *Majoranæ* subsimilibus), involucri appendicibus albis rubentibusve, majoribus vel minoribus etc.

774. EUPHORBIA *pilulifera*, Linn.—Mexico to Guayaquil.

775. EUPHORBIA *hypericifolia*, Linn.—Mexico to Guayaquil, with a very hairy variety from Peita.

776. EUPHORBIA *nudiflora*, Lam. Dict. 2. p. 426.—Acapulco.

777. EUPHORBIA *adianthoides*, Lam. Dict. 2. p. 426.—Tepic. This species extends from the warmer districts of Mexico to Guayaquil and Brazil.

778. EUPHORBIA *strigosa*, Hook. et Arn. Bot. Beech. p. 310.—Tepic.

779. EUPHORBIA (Exstipulatæ, Alternifoliæ, Erectæ, Capitatæ) *restiacea*, sp. n., suffruticosa, glabra, ramis erectis junceis subdichotomis, foliis caulinis perparvis lineari-subulatis vel nullis, floralibus in apicibus ramorum paucis lanceolatis coloratis, involucris terminalibus solitariis (aggregatisve?) subsessilibus turbinatis, lobis exterioribus reniformibus coloratis crenulatis.—Between San Blas and Tepic.

Caules e basi crassa tuberiformi lignosa complures, 1-1½-pedales, tenues, rigidi, virides, nitiduli, teretes, substriati, in parte inferiore ramis paucis strictis instructi. Folia rarissima, minima vel vix semipollicaria, floralia ad apices ramulorum per 3-4 approximata, 6-9 lin. longa, 1-2 lin. lata, utrinque acuta, integerrima, colorata. Involucra subsessilia, linea paullo longiora.

There being but a single perfect involucrum in the several specimens of this curious plant, I have refrained from cutting it up to examine the internal structure, having seen enough to have no doubt of its genus.

780. EUPHORBIA (Exstipulatæ, Verticillatæ, Fruticosæ, Cymosæ) *colletioides*, sp. n., ramis articulatis glabris, foliis ternatim verticillatis oppositisve petiolatis ellipticis obtusis basi angustatis subtus puberulis glaucis, cymis terminalibus sessilibus densis, bracteis parvis subulatis, involucri pubescentis lobis exterioribus orbiculatis crenulatis tubo subbrevioribus.—Acapulco.

Rami rigidi, teretes, virides, substriati, ad nodos tumidi et facile (præsertim juniores) in articulos secedentes, internodiis 3-6-pollicaribus, ramulis sæpius ternatim verticillatis. Folia 1-1½ poll. longa, 5-7 lin. lata, petiolo 3-lineari; ultima minora angustiora; omnia membranacea, opaca, impunctata, tenuiter penninervia, costa media subtus prominente. Cyma inter folia suprema sessilis, dichotoma, polycephala, foliis tamen brevior. Bracteæ ad dichotomias oppositæ, quam involucra multo breviores. Involucra brevissime pedicellata, turbinato-campanulata, linea paullo longiora, pube canescentia; lobi 5 exteriores lineam lati, colorati, crassiusculi, glandulis baseos majusculis orbiculatis duplicatis; lobi interiores inflexæ, membranaceæ, orbiculato-cuneatæ, fimbriatæ. Bracteolæ setaceæ, pilosulæ. Flores masculi diantheri, numerosi. Ovarium glabrum. Stylus usque ad basin fissus, lobis bipartitis. Capsula junior exserta, lævis, glabra, maturam non vidi.

781. EUPHORBIA (Exstipulatæ, Alternifoliæ, Fruticosæ, Umbellatæ) *Sinclairiana*, sp. n., glabra, foliis amplis obovali-oblongis acutis basi longe angustatis, umbella sessili (2-3-fida?) ramis elongatis dichotomis, bracteis ovato-orbiculatis foliaceis, involucri campanulati sessilis lobis 4 exterioribus orbiculatis crassis integerrimis.—Island of Gorgona.

Rami crassiusculi. Folia usque ad pedalia (vel longiora?), 3-4 poll. lata, breviter et acute acuminata, costa media subtus prominente, venis primariis obscuris tenuibus ad angulum fere rectum a costa divergentibus. Petioli 1-1½-pollicares, basi nodoso-incrassati. Umbella supra folium supremum sessilis, foliis brevior; rami primarii 2 (vel ex cicatricibus interdum 3), supra medium ter quaterve bifidi, ramis ultimis brevissimis. Bracteæ 8-10 lin. longæ, paullo angustiores, obtusæ vel mucronulatæ, basi subcordatæ. Involucra fere 3 lin. longa, lobis exterioribus patentibus glanduliformibus, interioribus erecto-inflexis membranaceis orbiculatis leviter fimbriatis. Bracteolæ glabræ, in laminas membranaceas apice laceras coalitæ. Flores masculi diantheri. Ovarium glabrum. Stylus vix ad medium trifidus, lobis semibifidis.

782. DALECHAMPIA *sidæfolia*, Humb. et Kunth, Nov. Gen. et Sp. 2. p. 100. — *D. hibiscoides*, Hook. et Arn. Bot. Beech. p. 443. non Humb. et Kunth.—Folia sæpius ultra medium 3-5-fida, sed nunquam ad basin partita.—Realejo, Panama, and other parts of Central America.

783. HIPPOMANE *Mancenilla*, Linn.—Culebra, Atacames.

784. ACALYPHA *obovata*, sp. n., (Plate LIII.) arborescens, ramulis subteretibus glabris, foliis obovatis vel obovato-oblongis breviter acuminatis subserratis basi longe angustatis glabris punctato-scabriusculis, spicis sexu distinctis axillaribus folio brevioribus pubescentibus, fœmineis gracilibus interruptis, involucris flore brevioribus.—Atacames.

Rami lignosi, cortice cinereo; ramuli læves, juniores vix obtuse angulati. Stipulæ lineari-lanceolatæ, sæpe falcatæ, 3-4 lin. longæ, rigidæ. Petioli stipulos vulgo superantes. Folia majora 6-8 poll. longa, supra medium 2½-3 poll. lata, pleraque a medio usque ad basin longe angustata, ima basi obtusa vel leviter cordata, a medio ad apicem irregulariter serrata et interdum sinuata, summo apice in acumen breve obtusum vel acutum producta, utrinque glaberrima, sed punctis minutis sub lente conspicuis et subpellucidis utrinque scabriuscula; costa media venæque primariæ pinnatim divergentes subtus prominulæ. Spicæ in axillis solitariæ, breviter pedunculatæ, aliæ masculæ aliæ fœmineæ, masculæ nunc superiores nunc inferiores; masculæ pollicares, glomerulis approximatis multifloris bracteis minutis subtensis. Pedicelli basi hispidi, superne glabri, ¼ lin. longi. Flores minuti. Perigonium 4-partitum. Stamina 8. Spicæ fœmineæ masculis 2-3-plo longiores. Involucra dissita, reniformia, concava, dentata, extus pilis paucis hirta, lineam longa, singula biflora. Flores sessiles, perigonii segmentis 3 brevibus ovatis acutis hispidis. Ovarium hirsutissimum. Styli multifidi uti ovarii loculi in altero flore cujusve involucri tres, in altero (an constanter?) duo tantum. Fructus non vidi.

This species is probably near to the *A. cuneata*, Pœpp. et Endl., but in the latter the branches are described as acutely angled, the leaves downy underneath, and the spikes very much longer.

Plate LIII. fig. 1. male flower; fig. 2. female involucre; fig. 3. female flower; all magnified.

785. ACALYPHA *vestita*, sp. n., fruticosa vel arborea, ramis hirsutis, foliis cordato-ovatis acuminatis crenatis utrinque pubescentibus villosisve, spicis androgynis in axillis subfasciculatis folio brevioribus vel raro longioribus.—Guayaquil.

Ramuli lignosi, teretes, crassitie pennæ anserinæ, undique pilis patentibus hirsuti. Folia adulta 3-4 poll. longa, 1½-2 poll. lata, basi rotundata et sinu subclauso cordata, apice longius breviusve in acumen producta, pube molle brevi utrinque vestita et ad costas venasque primarias utrinque hirsuta; costæ 5-7, a basi digitatæ, quorum intermedia utrinque, laterales a latere tantum exteriore, venas emittunt primarias. Petioli hirsuti, 1-1½-pollicares. Spicæ sæpius ad axillas foliorum per 2-3 cum foliis totidem parvis fasciculatæ (ramulis floriferis axillaribus brevissimis), superiores solitariæ. Involucra 2-3 ad basin spicæ fœmineæ, cyathiformia demum 4 lin. lata, herbacea, puberula, margine minute denticulata. Flores circiter 8, sessiles, ovario villoso, stylis multifidis. Capsulæ hirtæ. Semina læviuscula. Flores masculi minuti, in maxima parte spicæ in glomerulos distinctos multifloros dispositi. Perigonium 4-partitum. Stamina 8.

786. ACALYPHA *leptoclada*, sp. n., fruticosa, ramulis gracilibus petiolisque tomentoso-pubescentibus, foliis ovatis vel ovato-lanceolatis acuminatis serrato-crenatis basi cuneatis integerrimis tenuibus pubescentibus, spicis sexu distinctis axillaribus tenuibus petiolos vix æquantibus.—Tepic.

Ramuli teretes, pilis crispulis albidis undique vestiti, juniores fere filiformes. Stipulæ minutæ. Petioli 1-2-pollicares, villosi, tenues. Folia tenuiter membranacea, 2-3 poll. longa, 9-10 lin. lata, pleraque longe acuminata, dentibus grossis obtusis vel acutis, basi 5-nervia, costa media utrinque, lateralibus e latere tantum exteriore venas laterales emittentibus, costis utrinque hirtellis. Spicæ fœmineæ gracillimæ, raro pollicem longæ. Involucra dissita, lineam longa, cyathiformia, herbacea, crenulata, pleraque biflora. Ovarium pilis longis hispidum. Styli 3, trifidi. Spicæ masculæ fœmineis breviores, graciles, glomerulis multifloris approximatis, floribus minutis; adest etiam sæpe involucrum fœmineum unicum ad basin spicæ masculæ.

787. ACALYPHA *pilosa*, Cav. Ic. 6. p. 46. t. 568. f. 2.—Some specimens agree well with the figure and description, whilst others are above a foot long.—Acapulco.

788. ALCHORNEA *grandis*, sp. n., foliis amplis late ovalibus breviter acuminatis rigide chartaceis

supra glabris subtus pubescentibus trinervibus basi biglandulosis, spicis fœmineis fasciculatis petiolo longioribus simplicibus ovarioque leviter pulveraceo-puberulis.—Tumaco.

Rami fœminei adest frustulum crassum, lignosum, teres, cortice verrucoso. Folia 10 poll. longa, 7 poll. lata, supra nitidula, subtus ferruginea; costa media supra medium folii venas emittit primarias divergentes utrinsecus 3-4; costæ laterales ad latus exterius tantum venis præditæ sunt 7-9; costæ venæque majores quæ ad marginem attingunt ibidem sæpius in denticulum glandulæformem excurrunt; omnes in pagina superiore folii depressæ sunt, in inferiore valde elevatæ; venæ secundariæ minus elevatæ, transversales et subparallelæ, rete venularum minorum minus conspicuum; glandulæ orbiculares, depressæ, in pagina inferiore in axillis costarum. Petiolus 4 poll. longus. Spicæ interruptæ, 5-6-pollicares, sæpius geminæ, basi squamis paucis lanceolatis setaceo-acuminatis stipatæ. Flores singuli ad axillam bracteæ parvæ squamæformis subsessiles, dissiti vel per 2-3 approximati. Calyx minutus, 4-fidus. Fructus nondum maturus jam magnitudine pisi, 2-3-coccus, stylis 2-3, semipollicem longis, acutis, glabris, summo apice minute papillosis.

789. MABEA *Piriri*, Aubl. Pl. Gui. 2. p. 867. t. 334. f. 1.—The leaves are very white underneath, as described by Aublet, which is not the case with my specimens of Hostmann's n. 1320, from Surinam, referred to this species by Steudel.—Isthmus of Darien. I have it also from Santa Martha.

790. JATROPHA *nudicaulis*, sp. n., glaberrima, foliis peltatis 5-lobis, lobis ovatis acutis eciliatis, stipulis glanduliformibus, panicula pedunculata corymbosa.—Monte Christi, in Columbia; in flower when everything else is burned up.

Caulis crassus, mollis, rugosus, sexpedalis, apice tempore florescentiæ foliis paucis parvis nascentibus coronatus; dum fructus maturescit folia evolvuntur 3 pollices lata, vix ad medium lobata, lobis apice rotundatis cum acumine abrupto brevi acuto; ciliæ glanduliferæ omnino desunt. Stipulæ brevissimæ, irregulariter glandulæformes, pilis coronatæ longissimis tenuissimis implexis caducissimis. Inflorescentia et flores *J. panduræformis* et petala pariter coccinea videntur. Capsulæ glabræ, glaucescentes, semipollicem diametro.

791. JATROPHA, *sp. n.?*—Peduncle very long, and flowers smaller than in the preceding species; leaves nearly the same, but as they are loose it is not certain that they belong to the same plant as the flowers.—Columbia.

792. CURCAS *purgans*, Medic.—Columbia.

793. CNIDOSCOLUS *quinquelobus*, Pohl, Pl. Bras. Ic. 1. p. 63.—Realejo; Gulf of Fonseca; Isle of Taboga, Bay of Panama.

794. CROTON *riparius*, Humb. et Kunth, Nov. Gen. et Sp. 2. p. 90.—This should probably be referred to Klotzsch's genus *Astræa*.—Columbia.

795. CROTON *rivinæfolia*, Humb. et Kunth, Nov. Gen. et Sp. 2. p. 80. vel species ei valde affinis.—This is the same as Hartweg's n. 695, but in both cases I have only seen male flowers, and therefore cannot satisfy myself as to its identity with the female plant described by Kunth, nor yet as to the genus to which it ought now to be referred.—Guayaquil.

796. CAPERONIA *castaneæfolia*, A. de St. Hil.—Guayaquil.

797. PHYLLANTHUS *Niruri*, Linn.—Salango.

798. PHYLLANTHUS *tenellus*, sp. n., fruticosus?, glaber, ramulis angulato-subcompressis, foliis

distinctis parvis obovatis orbiculatisve obtusissimis retusisve basi subcuneatis, floribus axillaribus aggregatis, pedicellis capillaceis, fructiferis folia superantibus.—Columbia.

Affinis videtur *P. orbiculari*, Humb. et Kunth, sed diversus. Ramuli tenelli, uti folia exacte alterni, pinnatim dispositi, ultimi tenues. Stipulæ lanceolatæ, membranaceæ, scariosæ, petiolo breviores. Folia 3-3½ lin. longa, 2½-3 lin. lata, omnia apice obtusissime truncata vel retusa, costa media interdum in mucronulam brevem excurrente, basi obtusa vel breviter cuneata, membranacea; petiolo tenui ½-1 lin. longo. Flores utriusque sexus ex iisdem axillis orti, fœminei solitarii, masculi numerosi in cymam trichotomam dispositi, pedunculo tamen communi ramisque ita brevibus ut pedicelli fasciculati videntur. Pedicelli singuli ex axilla bracteæ parvæ orti, graciles, fere capillacei, 3-5 lin. longi. Calycis segmenta 5 vel 6, ovata, medio viridia, margine alba, inter se inæqualia. Columna staminea in maribus brevissima, antheris 3 subsessilibus. Ovarium in flore fœmineo sessile. Styli tres, brevissimi, obtuse bilobi, lobis brevissimis crassiuscule stigmatosis radiantibus. Capsulam non vidi.

799. PHYLLANTHUS *floribundus*, Humb. et Kunth? Nov. Gen. et Sp. 2. p. 116.—Columbia.

800. CICCA *macrostachya*, sp. n., racemis longissimis, calycis segmentis exterioribus villosis, staminibus 3.—San Blas to Tepic.

Rami tenuiores quam in *C. disticha*, cortice cinereo. Ramuli steriles foliati, semipedales, folium pinnatum simulantes, leviter pubescentes. Folia 1-2-pollicaria, forma *C. distichæ*, sed in sicco non glaucescentia, supra lucidula, subtus ad venas pubescentia vel omnino glabra, minute pellucido-punctata. Racemi seu ramuli floriferi ultrapedales, graciles, pilis sparsis adpressis pubescentes, aphylli. Flores in glomerulis numerosi, magnitudine eorum *C. distichæ*, in speciminibus suppetentibus omnes masculi. Calyx 6-partitus, segmentis 3 exterioribus ovatis extus hirsutis, 3 interioribus paullo angustioribus glabris. Stamina 3, filamenta libera, calyce longiora, sub disco centrali trilobo inserta.

ARISTOLOCHIACEÆ.

801. ARISTOLOCHIA *taliscana*, Hook. et Arn. Bot. Beech. p. 309.—Manzanilla Bay.

802. ARISTOLOCHIA *odoratissima*, Linn.—*A. inflata*, Humb. et Kunth? Nov. Gen. et Sp. 2. p. 145. t. 111.—A variable plant, spreading on the ground, or creeping on shrubs; the leaves as well as the lip of the flower sometimes scarcely mucronate, at others bearing a rather long point. The smell, resembling that of *A. clematitis*, is very strong, even in dry specimens.—Panama.

PIPERACEÆ.

803. ACROCARPIDIUM *brevipes*, sp. n., ramis filiformibus pilosis, foliis alternis brevissime petiolatis orbiculatis uninervibus carnosis punctatis, junioribus hirsutis, adultis glabratis ciliatis, pedunculis hirtis, baccis ovoideis.—Conchagua.

Affine *A. nummulariæfolio*, sed folia crassiora, petiolo raro semilineam excedente. Amenta terminalia vel (ramulis abortientibus) oppositifolia, gracilia, confertiflora, semipollicaria in pedunculo 3-5-lineari. Bracteæ breviter stipitatæ, orbiculatæ, peltatæ. Stamina longiuscule exserta. Bacca basi brevissime in stipitem contracta.

804. POTHOMORPHE *peltata*, Miq. Pip. p. 203. var. venis foliorum supra hirtis.—Columbia.

805. ENCKEA *platyphylla*, sp. n., glaberrima, foliis amplis ovato-orbiculatis acuminatis basi oblique vel subæqualiter truncatis vel inæqualiter subcordatis 9-nervibus subtilissime pellucido-punctatis, amentis bacciferis folio 3-4-plo brevioribus, baccis subgloboso-depressis. — Manzanilla Bay.

Folia usque ad 10 poll. longa, 8 poll. lata, membranacea, supra demum nitidula, juniora tactu scabriuscula; nervis subtus valde prominentibus, 3 intermediis usque ad apicem ductis, extimis tenuioribus; margo foliorum sæpius angustissime revolutus, glaber. Petioli 6-9 lin. longi, crassiusculi, basi teretes, apice sub lamina canaliculati, glabri. Amentum unicum vidi tripollicare, breviter pedunculatum, baccis jam auctis sed immaturis. Bracteæ parvæ, concavæ, ciliatæ. Baccæ numerosæ, confertæ, apice umbonato-depressæ, stigmatorum vestigiis obscuris, basi parum contractæ et filamentorum (4?) vestigiis stipatæ. Pericarpium crassum. Semen tetragono-sulcatum. Specimina etiam vidi Andersoniana in insula St. Vincentis lecta ad hanc speciem ut videtur referenda, quibus baccæ minus depressæ, fere obovoideæ, mutua pressione subtetragonæ, spiraliter dispositæ.

806. ENCKEA *decrescens*, Miq. Lond. Journ. Bot. 4. p. 440, there described from Barclay's specimens, which I have not seen.—Central America.

807. ENCKEA *miconiæfolia*, sp. n., glaberrima, foliis ovato-oblongis acuminatis basi inæquali cuneatis vel hinc rotundatis subcoriaceis membranaceis subtilissime pellucido-punctatis læte viridibus nitidis 5-nervibus, amentis folio brevioribus, bracteis minutis concavis, baccis ovoideo-oblongis quinque-sulcis.—Salango.

Pluribus characteribus convenit cum *E. tenui*, sed petioli et rami in specimine glabri. Folia 3-6 poll. longa, 1-2 poll. lata, basi pleraque inæqualia et fere semper angustato-cuneata, rarius uno latere rotundata. Amenta fructifera 2-3 poll. longa, interdum folium subæquant. Baccæ distinctæ, subdistantes, sessiles, lineam longæ, apice et basi obtusæ.

808. ARTANTHE *granulosa*, Miq. Pip. p. 435.—Scarcely distinct from *A. adunca*.—Atacames.

809. ARTANTHE *Sororia*, Miq. Lond. Journ. Bot. 4. p. 443.—Gulf of Fonseca.

810. ARTANTHE *leucophylla*, Miq. Pip. p. 460. — Probably the same as *A. scabrifolia*.—Acapulco.

811. ARTANTHE *cornifolia*, Miq. Pip. p. 479.—Salango.

812. ARTANTHE *Barclayana*, Miq. Lond. Journ. Bot. 4. p. 460. — West Coast of Columbia, described by Miquel from a specimen of Barclay's, which I have not seen.

813. ARTANTHE *tuberculata*, Miq. Pip. p. 497.—*Piper begoniæfolium*, Hook. et Arn. Bot. Beech. p. 310.—Atacames, Guayaquil.

814. ARTANTHE *tuberculata*, var.? *obtusifolia*, nonnisi foliis obtusissimis a præcedente differre videtur.—*Piper ellipticum*, Hook. et Arn. Bot. Beech. p. 443.—*Artanthe Beecheyana*, Miq. Pip. p. 403.—Realejo.

815 ARTANTHE *brachypoda*, sp. n., (Plate LIV.) ramis glabris maculatis, foliis brevissime petiolatis amplis ovatis acuminatis basi inæquilateris, hinc 4-costatis basi resectis, illinc 6-costatis basi rotundatis, rigidis subcoriaceis utrinque glabris tactu scabris, amentis brevibus breviter pedun-

culatis densissimis, bracteis apice subpeltatis glabriusculis, stigmatibus staminibusque tribus.—Isle of Gorgona.

Ramuli obsolete trigoni. Folia 10 poll. longa, 5 poll. lata, petiolo crasso vix 3 lin. longo; costæ fere omnes infra medium folii a costa media divergentes, subtus valde prominentes. Punctæ pellucidæ subtilissimæ. Amenta florifera vix semipollicaria, floribus confertissimis annulatim simulque spiraliter dispositis. Stigmata recurva.

This species is very distinct from any I am acquainted with, and is allied on the one hand to Miquel's section *Churumayu*, on the other to *Hemipodium*.

Plate LIV. fig. 1. section of the flowering spike; fig. 2. flower and bract; fig. 3. section of the ovary; fig. 4. side view of a portion of the spike in fruit; fig. 5. bract and berry; all magnified. The fruit represented in the two last figures is not yet ripe, but appears to have attained nearly its full size.

JULIFLORÆ.

816. MYRIOCARPA *stipitata*, gen. nov. *Urticacearum* (Plate LV.)—Tumaco.

CHAR. GEN. Flores dioici. Masculi ignoti. Fœminei: Perigonium bifoliolatum, foliolis parvis patentibus vel interdum (additis 2 foliolis minutis) 4-partitum. Ovarium compressum. Stylus unicus, simplex, ab apice ultra medium hinc crasse papilloso-stigmatosus. Achænium lenticulare, marginatum, stylo coronatum. Semen erectum. Albumen parcum. Cotyledones ovatæ. Radicula brevis, supera.—Arbores. Folia alterna ovata, basi trinervia et pennivenia, supra pilis appressis eleganter stellato-radiantibus vix nisi sub lente conspicuis obtecta. Cymæ axillares, dichotomæ, pedunculo communi brevi, ramulis paucis ultimis simplicibus longissimis pendulis, floribus numerosissimis secus ramos ultimos laxe spicatis.

M. stipitata, foliis subtus glabriusculis, ovario achænioque longiuscule stipitatis.—Ramuli crassiusculi, pube brevissima canescentes, mox glabrati. Squamæ gemmas obtegentes (an stipulæ?) lanceolatæ, 4-5 lin. longæ, rufescentes, extus canescentes, cito deciduæ. Folia petiolata, ovata, semipedalia, 3-4 poll. lata, supra demum bullato-rugosula, breviter acuminata, margine grosse crenata, basi rotundata; costa media et venæ primariæ utrinsecus 4-5 (quarum 2 inferiores oppositæ validiores) subtus prominentes, hinc inde sparse hirtellæ; venulæ transversæ anastomosantes et hinc inde in punctas pellucidas convergentes; pili brevissimi nonnisi ope lentis conspicui, in pagina inferiore rari sparsi, in pagina superiore creberrimi, arcte appressi et a punctis pellucidis hinc inde stellato-radiantes. Pedunculi communes 1-3 lin. longi, bis terve 2-3-chotomi; rami primarii breves, ultimi sæpe pedales secus totam longitudinem floribus parvis creberrimis onusti. Perigonii foliola (seu bracteæ?) minima, lineari-lanceolata, patentia, apice recurva, sub fructu persistentia et immutata, sæpius 2 subæqualia, additis interdum 2 multo minoribus. Ovarium stipite suo subbrevius, pilis paucis marginalibus hispidum. Stylus ovario longior, a tertio circiter parte usque ad apicem crasse papillosum. Achænium cum stipite suo vix semilinea longius, lenticulare, marginibus incrassatis et pilis paucis hispidis a faciebus glabris chartaceis facile secedentibus, stylo persistente terminatis. Semen minutum, ovatum, compressum.

Plate LV. fig. 1. portion of the upper surface of the leaf showing the hairs; fig. 2. female flower; fig. 3. section of the ovary; fig. 4. fruit; fig. 5. seed; fig. 6. embryo; fig. 7. transverse section of the seed; all magnified.

A second species of this genus* has been gathered in Peru by Mathews (n. 2040). In it the racemes or branches of the cyme are full as long as in *M. stipitata*, and the flowers still smaller and more crowded. I counted 150 in considerably less than an inch, which would give about 2000 to each raceme, or above 30,000 in the two cymes of a single specimen or fragment contained in my herbarium. Other specimens in Sir W. Hooker's herbarium, from the hot region of Mexico (Galeotti n. 331, Linden n. 49), belong either to *M. densiflora* or to a species closely allied to it. In all these there are only female flowers.

817. URERA, sp.—A single female specimen, allied to *V. baccifera*, but not in a state to determine satisfactorily. It is said to be a tree as stinging as our common nettles.—Tumaco.

818. ARTOCARPUS *incisa*, Linn.—Columbia; not common, and the fruit inferior to that of the Society Islands.

819. SPONIA *canescens*, Decaisne.— *Celtis canescens*, Humb. et Kunth, Nov. Gen. et Sp. 2. p. 28.—Folia proportione latiora, crassiora et brevius acuminata quam in cæteris speciebus. Florum cymæ in glomerulos brevissimos contractæ.—Isthmus of Darien.

820. QUERCUS *aristata*, Hook. et Arn. Bot. Beech. p. 444.—Tepic.

821. QUERCUS *elliptica*, Née? in Willd. Spec. 4. p. 428.—Sierra Pueblo Nuevo, near Acapulco, at the height of 1,500 feet above the sea.

PALMÆ.

822. MORENIA *fragrans*, Ruiz et Pav.—Kunth Enum. 3. p. 174. vel species ei affinis.— A palm of about forty feet in height, of which there are only portions of leaves and male panicles in the collection.—Salango.

823. MARTINEZIA *caryotæfolia*, Humb. et Kunth.— Kunth. Enum. 3. p. 270.— Isle of Gorgona.

824. ACROCOMIA *sclerocarpa*, Mart?—Kunth? Enum. 3. p. 271.—Bay of Panama.—This is certainly an *Acrocomia*, and, as far as the specimen goes, agrees with Kunth's character of *A. sclerocarpa*, but there is an *A. mexicana*, quoted as figured in Martin's work, the distinctive characters of which, as well as the figures, are unknown to me.

There are also in the collection fragments of two or three other palms not determinable.

AROIDEÆ.

825. PISTIA *stratiotes*, Linn.—Tepic to Guayaquil.

---

* *M. densiflora*, foliis subtus molliter tomentosis, achœniis subsessilibus.

I confess I am unable to distinguish the characters by which nine species of **Pistia** have been separated by Schleiden. Amongst the flowers I have examined, I have not found two in which the stamens are precisely the same in number and position. I have seen from three to seven (they are said to vary from two to eight), sometimes arranged nearly in a ring just below the summit of the spadix (which would constitute the section " Spadix antheras processu elevato superans "), sometimes more irregularly placed and closer to the summit; the form of the leaves varies from that of a very long wedge to nearly orbicular, rounded truncate or obcordate at the extremity, narrowed at the base into a slender petiole, or almost as broad at the base as at the extremity; the nerves free from the base, or confluent, entire, or forked, without any of these differences assuming a sufficiently tangible shape to indicate specific characters, and often depending on the age or degree of vigour of the specimen. The seeds are described by some as cylindrical, by others as pyriform and smooth. In numerous fructifying specimens from Asia, Africa, and America, they have always appeared to me nearly cylindrical, with a very slight tendency to the pear shape, truncate at both extremities, and pitted on the sides.

826. ANTHURIUM *Humboldtianum*, Kunth Enum. 3. p. 78.—A single membranous leaf, a foot and a half long, and a foot broad, with pedate nerves, and a broken spadix, belong either to this species, or one closely allied to it.—Salango.

SCITAMINEÆ.

827. HELICONIA *latispatha*, sp. n., foliis longe petiolatis oblongo-ellipticis subacuminato-acutis basi inæqualibus rotundatis vel hinc acutiusculis, scapis valde flexuosis dissitifloris, spathis 7-9 patentissimis late lanceolatis canaliculato-complicatis plurifloris, inferioribus longissime acuminatis, spathillis membranaceis ovato-lanceolatis flore paullo brevioribus, perigonii laciniis interioribus apice liberis.— Salango.

Petioli ultrapedalis pars inferior deest. Folia bipedalia, 6-8 poll. lata, apice rotundata et abrupte in acumen breve acutissimum producta, basi ad unum latus breviora angustiora et acutiora, pagina inferior superiore pallidior; venæ parallelæ, creberrimæ, validiores tamen inter se lineas 2-3 distantes. Scapus ultrapedalis. Inflorescentiæ rhachis valde flexuosa, semipedalis, sub spathis parum incrassata. Spathæ rigidæ, basi a carina ad marginem 8-10 lin. latæ, inferiores 8-12 poll. longæ, superiores dimidio breviores. Flores plures (10-12?) breviter pedicellati, pleræque tamen in speciminibus suppetentibus a vermibus exesæ. Spathillæ 1-1¼ pollicares, hyalinæ, acutæ, latiores quam in affinibus. Perigonium glabrum, sesquipollicare; foliolum exterius inferius carinatum, angustum, acutiusculum, ex sicco viridi-marginatum; 2 superiora et 3 interiora alte connata sed facile separabilia, lineari-lanceolata, 2 exteriora paullo breviora, membranacea, acuta, usque ad apicem colorata, 3 interiora æqualia, apicibus acutissimis liberis in sicco viridibus. Genitalia perigonium æquantia. Antheræ angustæ, longe adnatæ, connectivi apice acuta virescente apiculatæ. Stylus apice leviter clavatus, papillis stigmatosis apicem obtegentibus brunneis.

The above description is taken as well from Mr. Hinds's specimen, as from another gathered by Hartweg near Bogota. It is very distinct from all the species I am acquainted with, but agrees in several points with the character given by Miquel of his *H. Richardiana*. The leaves and spathæ are, however, longer, the bracts or spathillæ much broader, and the stalk scarcely thickened under the spathæ. There is also a *H. flexuosa* of Presl, but I have not access to any description of it.

828. HELICONIA *vaginalis*, sp. n., foliis caulinis oblongo-lanceolatis utrinque longe angustatis, petiolo fere ad apicem vaginante, spathis (4) lanceolatis acuminatis complicatis 8-12-floris, spathillis lanceolatis, perigonii laciniis interioribus usque ad apicem concretis.—Isle of Gorgona.

Folia tria adsunt, inferius sesquipedale, superius 7-pollicare, omnia $1\frac{1}{2}$-2 poll. lata, vaginis elongatis scapum arcte involventibus, lamina fere ad vaginam decurrente, apice longe (nec ut in *H. acuminata* abrupte) acuminata. Scapus e folio superiore breviter exsertus. Rhachis 3-pollicaris, flexuosus. Spathæ in specimine 4, infima 5 poll., suprema 2 poll. longa, omnes extus leviter puberulæ. Spathillæ acutissimæ, membranaceæ, complicatæ, exteriores sesquipollicares. Pedicelli fructiferi e spatha exserti. Perigonium sesquipollicare, undique coloratum; foliolum exterius infimum canaliculatum, 2 superiora interioribus alte adnata et paullo breviora; interiora connata in unum acutissimum integerrimum. Genitalia non vidi. Capsula baccata, fere hemisphærica, truncata, 5 lin. lata.

829. CANNÆ, sp. *A. glaucæ* affinis.—Guayaquil.

This is the same as Hartweg's n. 698, from the same locality. The species of this genus have been so multiplied and distinguished by characters, of so little value or fixity, that it is impossible to determine these from dried specimens, until the whole genus shall have been worked up by a competent botanist.

830. MARANTA *arundinacea*, Linn.—Panama.

It is surprising that, after the structure of the flower in this and allied genera has been so well explained by Nees and others, the outer sterile petaloid stamens should be still described in general works as inner lobes of the corolla. The ovary is, in a young stalk, three-celled, although, even at the time of flowering, two of the cells are already much smaller and empty.

831. RENEALMIA *racemosa*, Pœpp. et Endl. Nov. Gen. et Sp. 2. p. 26.—Caulis 8-pedalis. Racemus compositus, fere glaber, ramis 3-5-floris.—Salango.

In one of the flowers which I examined of this plant, the central lobe of the so-called *labellum* of some botanists, or *synème* of Lestiboudois, was converted into two perfect stamens, the anthers being borne on short filaments, with a dilated connectivum, one perfect cell, similar to the larger one of the stamen usually fertile, and one smaller rudimentary cell. The two lateral lobes of the *synème* were larger than usual, oblong, but contracted at the base; there was no trace of the sixth stamen, whose place would be between the pair of antheriferous lobes.

Another flower from the same raceme had the usual structure of the genus. The above deviation fully confirms the views of Lestiboudois, Nees, and others, as to the real structure of the *Zingiberaceæ* of Endlicher, which, with the *Museæ* and *Canneæ*, ought surely to form but one very natural order, though divisible into three tribes.

ORCHIDACEÆ.

(Determined by Dr. LINDLEY.)

832. EPIDENDRUM *macrochilum*, Hook. Bot. Mag. t. 3534.—Panama.

833. EPIDENDRUM *radicans*, Pav.—Lindl. Orch. Gen. et Sp. p. 104.—Realejo.

834. EPIDENDRUM *glumaceum*, Lindl.—Columbia.

835. EPIDENDRUM (Encyclium) *trachycarpum*, Lindl. sp. n., pseudobulbis elongato-conicis 2-3-phyllis, foliis rigidis ensiformibus canaliculatis acutis, scapo subpaniculato ramulis pedunculisque scaberrimis, floribus carnosis, sepalis petalisque oblongis obtusis, labelli trilobi laciniis lateralibus nanis semiovatis acutis, intermedia rotundata undulata emarginata lævi, capsula scaberrima.—Bay of Manzanilla.

Affine *E. adenocarpo*. Folia rigidissima. Flores carnosi nec membranacei.

836. BRASSAVOLA *grandiflora*, Lindl. Bot. Reg. 1839, Misc. p. 14.—Guayaquil.

837. CATTLEYA *Skinneri*, Lindl. Bot. Reg. 1840, Misc. p. 83.—Columbia.

838. BLETIA *acutipetala*, Hook. Bot. Mag. t. 3217.—Panama.

839. ORNITHOCEPHALUS *bicornis*, Lindl. sp. n., foliis ensiformibus erectis racemo hirsuto longioribus, sepalis subrotundis apiculatis petalisque conformibus unguiculatis ciliatis, labelli carnosi bipartiti laciniis lanceolatis recurvis canaliculatis.—Panama.

840. SCAPHYGLOTTIS? *fasciculata*, Hook. Ic. Pl. t. 317.—Realejo.

841. IONOPSIS *utricularioides*, Lindl. Orch. Gen. et Sp. p. 194.—Panama.

842. ONCIDIUM *iridifolium*, Humb. et Kunth.—Lindl. Orch. Gen. et Sp. p. 202.—Columbia.

843. ONCIDIUM *stipitatum*, Lindl. sp. n., foliis longissimis arcuatis semiteretibus canaliculatis, panicula contracta, sepalis petalisque liberis undulato-crispis obtusis æqualibus, labello trilobo laciniis lateralibus linearibus sepalis paullo brevioribus, intermedia longe unguiculata biloba dentata, callo solitario in unguem.—Panama.

Affine *O. variegato* et *O. tetrapetalo*.

844. DICHÆA *graminoides*, Lindl. Orch. Gen. et Sp. p. 209.—Choco on Mangrove trees.

Bromeliaceæ.

845. Æchmea *laxiflora*, sp. n., foliis remote spinoso-serratis, panicula elongata multiflora, ramulis flexuosis dissite 10-20-floris, bracteis primariis lanceolatis membranaceis, ultimis sub floribus complicatis striatis brevissime mucronatis, perigonii foliolis exterioribus æqualibus ovatis muticis apice hinc dilatatis.—Acapulco.

Folium adest rigidum, concavum, fere bipedale, basi $1\frac{1}{2}$ poll. latum, aculeis marginalibus remotis sursum uncinatis, pagina utraque punctis lepidotis minutis conspersa, cæterum glabra. Panicula sesquipedalis, oblonga, ovariis exceptis fere glabra. Rami secus rhachin creberrimi, 3-4-pollicares, inferiores subramosi, cæteri simplices, glabri, flexuosi, patentes, apicibus pendulis, rhachidibus bractearum decurrentia subancipitibus. Bracteæ ramos subtendentes, inferiores ramulos subæquantes, planæ, membranaceæ, striatæ, coloratæ; cæteræ gradatim decrescentes, summæ parvæ concavæ vel complicatæ. Bracteolæ sub floribus singulis 2-3 lin. longæ, rigidæ, complicatæ, striatæ, basi verticaliter adnatæ carina breviter decurrente, apice mucrone brevi acutatæ. Perigonium intra bracteam sessile, pars ovario adnata extus lanata, subtriquetra, bractea paullo brevior; laciniæ exteriores $2\frac{1}{2}$ lin. longæ, interiores liberæ, exterioribus longiores, convolutæ, obovali-oblongæ, basi angustatæ, intus bisquamatæ. Filamenta filiformia, 3 libera, 3 perigonio interiori usque ad squamas adnata. Antheræ oblongæ, circa styli apicem obtusum clavatum subintegrum arcte approximatæ (vel connatæ?). Ovarium triloculare, loculis multiovulatis.

846. Æchmea *pyramidalis*, sp. n., foliis longiuscule spinoso-serratis, panicula elongata rigida multiflora, ramulis reflexis approximatim 8-15-floris, bracteis primariis lanceolatis membranaceis, ultimis sub floribus complicatis mucronato-acuminatissimis subpungentibus, perigonii foliolis exterioribus ovatis coriaceis duobus acutis tertio obtuso.—Guayaquil.

Folium adest pedale, rigidum, aculeis marginalibus crebris 2-3 lin. longis rectiusculis vel leviter incurvis, pagina inferiore squamulis albidis peltatis lepidota. Panicula (an completa?) sesquipedalis, ramulis inferioribus semipedalibus ramosis, cæteris a medio ad apicem crebris 1-$1\frac{1}{4}$-pollicaribus rigide divaricato-recurvis. Flores distichi, approximati at non imbricati. Bracteæ fere *Æ. laxifloræ*, sed ultimæ majores et longius acuminatæ. Rhachides et perigonia lana laxa alba detergibili vestita. Flores fere *Æ. laxifloræ*.

847. Æchmea, sp. foliis inermibus.—Too much injured to describe accurately.—Salango.

848. Tillandsia, sp.—Apparently allied to *T. uniflora*, but there are no flowers.—Realejo.

849. Tillandsia *complanata*, sp. n., glabra, foliis inferioribus lanceolatis breviter acuminatis basi laxe vaginantibus, scapo simplici, squamis angustis acutis erectis vaginantibus, spica solitaria oblonga compressa, bracteis complicatis acutis imbricatis, perigonii exterioris foliolis liberis subæqualibus.—Atacames.

Folia (ad basin caulis approximata?) semipedalia, 7-8 lin. lata, basi latiora et in vaginam laxam convoluta, superne plana et in acumen angustum acutum 3-5 lin. longum producta, subtus pallida et punctis minutis subfurfuraceis rubentibus conspersa. Scapi 8-10-pollicares, erecti, stricti. Squamæ vaginantes 10-12 lin. longæ, scapum vix omnino obtegentes, apice sæpe rubentes, et mucrone acutissimo terminatæ; superiores latiores, laxiores, in bracteas abeunt. Spicæ, in speciminibus juveniles, vix pollice longiores, valde compressæ, apice et basi acutæ, 4-5 lin. latæ. Bracteæ distiche imbricatæ, carinatæ, venosæ, margine subscariosæ, apice rubentes et mucrone acuto terminatæ, 7-8 lin. longæ. Perigonium intra bracteam sessile, in specimine examinato nondum expansum; foliola 3 exteriora 5 lineas longa, glumacea, convoluta, acuta;

interiora corollina, basi in tubum connata. Stamina 6, antheris oblongis. Ovarium liberum. Stylus filiformis, apice terminatus lobis 3 brevibus filiformibus stigmatosis.

850. TILLANDSIA *disticha*, Humb. et Kunth.—Schult. Syst. 6. p. 1218.—Atacames; gathered also by Cuming, near Panama, n. 1188.

851. TILLANDSIA *divaricata*, sp. n., foliis caulinis subulato-acuminatis, spicis plurimis breviter pedunculatis divaricatis multifloris compressis, floribus distichis imbricatis, bracteis acutis argenteo-lepidotis perigonii interioris tubum æquantibus.—Columbia.

Folia inferiora desunt. Caulis obtectus vaginis angustis in folia brevia subulata pilosiuscula abeuntibus. Bracteæ ad basin spicarum ovato-lanceolatæ, vix striatæ, subulato-acutæ, 1-1½-pollicares, erectæ, rigidæ, extus lepidoto-canescentes. Spicæ 1½-2-pollicares, verticaliter compressæ, 6 lin. latæ, basi in pedunculum brevem attenuatæ, 12-15-floræ. Bracteæ sub floribus singulis complicatæ, semipollicares, arcte imbricatæ, acutiusculæ. Perigonium exterius triquetrum, rigide glumaceum, bractea vix brevius, diphyllum, foliolo altero bicarinato (e duobus connatis constante), altero convexo; interius tenue, tubo bracteam æquante, laciniis 3 oblongo-lanceolatis, minus fugacibus quam in plerisque speciebus.

852. TILLANDSIA *multiflora*, sp. n., foliis lanceolato-ligulatis apice convolutis superioribus subulatis, panicula oblonga ramosa, spiculis 8-20-floris distichis laxiusculis, perigonii foliolis exterioribus ovatis liberis carinatis bractea longioribus, interioribus apice patentibus exsertis.—Guayaquil.

Folia inferiora ultrapedalia, medio 6-8 lin. lata, basi latiora, longe vaginantia, apice longe convoluto-acuminata, glabra vel minute lepidoto-candicantia. Scapi pars adest cum panicula sesquipedalis. Folia, e vagina laxa longiuscule convoluto-subulata, gradatim abeunt in bracteas sub paniculæ ramis primariis oblongas, concavas, sesquipollicares, acumine gradatim breviore terminatas; bracteæ sub ramis secundariis spicisque ultimis multo minores, sub floribus singulis 1-1⅓ lin. longæ, muticæ, acutæ vel obtusiusculæ, omnes ovatæ, concavæ. Panicula pedalis, bis terve ramosa, ramis brevibus. Spicæ ultimæ subsessiles, pleræque fere pollicares, 10-15-floræ, nonnullæ longiores vel breviores. Rhachis flexuosa. Flores regulariter distichi, semilineam ad lineam inter se distantes, divaricati, sessiles. Perigonium exterius ovato-triquetrum, 2½ lin. longum, foliolis rigide glumaceis carinatis acutiusculis; interius dimidio longius, membranaceum, foliolis liberis basi latis, sese a latere valde obtegentibus. Filamenta 3 libera, 3 cum perigonio interiore basi connata. Stylus brevis, obsolete trilobus. Capsula oblonga, styli vestigiis mucronata, 4-6 lin. longa. Semina linearia, pendula, apice pilis longis comata.—Species affinis videtur *T. parvifloræ*, Ruiz et Pav.

853. GUSMANNIA *tricolor*, Ruiz et Pav.—Schult. Syst. 6. p. 1231.—Columbia.

854. PUYA *heterophylla*, Lindl. in Bot. Reg. 1840, t. 71.—Realejo.

AMARYLLIDACEÆ.

855. CRINUM *americanum*, Lhér.—Herb. Amaryll. p. 254.—Flores in umbella 4, rosei.—San Blas.

856. CRINUM *erubescens*, Herb.? Amaryll. p. 251.—Flores in umbella 5, tubo sexpollicari.—Guayaquil.

857. CALLIPSYCHE *eucrosioides*, Herb. in Bot. Reg. 1845, t. 45.—Guayaquil, unless it may have been mislaid from the Mexican parcel. The bulbs described by Mr. Herbert were from San Blas.

858. ALSTRŒMERIA *chorullensis*, Herb.? in Bot. Reg. 1843, Min. p. 95.—Huamantango.

859. BOMAREA *edulis*, Herb. Amaryll. p. 111.—Columbia.

HYDROCHARIDACEÆ.

860. LIMNOBIUM *Sinclairii*, sp. n., floribus monoicis, spathis unifloris, masculis in scapo brevi pluribus, fœmineis solitariis.—Guayaquil.

Planta natans, stolonifera, acaulis. Folia radicalia petiolo ½-1-pollicari, ovata vel orbiculata, obtusa, integerrima, basi rotundato-truncata, rarius leviter cordata vel in petiolum angustata, 10-15 lin. longa, venulis evidentioribus circa quinque in petiolum convergentibus, minoribus pluribus subparallelis et fenestrato-reticulatis. Scapi masculi nunc 2-6 lin. longi, nunc subnulli, spathis 2-3 brevibus laxis membranaceis hinc fissis terminati. Pedunculi intra spathas solitarii, uniflori, 2-4 poll. longi. Perigonium corollinum, 6-partitum, laciniis subæqualibus elliptico-oblongis, 3 exterioribus viridioribus. Stamina 6; filamenta brevissima, plana, basi connata; antheræ oblongæ. Styli rudimenta 2, filiformia. Spathæ fœmineæ, certe in eadem planta cum maribus, subsessiles, solitariæ, tubulosæ, 3-5 lin. longæ, hinc fissæ, demum explanatæ. Pedunculus vix spatham superans vel interdum ei brevior. Perigonium fere maris sed superum (vel potius tubo ovario adhærente donatum). Stamina nulla. Styli 6, filiformes, bifidi, lobis stigmatosis. Ovarium triloculare, omnino inferum. Ovula in loculis numerosa, hyalina. Capsula (immatura) ovoidea, nuda. Semina pauca, more *Hydrocharidacearum* echinulata.

The female flowers are so imperfect that I am not quite certain as to the details of their structure.

SMILACEÆ.

861. SMILAX *obtusa*, sp. n., glaberrima, ramis angulatis inermibus, foliis ramealibus brevissime petiolatis oblongis apice obtusis cum mucrone brevissimo vel muticis basi rotundatis angustatisve coriaceis utrinque 5-nervibus reticulatisque nitidulis, pedunculo fœmineo petiolum æquante, receptaculo globoso.—Manzanilla Bay.

Adsunt tantum plantæ fœmineæ rami ultimi fructiferi. Folia in his sesquipollicaria, 6 lin. lata, petiolo 3-lineari. Cirrhi e petiolo nati. Receptaculum fructiferum 1½-3 lin. diametro. Baccæ globosæ, breviter pedicellatæ, 2 lin. diametro.

ALISMACEÆ.

862. SAGITTARIA *sagittifolia*, Linn.—Kunth, Enum. 3. p. 156.—var.? foliorum lobis baseos divaricatis terminali æquilongis et vix angustioribus. An species propria? Flores in specimine manci.—Guayaquil.

Commelynaceæ.

863. Commelyna *agraria*, Kunth, Enum. 4. p. 38.—San Blas, Acapulco, Realejo, Panama.

864. Commelyna *acuminata*, Humb. et Kunth.—Kunth, Enum. 4. p. 38.—A single specimen, rather more downy than described by Kunth.—Between San Blas and Tepic.

865. Commelyna *cœlestis*, Kunth, Enum. 4. p. 45.—Realejo.

866. Commelyna *elegans*, Humb. et Kunth.—Kunth, Enum. 4. p. 55.—Panama and Guayaquil. These specimens are smoother than those described by Kunth. There is also a small variety from Acapulco, and a tall narrow-leaved form from Guayaquil.

867. Commelyna? *leiocarpa*, sp. n., caule geniculato glabro, vaginis ore ciliatis, foliis ovatis vel ovato-lanceolatis glabris, pedunculis hinc hirtellis, spatha complicata, pedicello altero 2-3-floro altero minuto sterili, perigonii foliolis interioribus parum inæqualibus, fructu globoso nitido indehiscente.—Tiger Island, Gulf of Fonseca.

Caules ultrapedales, basi procumbentes, ad quemquam fere nodum geniculati et ramosi, hinc sulcati et interdum longitudinaliter scabro-puberuli, cæterum glabri. Vaginæ breves, hinc fissæ. Folia 1½-2-pollicaria, pleraque complicata, subsessilia, basi rotundata. Pedunculi sub spatha semipollicares ad pollicares. Perigonii exterioris foliolum exterius 2 lin. longum, lateralia paullo breviora, latiora, inter se libera; interioris foliola 2 orbiculata, brevissime unguiculata, tertium lato-ovatum, sessile, glanduloso-lineolatum. Stamina fertilia tria; antheræ 2 ovato-sagittatæ, loculis oblongis arcuatis subcontiguis, tertia longior incurva loculis contiguis parallelis lineari-oblongis. Stamina sterilia 2, antheris more *Commelynarum* cruciato-lobatis; sextum omnino deest. Stylus filiformis, apice obtusus, tenuissime stigmatosus. Fructus 3 lin. diametro, trilocularis, pericarpium membranaceum nitidum, in sicco nigro-plumbeum. Semina in quoque loculo 2, superposita, nigra, grosse rugosa, fructum fere implentia, sed tanquam ex sicco apparet pulpa tenui nidulantia.

The fruit of this species is so different from that of any other *Commelyna* I am acquainted with, that I should have considered it as forming a distinct genus, were it not that the habit, inflorescence, and flowers are so precisely those of *Commelyna*, that its separation would break through the present very natural circumscription of that genus.

868. Tradescantia *cordifolia*, Sw.—Kunth, Enum. 4. p. 91.— Pedunculi terminales, gemini, filiformes, apice 5-7-flori; pedicelli pubescentes; filamenta imberbia, perigonio interiore breviora at non brevissima. Cætera cum descriptionibus auctorum omnino conveniunt.—Atacames.

869. Tradescantia *triandra*, Kunth, Enum. 4. p. 93.—Panama.

870. Tradescantia *cumanensis*, Kunth, Enum. 4. p. 96.—Panama.

This is the same plant as Cuming's n. 1140, from the same locality. It agrees, in some respects, rather with *T. Schlechtendahlii* than with *T. cumanensis*, but the outer perigon is not smooth. The stem, on the other hand, is smooth, with the exception of a longitudinal line of short hairs below each leaf-sheath. The flowers agree precisely with Kunth's description of *T. cumanensis*. Possibly the two described plants may be but varieties of one species. The plant referred here by Hooker and Arnott, Bot. Beech. p. 311, under the name of *Aneilema floribunda*, is a very distinct species, described by Martens and Galeotti under the name of *Tradescantia filiformis*.

CYPERACEÆ.

871. ELEOCHARIS *constricta*, Rœm. et Schult.—Kunth, Enum. 2. p. 153.—Spica ovato-conica, brevior et crassior quam illa *E. geniculatæ*.—Guayaquil.

872. DICHROMENA *ciliata*, Vahl.—Kunth, Enum. 2. p. 276.—Panama.

873. HYPOLYTRUM *pycnocephalum*, sp. n., culmo triquetro, spicis numerosis capitato-congestis, involucro inæqualiter plurifoliato.—Island of Gorgona.

Folia desunt. Culmi adest summitas rigida, triquetra, angulis scabris. Involucri folium exterius culmo continuum, ultrapedale, pollicem latum, rigidum, alterum paullo brevius, tertium semipedale, omnia subulato-acuminata, superne ad margines serrulato-scaberrima; quartum et quintum multo minora, subulata, basi breviter dilatata. Spiculæ ultra 30, densissime congestæ, semipollicares, ovato-conicæ, multifloræ. Squamæ undique imbricatæ, obtusæ vel retusæ. Squamulæ carinatæ, angustæ, squamis longiores. Stamina 2 (vel interdum abortientia?). Achænium lenticulari-turgidum, læve. Stylus longus, ad medium bifidus, basi persistente non dilatata.

874. SCLERIA *bracteata*, Cav.—Kunth, Enum. 2. p. 345.—Isle of Taboga, Bay of Panama.

GRAMINEÆ.

875. PASPALUM *paniculatum*, Linn.—Kunth, Enum. 1. p. 59.—Realejo.

876. OLYRA *latifolia*, Linn.—Kunth, Enum. 1. p. 69.—Gulf of Fonseca.

877. PANICUM *brevifolium*, Linn.—*P. trichodes*, Sw.—Kunth, Enum. 1. p. 112.— Gulf of Fonseca.

878. SETARIA *glauca*, Beauv.—Kunth, Enum. 1. p. 149.—Central America.

879. OPLISMENUS *Burmanni*, Beauv.—Kunth, Enum. 1. p. 139.—Forma mollissime villosa.—Gulf of Fonseca.

880. PENNISETUM *purpurascens*, Humb. et Kunth.—Kunth, Enum. 1. p. 160.—Acapulco.

881. DACTYLOCTENIUM *ægyptiacum*, Wild.—Kunth, Enum. 1. p. 261.—Gulf of Fonseca.

882. ERAGROSTIS, sp. near *Poa tenax* and *P. aturensis*, Humb. et Kunth (Kunth, Enum. 1. p. 327, 328), with dense panicles, a foot to a foot and a half long, and very numerous small shining flowers, about seven in each spikelet, but the leaves are wanting.—Conchagua.

883. UNIOLA *paniculata*, Linn.—Kunth, Enum. 1. p. 425.—Isthmus of Darien; Atacames.

884. ANDROPOGON *incompletus*, Presl.—Kunth, Enum. 1. p. 503.—Realejo.

885. DIECTOMIS *fastigiata*, Beauv.—Kunth, Enum. 1. p. 510.—Realejo.

There are also in the collection a considerable number of Ferns, which have been intrusted to Sir William Hooker for publication in his *Species Filicum*.

IV.—PERU AND CHILI.

The collection contained a parcel marked Callao, and several from Valparaiso, but as they had been made up in the earlier part of the voyage, they had suffered more than any others from insects. Most of the specimens were, indeed, reduced to powder. Out of what remained, I was enabled to recognise about fifty species, but none of them either new or deserving any special mention on this occasion.

V.—ISLANDS OF THE PACIFIC.

The collections made in the Sandwich Islands, the Marquesas, and Taiti, amounted to rather more than two hundred species, but with the exception, perhaps, of two or three doubtful Compositæ and Rubiaceæ, the whole are already described. A tolerably complete enumeration of the plants of the Society Islands, may be found in the first volume of the Annals of the Vienna Museum, and in Guillemin's *Zephyritis Taitensis* in the Annales des Sciences Naturelles, 2nd series, vols. vi. and vii. The Sandwich Island flora is much less completely known, and can only be collected either from general works, or from the botanical portions of different voyages, such as those of Captain Freycinet's voyage, published by Gaudichaud; of Captain Kotzebue's, by Chamisso and others in the Linnæa; of Captain Beechey's, by Hooker and Arnott, etc. A complete enumeration of the botanical productions of the Sandwich Islands, as far as known, would be a valuable work, and very considerable materials might be found in our herbaria, but the collection made by the Officers of the SULPHUR, bears too small a pro-

VI.—NEW GUINEA REGION.

portion to the whole number, and the space to which we are limited too small to undertake it here, and a mere list of the few collected of too little interest for insertion.

VI.—NEW GUINEA REGION.

The plants collected during this portion of the voyage, were already published in a paper, inserted in the London Journal of Botany, vol. i. p. 669, and vol. ii. p. 211, before any arrangements were made for the separate publication of the Botany of the voyage. It was, it is believed, the intention of the Editor to reprint that paper, as well as a previous one on the Hong Kong collection (London Journal of Botany, vol. i. p. 476) in the present work, but the space to which we are limited now precludes any farther mention of them than the repetition of the descriptions of the five following species now figured.

Chætosus *volubilis*, gen. nov. (Plate LVI.)—New Guinea.

Char. Gen. Calyx brevis, 5-partitus, sepalis æstivatione imbricatis. Corollæ tubus brevis, ovoideus, faux leviter contracta, subnuda; limbi laciniæ 5, oblongo-lineares, æstivatione leviter contorta. Stamina 5, imo tubo inserta. Antheræ exsertæ, in conum connatæ. Glandulæ hypogynæ 5, conicæ, ovario æquilongæ. Ovarium biloculare, ovulis in quoque loculo numerosissimis, placentis dissepimento adnatis. Stylus filiformis. Stigma basi orbiculari impositum, oblongum, apice breviter bilobum. Bacca bilocularis, crustacea, polysperma, seminibus peltatis dissepimento affixis.

C. volubilis. Frutex glaber, ramulis volubilibus. Folia opposita, petiolata, ovata breviter acuminata, penninervia, subtripollicaria. Stipulæ interpetiolares brevissimæ, breviter multisetæ. Cymæ pedunculatæ, axillares, 2-3-chotomæ, petiolo paullo longiores. Calyx ½ lin. longus. Corolla intus extusque glabra, tubo lineam, limbi laciniis sesquilineam longis. Faux annulo obscuro aucta; filamenta crassiuscula, pilis paucis hirtella, tubo corollæ paullo longiora. Ovarium gynophoro crasso-carnoso impositum, tetragono-conicum. Baccæ, in speciminibus immaturæ, late obovoideo-globosæ, 4-5 lin. longæ et latæ, nonnullæ loculo uno abortiente ovoideæ incurvæ. Semina in quoque loculo 4-5, matura non vidi. (Benth. in Lond. Jour. Bot. 2. p. 226.)

The central placentation and stipulary ciliæ indicate the affinities of this genus rather with *Loganiaceæ* than with *Apocynaceæ*, and it is probably near to the imperfectly known genus *Picrophlæus* of Blume.

Plate LVI. fig. 1. flower; fig. 2. corolla cut open; fig. 3. stamen; fig. 4. nectarium, ovary and style; fig. 5. longitudinal section of the ovary; all magnified.

Leucosmia *Burnettiana*, gen. nov. *Aquilarinearum* (Plate LVII.)—Feejee Islands.

CHAR. GEN. Perigonium longe tubulosum, limbo 5-fido, laciniis æstivatione imbricatis. Squamæ ad faucem 5, laciniis alternæ. Stamina 10, 5 ad faucem laciniis perigonii opposita, 5 paullo inferius inserta, squamis opposita; filamenta brevia; antheræ lineares, versatiles, biloculares, loculis longitudinaliter dehiscentibus. Vagina brevis, ovarii basin cingens. Ovarium biloculare, ovulis in quoque loculo solitariis, ab apice anguli interioris pendulis. Stylus longus, filiformis, apice incrassatus in stigma oblongum leviter emarginatum. Drupæ sarcocarpium tenue, putamen crassum lignosum biloculare dispermum. Semina pendula, exalbuminosa, cotyledonibus crassis, radicula brevissima supera.

S. Burnettiana. Frutex (vel arbor?) glaberrimus. Folia opposita, exstipulata, breviter petiolata ovatoelliptica vel suprema fere orbicularia, brevissime acuminata, integerrima, subcoriacea, nitidula, penninervia, reticulato-venosa, 2½-3½ poll. longa. Flores in capitulo terminali breviter pedunculato circa 10, sessiles. Involucrum in speciminibus nullum, sed cicatrices supersunt bractearum vel deciduarum, vel abortientium. Perigonium gracile, basi et apice leviter ampliatum, extus glabrum, bipollicare; laciniæ limbi crassæ, oblongæ, obtusæ, concavæ, 3-4 lin. longæ, in alabastro valde imbricatæ; tubus intus hirsutus. Squamæ faucis parvæ, ovatæ, vagina brevissima, glabra, integra. Ovarium oblongum, leviter compressum, villosum. Drupa magnitudine nucis avellanæ, compresso-globosa, siccitate rugosa, et interdum subdidyma, putamine crassissimo lignosofibroso. Seminum testa nigro-fusca. (Benth. l. c. pp. 231, 232.)

At the request of Mr. Hinds, I dedicated this species to Sir William Burnett, Inspector-General of the Navy, a zealous promoter of natural history, and much respected by the medical officers of the navy; regretting, at the same time, that a genus existing already of the name of *Burnettia*, precluded my fulfilling entirely the wishes of Mr. Hinds, to dedicate one to Sir William.

Plate LVII. fig. 1. perigonium cut open; fig. 2. section of the ovary; fig. 3. fruit; fig. 4. transverse section of the fruit; fig. 5. seed; fig. 6. embryo: figs. 3 and 4, natural size, the remainder magnified.

DENDROBIUM *bifalce*, Lindl. sp. n., (Plate LVIII.) caule tereti lævigato, folio (solitario?) coriaceo obovato acuto oblique emarginato, pedunculis longissimis rigidis nudis apice paucifloris, pedicellis racemosis erectis floribus triplo longioribus, petalis lanceolatis trinerviis membranaceis labello unguiculato tripartito supra unguem crista duplici carnosa biloba undulata aucto, laciniis lateralibus linearibus obtusis falcatis intermedia subrotunda, cornu obtuso incurvo.

This very singular plant exists in an imperfect state in the collection. Its habit is different from that of any *Dendrobium* I am acquainted with; but since this genus presents great diversity of habit, I cannot attach importance to that circumstance, in the absence of a more complete knowledge of the structure of the fructification. In my solitary specimen the main stem is gone, and I have only a couple of rigid peduncles proceeding from a common point, with a surface like that of a small bamboo, and a foot and a half long. With them, but separate from them, is a remarkably coriaceous leaf, six inches long and two inches broad at the broadest part, but how it fits on the stem there is no evidence to show. The flowers are inserted in a few-flowered raceme at the end of the peduncles; they appear to have been purple and some pale colour, and are about as large as those of *Aporum anceps*. At the base of the middle lobe of the lip are two parallel sharp-ridged fleshy tubercles, which occupy the middle of a short unguis belonging to the middle lobe (Lindl. in Lond. Journ. Bot. 2, p. 237).

Plate LVIII. fig. 1. flower; fig. 2. labellum and column, side view; fig. 3. labellum, seen from above; all magnified.

DENDROBIUM (Spathulata) *antennatum*, Lindl. sp. n., (Plate LIX.) foliis lanceolatis carnosis oblique emarginatis racemo oppositifolio brevioribus, sepalis acuminatis, petalis linearibus duplo longioribus reflexis, labello trilobo, venis quinque elevatis rectis per axin, lobo medio ovato acuto plano tricostato.—New Guinea.

The petals of this curious plant are two inches long, and scarcely half a line wide. The leaves are succulent, brittle, and veinless when fresh (Lindl. l. c. p. 236).

Plate LIX. fig. 1. labellum, magnified.

DENDROBIUM (Spathulata) *veratrifolium*, Lindl. sp. n., (Plate LX.) foliis oblongis (ovatisve) obtusis amplexicaulibus 9-11-nervibus, racemo terminali elongato multifloro, sepalis undulatis acutis, petalis spathulatis obtusis planis vix duplo longioribus, labello oblongo obtuso membranaceo, venis tribus elevatis per axin duabusque minoribus lateralibus, lobis lateralibus nanis obtusis, intermedio oblongo undulato.—New Guinea.

A most beautiful plant, with racemes a foot and a half long, loaded with flowers, whose spatula-shaped petals are an inch and more in length (Lindl. l. c. p. 236).

Plate LX. fig. 1. labellum, magnified.

The plant which I described in the above quoted paper, under the name of *Cardiophora Hindsii* (Benth. in Lond. Journ. 2, p. 216), has been shown by Dr. Planchon to be the *Soulamea amara*, Lam., which is usually enumerated amongst *Polygalaceæ*, with which it has but little affinity. Dr. Planchon refers it to *Simarubaceæ*.

The *Piper fragile*, Benth. l. c. p. 234, with other species formerly included by Miquel under *Piper*, has now, in his excellent monograph of *Piperaceæ*, been removed to his new genus *Chavica*, under the name of *Chavica Benthamiana*.

The genus *Serophyton*, p. 52, is the same as *Aphora*, Nutt., which not having been taken up in Endlicher's *Genera*, I had overlooked, as shown by Gray and Engelmann, Plantæ Lindheimerianæ, p. 25.

The undescribed Euphorbiaceous plant, from California, mentioned in this work, p. 54, is the same as the one since described by Nuttall under the name of *Simmondsia Californica*.

The *Ipomœa* mentioned, p. 135, as *I. cymosa*, is *I. umbellata*, Mey.—Chois. in DC. Prod. 9, p. 377,—an American species, which closely resembles the Asiatic *I. cymosa* in everything except the colour of the flower, which is yellow in *I. umbellata*, of a pure white in *I. cymosa*.

The Editor having left Europe shortly after the publication of the Fourth Part of this Work, the two last parts, commencing at p. 97, have been completed by the Author of the Botanical Descriptions, who avails himself of this opportunity of adverting to the materials from which this work is compiled.

The principal collection placed in his hands was that made by the Editor himself, Mr. Hinds, through whose liberality the original specimens have been deposited in the subscriber's herbarium. This extends over the whole of the stations mentioned in the work. A second collection was made likewise at the whole or the greater part of the stations, by Mr. Barclay, the collector sent out by the Royal Garden of Kew, and, through the kindness of Sir William Hooker, the subscriber has been enabled to avail himself of a set of these plants deposited in Sir William's herbarium.

A considerable portion of the specimens described from Western Tropical America, were gathered by Dr. Sinclair, and presented by him to Sir William Hooker, in whose herbarium the originals of these species will be found, and many of them likewise in the subscriber's collection, who owes a very valuable set of them to Sir William's liberality.

The original specimens of the *Orchiduceæ* are in Dr. Lindley's herbarium, and those of the *Ferns* in Sir William Hooker's.

The total number of species gathered in the voyage amounts to near two thousand, of which above four hundred were previously undescribed.

GEORGE BENTHAM.

January, 1846.

INDEX OF SPECIES.

(THE SYNONYMS ARE IN ITALICS.)

	Page
Abronia arenaria, Menz.	43
gracilis, Benth.	44
umbellata, Lam.	43
Abutilon californicum, Benth.	8
graveolens, Wight. et Arn.	69
pedunculare, Humb. et Kunth	69
reflexum, Sw.	68
Acacia *acantholoba, Humb. et Kunth*	90
Hindsii, Benth.	90
macracantha, Humb. et Kunth	90
pellacantha, Vog.	90
villosa, Willd.	90
Acalypha californica, Benth.	51
leptoclada, Benth.	164
obovata, Benth. (Plate LIII.)	163
pilosa, Cav.	164
vestita, Benth.	164
Achillea millefolium, Linn.	32
Achyranthes aspera, Linn.	157
Acnistus arborescens, Schlecht.	142
Acoma dissecta, Benth. (Plate XVII.)	29
Acourtia formosa, Don	122
Acrocarpidium brevipes, Benth.	166
Acrocomia selenocarpa, Mart.	169
Adenaria purpurata, Humb. et Kunth	93
Adenostemma Swartzii, Less.	111
Adenostoma fasciculata, Hook. et Arn.	14
Æchmea laxiflora, Benth.	173
pyramidalis, Benth.	173
Ægiphila glomerata, Benth.	154
Æschynomene glandulosa, Poir.	82
Æschynomene sensitiva, Sw.	82
Æsculus californicus, Benth.	9
Ageratum conyzoides, Linn.	111
Alchornea grandis, Benth.	164
Alsodeia deflexa, Benth.	67
Alstrœmeria chorullensis, Herb.	175
Amaranthus retroflexus, Linn.	158
scariosus, Benth. (Plate LI.)	158
spinosus, Linn.	157
urceolatus, Benth.	158
Amauria rotundifolia, Benth.	31
Ambrina ambrosioides, Moq.	159
Ambrosia artemisiæfolia, Linn.	25, 115
Amerimnum Brownei, Sw.	87
Amphilophium paniculatum, Humb. et Kunth	129
Anacardium occidentale Linn.	79
Andropogon incompletus, Presl.	178
Anoda hastata, Cav.	69
lanceolata, Hook. et Arn.	69
Anona reticulata, Linn.	64
Anotis thymifolia, DC.	106
Anthurium Humboldtianum, Kunth	170
Antigonon leptopus, Hook. et Arn.	47, 160
Antirrhinum cyathiferum, Benth. (Plate XIX.)	40
Aphelandra pectinata, Nees	146
Sinclairiana, Nees (Plate XLVII.)	146
Aphragmia Hænkei, Nees	146
rotundifolia, Nees	146
Aplopappus arenarius, Benth.	24
baccharoides, Benth.	24
Apodanthera gracilis, Benth.	99

INDEX OF SPECIES.

	Page
Arceuthobium oxycedri, Bieb.	18
Ardisia cuspidata, Benth.	123
Argemone mexicana, Linn.	64
Argyreia oblonga, Benth.	133
Aristolochia *inflata, Humb. et Kunth*	166
odoratissima, Linn.	166
taliscana, Hook. et Arn.	166
Armeria *humilis, Link.*	43
vulgaris, Willd.	43
Artanthe Barclayana, Miq.	167
Beecheyana, Miq.	167
brachypoda, Benth. (Plate LIV.)	167
cornifolia, Miq.	167
granulosa, Miq.	167
leucophylla, Miq.	167
sororia, Miq.	167
tuberculata, Miq.	167
Artemisia pachystachya, DC.	32
vulgaris, Linn.	32
Artocarpus incisa, Linn.	169
Asclepias curassavica, Linn.	127
incarnata, Hook. et Arn.	127
longicornu, Benth.	127
Aster chilense, Nees	23
divaricatus, Torr. et Gr.	113
Astragalus ervoides, Hook. et Arn.	81
Astrephia mexicana, Hook. et Arn.	109
Avicennia Meyeri, Miq.	155
Baccharis cinerea, DC.	114
consanguinea, DC.	25
Douglasii, DC.	25
pilularis, DC.	25
rhexioides, Humb. et Kunth	114
spartea, DC.	114
Bahia latifolia, Benth.	30
Barleria discolor, Nees	146
micans, Nees	146
Bastardia crispa, St. Hil.	68
viscosa, Humb. et Kunth	68
Batatas acetosæfolia, Chois.	134
crassicaulis, Benth.	134
paniculata, Chois.	134
pentaphylla, Chois.	134
quinquefolia, Chois.	134
Bauhinia *columbiensis, Vog.*	89
grandiflora, Juss.	89
inermis, Pers.	89
latifolia, Cav.	88
lunaria, Hook. et Arn.	88
Pes-capræ, Cav.	88
subrotundifolia, Cav.	88
Begonia filipes, Benth.	101
humilis, Dryand.	101
Beloperone californica, Benth.	38
Bertiera angustifolia, Benth.	103
Bertolonia hirsuta, Benth.	94
Bidens hispida, Humb. et Kunth	117
leucantha, Willd.	117
tereticaulis, DC.	116
Bignonia alliacea, Lam.	128
longiflora, Cav.	128
obovata, Hook. et Arn.	125
patellifera, Schlecht.	128
Sinclairi, Benth.	129
Bixa orellana, Linn.	65
Blakea glabrescens, Benth.	94
Blechum Linnæi, Nees	149
Blepharodon mucronatum, Decaisne	127
Bletia acutipetala, Hook.	172
Boerhaavia polymorpha, A. Rich.	43, 155
viscosa, Lag.	156
Boldoa lanceolata, Lag.	155
ovatifolia, Lag.	155
Bomarea edulis, Herb.	175
Bouvardia linearis, Hook. et Arn.	105
scabra, Hook. et Arn.	105
Brandesia pubiflora, Benth.	157
pycnantha, Benth.	157
Brassavola grandiflora, Lindl.	172
Brickelia hastata, Benth.	21
Bronnia spinosa, Humb. et Kunth	16
Browallia abbreviata, Benth.	144
demissä, Linn.	143
peduncularis, Benth.	143
Bryonia attenuata, Hook. et Arn.	99
Buchnera elongata, Sw.	144
lavandulacea, Cham. et Schlecht.	144
pilosa, Benth.	144
Bucholtzia frutescens, Mart.	157

INDEX OF SPECIES.

	Page
Buddleia americana, Linn.	144
Buena macrocarpa, Benth. (Plate XXXVIII.)	104
Buettneria glabrescens, Benth.	71
lanceolata, DC.	71
Cacalia cirsiifolia, Hook. et Arn.	21
Cæsalpinia corymbosa, Benth.	87
eriostachys, Benth.	88
præcox, Ruiz et Pav.	87
pulcherrima, Sw.	87
Calea prunifolia, Humb. et Kunth	120
Calliandra californica, Benth. (Plate XI.)	14
grandiflora, Benth.	91
portoricensis, Benth.	91
Callipsyche eucrosioides, Herb.	174
Calonyction speciosum, Chois.	134
Calycophyllum candidissimum, DC.	105
Camara tiliæfolia, Benth.	154
vulgaris, Benth.	154
Campderia floribunda, Benth. (Plate LII.)	159
Campomanesia crassifolia, Benth. (Plate XXXVII.)	97
Canavalia *brasiliensis, Mart.*	85
ensiformis, DC.	85
gladiata, DC.	85
multiflora, Hook. et Arn.	85
obtusifolia, DC.	85
Cantua buxifolia, Lam.	132
Caperonia castaneæfolia, St. Hil.	165
Capparis amygdalina, Linn.	65
avicenniæfolia, Humb. et Kunth	65
brevipes, Benth.	65
crotonoides, Humb. et Kunth	65
scabrida, Humb. et Kunth	65
Sinclairii, Benth. (Plate XXVII.)	65
Capraria biflora, Linn.	144
peruviana, Feuill.	144
Capsicum frutescens, Willd.	141
longum, DC.	141
Cardiophora Hindsii, Benth.	181
Cardiospermum coluteoides, Humb. et Kunth	75
hispidum, Humb. et Kunth	75
tortuosum, Benth. (Plate VI.)	9
Carica cauliflora, Jacq.	100
Papaya, Linn.	100
peltata, Hook. et Arn.	100
Carphephorus junceus, Benth.	21

	Page
Casearia pubiflora, Benth.	66
Casparia latifolia, Kunth	88
Pes-capræ, Kunth	88
subrotundifolia, Kunth	88
Cassia alata, Linn.	88
bacillaris, Linn.	88
bicapsularis, Linn.	88
biflora, Linn.	88
brasiliana, Lam.	88
diphylla, Lam.	88
occidentalis, Linn.	88
oxyphylla, Humb. et Kunth	88
pauciflora, Humb. et Kunth	88
picta, Don.	88
prostrata, Humb. et Kunth	88
punctulata, Hook. et Arn.	88
reticulata, Willd.	88
strobilacea, Humb. et Kunth	88
undulata, Benth.	88
viminea, Linn.	88
Cattleya Skinneri, Lindl.	172
Ceanothus thyrsiflorus, Eschsch.	10
verrucosus, Nutt.	10
Celosia cristata, Linn.	158
nitida, Vahl.	158
paniculata, Linn.	158
Celtis *canescens, Humb. et Kunth*	169
Cenchrus pauciflorus, Benth.	56
Centropogon surinamensis, Presl.	122
Centrosema angustifolium, Benth.	84
hastatum, Benth.	84
Plumieri, Benth.	84
Salzmanni, Benth.	84
virginianum, Hook. et Arn.	84
Cephælis tomentosa, Willd.	108
Cephalanthus occidentalis, Linn.	108
Cestrum Parqui, Lhér.	143
Chætogastra ferruginea, Hook. et Arn.	93
havanensis, DC.	93
Chætosus volubilis, Benth. (Plate LVI.)	179
Chamissoa altissima, Sw.	158
Chavica Benthamiana, Miq.	181
Chenopodium murale, Linn.	159
Chiococca racemosa, Jacq.	106
Chloris alba, Presl.	56

INDEX OF SPECIES.

	Page
Chondrosium polystachyum, Benth.	56
Chrysobalanus Icaco, Linn.	91
Chrysophyllum Caimito, Linn.	123
Chrysopsis echioides, Benth.	25
Cicca macrostachya, Benth.	166
Cirsium cernuum, Lag.	121
Cissampelos guayaquilensis, Humb. et Kunth	64
Pareira, Linn.	64
Cissus obtusata, Benth.	77
salutaris, Humb. et Kunth	77
Clematis acapulcensis, Hook. et Arn.	63
Cleome pilosa, Benth.	65
polygama, Linn.	65
Clibadium acuminatum, Benth.	114
Clidemia barbinervis, Benth.	95
crenata, DC.	94
cyanocarpa, Benth.	94
fenestrata, Benth.	94
lacera, DC.	94
polyandra, Benth. (Plate XXXIV.)	95
rubra, Mart.	94
Clitoria arborescens, Ait.	84
brachystachya, Benth.	84
Poitæi, Benth.	84
Clusia subsessilis, Benth.	72
Cnidoscolus quinquelobus, Pohl	165
Cobæa macrostema, Pohl	132
Coccoloba acuminata, Humb. et Kunth	159
leptostachya, Benth.	159
Cocculus oblongifolius, DC.	64
Cochlospermum hibiscoides, Humb. et Kunth	72
Cœlestina corymbosa, DC.	111
petiolata, Hook. et Arn.	111
Combretum argenteum, Bertol.	92
erianthum, Benth.	92
farinosum, Humb. et Kunth	92
mexicanum, Humb. et Kunth	92
Commelyna acuminata, Humb. et Kunth	176
agraria, Kunth	176
cœlestis, Kunth	176
elegans, Humb. et Kunth	176
leiocarpa, Benth.	176
Condaminea corymbosa, DC.	105
Conocarpus erectus, Jacq.	92
Conostegia lasiopoda, Benth.	96
Conostegia polyandra, Benth. (Plate XXXV.)	96
xalapensis, DC.	96
Convolvulus *densiflorus, Hook. et Arn.*	135
nodiflorus, Lam.	138
Conyza apurensis, Humb. et Kunth	114
Corchorus tortipes, St. Hil.	71
Cordia angustifolia, Rœm. et Schult.	37
Bonplandii, Rœm. et Schult.	139
dasycephala, Humb. et Kunth	139
ferruginea, Rœm. et Schult.	139
gerascanthus, Jacq.	138
guayaquilensis, Alph. DC.	139
hispida, Benth.	139
microcephala, Willd.	139
peruviana, DC.	139
Coreocarpus parthenioides, Benth. (Plate XVI.)	28
Corethrogyne obovata, Benth.	22
Cornus glabrata, Benth.	18
Cosmos carvifolius, Benth.	117
cordatus, Humb. et Kunth	117
Coutoubea densiflora, Mart.	128
Cremanium compressum, Benth.	96
Crescentia cuneifolia, Gardn.	130
obovata, Benth. (Plate XLVI.)	130
Crinum americanum, Lhér.	174
erubescens, Herb.	174
Crotalaria *acapulcensis, Hook. et Arn.*	79
buplevrifolia, Schlecht.	79
eriocarpa, Benth.	80
Hookeriana, Alph. DC.	79
incana, Linn.	80
longirostrata, Hook. et Arn.	79
maypurensis, Humb. et Kunth	79
tepicana, Hook. et Arn.	79
Croton riparius, Humb. et Kunth	165
rivinæfolius, Humb. et Kunth	165
setigerus, Hook.	53
Crudya acuminata, Benth.	89
oblonga, Benth.	89
Crusea lucida, Benth.	109
parviflora, Hook. et Arn.	109
subalata, Hook. et Arn.	109
Cryptocarpus pyriformis, Humb. et Kunth	159
Cuphea Balsamona, Cham. et Schlecht.	93
bracteata, Hook. et Arn.	93

INDEX OF SPECIES.

Species	Page
Cuphea floribunda, Hook. et Arn.	93
Llavea, La Llav. et Lex.	93
Melvilla, Lindl.	93
Curatella americana, Linn.	64
Curcas purgans, Medik.	165
Cuscuta congesta, Benth.	138
globulosa, Benth.	138
laxiflora, Benth.	138
patens, Benth.	35
Cyclanthera leptostachya, Benth.	99
Dactyloctenium ægyptiacum, Willd.	177
Dalea canescens, Benth.	12
diffusa, Moric.	80
divaricata, Benth.	12
elata, Hook. et Arn.	80
elegans, Hook. et Arn.	80
gracilis, Hook. et Arn.	80
ramosissima, Benth. (Plate X.)	11
Dalechampia *hibiscoides, Hook. et Arn.*	163
sidæfolia, Humb. et Kunth	163
Datura stramonium, Linn.	143
Davila rugosa, Poir.	64
Decachæta Hænkeana, DC.	112
Dendrobium antennatum, Lindl. (Plate LIX.)	181
bifalce, Lindl. (Plate LVIII.)	180
veratrifolium, Lindl. (Plate LX.)	181
Desmanthus virgatus, Willd.	14
Desmodium adscendens, DC.	82
ancistrocarpum, DC.	82
axillare, DC.	82
Barclayi, Benth.	83
diversifolium, Schlecht	82
heterophyllum, Hook. et Arn.	82
incanum, DC.	82
molle, DC.	83
plicatum, Cham. et Schlecht.	82
podocarpum, Hook. et Arn.	82
radicans, Macfad.	82
reptans, DC.	82
scorpiurus, Desv.	82
Sinclairi, Benth.	82
stipulaceum, DC.	82
triflorum, DC.	82
Diastema racemifera, Benth.	132
Dichæa graminoides, Lindl.	172
Dichromena ciliata, Vahl.	177
Dicliptera confinis, Nees	149
multiflora, Humb. et Kunth	149
unguiculata, Nees	149
Diectomis fastigiata, Beauv.	178
Dioclea guianensis, Benth.	85
Diodia crassifolia, Benth.	108
setigera, DC.	108
Diplandra lopezioides, Hook. et Arn.	93
Dipteracanthus fœtidus, Nees	146
Distreptus spicatus, Cass.	110
Dodecas surinamensis, Linn.	93
Drepanocarpus microphyllus, Mey.	87
Drymaria crassifolia, Benth.	16
holosteoides, Benth.	16
Dunantia achyranthes, DC.	117
Duranta Plumieri, Jacq.	154
Dysodia anthemidifolia, Benth.	29
Echites biflora, Jacq.	126
hirtiflora, A. DC.	126
trifida, Jacq.	126
Eclipta erecta, Linn.	114
Elaphrium Hindsianum, Benth. (Plate VIII.)	11
rhoifolium, Benth. (Plate VII.)	10
Eleocharis constricta, Rœm. et Schult.	177
Elytraria apargiæfolia, Nees	145
ramosa, Humb. et Kunth	145
Encelia conspersa, Benth.	26
nivea, Benth.	27
Enckea decrescens, Miq.	167
miconiæfolia, Benth.	167
platyphylla, Benth.	167
Epidendrum glumaceum, Lindl.	172
macrochilum, Hook.	172
radicans, Pav.	172
trachycarpum, Lindl.	172
Eranthemum cordatum, Nees	147
cristatum, Willd.	146
Eremocarpus setigerus, Benth. (Plate XXVI.)	53
Ericameria diffusa, Benth.	23
microphylla, Nutt.	23
Erigeron glaucum, Ker	23
velutipes, Hook. et Arn.	114

INDEX OF SPECIES.

	Page
Eriodendron anfractuosum, DC.	70
Eriodyction crassifolium, Benth.	35
glutinosum, Benth.	36
tomentosum, Benth.	36
Eriogonum cinereum, Benth.	45
elongatum, Benth.	45
fasciculatum, Benth.	45
gracile, Benth.	46
intricatum, Benth. (Plate XXII.)	46
fasciculatum, Benth.	45
latifolium, Sm.	45
parvifolium, Sm.	45
Eryngium petiolatum, Hook.	18
Erythræa setacea, Benth.	128
Eugenia guayaquilensis, DC.	98
pacifica, Benth.	98
sericiflora, Benth.	98
Eupatorium Barclayanum, Benth.	112
compactum, Benth.	112
conyzoides, Vahl.	112
dissectum, Benth.	113
Neæanum, DC.	113
odoratum, Linn.	112
ovaliflorum, Hook. et Arn.	112
paniculatum, Schrad.	113
Schiedeanum, DC.	113
sericeum, Humb. et Kunth	113
Euphorbia adianthoides, Lam.	162
anceps, Benth.	162
californica, Benth. (Plate XXIII. B)	49
colletioides, Benth.	163
dioica, Humb. et Kunth	161
eriantha, Benth.	51
Hindsiana, Benth. (Plate XXIV.)	51
hypericifolia, Linn.	162
leucophylla, Benth.	50
Magdalenæ, Benth.	50
misera, Benth.	51
nudiflora, Lam.	162
ocymoides, *Hook. et Arn.*	162
pilulifera, Linn.	162
polycarpa, Benth.	50
restiacea, Benth.	162
serpens, Humb. et Kunth	50
Sinclairiana, Benth.	163

	Page
Euphorbia strigosa, Hook. et Arn.	162
Eustoma exaltatum, Griseb.	128
Evolvulus glabriusculus, Chois.	138
linifolius, Linn.	138
nummularius, Linn.	138
Exostemma occidentale, Benth.	104
Fagonia californica, Benth.	10
Fragaria chilensis, Eschsch.	14
Frankenia grandifolia, Cham. et Schlecht.	7
Franseria chenopodiifolia, Benth.	26
hispida, Benth.	25
Fraxinus latifolia, Benth.	35
Fugosia cuneata, Benth.	68
Galactia brevistyla, Schlecht	84
Galinsoga hispida, Benth.	119
Galphimia angustifolia, Benth. (Plate V.)	9
Galvesia limensis, Domb.	144
Garrya elliptica, Dougl.	55
Gaudichaudia Schiedeana, Ad. Juss.	7
Gaultheria odorata, Humb. et Kunth	129
Gaura fruticulosa, Benth.	18
Gesnera Deppeana, Cham. et Schlecht.	132
incurva, Benth.	131
petiolaris, Benth.	131
rhynchocarpa, Benth.	131
spicata, Humb. et Kunth	131
Gilia capitata, Dougl.	34
pharnaceoides, Benth.	34
Glycine oblonga, Benth.	84
Gnaphalium luteo-album, Linn.	120
palustre, Nutt.	32
Sprengelii, Hook. et Arn.	32
Gomphrena *celosioides, Mart.*	157
decumbens, Jacq.	157
globosa, Linn.	157
Gossypium barbadense, Linn.	68
Gouania corylifolia, Raddi.	79
Grindelia cuneifolia, Nutt.	24
Gronovia scandens, Linn.	101
Guazuma polybotrya, Cav.	71
Guettarda conferta, Benth.	106
Guzmannia tricolor, Ruiz et Pav.	174
Gustavia angustifolia, Benth.	99

INDEX OF SPECIES.

	Page
Gymnopsis divaricata, Benth.	116
Gynandropsis speciosa, DC.	64
trichopus, Benth.	64
Gynoxis Hænkei, DC.	120
scabra, Benth.	121
Sinclairi, Benth.	120
Gyrandra speciosa, Benth. (Plate XLV.)	127
Hæmadictyon tomentellum, Benth.	126
Hæmatoxylon campechianum, Linn.	87
Halenia multiflora, Benth.	128
Hamelia patens, Jacq.	106
Hasseltia floribunda, Humb. et Kunth	72
Hebanthe parviflora, Benth.	156
Hebeclinium tepicanum, Hook. et Arn.	112
Hedyotis asperuloides, Benth. (Plate XIII.)	19
mucronata, Benth.	19
thymifolia, Ruiz et Pav.	106
Heeria cupheoides, Benth. (Plate XXXIII.)	93
Heimia salicifolia, Link. et Otto	93
Helenium puberulum, DC.	30
Helianthemum glomeratum, Lag.	66
Helianthus annuus, Linn.	116
californicus, DC.	28
scaberrimus, Benth.	28
Heliconia latispatha, Benth.	170
vaginalis, Benth.	171
Helicteres altheæfolia, Lam.	71
baruensis, Lam.	70
guazumæfolia, Humb. et Kunth	71
Heliocarpus popayanensis, Humb. et Kunth	71
Heliophytum indicum, DC.	141
parviflorum, DC.	141
Heliotropium corymbosum, Ruiz et Pav.	141
curassavicum, Linn.	37, 141
Helogyne fasciculata, Benth. (Plate XIV.)	20
Hemizonia pungens, Torr. et Gr.	31
ramosissima, Benth.	30
rudis, Benth.	31
Hendecandra procumbens, Eschsch.	52
Henrya Barclayana, Nees	149
insularis, Nees (Plate XLIX.)	148
Herpestis Monnieria, Humb. et Kunth	144
Heterocentron mexicanum, Hook. et Arn.	94
Heteronoma diversifolium, DC.	93
Heteronoma mexicanum, Benth.	94
Heteropterys Beecheyana, Ad. Juss.	75
Mathewsana, Ad. Juss.	75
Heterotheca floribunda, Benth.	24
Hibiscus betulifolius, Humb. et Kunth	68
denudatus, Benth. (Plate III.)	7
Hippocratea excelsa, Humb. et Kunth	78
floribunda, Benth.	78
Hippomane mancenilla, Linn.	163
Hiræa Barclayana, Benth.	75
Hirtella americana, Aubl.	91
racemosa, Lam.	91
Hosta longifolia, Humb. et Kunth	154
Hydrolea spinosa, Linn.	141
Hypolytrum pycnocephalum, Benth.	177
Hyptis capitata, Jacq.	150
florida, Benth.	150
laniflora, Benth. (Plate XX.)	42
melissoides, Humb. et Kunth	150
pectinata, Poit.	150
polystachya, Humb. et Kunth	150
rhytidea, Benth.	150
spicata, Poit.	150
stellulata, Benth.	150
suaveolens, Poit.	150
verticillata, Jacq.	150
Indigofera anil, Linn.	80
lespedezioides, Humb. et Kunth	80
Inga guatemalensis, Hook. et Arn.	89
patens, Hook. et Arn.	89
Ionidium fruticulosum, Benth. (Plate II.)	7
Ionopsis utricularioides, Lindl.	172
Ipomæa brachypoda, Benth.	135
codonantha, Benth.	135
cymosa, Benth.	135, 181
evolvuloides, Moric.	137
microsepala, Benth.	136
oocarpa, Benth.	136
pedicellaris, Benth.	135
puncticulata, Benth.	136
trifida, Don.	136
umbellata, Mey.	181
urbica, Chois.	135
Iresine celosioides, Linn.	156

INDEX OF SPECIES.

	Page
Iresine interrupta, Benth.	156
Isertia coccinea, Vahl.	106
Isocarpha divaricata, Benth. (Plate XLI.)	110
Isomeria arborea, Nutt.	6
Jacquemontia abutiloides, Benth.	34
corymbulosa, Benth.	137
pycnocephala, Benth.	137
violacea, Chois.	137
Jacquinia armillaris, Jacq.	123
macrocarpa, Cav.	123
pubescens, Kunth	123
Janusia californica, Benth. (Plate IV.)	8
Jatropha nudicaulis, Benth.	165
Jussiæa calycina, Presl.	92
hirta, Hook. et Arn.	92
linifolia, Vahl.	92
macrocarpa, Humb. et Kunth	92
octofila, DC.	92
peploides, Humb. et Kunth	92
peruviana, Linn.	92
Justicia oxyphylla, DC.	146
serrata, Humb. et Kunth	146
Kosteletzkya sagittata, Presl.	68
Krameria parvifolia, Benth. (Plate I.)	6
Lablab vulgaris, Savi	86
Lagascea angustifolia, DC.	110
latifolia, DC.	110
rubra, Humb. et Kunth	110
suaveolens, Humb. et Kunth	110
Laguncularia racemosa, Gærtn.	14, 92
Lamourouxia cordata, Cham. et Schlecht.	145
multifida, Humb. et Kunth	145
viscosa, Humb. et Kunth	145
Lantana *camara, Linn.*	154
lippioides, Hook. et Arn.	153
salviæfolia, Jacq.	154
tiliæfolia, Cham. et Schlecht.	154
Lasionema glabrescens, Benth.	105
Leptoglossis schwenckioides, Benth.	143
Leptostachya crinita, Nees	147
Martiana, Nees	147
Leucæna macrophylla, Benth.	90

	Page
Leucosmia Burnettiana, Benth. (Plate LVII.)	180
Licania hypoleuca, Benth. (Plate XXXII.)	91
Limnanthemum Humboldtianum, Griseb.	128
Limnobium Sinclairi, Benth.	175
Lindenia rivalis, Benth.	105
Linociera compacta, Br.	123
Linum Schiedeanum, Cham. et Schlecht.	67
Lipochæte macrocephala, Hook. et Arn.	117
umbellata, DC.	117
Lippia asperifolia, Rich.	153
cardiostegia, Benth.	153
geminata, Humb. et Kunth	153
myriocephala, Cham.	154
nodiflora, Rich.	153
Loasa chelidoniifolia, Benth.	101
Lobelia laxiflora, Humb. et Bonpl.	122
Lœselia amplectens, Benth.	132
coccinea, G. Don	132
glandulosa, G. Don	132
involucrata, G. Don	132
Lonchocarpus maculatus, DC.	81
Lonicera involucrata, Banks	19
Lopezia hirsuta, Jacq.	93
Lopimia malacophylla, Mart.	68
Loranthus *calyculatus, Hook. et Arn.*	103
inconspicuus, Benth.	102
obovatus, Benth.	103
rhynchanthus, Benth.	102
Schiedeanus, Schlecht.	102
Luhea rufescens, St. Hil.	72
Lupinus sericeus, Pursh.	11
Lycium brevipes, Benth.	40
salsum, Ruiz et Pav.	142
Lycopersicum esculentum, Mill.	142
peruvianum, Mill.	142
Lycoseris bracteata, Benth.	121
squarrosa, Benth.	121
Lysiloma Schiedeana, Benth. (Plate XXXI.)	91
Lythrum maritimum, Humb. et Kunth	93
Mabea Piriri, Aubl.	165
Machærium angustifolium, Vog.	87
Madaria corymbosa, DC.	31
Malachra humilis, Benth.	70
Malpighia retusa, Benth.	74

INDEX OF SPECIES.

	Page
Malvaviscus acapulcensis, Humb. et Kunth	68
brevipes, Benth.	68
mollis, DC.	68
pilosus, DC.	68
Mammea americana, Linn.	73
Manettia cuspidata, Benth.	105
Mangifera indica, Linn.	79
Maranta arundinacea, Linn.	171
Marila macrophylla, Benth.	72
Martinezia caryotæfolia, Humb. et Kunth	169
Martynia altheæfolia, Benth.	37
Maurandia juncea, Benth.	41
Maytenus phyllanthoides, Benth.	54
Melampodium tenellum, Hook. et Arn.	115
Melanthera deltoidea, Reichb.	116
oxylepis, DC.	116
Melilotus parviflora, Desf.	80
Melochia inflata, DC.	71
nodiflora, Sw.	71
pyramidata, Linn.	71
serrata, Vent.	71
tomentosa, Linn.	8, 71
Mendozia puberula, Mart.	145
Mentzelia adhærens, Benth.	15
Metastelma californicum, Benth. (Plate XVIII.)	33
Miconia attenuata, DC.	96
guayaquilensis, Don	96
Micromeria Douglasii, Benth.	43
Mikania angularis, Humb. et Kunth	113
gonoclada, DC.	113
guaco, Humb. et Bonpl.	113
tamoides, DC.	113
Mimosa acantholoba, Benth.	90
æschynomenis, Benth.	89
asperata, Linn.	89
elliptica, Benth.	89
floribunda, Willd.	89
guatemalensis, Benth.	89
pudica, Linn.	89
pusilla, Benth.	90
Mitracarpium lineare, Benth.	20
pallidum, Hook. et Arn.	109
schizangium, DC.	109
villosum, Cham. et Schlecht.	108
Mohlana secunda, Mart.	158
Momordica quinquefida, Hook. et Arn.	99
Monardella villosa, Benth. (Plate XXI.)	42
Morenia fragrans, Ruiz et Pav.	169
Mouriria parvifolia, Benth. (Plate XXXVI.)	97
Mozinna canescens, Benth. (Plate XXV.)	52
Muntingia calaburu, Linn.	72
Myosotis californica, Fisch. et Mey.	37
Myrica acuminata, DC.	98
aromatica, Schlecht.	98
californica, Cham.	55
gale, Linn.	55
Myriocarpa densiflora, Benth.	168
stipitata, Benth. (Plate LV.)	167
Myrsine erythroxyloides, Benth.	123
Nectandra glabrescens, Benth.	161
Neptunia plena, Benth.	89
Neurolæna lobata, Br.	120
Nicandra physalodes, Gærtn.	141
Obione Barclayana, Benth.	48
microcarpa, Benth.	48
tetraptera, Benth.	48
Ocotea salicifolia, Hook. et Arn.	161
Œnothera cheiranthifolia, Hornem.	15
Lindleyana, Dougl.	14
purpurea, Curt.	15
rosea, Ait.	92
Olyra latifolia, Linn.	177
Oncidium iridifolium, Humb. et Kunth	172
stipitatum, Lindl.	172
Oplismenus Burmanni, Beauv.	177
Oreodaphne californica, Nees	49
Ornithocephalus bicornis, Lindl.	172
Orthotactus oblongus, Nees	147
Oxalis microcarpa, Benth.	77
Neæi, DC.	77
Oxymeris macrophylla, Benth.	95
Oxypappus scaber, Benth. (Plate XLII.)	118
Pachira sessilis, Benth.	20
Palicourea guianensis, Aubl.	107
parviflora, Benth.	107
Panicum brevifolium, Linn.	177
californicum, Benth.	55

INDEX OF SPECIES.

	Page
Panicum *trichodes*, Sw.	177
Paritium tiliaceum, St. Hil.	68
Parkinsonia aculeata, Linn.	87
Paspalum paniculatum, Linn.	177
Passiflora biflora, Linn.	100
fœtida, Linn.	100
littoralis, Humb. et Kunth	100
quadrangularis, Linn.	100
rubra, Linn.	100
suberosa, Linn.	100
Paullinia barbadensis, Jacq.	76
curassavica, Linn.	76
fuscescens, Humb. et Kunth	76
Pavonia mexicana, Humb. et Kunth	68
typhaleoides, Humb. et Kunth	68
Pectis arenaria, Benth.	110
multiseta, Benth.	20
taliscana, Hook. et Arn.	110
Pedilanthus macrocarpus, Benth. (Pl. XXIII. A.)	49
Pennisetum purpurascens, Humb. et Kunth	177
Pentagonia macrophylla, Benth. (Plate XXXIX.)	105
Perityle californica, Benth. (Plate XV.)	23
microglossa, Benth.	119
Petiveria alliacea, Linn.	158
Phaca candidissima, Benth.	13
vestita, Benth.	13
Pharbitis heterosepala, Benth.	134
hispida, Chois.	134
nil, Chois.	135
Phaseolus amplus, Benth.	85
filiformis, Benth.	13
gracilis, Benth.	85
truxillensis, Humb. et Kunth	85
vulgaris, Linn.	85
Photinia arbutifolia, Lindl.	14
Phyllanthus floribundus, Humb. et Kunth	166
Niruri, Linn.	165
tenellus, Benth.	165
Physalis crassifolia, Benth.	40
glabra, Benth.	39
Linkiana, Nees	141
Phytolacca octandra, Linn.	159
Picrosia longifolia, Don	122
Pinguicula lilacina, Cham. et Schlecht.	155
Pinus insignis, Dougl.	55
Piper begoniæfolium, Hook. et Arn.	167
ellipticum, Hook. et Arn.	167
fragile, Benth.	181
Piptadenia patens, Benth.	89
Piqueria densiflora, Benth.	110
trinervis, Cav.	110
Piscidia erythrina, Linn.	81
Pistia stratiotes, Linn.	169
Pithecoctenium muricatum, DC.	129
Pithecolobium candidum, Benth.	91
dulce, Benth.	91
macrostachyum, Benth.	91
multiflorum, Benth.	91
oblongum, Benth.	91
Planarium latisiliquum, Desv. (Plate XXX.)	81
Platanus californicus, Benth.	54
Plumbago scandens, Linn.	155
Plumeria rubra, Linn.	126
Podopterus mexicanus, Humb. et Kunth	160
Poinciana pulcherrima, Linn.	87
Poinsettia pulcherrima, Grah.	161
Polygala hebantha, Benth.	67
paniculata, Linn.	67
rivinæfolia, Humb. et Kunth	67
Polygonum acre, Humb. et Kunth	159
persicarioides, Humb. et Kunth	159
Porophyllum gracile, Benth.	29
tridentatum, Benth.	30
viridiflorum, DC.	118
Portulaca oleracea, Linn.	102
Posoqueria decora, DC.	103
Pothomorphe peltata, Miq.	167
Priva lappulacea, Pers.	152
Psidium pyrifolium, Linn.	97
Psoralea macrostachya, DC.	11
orbicularis, Lindl.	11
Psychotria acuminata, Benth.	107
fimbriata, Benth.	107
justicioides, Schlecht.	107
micrantha, Humb. et Kunth	106
viridis, Benth.	106
Pterostegia macroptera, Benth.	44
Puya heterophylla, Lindl.	174
Quamoclit coccinea, Chois.	133

INDEX OF SPECIES.

	Page
Quamoclit hederæfolia, Chois.	133
vulgaris, Chois.	133
Quassia amara, Linn. fil.	78
Quercus agrifolia, Née.	55
aristata, Hook. et Arn.	169
Douglasii, Hook.	55
elliptica, Née.	169
Hindsii, Benth.	55
Quinchamalium chilense, Lam.	160
Randia glomerata, Benth.	103
Renealmia racemosa, Pœpp. et Endl.	171
Rhamnus oleæfolius, Hook.	10
Rhinocarpus excelsus, Humb. et Kunth	79
Rhizophora Mangle, Linn.	14, 92
racemosa, Mey.	92
Rhopala complicata, Humb. et Kunth	161
Rhus laurina, Nutt.	11
macrophylla, Hook. et Arn.	79
terebinthifolia, Schlecht.	79
Rhynchosia grandiflora, Schlecht.	87
minima, DC.	87
Ribes malvaceum, Sm.	17
Menziesi, Pursh.	17
tortuosum, Benth.	17
Riedleia inflata, DC.	71
nodiflora, DC.	71
serrata, DC.	71
Rivina humilis, Linn.	158
inæqualis, Hook.	151
secunda, Ruiz et Pav.	158
Raso californica, Cham. et Schlecht.	14
Rubus ursinus, Cham. et Schlecht.	14
Ruellia albicaulis, Bert.	146
Rumex crispus, Linn.	47
Russelia rotundifolia, Cav.	144
sarmentosa, Jacq.	144
Ruyschia bicolor, Benth. (Plate XXIX.)	73
subsessilis, Benth.	73
Rytidostylis gracilis, Hook. et Arn.	100
Sagittaria sagittifolia, Linn.	175
Sagræa sessilifolia, DC.	94
Salmea angustifolia, Benth.	117
Salvia Cruikshanksii, Benth.	151

	Page
Salvia elsholtzioides, Benth. (Plate L.)	152
lasiocephala, Hook. et Arn.	152
membranacea, Benth.	151
occidentalis, Sw.	150
orbicularis, Benth.	151
prasiifolia, Benth.	151
privoides, Benth.	150
scorodonia, Poit.	151
thyrsiflora, Benth.	151
Sarcostemma arenarium, Benth.	34
bilobum, Hook. et Arn.	127
cumanense, Humb. et Kunth	127
Sauvagesia erecta, Linn.	67
Scaphyglottis fasciculata, Hook.	172
Schinus discolor, Benth. (Plate IX.)	11
Schnella columbiensis, Benth.	89
Schradera stellata, Benth. (Plate XL.)	106
Sciodaphyllum sphærocoma, Benth.	102
Scleria bracteata, Cav.	177
Sclerocalyx mexicanus, Nees	145
Scoparia dulcis, Linn.	144
Scorodoxylum terminale, Nees	145
Scrophularia *californica, Cham.*	40
nodosa, Linn.	40
Securidaca volubilis, Linn.	67
Semeiandra grandiflora, Hook. et Arn.	92
Serjania brevipes, Benth.	76
glabrata, Humb. et Kunth	76
lupulina, Schum.	76
mexicana, Willd.	76
paniculata, Humb. et Kunth	76
racemosa, Schum.	76
Serophyton Drummondi, Benth.	53
lanceolatum, Benth.	52
pilosissimum, Benth.	53
Setaria glauca, Beauv.	177
Sida betonicæfolia, Balb.	69
carpinifolia, Linn.	70
depressa, Benth.	69
divergens, Benth.	69
Dombeyana, DC.	69
dumosa, Hook. et Arn.	69
excelsior, Cav.	69
glanduligera, Benth.	69
hondensis, Humb. et Kunth	70

3 E

INDEX OF SPECIES.

	Page
Sida malvæflora, DC.	8
nudiflora, Lhér.	69
paniculata, Linn.	69
reflexa, Cav.	68
rhombifolia, Linn.	70
rhomboidea, Roxb.	70
urens, Linn.	70
Simmondsia californica, Nutt.	181
Sinclairia discolor, Hook. et Arn.	100
Smilax obtusa, Benth.	175
Solanum diphyllum, Linn.	141
flexicaule, Benth.	141
Hindsianum, Benth.	39
nigrum, Linn.	39, 141
scabrum, Vahl.	142
torvum, Sw.	142
verbascifolium, Linn.	141
Soulamea amara, Lam.	181
Spartina leiantha, Benth.	56
Spennera aquatica, Mart.	93
Spergularia rupestris, Camb.	17
Spermacoce parviflora, Mey.	108
tenuior, Linn.	108
Spondias purpurea, Linn.	79
Sponia canescens, Decaisne	169
Stachys ajugoides, Benth.	43
Macræi, Benth.	43
Stachytarpheta dichotoma, Humb. et Kunth	152
Statice Limonium, Linn.	43
Stegnosperma halimifolia, Benth. (Plate XII.)	17
Stemmadenia glabra, Benth. (Plate XLIV.)	124
mollis, Benth.	125
pubescens, Benth.	125
Stemodia durantifolia, Sw.	144
pusilla, Benth.	144
Stenolobium cœruleum, Benth.	84
Stephanomeria virgata, Benth.	32
Stevia elliptica, Hook. et Arn.	112
Hænkeana, DC.	112
Stigmaphyllum ellipticum, A. Juss.	74
fulgens, A. Juss.	74
Stylosanthes humilis, Humb. et Kunth	82
Styphonia integrifolia, Nutt	11
Swartzia grandiflora, Willd.	88
Synedrella nodiflora, Gærtn.	118

	Page
Tabebuia cordata, Benth.	129
rosea, DC.	130
Tacsonia lævis, Benth.	100
sanguinea, Cav.	101
Tagetes microglossa, Benth.	115
multiseta, DC.	115
Tecoma Gaudichaudi, DC.	130
stans, Juss.	130
Tephrosia crassifolia, Benth.	80
glabrescens, Benth.	81
glandulifera, Benth.	81
leucantha, Humb. et Kunth.	80
mollis, Humb. et Kunth	81
oroboides, Humb. et Kunth	81
piscatoria, Pers.	80
toxicaria, Pers.	80
Teramnus volubilis, Sw.	81
Ternstrœmia clusiæfolia, Humb. et Kunth	75
Tetracera volubilis, Linn.	64
Tetramerium nervosum, Nees (Plate XLVIII.)	148
polystachyum, Nees	148
Tetrapterys acapulcensis, Humb. et Kunth	74
Theobroma Cacao, Linn.	7
Thevetia neriifolia, Juss.	124
plumeriæfolia, Benth. (Plate XLIII.)	124
Thinogeton maritimus, Benth.	145
Tillandsia complanata, Benth.	174
disticha, Humb. et Kunth	174
divaricata, Benth.	174
multiflora, Benth.	174
Tithonia angustifolia, Hook. et Arn.	110
tagetiflora, Desf.	110
Tococa acuminata, Benth.	93
Tournefortia calycina, Benth.	139
hirsutissima, Linn.	139
lævigata, Linn.	139
leptostachya, Benth.	140
obtusiflora, Benth.	140
rufipila, Benth.	140
velutina, Humb. et Kunth	140
Tradescantia cordifolia, Sw.	174
cumanensis, Kunth	174
triandra, Kunth	174
Tridax procumbens, Linn.	121
Trigonia rugosa, Benth.	7

INDEX OF SPECIES.

	Page
Triplandron lineatum, Benth. (Plate XXVIII.)	73
Triplaris Cumingiana, Fisch. et Mey.	160
Tripolium subulatum, Nees	113
Triumfetta dumetorum, Hook. et Arn.	71
heterophylla, Lam.	71
rhomboidea, Jacq.	71
Trixis frutescens, P. Br.	32, 122
latifolia, Hook. et Arn.	122
obvallata, Hook. et Arn.	122
Turnera *cuneiformis*, Hook. et Arn.	101
Hindsiana, Benth.	101
ulmifolia, Linn.	101
Uniola paniculata, Linn.	178
Urvillæa Berteriana, DC.	76
Utricularia aphylla, Ruiz et Pav.	155
Vallesia *chiococcoides*, Humb. et Kunth	124
dichotoma, Ruiz et Pav.	33, 124
glabra, Cav.	124
Varronia calyptrata, DC.	138
rotundifolia, A. DC.	138
Verbena fasciculata, Benth.	153
lasiostachys, Link.	41
littoralis, Humb. et Kunth	152
paniculata, Lam.	41
veronicæfolia, Humb. et Kunth	152
Vernonia lanceolaris, DC.	109
scorpioides, Pers.	109
Sinclairi, Benth.	109
Vicia bidentata, Hook.	84
Vigna brachystachys, Benth.	86
carinalis, Benth.	86
villosa, Savi.	86
Viguiera subincisa, Benth.	27
Vilfa virginica, Beauv.	56
Vinca rosea, Linn.	126
Viscum flavescens, Pursh.	18
Kunthianum, DC.	102
tomentosum, DC.	102
Vitex californica, Benth.	10
caribæa, Hook. et Arn.	10
gigantea, Humb. et Kunth	154
lasiophylla, Benth.	155
mollis, Hook. et Arn.	155
Waltheria americana, Linn.	71
ovata, Cav.	71
Wedelia acapulcensis, Humb. et Kunth	115
cordata, Hook. et Arn.	115
grandiflora, Benth.	115
paludosa, DC.	115
populifolia, Hook. et Arn.	115
strigosa, Hook. et Arn.	115
subflexuosa, Hook. et Arn.	115
Wigandia *californica*, Hook. et Arn.	36
Kunthii, Chois.	141
scorpioides, Chois.	141
Wissadula excelsior, Presl.	69
nudiflora, Benth.	69
Witheringia montana, Dun.	141
phyllantha, Dun.	141
Ximenia americana, Linn.	160
Xuaresia biflora, Ruiz et Pav.	144
Xylopia grandiflora, St. Hil.	64
Zauschneria californica, Presl.	15
Zinnia angustifolia, Humb. et Kunth	115
Zizyphus acuminata, Benth.	78
thyrsiflora, Benth.	78

London:
Printed by STEWART and MURRAY,
Old Bailey.

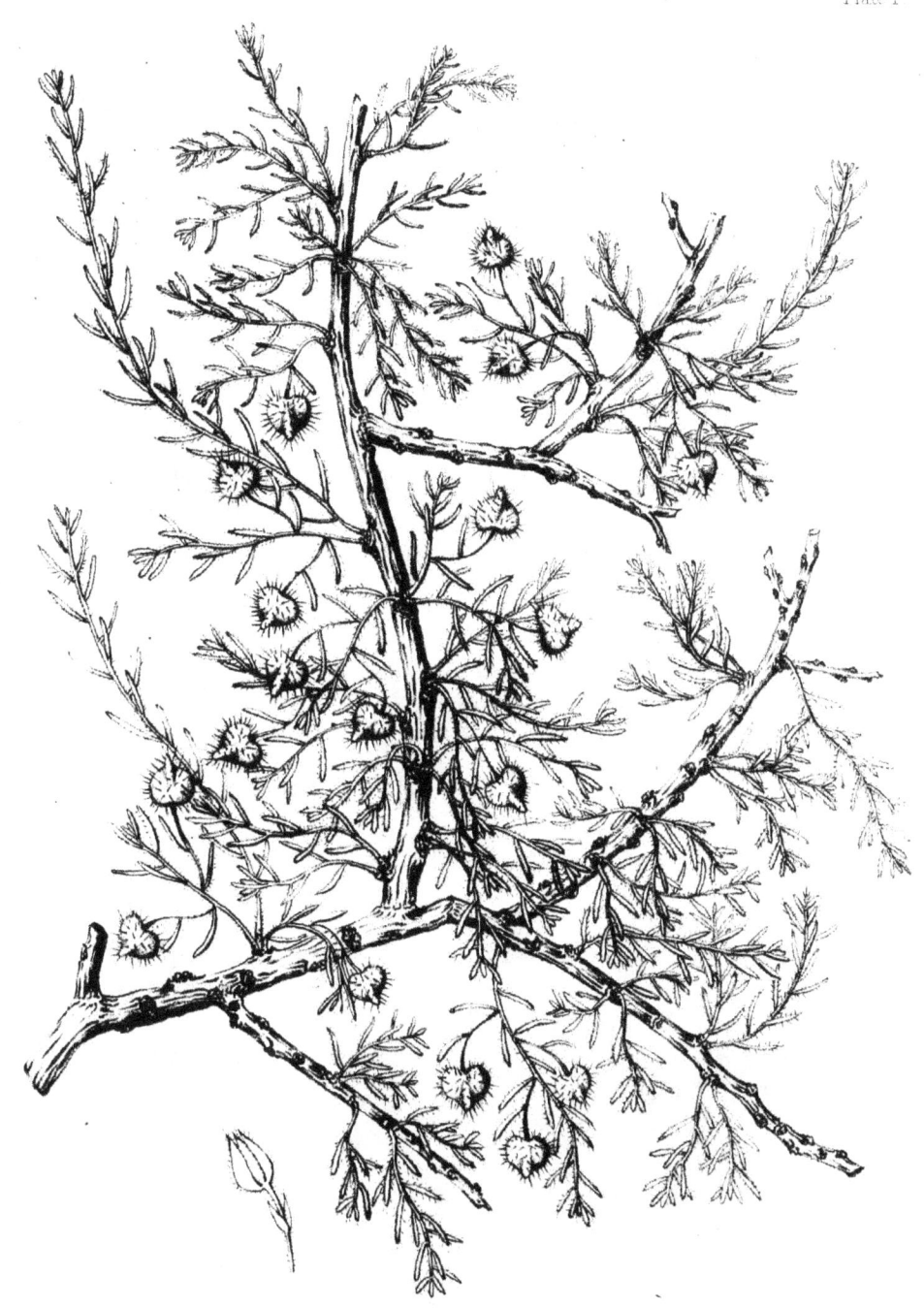

KRAMERIA PARVIFOLIA.

Plate 2.

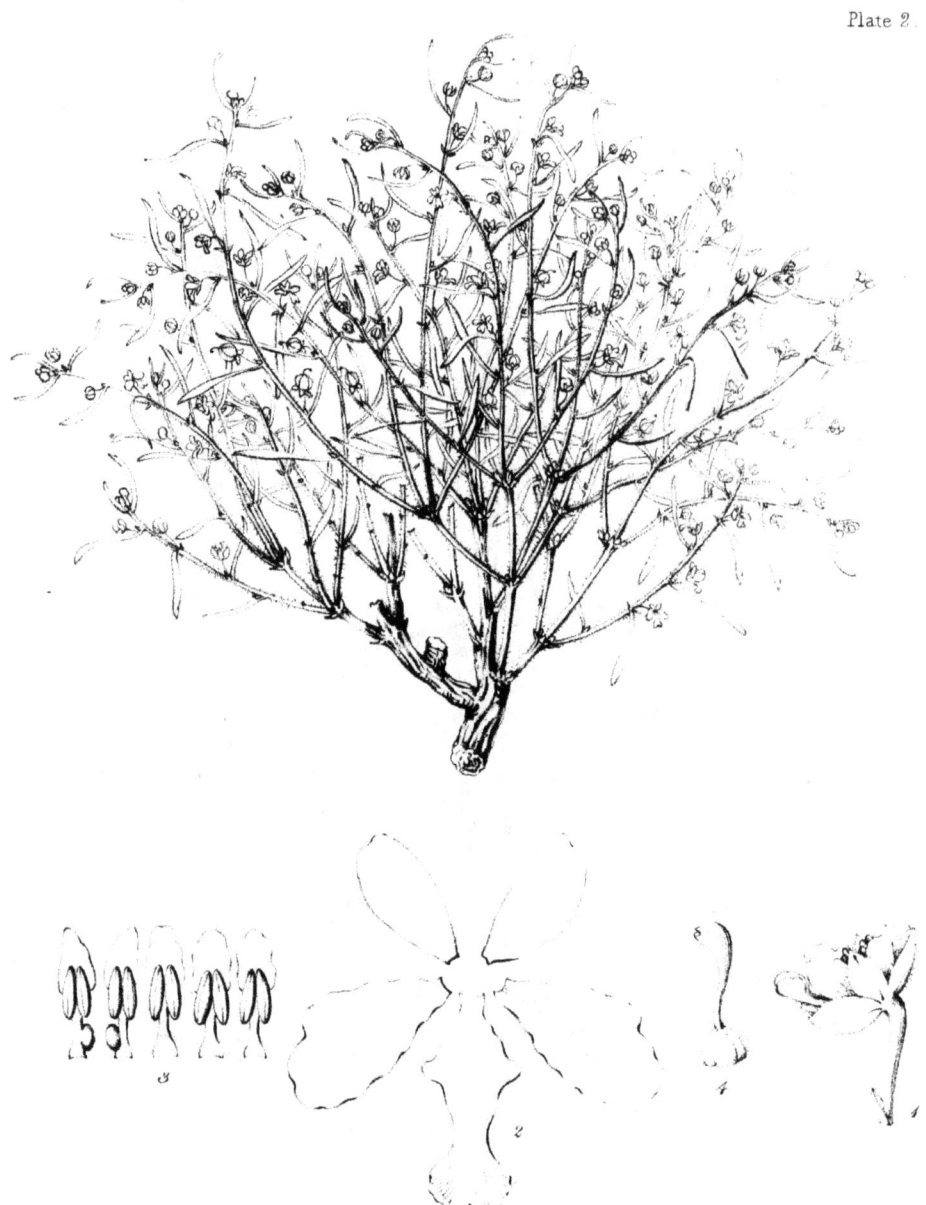

Drawn from Nature and on Stone by Miss Drake.　　　　Printed by Hullmandel.

IONIDIUM FRUTICULOSUM

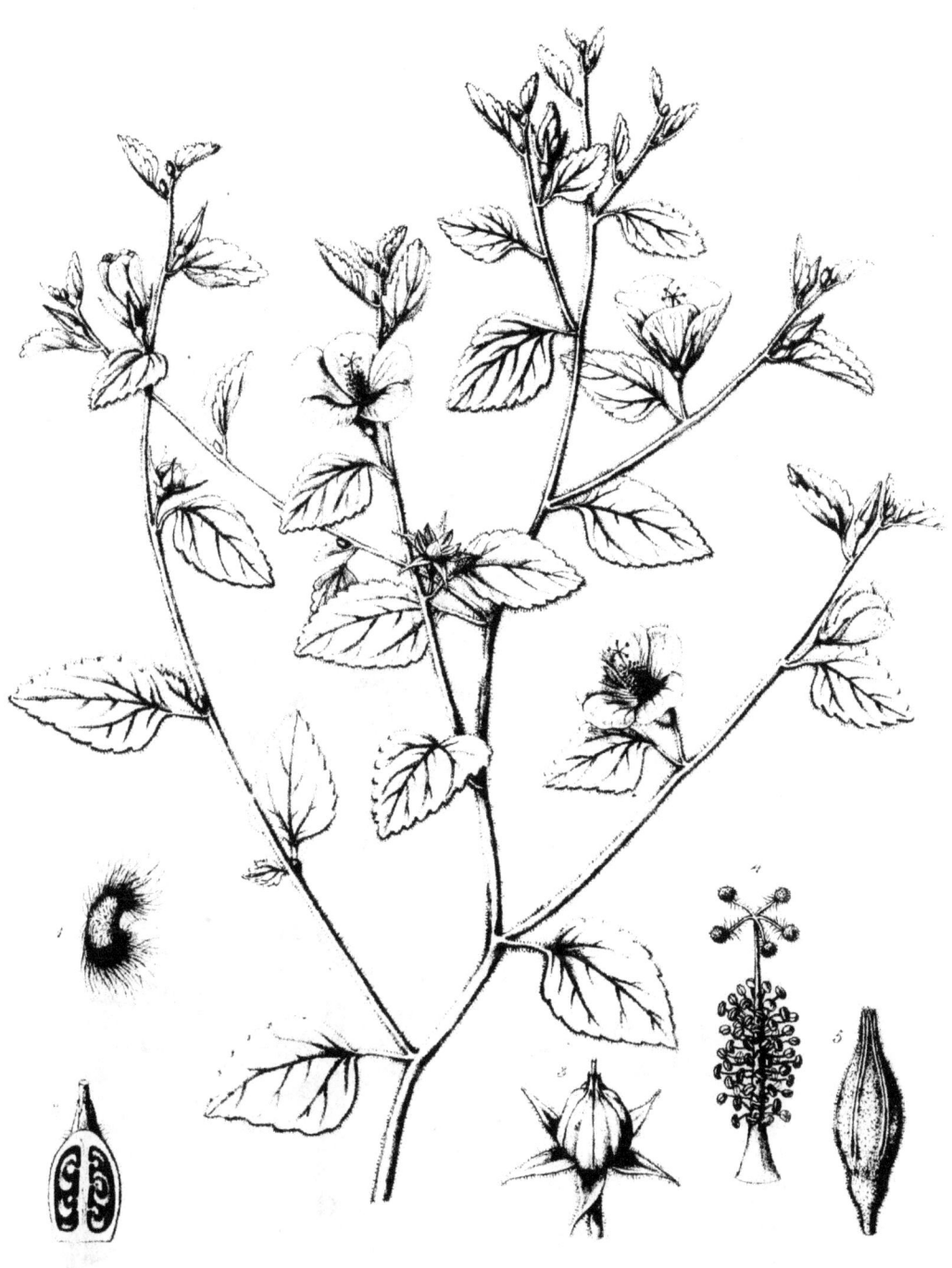

HIBISCUS DENUDATUS

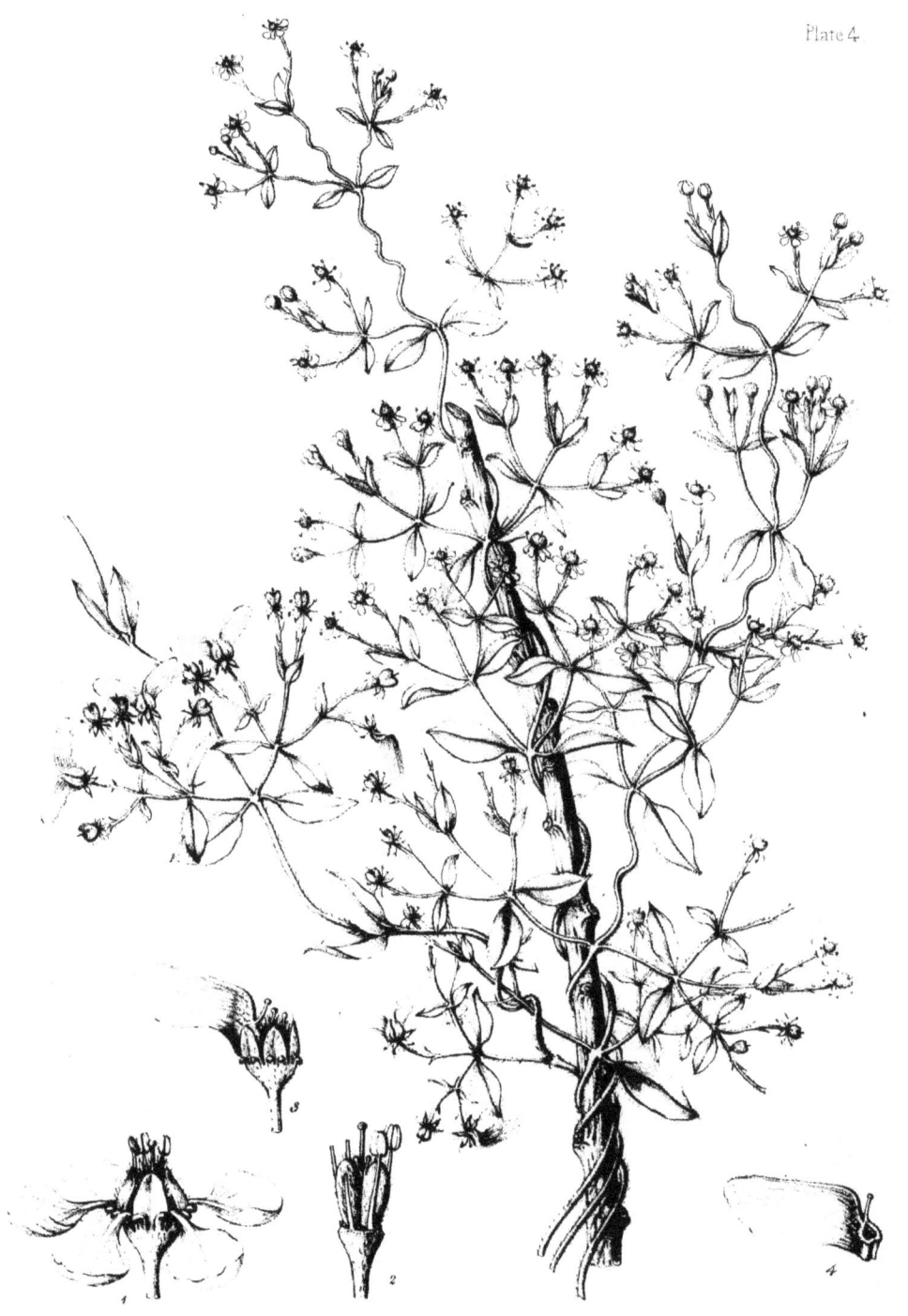

JANUSIA CALIFORNICA.

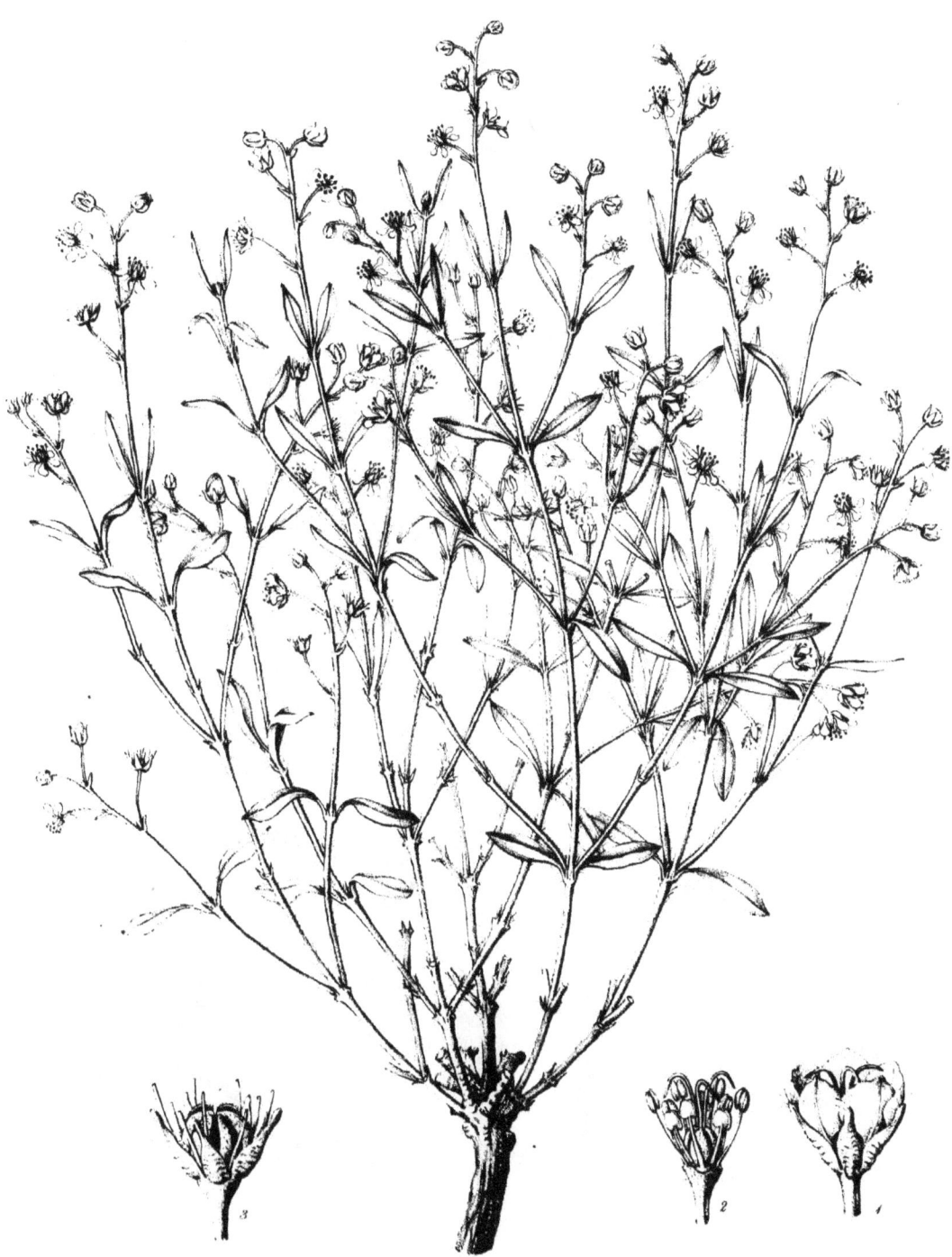

GALPHIMIA ANGUSTIFOLIA

ELAPHRIUM RHOIFOLIUM.

ELAPHRIUM HINDSIANUM.

Plate 9

SCHINUS DISCOLOR

DALEA RAMOSISSIMA.

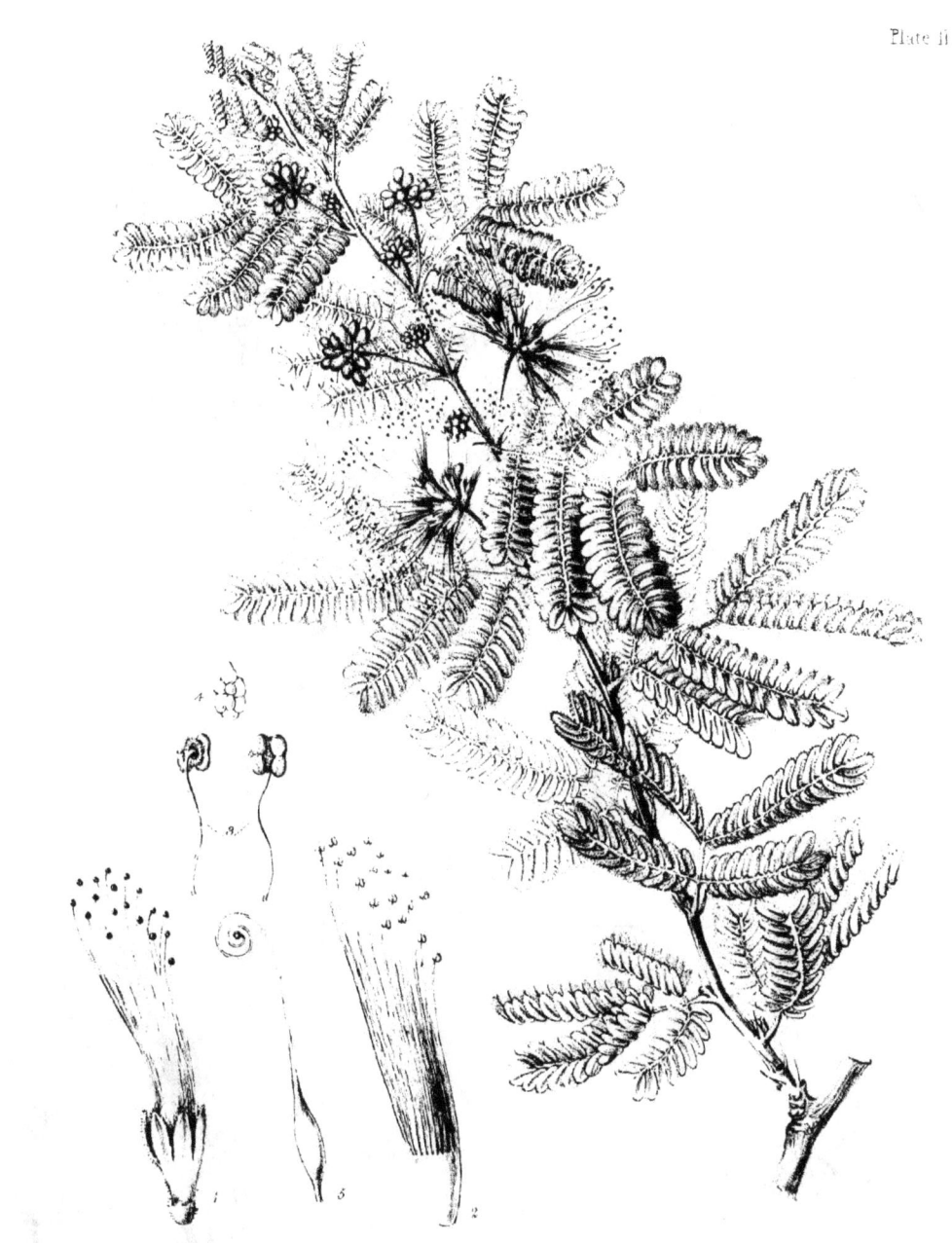

CALLIANDRA CALIFORNICA

Plate 12

STENOSPERMA HALIMIFOLIA.

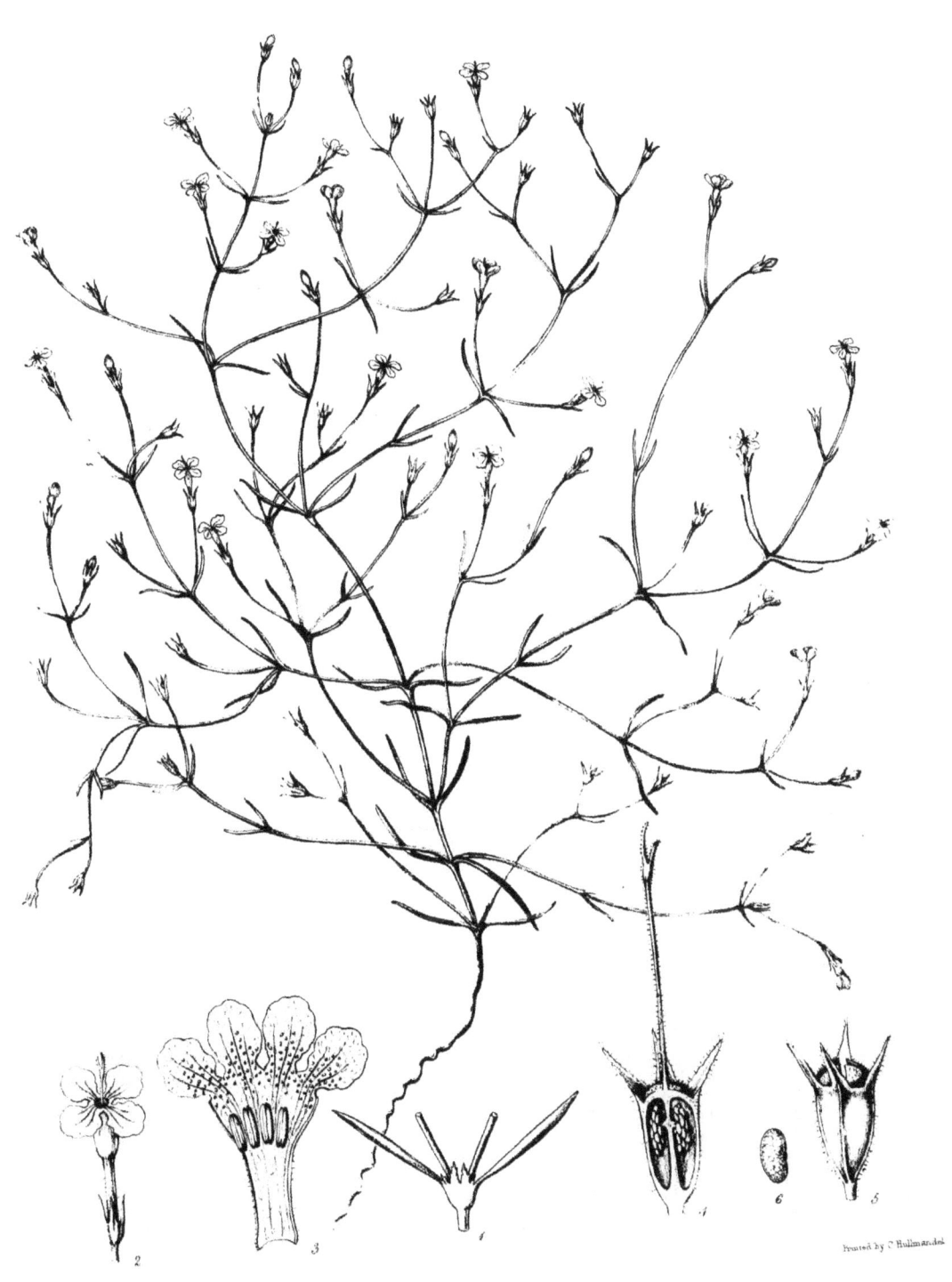

Plate 13.

HEDYOTIS ASPERULOIDES

Plate 14.

HELOGYNE FASCICULATA

Plate 15.

ERIPYLE CALIFORNICA.

Plate 16.

COREOCARPUS PARTHENIOIDES

ACOMA DISSECTA

METASTELMA CALIFORNICUM

Plate 20.

HYPTIS LANIFLORA.

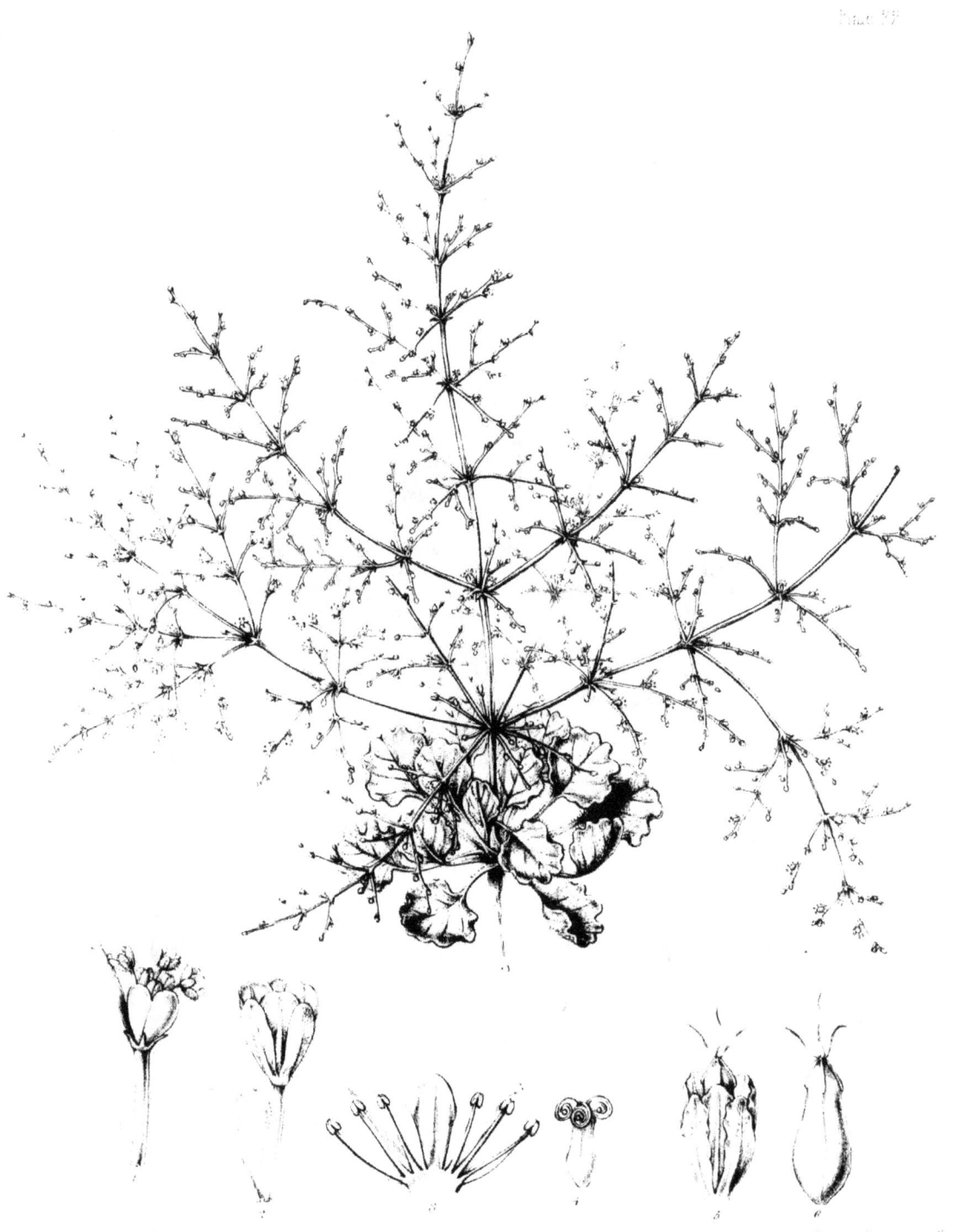

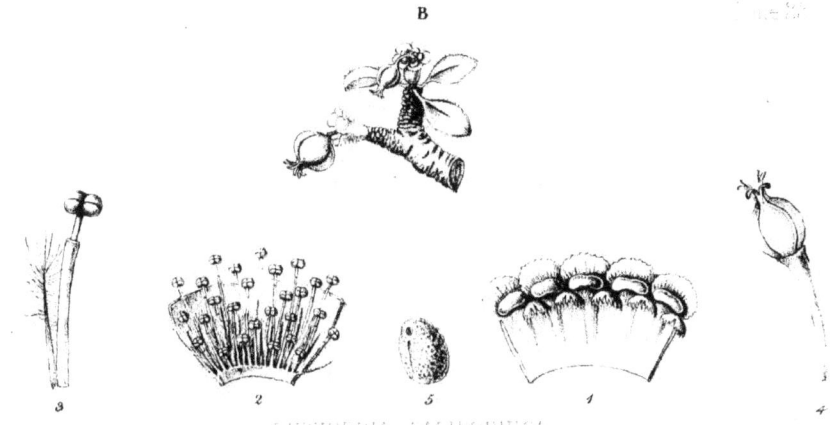

EUPHORBIA CALIFORNICA

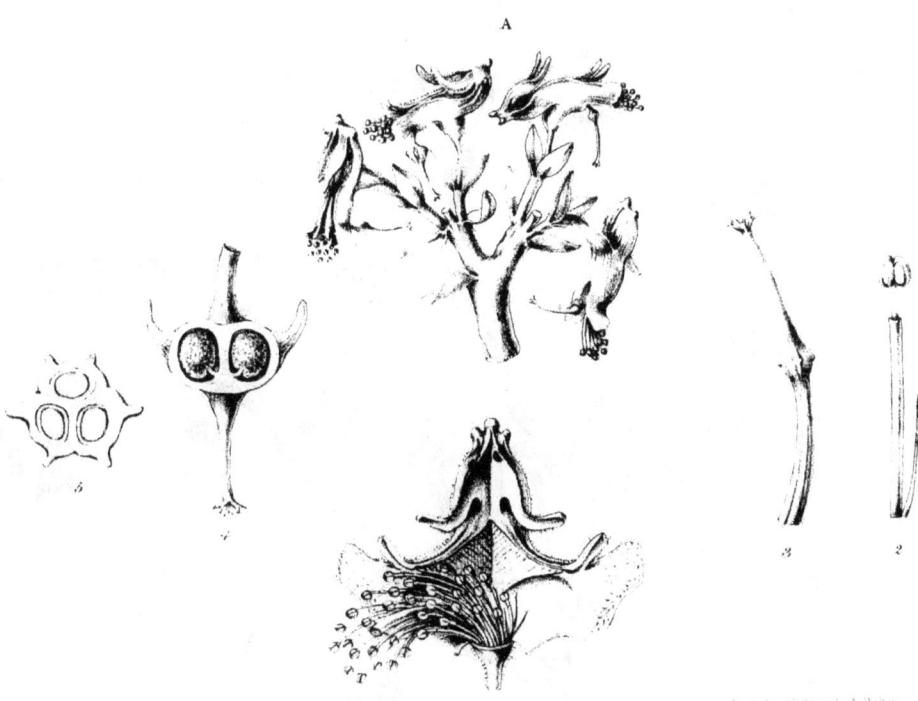

PLEURACANTHUS MACROCARPUS

EUPHORBIA HINDSIANA.

MOLINNA CANESCENS

Plate 26.

EREMOCARPUS SETIGERUS

CAPPARIS SINCLAIRII

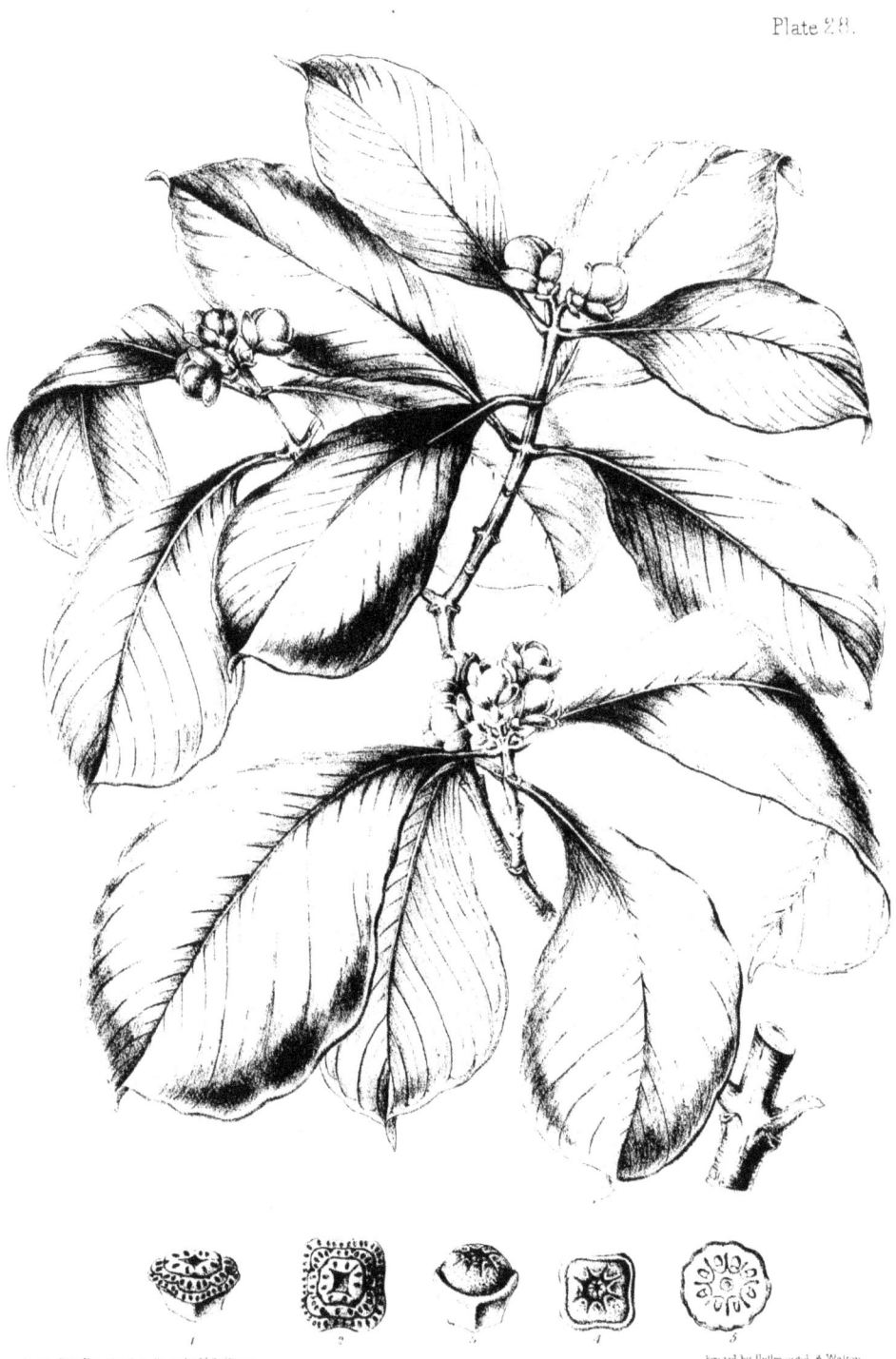

Plate 28.

TRIPLANDRON LÆVIGATUM.

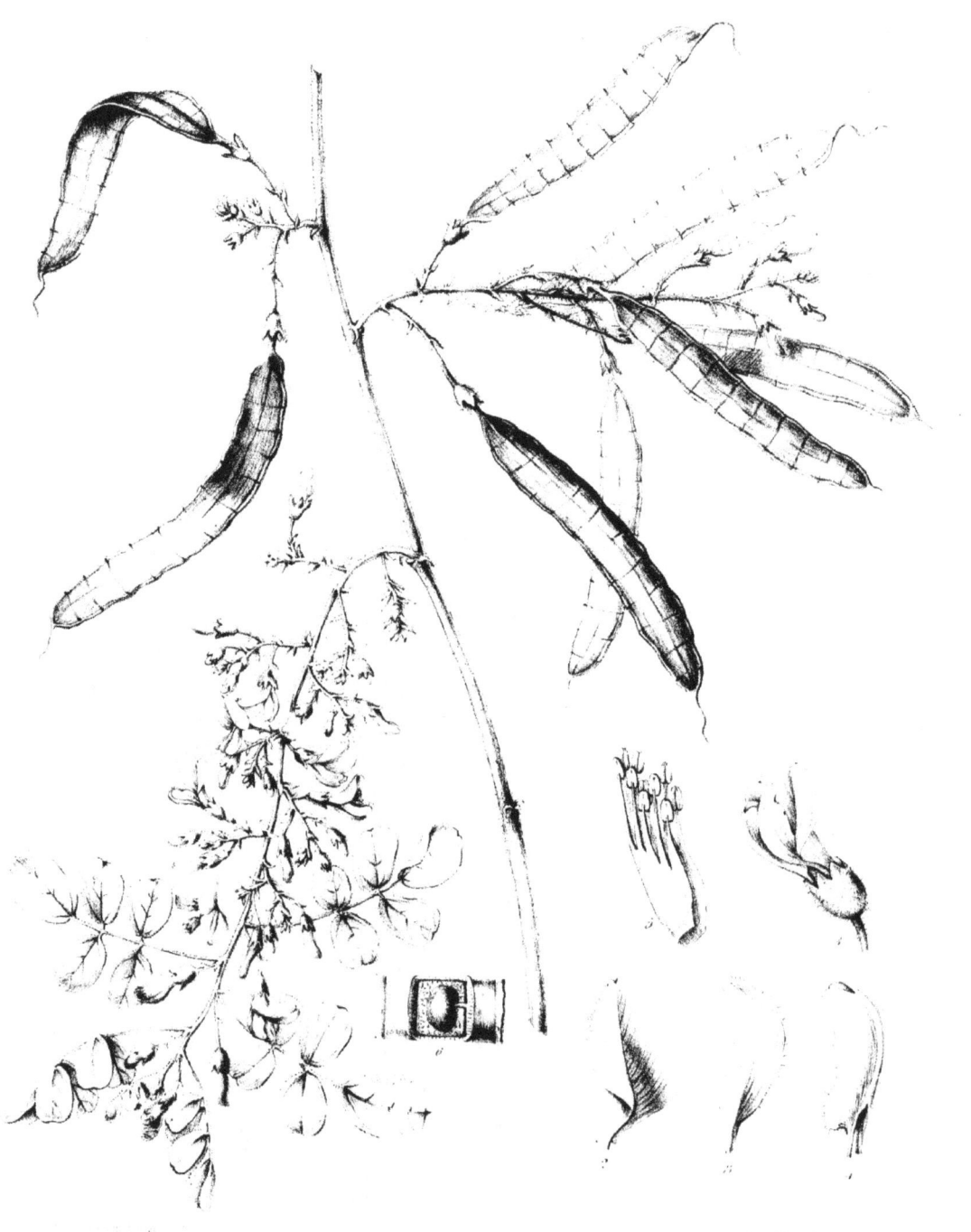

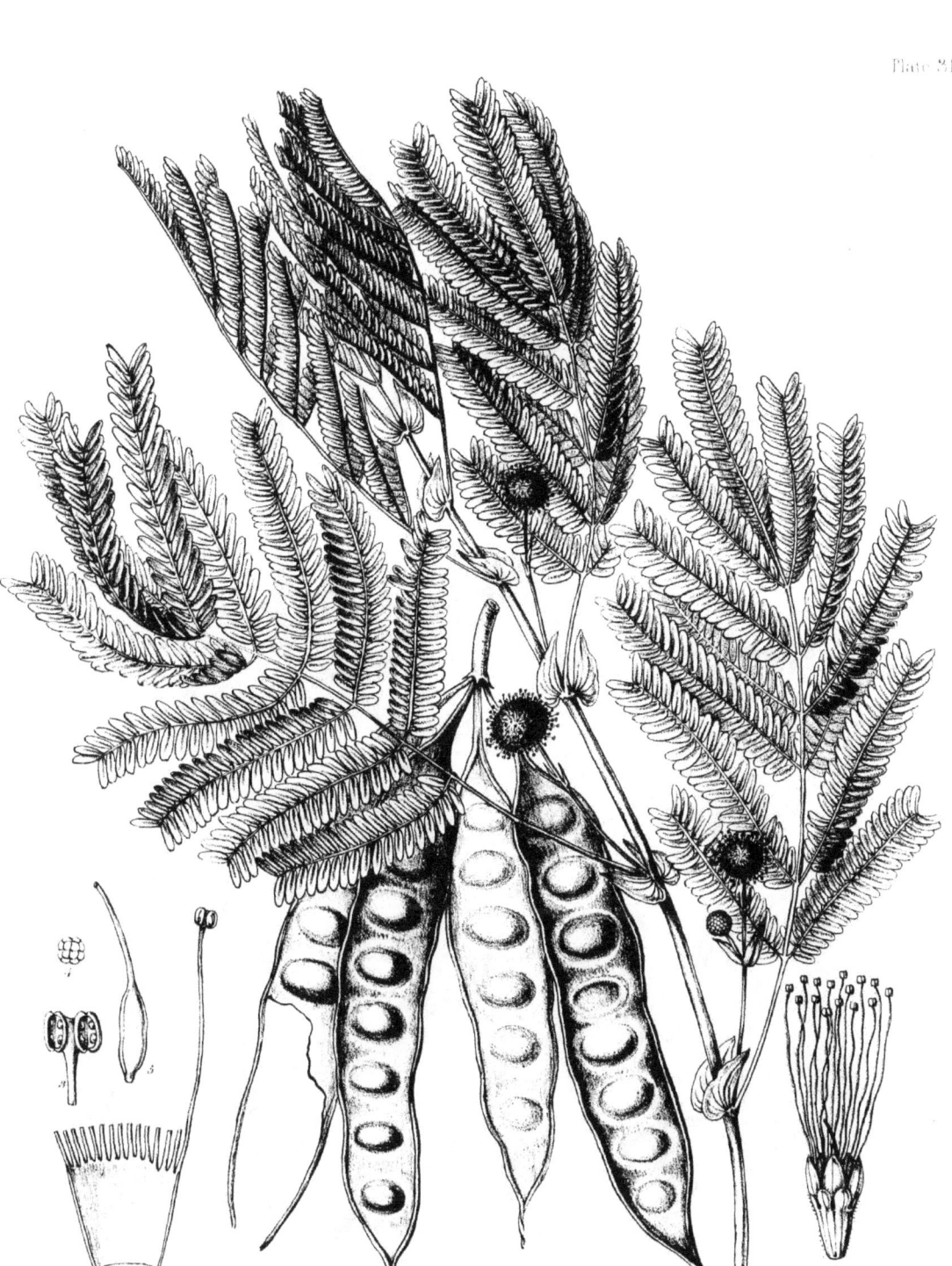

LYSILOMA SCHIEDEANA.

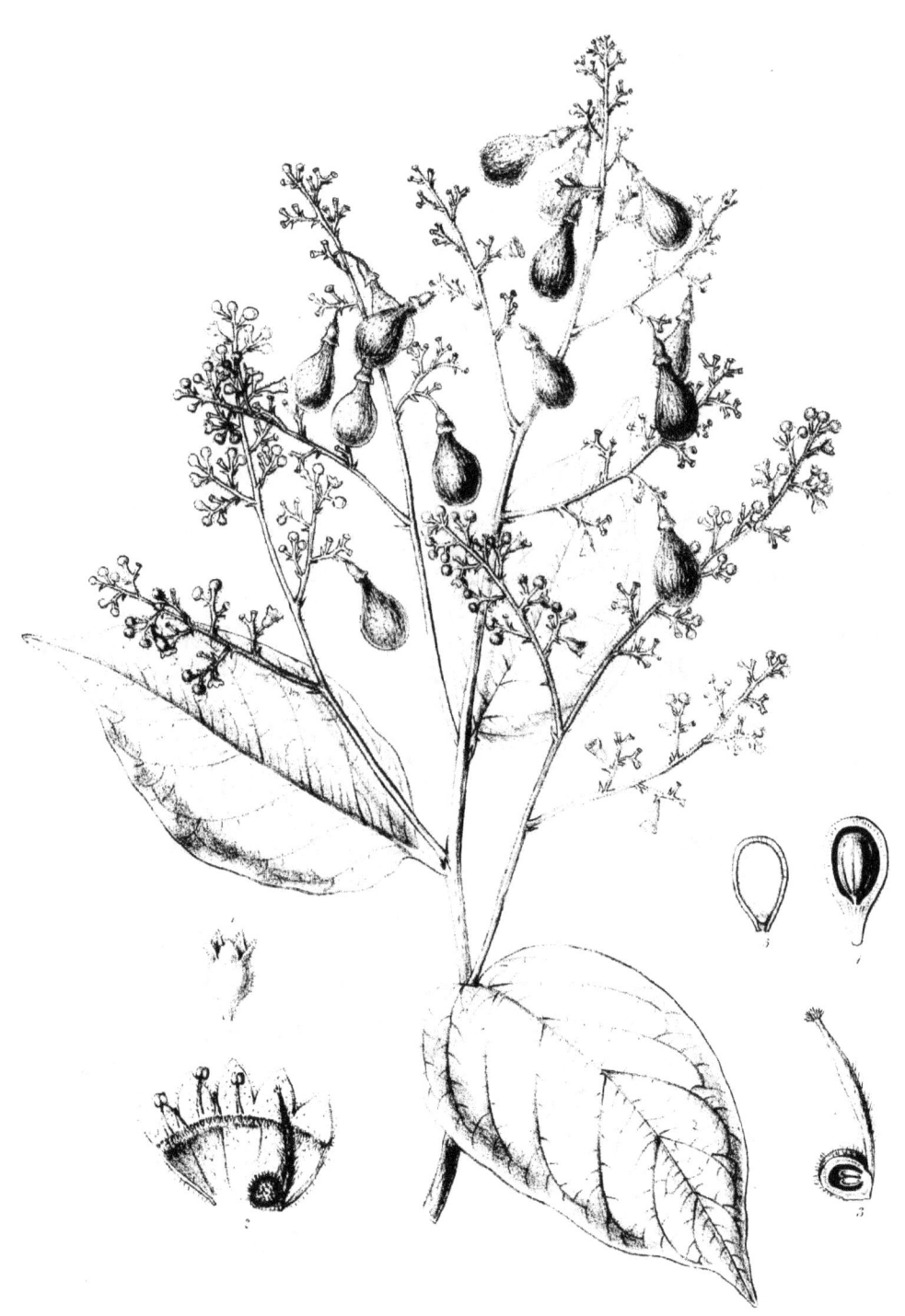

CLIDEMIA POLYANDRA

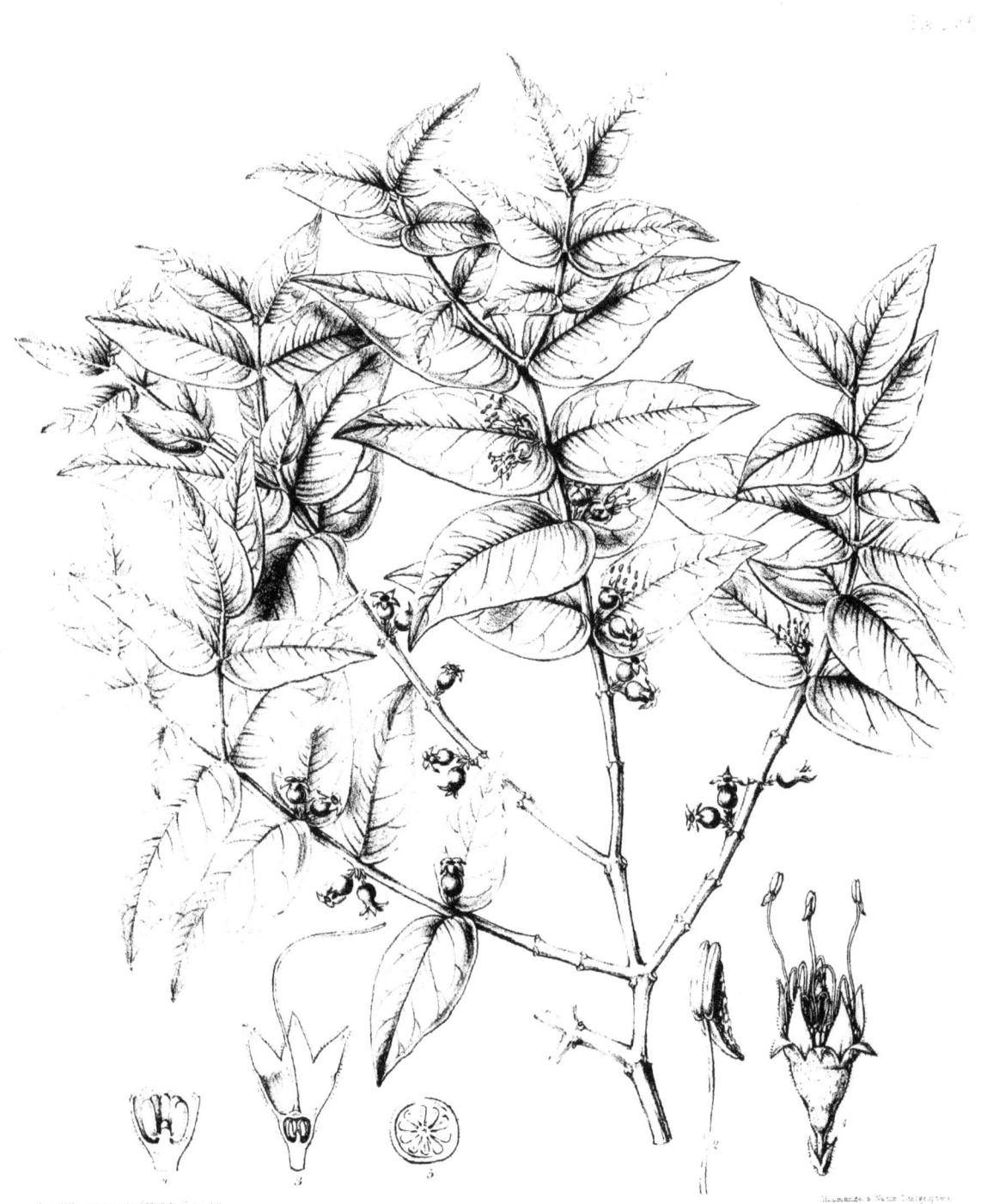

Plate 37.

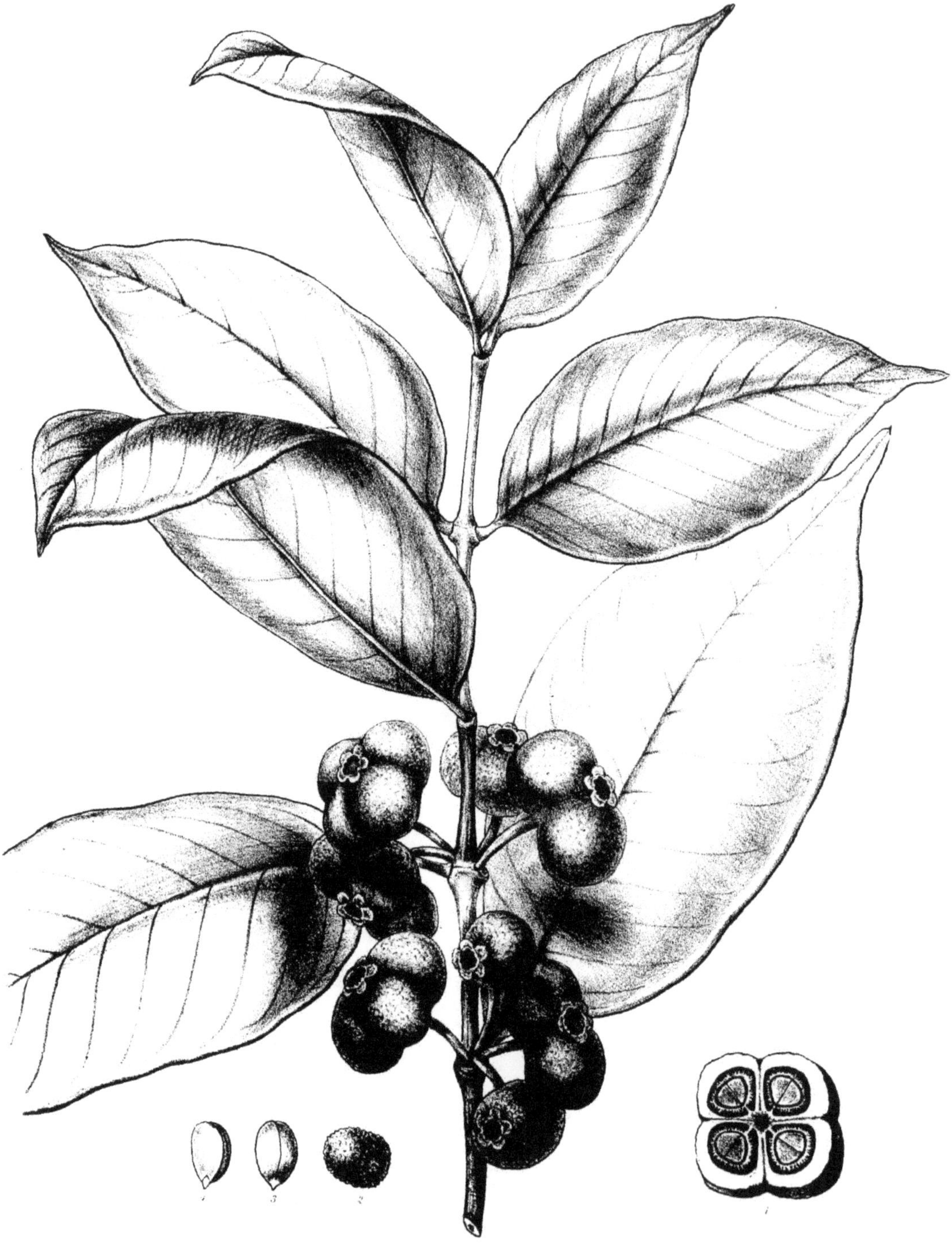

Drawn from Nature and on Stone by Miss Drake

Hullmandel & Walton Lithographers

CAMPOMANESIA CRASSIFOLIA

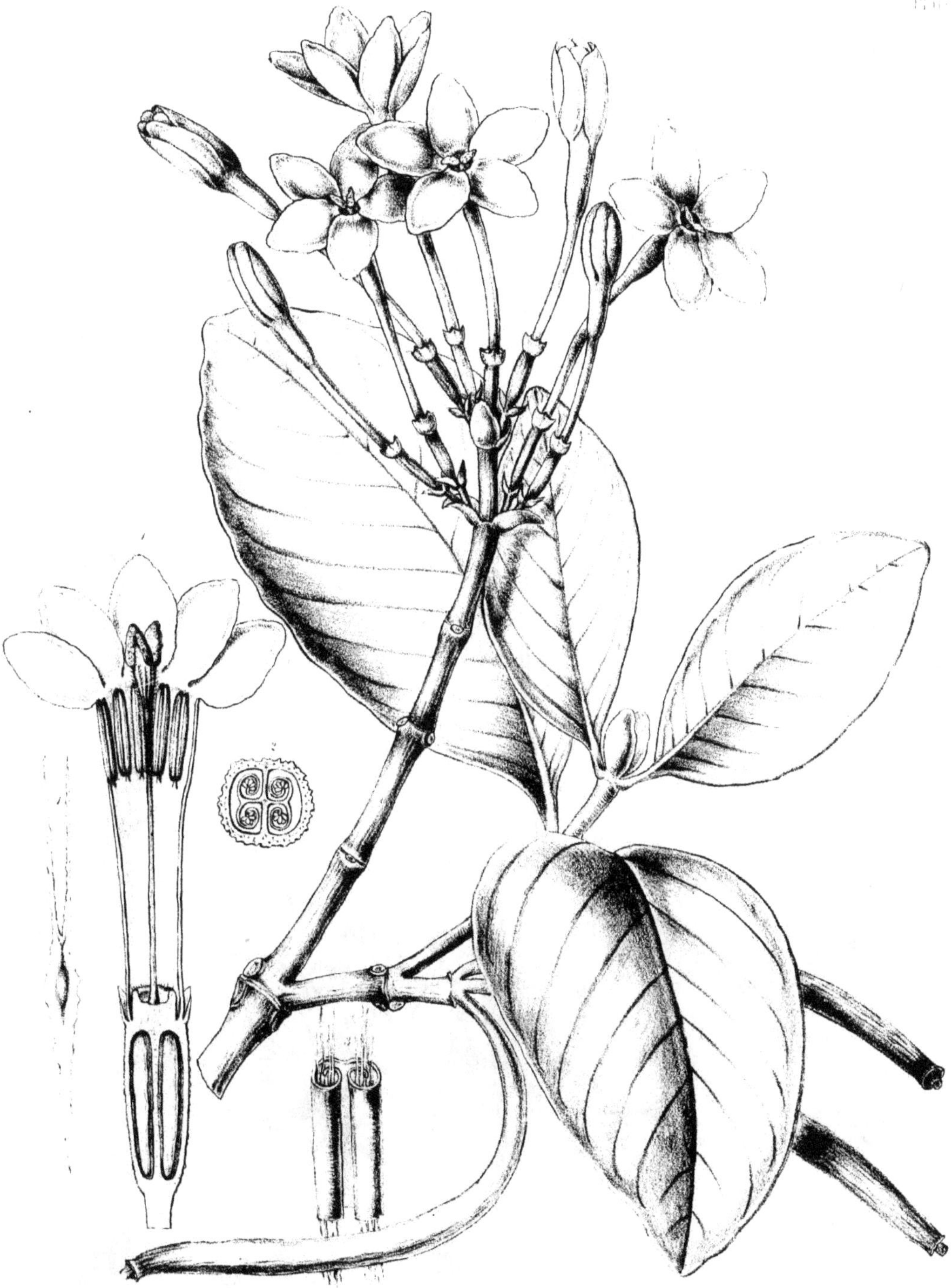

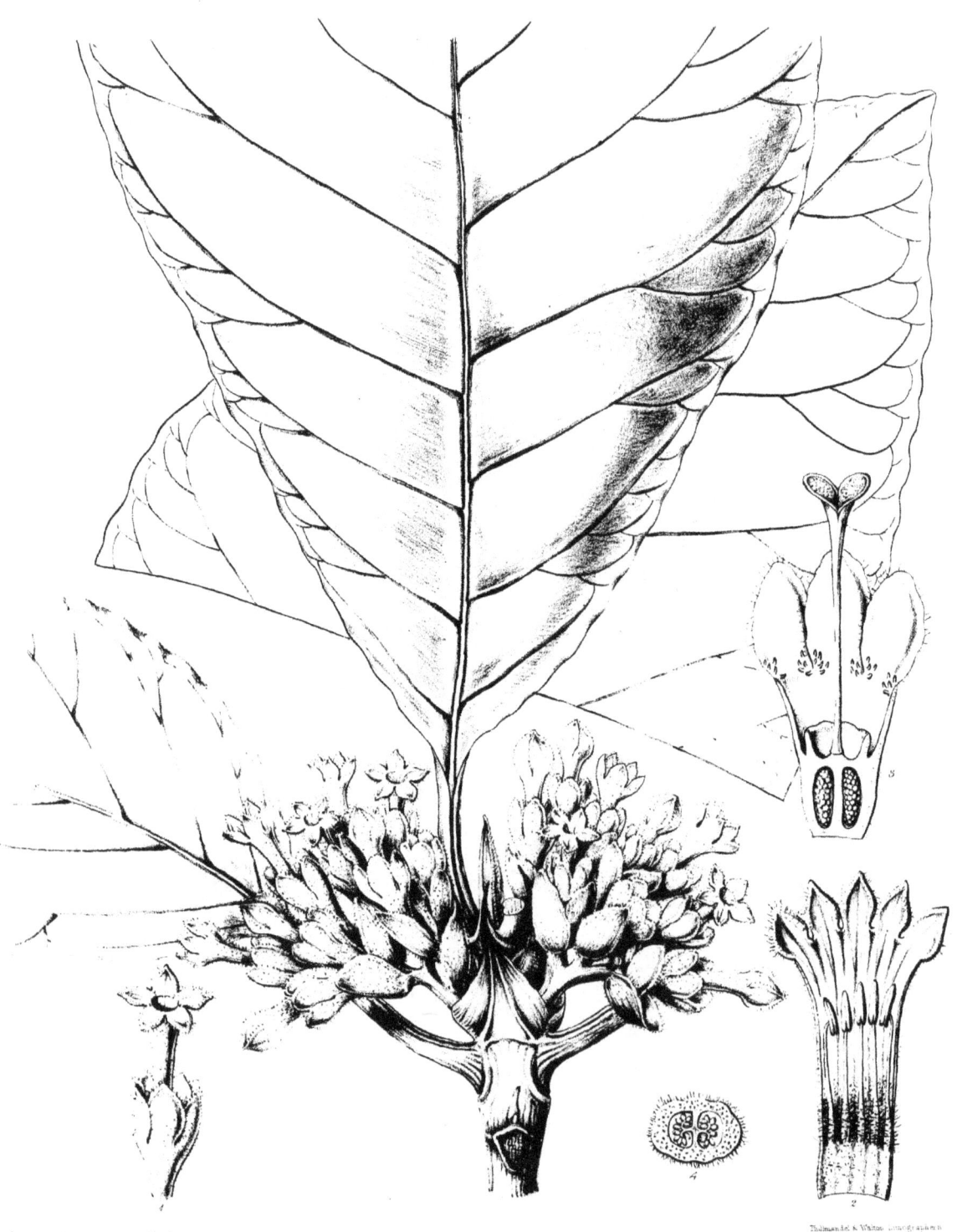

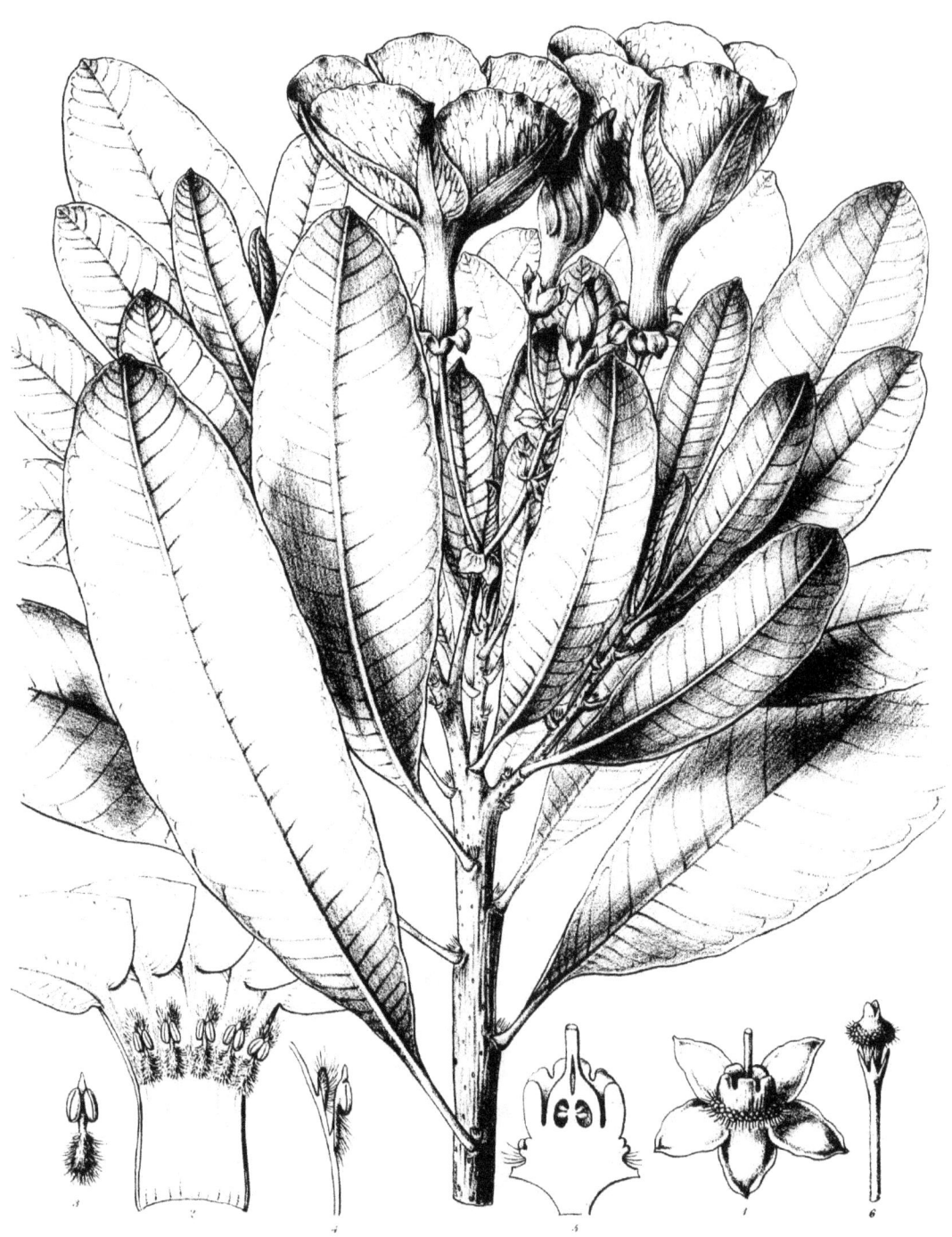

STEMMADENIA GLABRA

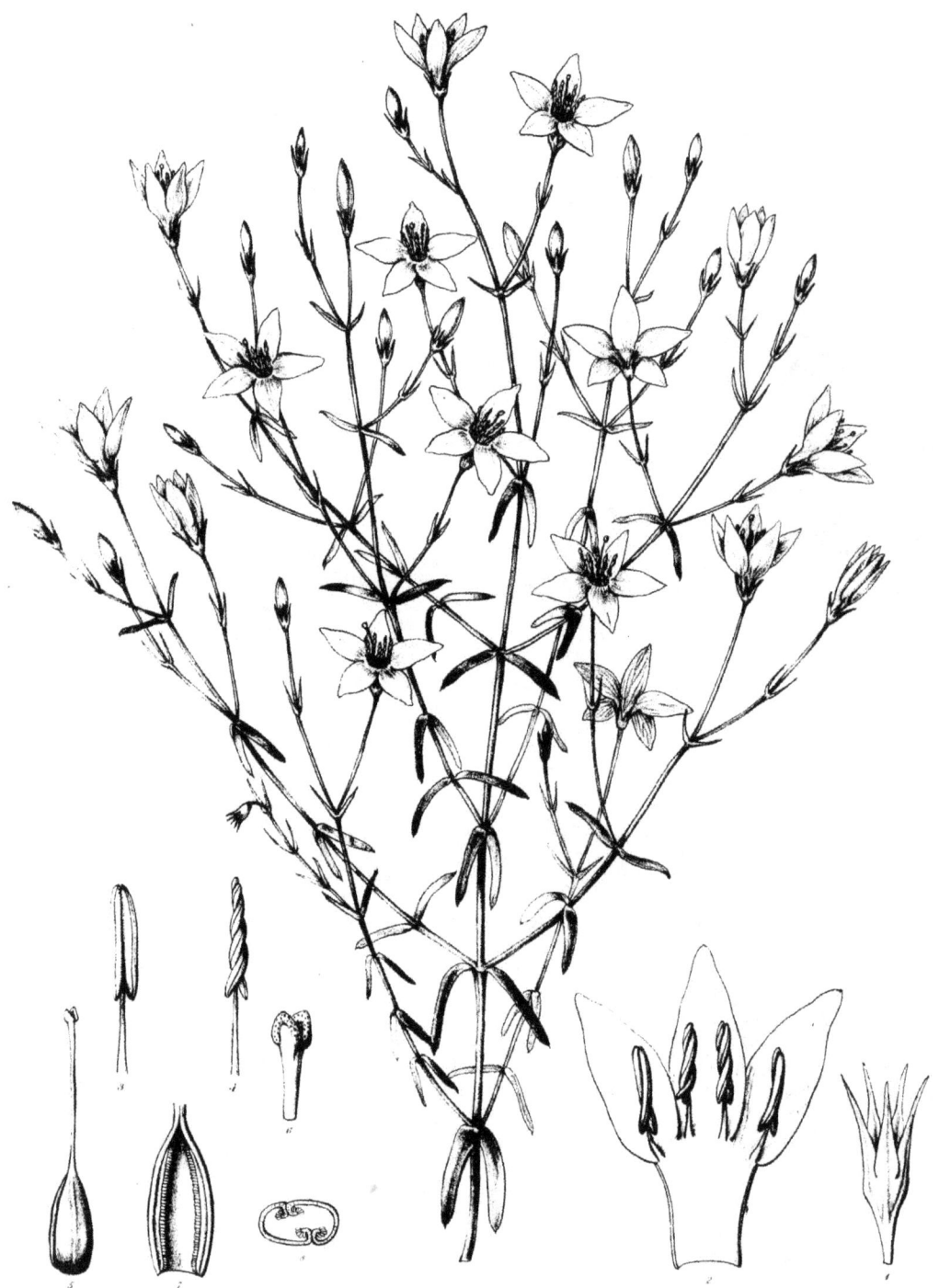

Plate 45

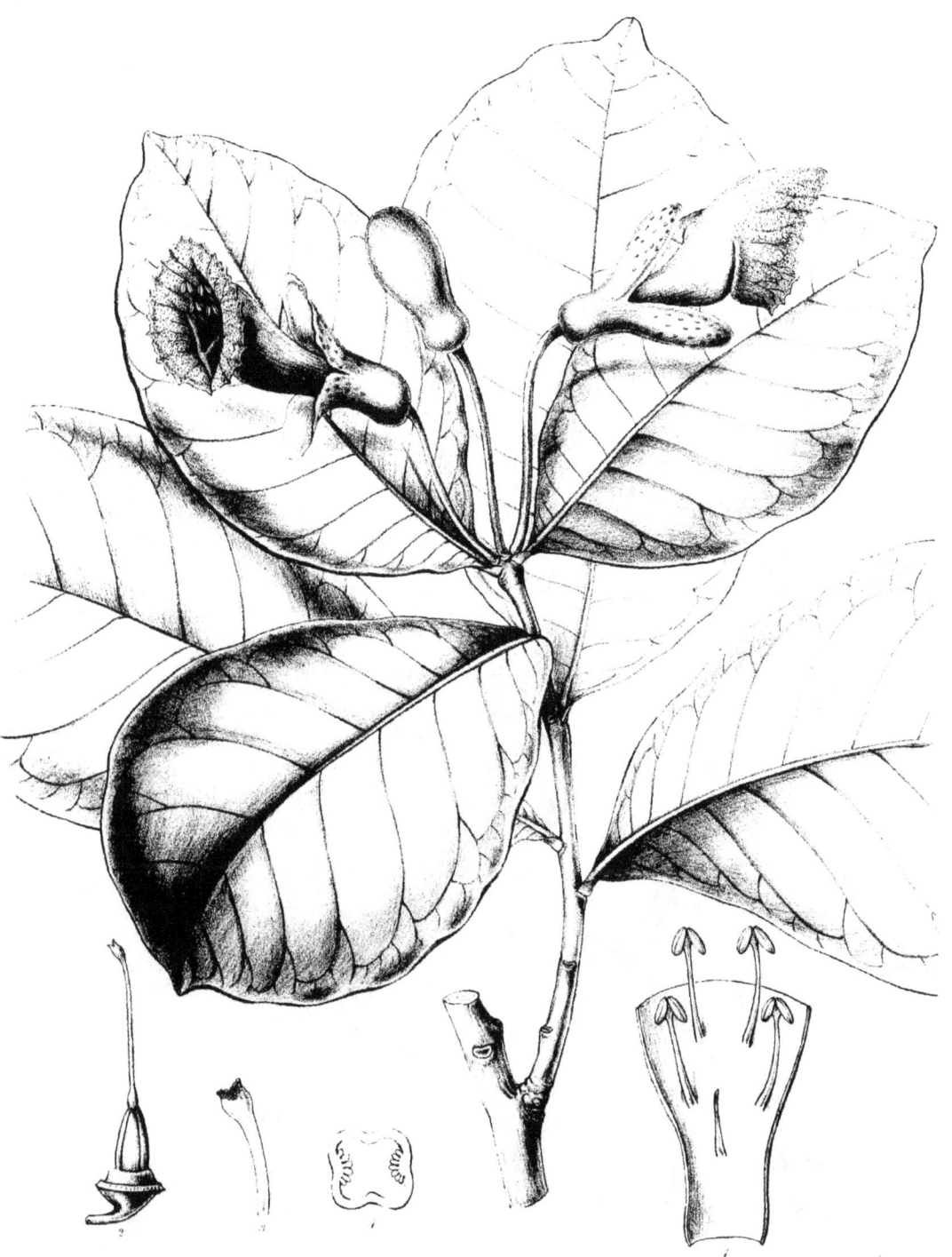

CRESCENTIA OBOVATA.

Plate 47.

APHELANDRA SINCLAIRIANA

SALVIA ELSHOLTZIOIDES

AMARANTHUS FLORIDUS

ACALYPHA DENTATA

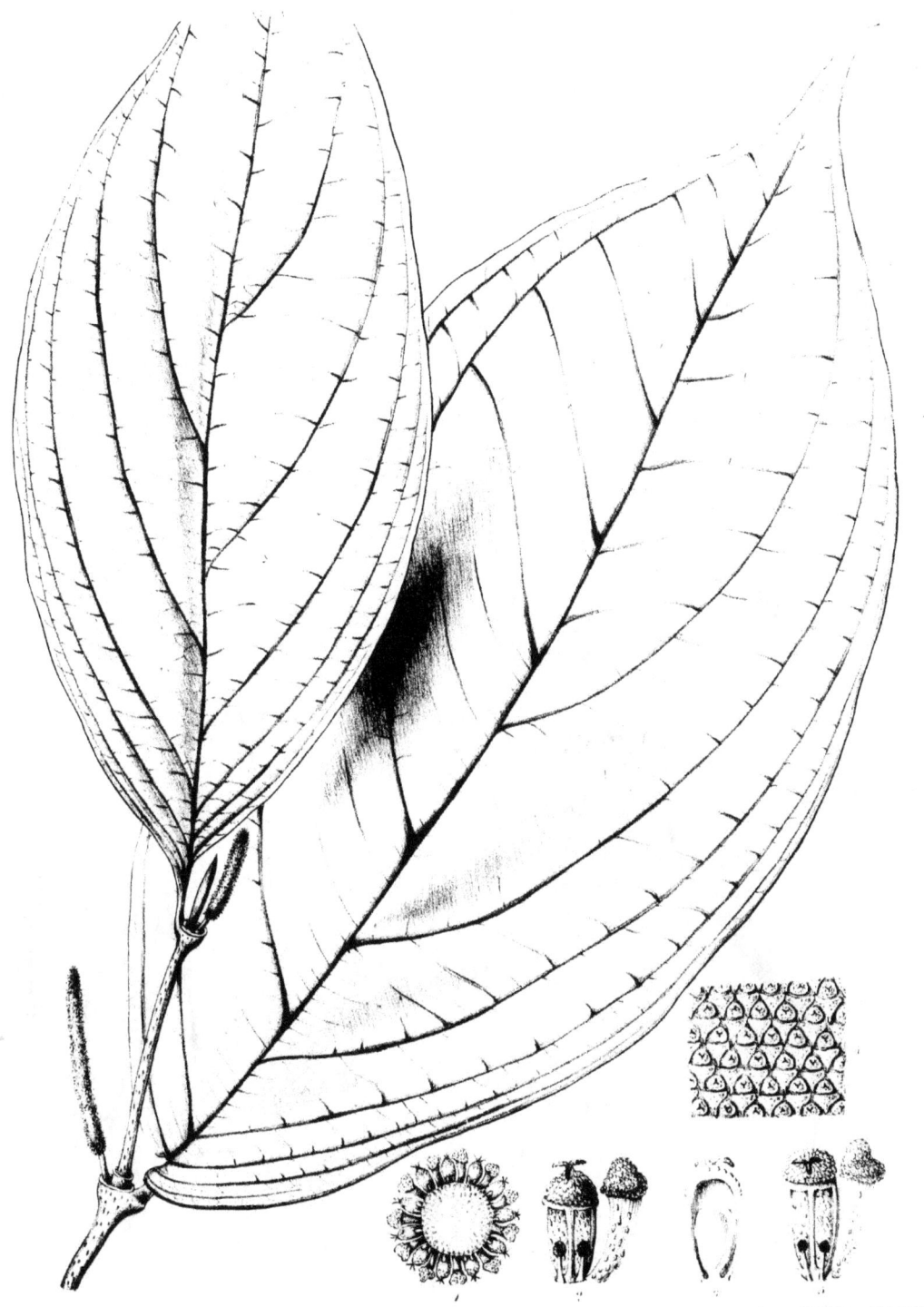

ARTANTHE BRACHYPODA

PYRIOCARPA STIPITATA

CHAETOSUS VOLUBILIS.

DENDROBIUM BIFALCE.

DENDROBIUM ANTENNATUM

DENDROBIUM VERATRIFOLIUM.

www.ingramcontent.com/pod-product-compliance
Lightning Source LLC
Chambersburg PA
CBHW081324090426
42737CB00017B/3030